Dedication

In memory of Geoff Sampson
(1947–2019)

Rome, Blood and Power

Reform, Murder and Popular Politics in the Late Republic 70–27 BC

Gareth C Sampson

Pen & Sword
MILITARY

First published in Great Britain in 2019 by
Pen & Sword Military
An imprint of
Pen & Sword Books Ltd
Yorkshire – Philadelphia

ISBN 978 1 52671 017 8

A CIP catalogue record for this book is
available from the British Library.

Printed and bound in the UK by TJ International Ltd,
Padstow, Cornwall.

Pen & Sword Books Limited incorporates the imprints of Atlas,
Archaeology, Aviation, Discovery, Family History, Fiction, History,
Maritime, Military, Military Classics, Politics, Select, Transport,
True Crime, Air World, Frontline Publishing, Leo Cooper, Remember
When, Seaforth Publishing, The Praetorian Press, Wharncliffe
Local History, Wharncliffe Transport, Wharncliffe True Crime
and White Owl.

For a complete list of Pen & Sword titles please contact

PEN & SWORD BOOKS LIMITED
47 Church Street, Barnsley, South Yorkshire, S70 2AS, England
E-mail: enquiries@pen-and-sword.co.uk
Website: www.pen-and-sword.co.uk

Or

PEN AND SWORD BOOKS
1950 Lawrence Rd, Havertown, PA 19083, USA
E-mail: Uspen-and-sword@casematepublishers.com
Website: www.penandswordbooks.com

Contents

Acknowledgements

The first and greatest acknowledgement must go out to my wonderful wife Alex, without whose support none of this would be possible.

Special thanks go out to my parents who always encouraged a love of books and learning.

There are a number of individuals who through the years have inspired the love of Roman history in me and mentored me along the way: Michael Gracey at William Hulme, David Shotter at Lancaster and Tim Cornell at Manchester. My heartfelt thanks go out to them all.

A shout goes out to the remaining members of the Manchester diaspora: Gary, Ian, Jason, Sam. Those were good days.

As always, my thanks go out to my editor Phil Sidnell, for his patience and understanding.

List of Plates

List of Maps

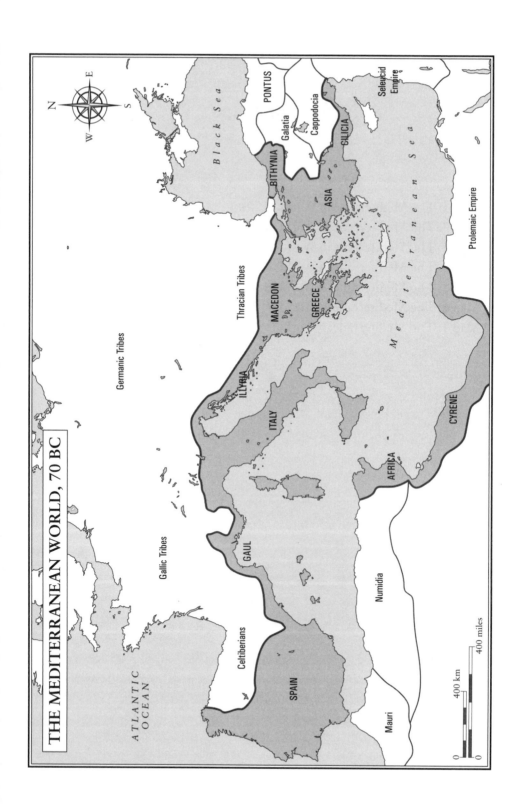

THE MEDITERRANEAN WORLD, 70 BC

N

Germanic Tribes

ATLANTIC
OCEAN

Gallic Tribes

GAUL

Celtiberians

SPAIN

Mauri

Numidia

ITALY

ILLYRIA

Thracian Tribes

MACEDON

GREECE

AFRICA

CYRENE

Mediterranean Sea

Black Sea

BITHYNIA

ASIA

PONTUS

Galatia

Cappodocia

CILICIA

Seleucid
Empire

Ptolemaic Empire

0   400 km

0   400 miles

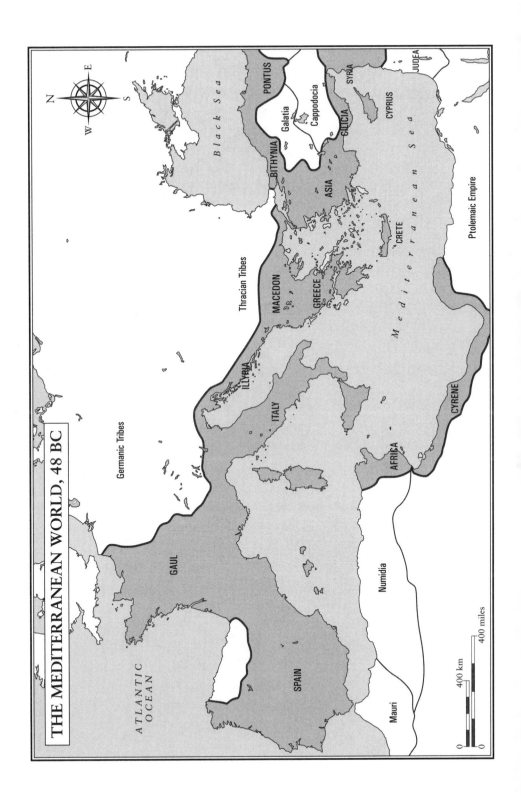

THE MEDITERRANEAN WORLD, 48 BC

Germanic Tribes

ATLANTIC OCEAN

GAUL

SPAIN

Mauri

Numidia

ITALY

ILLYRIA

Thracian Tribes

MACEDON

GREECE

CRETE

AFRICA

CYRENE

Mediterranean Sea

Black Sea

BITHYNIA

PONTUS

Galatia

Cappadocia

ASIA

CILICIA

SYRIA

CYPRUS

JUDEA

Ptolemaic Empire

N
E
S
W

0   400 km

0   400 miles

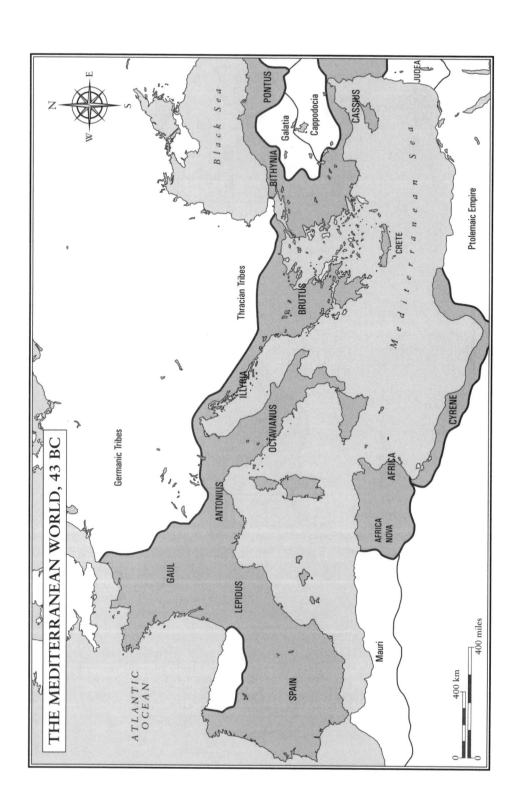

THE MEDITERRANEAN WORLD, 43 BC

ATLANTIC OCEAN

Germanic Tribes

Black Sea

Thracian Tribes

N E S W

GAUL

ANTONIUS

ILLYRIA

OCTAVIANUS

BRUTUS

BITHYNIA

PONTUS

Galatia

Cappadocia

CASSIUS

JUDEA

LEPIDUS

SPAIN

Mauri

AFRICA NOVA

AFRICA

CYRENE

CRETE

Mediterranean Sea

Ptolemaic Empire

400 km

400 miles

0

0

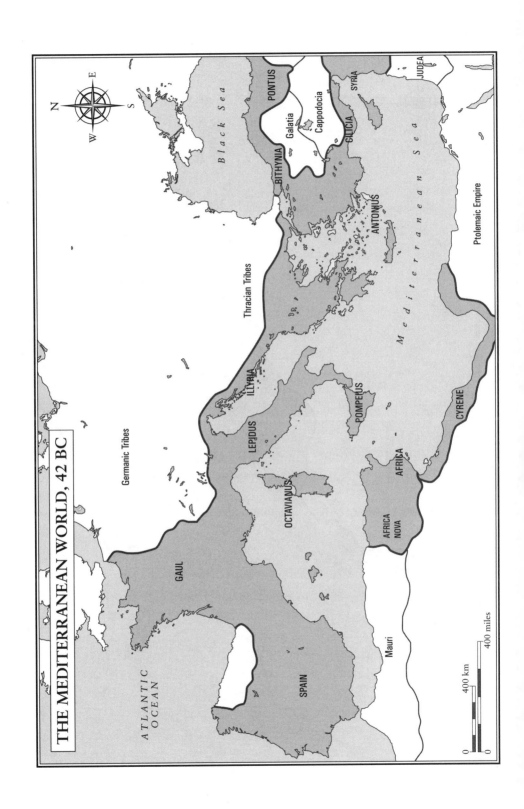

THE MEDITERRANEAN WORLD, 42 BC

ATLANTIC OCEAN

Germanic Tribes

Black Sea

Thracian Tribes

GAUL

SPAIN

Mauri

AFRICA NOVA

OCTAVIANUS

LEPIDUS

ILLYRIA

POMPEIUS

AFRICA

CYRENE

Mediterranean Sea

ANTONIUS

BITHYNIA

PONTUS

Galatia

Cappadocia

CILICIA

SYRIA

JUDEA

Ptolemaic Empire

400 km

400 miles

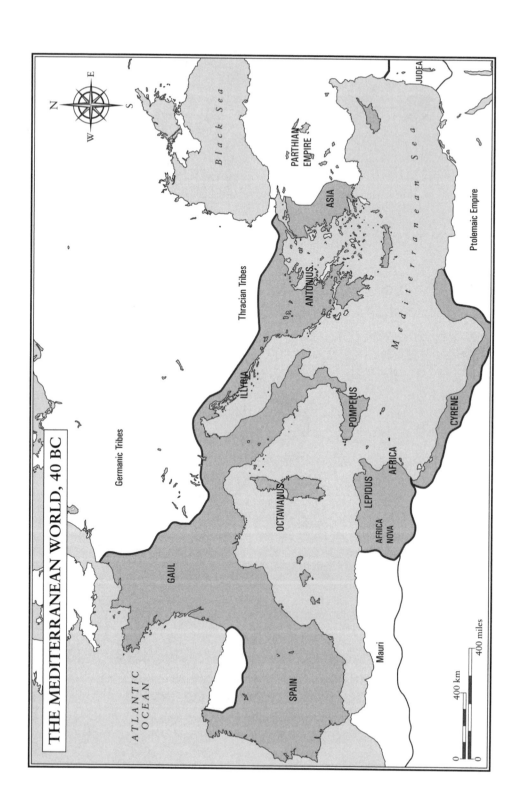

THE MEDITERRANEAN WORLD, 40 BC

ATLANTIC
OCEAN

Germanic Tribes

Black Sea

Thracian Tribes

PARTHIAN
EMPIRE

ASIA

ANTONIUS.

ILLYRIA

POMPEIUS

Mediterranean Sea

JUDEA

Ptolemaic Empire

CYRENE

AFRICA

LEPIDUS

AFRICA
NOVA

OCTAVIANUS

GAUL

SPAIN

Mauri

400 km

400 miles

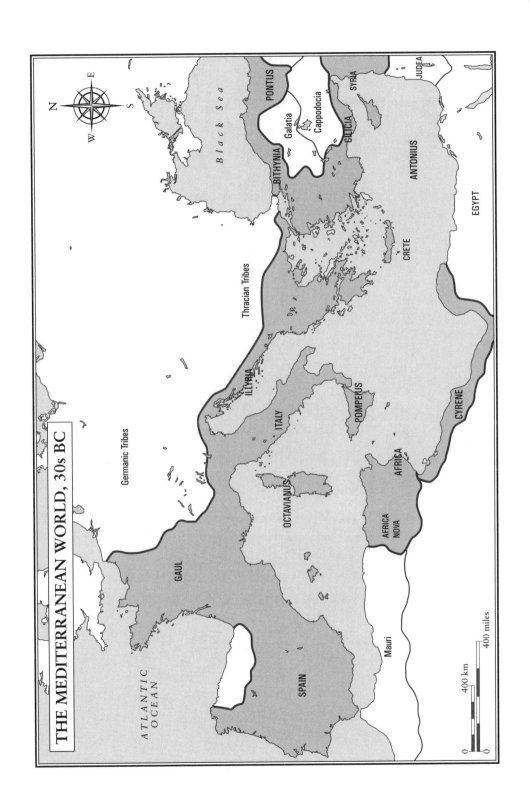

THE MEDITERRANEAN WORLD, 30s BC

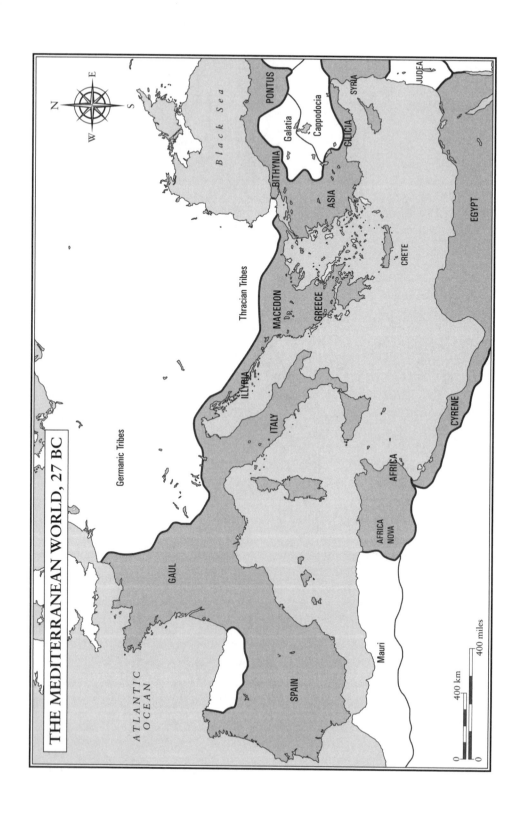

THE MEDITERRANEAN WORLD, 27 BC

ATLANTIC
OCEAN

Germanic Tribes

Black Sea

GAUL

SPAIN

Mauri

ITALY

ILLYRIA

AFRICA
NOVA

AFRICA

Thracian Tribes

MACEDON

GREECE

CRETE

CYRENE

BITHYNIA

PONTUS

Galatia

Cappodocia

ASIA

CILICIA

SYRIA

JUDEA

EGYPT

0   400 km

0   400 miles

Introduction: Out of the Ashes, the Struggle for Stability

The year 70 BC saw the Roman Republic emerge from twenty years of civil war and bloody slaughter, which had brought the Roman Republic and its growing empire to the very brink of collapse. Out of the ashes of this conflict emerged a 'New' Republic, or a re-founded one, as its architects (Pompeius and Crassus) would have preferred. Whilst this Republic maintained the offices and power structures identical to those from before the collapse, the key questions were whether this renewal would be permanent or merely an illusion; nothing more than a breathing space between bouts of civil war in a system that was locked into terminal decline. Was the Roman Republic and its ruling oligarchy capable of maintaining peace and stability whilst engaging in the age-old struggle for political advancement and the growth of empire?

The forty years which sit between the end of the First Civil War and the rise of Augustus are perhaps the most well known of all of Roman history, containing such dazzling figures as Pompeius and Caesar, Cato and Cicero, Catilina and Clodius, Antonius and Cleopatra. Yet aside from the larger-than-life personalities, immortalised in verse and now film, lies the functioning of the Roman Republican system and how it was able to recover from the devastating bloodshed of the Civil War and continue to function and rule an ever-growing Mediterranean and European empire.

The Roman Republican system had always had to manage the twin tensions of maintaining the public good (the *res publica*) against the ambitions of its ruling oligarchy. Yet seemingly as Rome's overseas empire expanded then the system was increasingly unable to keep these tensions under control and had seen escalating outbursts of political bloodletting (133, 121 and 100 BC). This culminated in a full-scale war in Italy and then across the empire, between the various ethnic groups and individuals that made up the Republic, with Rome itself attacked on no less than four occasions in just over a decade. Yet when the bloodletting subsided it was up to a new generation of Roman politicians to restore the *res publica*, expand the empire and keep their ambitions under control.

As will be seen with the following volume, maintaining this balance proved to be equally, if not more difficult than before, and saw the Republican system continue its evolution and undergo a number of political experiments in an ever-increasing and desperate search for stability. This search for stability culminated in the 20s BC with the rise of one man with a vision for how he could re-introduce stability to the Republican system.

Central to this study is a unique political office, the Tribunate of the Plebeian Order, which evolved from humble origins as the mouthpiece of a disenfranchised section of the Roman populace to being the most powerful, and most dangerous, political office in the Roman Republican system, and ultimately the foundation for the role of Emperor. The origins of the current work lies in my doctoral thesis from the early twenty-first century: *A re-examination of the office of the Tribunate of the Plebs in the Roman Republic (494–23 BC)*,[1] whose dry title concealed an analysis of what lay behind five centuries of political clashes and bloodshed; the very heart of the Roman Republican system.

The aim of this work is to examine this process and understand how a political system could bring itself back from the brink of collapse and not only renew itself but attempt to maintain the stability that had been so lacking in the preceding fifty years. It is also an examination of the key political events that happened in the period 70–27 BC. Whilst this period also covers a significant portion of Roman military history, in terms of conquest and civil wars, the military aspect will not be covered in detail, merely their political significance and impact.

This work does follow on from my earlier volume, '*Rome, Blood and Politics: Reform, Murder and Popular Politics in the Late Republic*' but is also designed to be a stand-alone volume analysing the late Republic, from the end of the First Civil War to the Settlements of Augustus.

Timeline of the Key Events
of the Period 70–27 BC

BC

91–70 First Civil War
70   End of the First Civil War
     Pompeian-Crassan Political Settlement
69   Pompeius and Crassus step down from office
67   Pompeius is granted a Mediterranean wide command against the pirates.
66   Pompeius is granted command of the Great Eastern War
65   Censorship of Crassus, attempted annexation of Egypt

63–62 Second Civil War
63   Attempted Coup in Rome
     SCU Passed, Execution of Cornelius Lentulus and colleagues
62   Battle of Pistoria – Catilina and Manlius defeated by Antonius
     Revolt of the Allobroges
     Pompeius returns to Rome
60   Pompeius and Crassus combine forces to elect Caesar as Consul
59   Consulship of Caesar
58   Tribunate of Clodius, exile of Cicero
57   Tribunate of Milo, battles on the streets of Rome
56   Conference at Luca – Pompeius, Crassus and Caesar combine forces once more
55   Second Consulship of Pompeius and Crassus
53   Battle of Carrhae – Crassus defeated by the Parthians, killed in retreat
52   Murder of Clodius, Pompeius assumes a sole Consulship in Rome

49–27 Third Civil War

49   Caesar invades Italy, captures Rome

48   Battle of Pharsalus, Caesar victorious, Pompeius murdered in Egypt

46   Battle of Thapsus, Caesar victorious, Metellus Scipio and Cato commit suicide

45   Battle of Munda, Caesar victorious, Cn. Pompeius killed

44   Assassination of Iulius Caesar in the Senate House

43   War between Octavius and M. Antonius
     Battles of Forum Gallorum and Mutina, death of both Consuls
     Formation of Triumvirate of Antonius, Lepidus and Octavius

42   Two Battles of Philippi, Brutus and Cassius commit suicide

41   War between Octavianus and L. Antonius

40   Siege of Mutina ends with Octavianus victorious.
     Renewal of alliance between Octavianus and M. Antonius

39   Peace treaty between Triumvirate and Sex. Pompeius

37   Final Renewal of the Triumvirate

36   Octavianus and Agrippa defeat Sex. Pompeius. Lepidus removed from Triumvirate

35   Murder of Sex. Pompeius

32   Triumvirate Expires. Final breach between Octavianus and M. Antonius

31   Battle of Actium – Octavianus and Agrippa defeated Antonius and Cleopatra

30   Roman Conquest of Egypt
     Deaths of Antonius and Cleopatra

27   Octavianus becomes Augustus
     First Constitutional Settlement of Augustus

23   Second Constitutional Settlement of Augustus

Notes on Roman Names

All Roman names in the following text will be given in their traditional form, including the abbreviated first name. Below is a list of the Roman first names referred to in the text and their abbreviations.

A.	Aulus.
Ap.	Appius
C.	Caius
Cn.	Cnaeus
D.	Decimus
K.	Kaeso
L.	Lucius
M.	Marcus
Mam.	Mamercus
P.	Publius
Paul.	Paullus
Q.	Quintus
Ser.	Servius
Sex.	Sextus
Sp.	Spurius
T.	Titus
Ti.	Tiberius

Part I

The Collapse and Recovery of the Roman Republic (146–70 BC)

Chapter One

The Collapse and Recovery of the Roman Republic (146–70 BC)

In the summer of 71 BC the inhabitants of Rome looked on nervously as two great, battle-hardened armies, approached the walls of Rome. The fact that both armies were Roman brought little comfort as for the previous two decades the Roman Republic had collapsed into a series of interconnected civil wars, which had seen Rome itself attacked on numerous occasions and even brutally sacked by her own forces in 87 BC. Just six years previously another Roman army had marched on Rome and been defeated just to Rome's north by the Milvian Bridge and throughout the previous year there was a genuine fear that a slave army would attack and sack the city.

At the head of these two great armies were Rome's two foremost generals of their day. From the north came Cn. Pompeius 'Magnus' (the Great), fresh from winning a civil war in Spain, whilst from the south came M. Licinius Crassus, fresh from saving Rome from the slave armies of Spartacus. The two men were natural rivals, whose careers had followed strangely similar paths. Both were the sons of Consuls who had died in 87 BC during the civil war that year; Cn. Pompeius Strabo (Cos. 89 BC) of plague and P. Licinius Crassus (Cos. 97 BC) having been murdered during the sack of Rome. In the years that followed, both men had raised their own armies and joined the forces of the civil war commander L. Cornelius Sulla and had fought their way up through Italy when Sulla had invaded from Greece. With Sulla victorious, thanks to Crassus' victory at the Battle of the Colline Gate, their career paths had differed, with Pompeius continuing to command Roman armies in the ongoing civil wars (Sicily, Africa, Italy and Spain), whilst Crassus had built up a vast fortune and was content to politic in the Senate. When Rome faced its largest ever slave rebellion, in southern Italy, commanded by none other than Spartacus, it was Crassus who took command and ensured a total Roman victory, with Pompeius returning from Spain too late to do anything other than mop up.

Now these two rivals marched their victorious armies towards Rome and the rewards they felt they deserved. Given the blood-soaked reputations of both men, many in Rome (both the Senate and People) would have had every right to be fearful that their arrival would herald a fresh chapter in Rome's bloody First Civil War. Yet it seems that the two men themselves, whilst rivals, shared a common understanding of Roman politics, perhaps borne out of being the second generation of their families to be involved in the civil war and having lost family to the war's bloodier early phases. Both men realised that there was no need to go to war with the other when their combined forces could dominate the Republic and ensure they received what they considered to be their due rewards. Thus was born a temporary Duumvirate (of Pompeius and Crassus), with both men riding roughshod over the constitution to ensure that they were elected as the two Consuls for 70 BC. Yet despite the methods used, both men wanted to use this temporary ascendancy not just to satisfy their own sense of entitlement and rewards for their endeavours, but to mould the very Republic itself and hopefully end the crises and bloodshed that had plagued the Republic for the previous sixty years and had seen it collapse into a brutal and bloody civil war.

1. The Crisis: Political Reform and Bloodshed (146–91 BC)[1]

For Roman historians such as Sallust, it was not a coincidence that the Roman Republic started its descent into internal collapse just as it achieved a position of unparalleled dominance in the Mediterranean World. The year 146 BC saw Republican armies destroy the ancient cities of Carthage and Corinth and annex the territories of Carthage and Macedon, two of the Mediterranean world's former leading powers, along with the states of mainland Greece (including Athens and Sparta). This left the Republic with imperial territories in North Africa and Greece, to go with their conquests in Italy and Spain. Furthermore, it confirmed Rome's status as the leading power in the Mediterranean, with the two surviving Hellenistic empires (Seleucid and Ptolemaic) acknowledging Rome's superiority, as did the myriad of smaller kingdoms. Outside of the Mediterranean was a different matter, with this hegemony not being recognised by either the native tribes of mainland Europe, including Spain, nor the growing Parthian Empire in the east.

Yet within just over a decade of this momentous year, Rome saw its first political murder in several centuries, which sparked off a series of bloodier clashes within the city of Rome itself, culminating in three massacres (133, 121 and 100 BC) as the Roman oligarchy turned on itself. The spark for this bloodshed came in 133 BC when a young blue-blooded aristocrat, Ti. Sempronius Gracchus, used his political post as the Tribune of the Plebs to propose what seemed like a modest law to distribute public land (*ager publicus*) to the landless. The reason he put forward for proposing this law was to cure what he, and others, had seen as a growing social (and military) problem: namely, that long service in Rome's armies was impacting on Rome's citizens who were losing their land and farms and being driven into cities. Thus he and many others seemed to believe that this was a growing social problem, a demographic shift away from the land to the cities, with an influx of slaves taking their place. Thus, like many politicians, they believed that society was changing and not for the better. In Roman terms there was also an additional military aspect to this change, namely a loss of manpower, as only citizens with land were eligible for recruitment into Rome's non-professional armies.

As with most political issues, it is far from clear whether there was a genuine issue facing Roman society and whether this measure would actually be able to 'turn the clock back' and restore Roman society to its agrarian ideal. Furthermore, many in the Senate did not see this as an altruistic act but as a factional one, merely another move in a political clash for dominance between the various factions that existed within the Roman oligarchy. Gracchus was none other than the brother-in-law of Rome's leading statesmen at the time, P. Cornelius Scipio Aemilianus 'Africanus', the conqueror of Carthage, who was at the time absent in Spain and had probably instructed the young Gracchus to pass this measure. Furthermore, the proposed legislation called for the creation of an Agrarian Commission to confiscate and distribute the public lands, complete with judicial powers. The three-man board would be Tiberius, his younger brother Caius, and his father in law Ap. Claudius Pulcher, (the *Princeps Senatus*).

For these reasons this proposal was blocked by one of Gracchus' Tribunician colleagues (M. Octavius), using his power of veto (*ius intercessio*). Up to this point there had been nothing unusual or untoward about this political clash; a blocked proposal, as such things happened every year in Roman politics, based as it was on the annual turnover of elected magistrates.

Yet Gracchus was unwilling to let this issue rest and took an innovative and some would say fateful step. Rather than accept that his proposal had been blocked and let the matter drop, he went a stage further and used the theoretical power of his office to depose his colleague for his legitimate opposition. The office he held was the Tribunate of the Plebeian order, which was a legacy from the earlier days of the Republic when politics and society were divided into two, sometimes antagonistic, factions: the Patricians and the Plebeians, themselves differentiations whose origins are far from clear but were passed down by birth. With the Patricians dominating the levers of power in the Republic, the Plebeians grouped together and elected their own magistrates (the Tribunes) and instituted their own Assembly.

This political, social and economic clash became known as the 'Struggle of the Orders' and lasted from the Fifth Century BC to the Third, when in c. 287 BC the Plebeians in theory gained full political parity in the Republic. In reality the elite families of the Plebeian order merged with the Patrician aristocracy to form a unified ruling oligarchy, leaving the poorer Plebeians to struggle with the long-standing social and economic issues of food supply and debt. Thus Ti. Sempronius Gracchus was technically a Plebeian but was the son of a Consul and brother-in-law to the leading Patrician politician, Scipio Africanus.

The Tribunate itself was still technically open only to Plebeians but was now no longer what has been described as an 'anti-office' to rival the official ones, but for young Plebeian aristocrats was a much sought-after junior office to be held as part of their fledgling political career path (whilst still not being part of the 'official' *cursus honorum*). As an aside the existing evidence does indicate that non-aristocratic Plebeians also held the Tribunate, alongside their more noble colleagues. Though the Tribunate was considered to be only a junior office in the *cursus honorum*, in theory it held unlimited power as its holders had the right to propose any legislation to the Tribal Assembly, which itself had unlimited powers to legislate on any matter they saw fit. Thus, Gracchus tapped into this theoretical power and proposed the removal of his colleague, arguing that his proposal was in the People's benefit (or at least the voting element) and that his colleague was stopping this. Swayed by his arguments and possibly thinking of their own benefit, the Assembly duly removed Octavius from office. Gracchus had thus shown that a Tribune controlling the Assembly could remove an elected official and a political opponent. This theoretically unlimited power was further demonstrated when Gracchus again proposed (and had passed) a measure which sequestered the riches of the Kingdom of Pergamum (recently bequeathed to Rome) to fund his legislation.

The final straw came when the end of Gracchus' year in office was approaching, which was the last check on a Roman magistrate. After his year had passed he would be a private citizen again, with no political power and no immunity from prosecution. Anticipating this, Gracchus again proposed that he would stand for re-election, which whilst technically was legal, was against custom and practice (*mos maiorum*) in the mid Republic. Thus, his opponents were faced with another year (if not more) of Gracchus and his legislative powers, with seemingly no legitimate way of opposing him (at least in their minds). On the day of the elections, an incident sparked by a group of Senators (and their adherents), led by a Scipio (P. Cornelius Scipio Nasica Serapio) who was Rome's Chief Priest (Pontifex Maximus), attacked Gracchus and his supporters. In the ensuing melee, Gracchus himself was killed (seemingly by one of his Tribunician colleagues), along with some three hundred of his supporters whose bodies were thrown into the Tiber. Thus, Rome had its first political bloodshed and murder since the early days of the Republic and the collegiality of the Roman oligarchy had been fractured (albeit temporarily). To make matters worse, Gracchus' murderers were not prosecuted, with Nasica being quietly exiled temporarily to the east, where he met a suspiciously quick death.

However, many of Gracchus' supporters were tried for their complicity in Gracchus' perfectly legal acts, with many being exiled. The surviving sources do not cover the aftermath of the massacre of 133 BC in any great depth, which is a pity as what we do know reveals that there were continuing political repercussions following Tiberius' death, which seemingly resulted in the murder of none other than Scipio Africanus (Aemilianus) himself in 129 BC. Scipio (Tiberius' absent patron) had returned from Spain and publicly stated that Tiberius' death was a just one (albeit illegal). Thus, both sides clearly hoped that the Senatorial aristocracy would pull together and heal the rift this murder had caused.

Yet it seems that Scipio's absence from Rome, which seemingly had an important part to play in the events of 133 BC, had led to a fracturing of his faction in the Senate, with a new Gracchan faction forming which intended to continue with Tiberius' policies. At the forefront of the subsequent events was the work of the Gracchan Agrarian Commission, who's continued existence and work was guaranteed by the Senate. Scipio found himself being drawn into opposing the work of the Commission (on behalf of a group of wealthy landowners) and was found dead on the morning of a key debate on the matter with suspicion falling on both his wife (Tiberius' sister) and C. Papirius Carbo, the leading surviving Gracchan. Thus, Rome's greatest living general and the conqueror of Carthage was seemingly murdered in a political feud.

Any hopes the Senate may have had of this split amongst them being healed fell upon the shoulders of one young man; Tiberius' younger brother Caius (who ironically had been serving with Scipio in Spain during 133 BC). He was faced with a choice between family honour (avenging the honour of his murdered brother) or not enflaming the tensions that existed within the Senatorial aristocracy. Given his Roman upbringing he chose the former with a vengeance. Thus, he bided his time until he too was able to stand for election to the Tribunate. Despite facing several half-hearted attempts at blocking him from standing, Caius Sempronius Gracchus was duly elected as Tribune in December 124 BC and immediately set about introducing legislation aimed at those who had opposed his brother, seemingly satisfying family honour. Yet Caius went far further and took up the mantle of reform and introduced a programme of legislation the likes of which had not been seen in the Republic.

Caius introduced over a dozen pieces of legislation, affecting everything from the military (army recruitment and equipment), the judiciary (equestrian jurors) to the economy (subsidised corn for the citizenry). It was Caius who truly revealed the full scope of the powers of the Tribunate as an office which could be used to reshape the Republic through popular legislation. We must not forget that neither Tiberius nor Caius were outsiders but were part of the upper echelons of the Plebeian aristocracy and the Senatorial order, yet here was Caius overriding Senatorial prerogative across multiple areas. This also showed that the powers of the Senate relied on custom and practice (*mos maiorum*) and that the People (guided by a Tribune) could override these powers whenever the legislation was passed.

For the first of Caius' Tribunates his opponents in the Senate seemed powerless, and we must not forget that Caius had his own supporters in the Senate, including the former Consul M. Fulvius Flaccus (Cos. 125 BC). Thus, Caius was able to surpass his brother and secure immediate re-election to the Tribunate, giving him a second consecutive year in office, something that had not been seen in the Tribunate since the early fourth century BC. Furthermore, Caius' close ally and mentor, the former Consul, M. Fulvius Flaccus, took the unprecedented opportunity (as far as we know) of seeking election to the Tribunate (which must have been his second) subsequent to a Consulship. On the face of it, such a move, holding a junior office following holding the highest office must have seemed a highly odd action, but this move just went to show the anomalous position of the Tribunate of the Plebs. Whilst technically it was a junior office, and not even part of the official *cursus honorum* (it being a Plebeian office), in practice it was the most powerful domestic political office in Rome. Whilst Consul, Flaccus had raised the issue of Roman citizenship for the peoples of Italy and been blocked. Now, holding the Tribunate and in conjunction with his colleague Gracchus he had a second, and more realistic, chance of passing legislation for reforming Rome's citizenship system.

Rome's current citizenship system had been in existence since the 330s BC and was the bedrock of Rome's political control of Italy and her military success ever since. In 341 BC the Romans suffered a major revolt of their Latin allies (the states nearest Rome, which were under their control). Following military success in the Latin War (341–338 BC), Rome introduced a new system of rule. The old Federation of states with Rome at its head was abolished, and in its place stood a series of individual treaties between

Rome and the individual cities and regions, which allowed them autonomy on domestic matters, at the price of supplying men to fight in Rome's armies. This gave Rome the ability to tap into the military manpower of her defeated opponents, which eventually covered the whole Italian peninsula, allowing Rome to field armies the size of which had not been seen in the ancient world since the Persian Empire. This allowed Rome to field multiple and sometimes replacement armies and absorb defeats, no matter how heavy, as both Pyrrhus and Hannibal found to their cost.

Supporting this system of alliances were three grades of citizenship. At the top level was full Roman citizenship, which was now no longer based on geography alone. As well as the original inhabitants of the city, any allied community or individuals could be granted citizenship, as reward for their loyalty. This brought full legal rights, including protection from arbitrary Roman justice and the right to a trial as well as full political rights in terms of voting in Rome and being allowed to stand for Roman public office. Thus, the elites of each of the regions became suborned into the Roman oligarchy, men such as M. Porcius Cato, and were effectively given a stake in ensuring the continuation of Roman rule in their own regions. Thus, just as the Patrician order had suborned the elites of the Plebeian order and created a new Senatorial oligarchy, the Senate now steadily absorbed the elites of Italian regions.

However, if you did not have a full grant of Roman citizenship then there were two lesser categories, each with fewer legal and political rights. The second level was Latin citizenship, again originally for the Latin allies of Rome, but which could be extended to other individuals or regions, as the Senate and People decreed. Finally, there was Italian status, which the majority of inhabitants of Italy held. Our surviving sources do not present us with evidence for a major upsurge in demands from the Latin and Italians for Roman citizenship until Flaccus raised the issue in 125 BC. Yet Flaccus' failure led to the town of Fregellae rebelling from Roman rule in a one sided and doomed armed insurrection. Nevertheless, the second century had seen an increased military burden on the Latin and Italian allies to provide soldiers for Rome's continuing overseas wars, whether in Spain or in Greece / Macedon, not to mention a slow extension of Roman domestic legislation applying through the supposedly autonomous regions of Italy (as best seen with the suppression of the Bacchus cult in 186 BC).

Yet Flaccus and Gracchus now raised the prospect of Tribunes altering the fundamental underlying system of Roman citizenship, with a massive extension of the franchise. Here as always Roman politicians on both sides fell afoul of the issue of state vs. self. Even if there was a pressing need for reform, the person or group that enfranchised large groups of new citizens would reap a major political reward, as these people would now be able to vote in the Assemblies (if they were close enough to Rome). Under the Roman political system only Roman citizens could vote in Rome, restricting the franchise to just under four hundred thousand people (though far less in practice as voting had to be in person in Rome itself). These proposals would bring about a large increase in potential voters and thus disrupt the traditional networks of patronage which all the Roman aristocratic families had. Thus, once again, the rest of the Senatorial aristocracy believed that it was in their interests to oppose this reform.

During Caius' first year in the Tribunate (124/123 BC) he had faced little effective opposition, but for the following year his opponents in the Senate finally hit upon an effective tactic: promoting their own Tribune with his own (watered down) reform programme. Thus, they fought fire with fire and used the full potential of the Tribunate, and its positive powers (legislation) rather than just its negative ones (the power of veto). The man in question was M. Livius Drusus, an equally charismatic speaker, and his proposals (many of which never became law) drew crucial support away from Gracchus and Flaccus and ensured that deadlock ensured in the Assembly. Drusus was so successful that Gracchus failed to be elected for a third consecutive Tribunate (for 122/121 BC) and thus became a private citizen again. This allowed the focus to shift from proposing/opposing new legislation to protecting/overruling existing legislation and Gracchus and his supporters found themselves having to defend the laws he had already passed from being overturned in the Assembly by the new Tribunes.

At this point, the Republican system seemed to have been stabilised, having successfully navigated the various flashpoints which had emerged in 133 BC; namely re-election to the Tribunate and opposing Tribunician proposals without violence or the deposition of magistrates. Yet just as factions within the Senate had felt that they had no recourse but to violence in 133 BC it was now the turn of Gracchus and Flaccus to feel this, even though they may well have had allies in office. Thus, Gracchus and Flaccus tried to disrupt an Assembly held to overturn their legislation, which in turn led to bloodshed and the murder of a Q. Antyllus, who was connected to the Consul L. Opimius (possibly a official). This violence gave Opimius the chance he needed, and he had the Senate pass the *senatus consultum ultimum* (SCU), the ultimate decree of the Senate, which charged Opimius with defending the Republic from named enemies of the state – Gracchus and Flaccus.

The SCU is an incredibly obscure decree, which, as a Senatorial decree, did not have the force of law. It has been likened to a grant of martial law allowing the authorities to suspend civil liberties, most notably the right to a trial before punishment. However, the SCU had no such powers and was merely the considered opinion of the Senate (or whoever had the majority in the Senate that day). However, it set a terrible precedent; namely that one group within the Senatorial oligarchy could decree their political opponents as enemies of the state, to be dealt with in an extra judicial manner.

Whilst Gracchus and Flaccus may have started this chain of events by using violence to disrupt an Assembly, the Consul Opimius, charged with defending the Republic, oversaw a massive escalation of the bloodshed and brought soldiers into Rome (including archers) to eliminate Flaccus and Gracchus. Facing a Consul at the head of an armed force, and with negotiations proving fruitless, Flaccus and Gracchus and their supporters made a stand on the Aventine Hill but were no match for professional soldiers and especially the archers. What followed was a one-sided massacre with two hundred and fifty of Gracchus' and Flaccus' supporters being killed in 'battle' on the Aventine Hill. Opimius then pressed home his advantage by hunting down and murdering the survivors of the clash and any other notable supporters of the men still in Rome, totalling some three thousand people, including both Gracchus and Flaccus.

Thus, we can see that the events of 121 BC presented a significant escalation in the political chaos and bloodshed into which the Republic had fallen. The murders of 133 BC were a seemingly spontaneous act by a group within the Senatorial oligarchy who may not have even contemplated murder until the violence escalated. Here, the Consul Opimius oversaw a massacre of mostly-unarmed opponents using soldiers and supported by a formal decree of the Senate (against some of their own members). The dubious legality of the SCU was shown by Opimius being brought to trial for his actions, but his subsequent acquittal de facto strengthened its authority.

Whilst in the long term this incident had introduced some disturbing new elements into Roman politics, in the short term it did bring about political stability. The vast majority of Gracchus' and Flaccus' supporters had been murdered, leaving few alive to take up their cause. The only surviving prominent faction member was C. Papirius Carbo who was able to be elected Consul that year (for 120 BC) but was subsequently put on trial for treason and committed suicide. The causes they had raised, political reform and especially that of the Roman citizenship for Italians (the Italian Question) fell into the background. The next decade was a relatively quiet one in Roman politics (aided by a dearth of surviving sources for the period). However, it was another member of the Scipionic circle, albeit a junior one, who came to dominate Roman politics and engineer a third outbreak of political bloodshed.

The man in question was an Italian nobleman (with Roman citizenship) named C. Marius. He had been a client of Scipio Aemilianus and served with him in Spain, and thus at least must have known Caius Gracchus. We do not know his role during the tumult of the 120s BC, but he was a Questor c. 121 BC and became a Tribune in 119 BC, at the tail end of the period, and became noted for proposing a reform to the method of voting in elections (relating to the physical set up of the voting lanes) and ended up threatening to imprison the Consuls, one of whom was a Metellus (L. Caecilius Metellus Delmaticus), a member of Rome's' leading political family who were Marius' sponsors. Naturally enough his subsequent political career plateaued, barely scraping a Praetorship, though he did secure a marriage alliance with an old though undistinguished Patrician family, the Iulii, which eventually made him the uncle of a certain C. Iulius Caesar. By 109 BC he found himself on the command staff of the Consul Q. Caecilius Metellus 'Numidicus', who had command of Rome's war against their former ally in North Africa, the Kingdom of Numidia and its king Jugurtha.

The war itself had been forced on the Senatorial oligarchy (which had tried to avoid becoming entangled in North Africa) by a Tribune (C. Memmius). The Tribunes of this period continued to play a role throughout the war, with the elections for 109 BC suspended whilst two Tribunes of 110 BC attempted to be re-elected, and a special court set up in 109 BC by the Tribune Mamilius (the Mamilian Commission) to search out and try those amongst the Senatorial oligarchy who were believed to be in league with Jugurtha.

It was against this backdrop that Marius made a bold and career defining move. Recognising the growing anger of the People and the Equestrian business class at the Senate's handling of the war he returned to Rome to stand for election himself, with a promise to end the war (and Senatorial incompetence). Despite his own position as a junior member of the Senatorial oligarchy, Marius, with his background and experience, recognised the changes that the Roman constitution had undergone in the previous twenty years, with the Senatorial oligarchy's control of the Republic being loosened. On the back of this anti-Senatorial message and being bankrolled by the business cartels, he not only secured election to the Consulship of 107 BC but had a Tribune pass legislation to transfer the command of the Numidian War from Metellus Numidicus to himself, trampling on the Senatorial privilege of selecting Roman commanders and providing a clear blueprint for any commander who wished to follow him.

In all fairness however, we must not ignore the role of Marius' old patron Scipio Aemilianus, who had also been the patron to Ti. Gracchus. It was Scipio who had actually pioneered the use of the Tribunate to secure a military command, when in 135 BC (albeit with the approval of the Senate), Tribunes had directed the Assembly to suspend the law governing the time span between repeat Consulships (to allow him to be elected) and granting him command in Numantia. Thus, Marius had a perfect blueprint and merely took it one stage further by doing it against the wishes of the Senate. He then went further by suspending (not abolishing) Rome's most ancient principle on military recruitment; that citizens must have land, which in the short term allowed him to boost the numbers that could be recruited into Rome's legions for this war in Africa, but in the long term again providing a blueprint for other generals to recruit landless citizens in their armies.

With Metellus having gained the upper hand over Jugurtha, Marius crossed into Africa with his new army and ended the war. Under normal circumstances Marius would have returned to Rome, held his Triumph and retired to the life of a 'backbench' Senator, basking in his military and political Triumph and avoiding the dominant Metellan faction, who he had again humiliated. Yet whilst Rome's attention had primarily been on the Numidian War in the south and its impact on Roman domestic politics, in the north a military crisis was developing which soon began to threaten Rome itself.[2]

As was common with mainland Europe, the various tribes were engaged in a periodic cycle of warfare and migration. This cycle however saw two major northern tribes, the Cimbri and Teutones, as well as several lesser tribes such as the Ambrones and Tigurini, move southwards towards the tribes bordering Rome's limited (but important) territory in southern Gaul. Naturally enough Roman armies moved to intercept them but suffered a series of defeats (133, 108 and 107 BC). Thus by 105 BC the situation was so serious that the Senate dispatched two commanders (a Consul of 106 and one of 105 BC) to end the tribal menace once and for all. The result was the Battle of Arausio in 105 BC which was the greatest Roman military defeat to date, with sources placing the casualty figure in the region of one hundred thousand dead (and thus on a par with the Battle of Cannae).

Whilst this was a disaster for Rome, it was a splendid opportunity for Marius who, fresh from his Numidian victory was appointed as Consul once more for 104 BC and continuously until 101 BC (five consecutive Consulships). Under his command the Roman army achieved stunning victories over the tribes at the Battles of Aquae Sextiae and the Raudine Plain (Vercellae). Upon his return to Rome in 100 BC, despite being the 'Saviour' of Rome, he was well aware that he would face opposition in the Senate, especially from the dominant Metellan faction, and so fell back on tried and tested methods, and thus sought out a Tribune to work with. The Tribune he selected was L. Appuleius Saturninus, who with his political ally C. Servilius Glaucia, had already made a name for themselves, being noted for legislation and tactics in the mould of C. Gracchus.

Thus in 101–100 BC Marius formed a temporary Triumvirate, with Saturninus and Glaucia, with Marius as a Consul (with a pliant colleague),

Glaucia as a Praetor and Saturninus as a Tribune. Marius lent them his political power and his veterans to use in the Assembly and in return the two men ensured that Marius had the legislation he needed; in this case veteran colonies for his demobilised troops (giving the landless ones land). Saturninus however was far from a passive agent for Marius but an active force in his own right and he and Glaucia used this support to pass further laws through the Assembly using violence to overcome any opposition. He and Glaucia then attempted to ensure their subsequent re-election for the following year (99 BC) with Saturninus seeking another Tribunate and Glaucia the Consulship. However, the two men overplayed their hand and having secured for Marius the legislation they needed found that he now no longer had any need for them.

Once again, an electoral assembly led to violence which gave the Senate (and Marius) the excuse they needed to pass the *senatus consultum ultimum* once again and called up Marius to defend the Republic (once more). As had happened in 121 BC with Opimius and Gracchus, this clash in the heart of Rome took on a quasi-military tone, with Marius bringing in his veteran soldiers and Saturninus and his supporters being besieged on the Capitol. Being hopelessly outnumbered and with no resources to resist a long siege, Saturninus and his supporters surrendered and were promptly (and conveniently for Marius) murdered, along with Glaucia (who had been hiding elsewhere in Rome). Thus, for the third time, serving Roman magistrates had been slaughtered in the heart of Rome.

The immediate years that followed this massacre saw the political repercussions being played out across a series of trials, though Marius himself was never brought to trial for the deaths, his defence being that they were not killed on his orders and his acting under the auspices of the SCU. There were also several Tribunes, such as Sex. Titius, who took up the mantle of reform legislation, with another agrarian bill. There was another notable political murder in 98 BC with the lynching of the former Tribune (99 BC) P. Furius during his trial.

However, as was common, Roman politics reset itself and the various factions amongst the oligarchy returned to their political manoeuvrings. By 92 BC one faction, led by three senior Senators – L. Licinius Crassus (Cos. 95, Cens. 92 BC), Q. Mucius Scaevola (Cos. 95 BC) and M. Antonius (Cos. 99, Cens. 97 BC) – proposed a reform programme for the Republic, fronted by the junior members of their number as Tribunes. The first of these was none other than the son of C. Gracchus' opponent; M. Livius Drusus, who was elected Tribune for 91 BC Ironically, the programme proposed was a similar one to that of Gracchus and Flaccus some thirty years before. Amongst the measures proposed were bills on land distribution and subsidised grain, and more importantly one to change the composition of the Senate by adding three hundred equestrians to its number and one to extend Roman citizenship to the Italian allies.

It seems that tensions with the Italian allies had been rising throughout this period. Italian soldiers had stood shoulder to shoulder with their Roman counterparts at the Battles of Aquae Sextiae and the Raudine Plain (Vercellae) to defend Italy yet were still third-class citizens in their own peninsula. In fact, the Consuls of 95 BC (Crassus and Scaevola) had expelled all Italians from Rome, who were apparently claiming the full privileges of Roman citizenship (including subsidised grain). Given the close links between the Roman nobility and their Italian counterparts, they must have been well aware of the resentment building in Italy.

Thus, on the one hand we have a group of senior Roman aristocrats, all acknowledged to be amongst the most talented of their generation, putting forward a programme of reforms to cure what they diagnosed as the major faults within the Republic, as shown by the previous forty years. On the other hand, however, it could be seen as one faction of the oligarchy attempting to gain political advantage by reaping the rewards of the people who would benefit from these reforms; three hundred new Senators and millions of new Roman citizens. In the mind of a Roman aristocrat, however, both serving the Republic and gaining personal glory were totally intertwined and were one and the same. Unfortunately for the Crassan-Scaevolan-Antonine faction however, their opponents within the Senate placed greater value on the dangers of allowing these reforms to pass rather than the benefits they might bring to the Republic. Thus, these reforms were defeated in the Senate and blocked. Unlike many of his predecessors, Drusus and his supporters did not turn to violence to push them through and had in fact lined up two of Drusus' colleagues to be Tribunes for the following two years (C. Aurelius Cotta, for 90 BC and P. Sulpicius, for 89 BC).

It seems, however, that the faction's opponents were not above turning to violence, with Crassus dying suspiciously at home in the middle of a major Senatorial debate on the reforms and Drusus being assassinated at night by unknown assailants, though Cicero names Q. Varius Severus Hybrida (Tr. 90 BC) as the prime suspect.[3] Yet it was outside of Rome that the major implications of these failed reforms were to be felt. During the Senatorial clashes on the matter, a force of ten thousand Italians marched on Rome, ostensibly to show their support for them, but were turned away. Furthermore, rumours of a plot to assassinate the Consuls on the Alban Mount circulated, though nothing actually happened. Having rejected these proposed reforms (for this year) the Senate did however take the matter of how their rejection would impact on the Italians seriously and dispatched envoys to the major Italian cities to keep an eye on the reaction. Unfortunately for the Senate, they dispatched the Praetor Q. Servilius to Asculum, who acted in such a heavy-handed manner that he (and his legate) were murdered, a spark which ignited Rome's First Civil War and brought the Republic to the brink of collapse.

2. The Collapse: The First Civil War (91–71 BC)[4]

The rising at Asculum sparked off a peninsula-wide revolt of Rome's Italian allies, bringing together a broad church of different Italian races, each with a different aspiration of the revolt; from political equality within Italy to full-blown independence and the destruction of the Roman system. Broadly, the rebels formed two main alliances, one block concentrated on northern and central Italy under the command of the Marsi, and one in central and southern Italy under the command of the Samnites. Together they could easily have defeated Rome and destroyed the Roman system within Italy.

Faced with a crisis of this magnitude the Senate acted with remarkable swiftness and clarity. Having spent thirty years denying the Italian peoples Roman citizenship they immediately offered it to any Italian city or region that did not join the rebellion. Thus, at a stroke the vast majority of the Italian regions got the legal and political equality they had wanted without taking up arms. This tactic immediately separated the hardcore rebels from the moderate ones and denied the two rebel alliances any additional sources of manpower.

With these alliances isolated within Italy, Rome then deployed the full resources of its loyal allies, supported by drawing on the wealth of their empire outside of Italy. In military terms, given such a disparity of resources, the rebels' only chance was for a quick victory. The year 90 saw the fighting in the balance, with Rome losing the Consul P. Rutilius Lupus in battle and the Proconsul Sex. Iulius Caesar (Cos. 91 BC). Yet by year end, C. Marius had taken up command of Rutilius' army and a number of talented Roman commanders won victories, such as Cn. Pompeius Strabo and L. Cornelius Sulla. Thus by 89 BC the tide had turned and both rebel alliances were being defeated, though Rome did lose the Consul L. Porcius Cato in battle, but by the end of the year victory was assured.

It was perhaps safe in the knowledge that victory was on hand that the Senatorial oligarchy underwent another period of internal infighting and bloodletting which nearly converted a hard-won victory into a total collapse. Having granted most of the Italian people Roman citizenship the Senate turned to the thorny issue of the mechanics of this enrolment and once again the old Roman insecurities surfaced. The Republic had several assemblies for elections and legislation, but the most commonly-used one for legislation was the Tribal Assembly, with all of Rome's citizenry split into thirty-five tribes, originally based on geography.

As time had passed however, and more and more people across Italy received citizenship, these tribes had lost their geographic cohesion and more importantly their relative equality in terms of members. Thus, each Tribe had a different number of citizens, yet they all had one vote each. Legislation would thus be passed by the Tribes voting in a set order and a simple majority achieved. Thus, if the first eighteen tribes voted in favour of a measure then it was passed, regardless of whether the next seventeen agreed or not, or had even voted. The legislation the Senate passed in 89 BC to enrol the Italian people into the Roman citizenship thus contained a crafty safeguard, the creation of ten new tribes (numbers thirty-six to forty-five) for the millions of new citizens to be enrolled. Thus, the voting rights of the original citizens would be safeguarded, as would the oligarchy's control of them. Only twenty-three tribes would be required to pass a measure and the new citizens would only be called on to vote (if they could even attend in person) if the matter was a close one. Yet whilst this certainly was a crafty safeguard for the existing Roman oligarchy and citizenry, it rendered the new citizens as second class once more in terms of voting rights, not that the vast majority of Italians would be bothered.

Yet this was still a Roman sleight of hand and a statement that the Italians were still not fully equal to their Roman counterparts, and more importantly acted as a political cause to be manipulated. Almost immediately a Tribune picked up this cause and proposed an immediate reform, namely the full distribution of the new citizens throughout the existing thirty-five tribes. The Tribune in question was P. Sulpicius, a surviving junior member of the Crassan-Scaevolan-Antonine faction (many having been judicially purged by the Tribune Varius in 90 BC) and a former colleague of Drusus himself.

Unsurprisingly, Sulpicius' proposals brought him into conflict with the two Consuls, a partnership of L. Cornelius Sulla (a protege of Marius) and Q. Pompeius Rufus. Rather than back down, Sulpicius followed the tactics innovated by Saturninus in 100 BC and used violence to pass his reforms through the Assembly, which also included a bill to recall his colleagues and a Senatorial debt measure. Matters however soon escalated, with the Consuls attempting to disband the Assembly by declaring that all public business was prohibited that day. During the ensuing violence the son of the Consul Pompeius (married to Sulla's daughter) was murdered and the Consuls driven from Rome. Sulla sought refuge in his former mentor Marius' house. We will never know what the two men discussed, but Sulla lifted the suspension on public business and left Rome to take command of his army which was in Italy prior to being dispatched to the east to fight the King of Pontus, Mithridates VI, who had used the Roman collapse into civil war to invade and annex Rome's eastern provinces; firstly, Asia Minor and then Greece itself.

What happened next is one of the most notorious incidents in Republican history. With the ban on public business lifted, Sulpicius returned to the Assembly and passed his legislation, but included additional bills stripping Pompeius Rufus of his Consulship (a first for Tribunician legislation) and then transferring the command of the

Mithridatic campaign to none other than Sulla's mentor C. Marius himself (now well into his seventies). In response Sulla then marched his army on Rome, ostensibly in his role as Consul, and along with his colleague Pompeius Rufus, in order to restore peace and order in Rome; others however would call it a military coup. Naturally enough, faced with the Roman army, Rome itself soon fell and the Consuls were once more in charge. The Consuls then continued this escalation by declaring that Marius, Sulpicius and ten of their allies were enemies of the state and were to be executed without trial (illegal under Roman law). Of the twelve men, only Sulpicius was captured and executed, with the others, including Marius, fleeing overseas, mostly to North Africa.

The Consuls then passed conditional reforms to strengthen the role of the state and lessen that of the People and their Tribunes and then began to prepare for the future. With Rome's Eastern Republic overrun, Sulla had no choice but to march his army east to fight Mithridates. There were however Roman armies still in Italy fighting the last of the rebels, the largest of which was commanded by the Proconsul Cn. Pompeius Strabo. The Consuls therefore had the command of this army transferred to Pompeius Rufus, who was promptly murdered, on Strabo's order, when he turned up to take command.

With Pompeius Rufus dead and Sulla in the East, it fell to the newly elected Consuls of 87 BC to maintain peace and stability. Unfortunately for the Republic it was the Consuls themselves (L. Cornelius Cinna and Cn. Octavius) who were the source of the political dissension this year and escalated matters further than ever before. Rather than let matters lie, Cinna picked up Sulpicius' proposal on citizen distribution and was opposed by his colleague. Matters came to a head when Octavius had Cinna expelled from Rome and stripped of his Consulship. Cinna responded, as Sulla had done before him, and appealed to a Roman army stationed in Italy, that as Consul it was his duty to defend the Republic and their duty to follow him.

Cinna also appealed to the Italians to come to his aid and help him be restored to power and so gain full political equality, and thus his opponents in the Senate now faced another large army marching on Rome. Of the other military forces in Italy, the largest by far were those under the command of Cn. Pompeius Strabo and he nominally supported the Senate, but was actually bartering his services to both sides. A force under Q. Caecilius Metellus Pius (son of Numidicus) also supported the Senate. Marius, in exile in Africa, saw his opportunity and returned to Italy raising fresh forces as he went. Thus Rome faced its first siege since the time of the Gallic Sack some three hundred years before.

Again, rather than come to a political compromise both sides chose a full-scale civil war to decide the matter, with Cinna and Marius laying siege to Rome, which fell (as it usually did) to the attacking force. What followed was a total massacre as Cinna and Marius ordered the wholesale extermination of their political opponents and the sack of Rome itself. When the bloodshed had died down Marius and Cinna were the conquerors and masters of Rome. The Republic now had a new ruling Duumvirate, who promptly declared themselves Consuls for 86 BC. Sulla, fighting Mithridates in Greece, suddenly found himself as an enemy of Rome, despite commanding a Roman army and fighting Rome's enemies.

The rule of two soon became the rule of one, as Marius died, ironically of natural causes (old age and physical exertion) and Cinna found himself master of Rome. Under Cinna's direction the Republic experienced an outbreak of peace and stability (though the war continued in Greece). Unfortunately, once the war in Greece was concluded, which at one point saw two antagonistic Roman armies fighting Mithridates, the civil war resumed. Again, Sulla and Cinna could have chosen to negotiate, but neither wanted to back down. Cinna had intended to invade Greece and fight Sulla there, but was murdered during a mutiny. Leadership of his faction fell to Cn. Papirius Carbo and C. Marius (son of the elder) who refused the Senate's demands to negotiate with Sulla, thus ensuring another two years of bloody warfare on the Italian peninsula following Sulla's invasion of Italy in 83 BC.

Following the peninsula-wide campaigns, the final battle in Italy was fought for Rome itself in 82 BC at the Colline Gate, where Sulla's forces defeated an alliance of the Marian-Cinnan forces and the Samnites, the only undefeated Italian rebels from the war of 91–87 BC. Thanks to the military genius of a certain M. Licinius Crassus, the Sullan forces won the day and ensured their control of Italy. Sulla followed up this victory with a wave of bloody purges, known as the Proscriptions, with official deathlists being published of 'enemies' to be killed. He cemented his rule with the formal appointment as Dictator (for the duration of the crisis, as defined by him) which again saw a major overhaul of the Roman constitution, including the emasculation of the Tribunate and the centralisation of all political power in the hands of a freshly purged Senate. Following this Sullan constitutional settlement, he resigned his Dictatorship, spent a year as Consul and then retired from public office, presumably to take up a role as a 'guardian' of the New Republic, supported by a wave of veteran colonies planted strategically through Italy. Unfortunately for Sulla, and perhaps the Republic, he was not able to maintain this role as he died soon after (again ironically of natural causes, a degenerative disease).

Although victory at the Colline Gate had given Sulla control of Italy, along with Greece and Asia, the rest of Rome's Western Republic lay outside of his control. Gaul and Spain were under the command of C. Valerius Flaccus, an intriguing figure who spent the whole of the 80s BC maintaining Rome's empire in Spain and Gaul and refusing to get involved in the various civil wars of the period (unlike his brother; L. Valerius Flaccus, who replaced Marius in 86 BC and died in a mutiny in Asia the following year). In an unusual and what must have been a welcome move, Sulla and Flaccus chose to negotiate rather than fight and thus spare Rome a further round of civil war. Flaccus returned to Rome in 81 BC and celebrated a Triumph (over the native tribes), before returning to the life of a 'backbench' Senator and returning control of Spain and Gaul to the Sullan Senate.

The rest of Rome's Western Republic did not fall to Sullan control so peacefully, with Sicily and Africa still under Marian-Cinnan faction control, with Carbo himself having fled to Sicily. The task of subduing these regions fell to Sulla's most famous protege; Cn. Pompeius (son of Pompeius Strabo) and soon to be christened Magnus (the Great). Having proved his military credentials during the peninsular war of 83–82 BC, he soon invaded and conquered both Sicily and Africa, slaughtering a number of surviving Marian-Cinnan commanders, most notoriously Carbo himself. Thus, ever so briefly in 81 BC it looked as though the First Civil War had ended and Rome's empire was united once more. Unfortunately, this was merely an illusion and proved only to be a lull (as had happened in 86–84 BC).

A group of surviving members of the Marian-Cinnan faction fled from Africa to Spain under the command of a Q. Sertorius, their most senior surviving member, and raised a rebellion amongst the native tribes, undoing the work of Valerius Flaccus. Thus, the civil war flared up once more in Spain and was not subdued until 72 BC when Pompeius defeated Sertorius' successor, M. Perperna. Civil War in Spain was soon followed by a renewal of the war in Italy, when the Consuls of 78 BC violently fell out (repeating the scenario of a decade earlier). On this occasion the two men, M. Aemilius Lepidus (father of the future Triumvir) and Q. Lutatius Catulus, were able to prevent their political clashes from turning violent during their year in office. With Sulla having died in 78 BC, Lepidus immediately took up the cause of overturning the Sullan constitutional settlement. However, once Lepidus had left Rome to take up a Proconsular command in Transalpine Gaul, the clash became violent and Lepidus marched his army on Rome itself; the fourth time a Consul or Proconsul had done so in just over decade (the others being 88, 87, and 82 BC).

Unlike in 88 and 87 BC, the defenders of Rome were better prepared, and he was faced by an army commanded by his former colleague Catulus and Pompeius Magnus himself. Lepidus' army was defeated but the survivors fled first to Sardinia, where Lepidus died of natural causes, and then to Spain to join Sertorius. The survivors included M. Perperna who was to murder Sertorius and assume command of the rebellion in Spain, and L. Cornelius Cinna, son of the Consul of 87–84 BC.

Although the civil war in Italy had been extinguished again, a second front opened in Asia when a group of the Marian-Cinnan faction led by M. Marius (whose relation to C. Marius is not clear) allied themselves to the Pontic King Mithridates during his third war with Rome in the east. Thus, Rome faced a civil war on two fronts; in the west (Spain) Rome faced a native rebellion led by the survivors of the Marian/Cinnan faction whilst in the east (Asia Minor) Rome faced a Pontic army spearheaded by the survivors of the Marian/Cinnan faction. To make matters worse, the devastation of Italy during the preceding near two decades of warfare had provided the perfect breeding ground for a slave rebellion, which unlike previous small-scale affairs soon escalated into a major war, enflamed by successive Roman defeats at the hands of a slave army led by a Thracian known as Spartacus.

Yet despite facing war on three fronts, the Sullan commanders slowly gained the upper hand. In the east, in 73 BC L. Licinius Lucullus defeated the Marian-Mithridatic forces at the Battle of Tenedos and ordered the murder of the captive M. Marius, removing the civil war element from the conflict, and then drove Mithridates further into Asia. The following year (72 BC) in Spain saw the Marian-Cinnan leader Sertorius murdered by his deputy, Perperna, who was easily dispatched by Pompeius. The same year saw the Senate appoint M. Licinius Crassus (the victor of the Colline Gate) to command the Roman forces against Spartacus. Faced with a large Roman army commanded by a talented general, the slave armies proved to be no match and were destroyed in 71 BC. Thus, Italy and Spain were at peace and another lull opened in the civil war.

Yet, almost inevitably, a new threat to the Republic's stability emerged when Cn. Pompeius marched his victorious army from Spain back into Italy (defeating a remnant of Spartacus's army fleeing Crassus). From the opposite direction Crassus marched his victorious army back to Rome. Thus, the two most talented and dangerous of Sulla's lieutenants marched towards Rome, both at the head of victorious armies, both expecting to receive their rewards for their campaigns. Naturally everyone amongst the Senate and People of Rome awaited their next actions.

3. The Recovery: The Pompeian-Crassan Settlement and the New Republic (71–70 BC)

What happened next was a milestone in the Republic; although both men acknowledged that they were rivals they came to the conclusion that they could achieve what they wanted by combining forces rather than fighting. Thus, Pompeius and Crassus combined forces, bringing together their respective political patronage, financial backing and popularity, presenting an unstoppable force which ensured that both men would be elected as Consuls for the following year, despite Pompeius' candidacy being against the Sullan constitution (due to his age and lack of previous offices). By choosing to pursue power in the Republic through peaceful means the two men ensured that the lull in the civil war was converted into its end. Furthermore, the two men provided a new blueprint for achieving temporary domination of the Republic – co-operation, forming an unstoppable temporary alliance whose resources could ensure that they overwhelmed the other factions in the Senate (albeit on a temporary basis). It was a tactic which the two men returned to repeatedly (60–59 and 55–53 BC) and was followed by others (men such as Caesar, Octavianus, Lepidus and Antonius).

Having achieved their Consulships, the two men set about reforming the Republic and introduced a series of measures overturning many elements of the Sullan settlement. The two key elements were the restoration of the powers of the Tribunate – far too useful a tool for either man to allow to remain unused – and the restoration of the Censorship. There is no clear evidence that Sulla abolished the Censorship, but he must have instructed the Senate not to use it as no Censors had been appointed since the Cinnan ones of 86 BC. Perhaps this was Sulla's method of avoiding the question of Italian citizenship, by not conducting a full census of the citizenry.

Both offices were put to immediate use. We only know the name of one of the Tribunes of this year; Plautius / Plotius, but he immediately passed a law restoring citizen rights to all those Romans who had been exiled during the civil war period, thus allowing the return to Rome of a whole swathe of politicians, including those who had supported Lepidus in 78–77 BC (and who had survived the intervening years). This allowed men such as L. Cornelius Cinna to return to Rome. Furthermore, these men would owe their restoration to Pompeius and Crassus and would form a new block in the Senate to counter balance the hardcore Sullan faction (who would not be amenable to Pompeius and Crassus). Furthermore, this amnesty was a very public declaration that the divisions of the civil war were now over, and that peace had been restored (by Pompeius and Crassus). We also hear of a *lex Plotia*, which was an agrarian bill and may have been passed by this Tribune to provide land for the discharged soldiers of the two men.[5]

As well as the Tribunate, Pompeius and Crassus made immediate use of the Censorship, with the two Consuls of 72 BC, who had endorsed Crassus' appointment to the Spartacan command, now getting their reward. In return they conducted the first full census of the Roman citizenry since the Italian rebellion and the full grant of citizenship. Its effects were immediately apparent as the number of Roman citizens had more than doubled from 463,000 in 86 BC to 910,000.[6] Thus, Pompeius and Crassus completed the work that had started some twenty years before and concluded the Italian citizenship question as well. The two men also made use of the powers of the Censorship to revise the Senate list, with some sixty-four Sullan Senators expelled or purged.[7] We can be certain that these men were no friends of either Pompeius or Crassus.

The two men also had Praetor L. Aurelius Cotta pass a law reforming the composition of juries; a long standing political issue (since C. Gracchus in the 120s BC). Rather than favour either the Senate or the Equestrians (the latter of which had supported Pompeius and Crassus), this law struck a balance with jury composition split evenly between three groups (Senators, Equestrians and a third obscure group, the *Tribuni aerarii*). Clearly the hope was that by favouring neither side but having a balancing group that this would make the juries fairer and stop it being a political issue. As it was Pompeius himself passed two further reforms to judicial proceedings later in his career.

Thus, we can see that both men introduced their own constitutional settlement (the Pompeian-Crassan settlement) which reformed the Republic once more. The long-standing offices of Censors and Tribunes were restored, there was a very public amnesty of all political exiles, a full census of Roman citizens was taken, the Senate lists revised and a compromise position on jury reform reached. Thus, a framework was devised to put an end to the First Civil War, which had raged for two decades, and a return to a normal working Republic, as proved by both men standing down and returning to the status of private citizens. Therefore, Pompeius and Crassus had ended the Sullan Republic and created a new post-civil war Republic. Of course, the crucial question would be that after forty years of political bloodshed, and twenty years of civil war, how strong and stable would this 'new' Republic be?

Part II

The New Republic Challenged (70–59 BC)

Chapter Two

An Outbreak of Peace? Political Reform and the 'New' Republic (69–64 BC)

Naturally, it is only with the benefit of hindsight that we can argue that the Consulships of Pompeius and Crassus marked a turning point in the history of the late Republic and brought an end to the First Civil War. Certainly, it was the first full year since 92 BC that there had been no civil warfare, but this did not automatically mean that the civil war had ended, as there had been lulls in the previous two decades. The key question which everyone at the time must have been asking was whether the Pompeian-Crassan settlement would bring about an end to civil warfare and more importantly end the political violence and bloodshed that had plagued the Republic for the four decades before the First Civil War.

1. A New Republic?

The reforms of Pompeius and Crassus overturned key elements of the decade-old political settlement of their former mentor, L. Cornelius Sulla, and ushered in a new period of the Republic. Yet this was not simply turning the clock back and overthrowing the whole Sullan settlement (as had been done in 87/86 BC)[1] but the bringing together of elements of the pre-Civil War Republic, the Cinnan and Sullan Republics, together with completely new features. In many ways, the Republican system that emerged was the Pompeian-Crassan Republic and these two men were at the heart of the system for the two decades of its existence.

The most obvious feature of the pre-Civil War Republic was a restoration of the powers of the Tribunate of the Plebs, an office which was unique in the Roman constitution in a number of ways (see Chapter One). This was certainly the most popular and contentious of the Pompeian-Crassan reforms, given that the Tribunate had been at the heart of the various

bouts of political reform and accompanying bloodshed throughout the
133–91 BC period and had contributed greatly to the outbreak of the First
Roman Civil War. Yet aside from this role, the office had developed over
the centuries into being the most efficient method of passing legislation
in Rome, on both important matters of state and the mundane day to day
affairs.

The key element of the Cinnan Republic, which was both retained and
built upon, was the full enrolment of all the peoples of Italy (south of
the River Po) into the Roman citizenship system. Whilst the citizenship
franchise had initially been granted to certain Italian peoples as far
back as 90 BC, their path to full integration was a rocky and sometimes
obscure one. We know that the issue of their full integration amongst the
thirty-five voting Tribes was a major factor in the bloodshed of both 88
and 87 BC. The Cinnan Census of 86 BC had clearly started the process
of integrating the new citizens, as the total number recorded rose from
394,000 in 115/114 BC to 463,000; the highest total to date.[2] Yet we also
know that this number falls way short of the total number of new citizens
in Italy. We have no record of any further censuses being held between
86 and 70 BC though the *Periochae* of Livy does state that c.84 BC, '*by
Senatorial decree, the new citizens received the right to vote*'.[3]

Frustratingly we have no further details, so are unable to properly
examine the evolution of this integration process. Furthermore, we are
not clear as to Sulla's actions in relation to these new citizens. Certainly he
had opposed their full integration in 88 BC and huge numbers of Italians
joined the Cinnan armies in opposing his invasion of Italy. However
even with full military control of Italy, Sulla would not have been able
to reverse the citizenship gains they had made (without sparking off a
fresh civil war), but he may well have frustrated their full integration.
The Pompeian-Crassan sponsored Census of 70 BC, therefore, seems to
have completed this integration process, with the number of new citizens
nearly doubling to 910,000.[4] Thus, the new Republican system of post-
70 BC had to contend with a potential electorate of nearly one million
citizens, though voting for Roman magistrates and laws still had to be
done in person in Rome itself.

Despite the high-profile restoration of the powers of the Tribunate,
large elements of the Sullan constitution survived, most notably the

reforms to the *cursus honorum* (the system of progression through the Roman political offices), not to mention the membership of the Senate, which had been fully re-stocked by Sulla himself. However, under the Pompeian-Crassan settlement the Senate had lost its control over the legislation and the juries. Furthermore, a decade of natural attrition would have lessened the number of hard-core Sullan Senators, as did the Census of 70 BC itself, which expelled sixty-four Senators, none of whom would have been allies of either Pompeius or Crassus. Nevertheless, there would still have been many Sullan loyalists in the Senate.

Other legacies of Sulla remained; notably his veteran colonies planted throughout Italy and his disenfranchisement of the relatives of those men who had been proscribed during his Dictatorship. The final legacy was a physical one; namely the next generation of the Cornelii Sullae, of which the most prominent were his son Faustus and his nephews Publius and Servius. Of the three, Publius was the eldest and was already in the Senate at this point and would have been eligible for the Praetorship shortly. These men would have to navigate the fine line between tapping into the positive aspects of Sulla's legacy without being tarred by the negative ones.

Finally, this new Republic had completely new elements, the most obvious of which was the three-way split on the composition of juries. Jury membership had been a contentious issue since the time of C. Sempronius Gracchus in the 120s BC. Originally manned solely by Senators, Gracchus had handed control of the juries, which tried cases of corruption and treason, to the Equestrian Order. Since that time, it had gone back and forth between the Senators and Equestrians and occasionally both. Sulla had firmly placed juries under the control of the Senate, but Pompeius and Crassus, using a Praetor (L. Aurelius Cotta), created a new tripartite solution, with Senators, Equestrians and a third (and obscure) group called the *Tribuni Aerarii*.

Thus, the Republican system which emerged from the Pompeian-Crassan Consulship of 70 BC was not simply a return to the pre-Sullan Republic but a new entity, a hybrid of elements from the various reforms to the Republican system over the previous twenty-year period of the First Civil War (91–70 BC). Yet, as we have seen, the Republic had seen numerous and sometimes drastic reforms imposed on it during these last twenty years and there was no reason that those of Pompeius and Crassus would be the final ones or be any more permanent than those of their former mentor Sulla. Thus, these reforms were not an end in themselves, but merely another stage in its evolution.

2. The Calm after the Storm, 69–68 BC

What happened next, after this tumultuous year in the history of the Republic, has long been seen as something of an anti–climax. For the next two years (69 and 68 BC) we see virtually nothing of note reported in terms of Roman domestic politics. In fact, the surviving narrative of the year which followed is dominated by the trial of C. Verres, who had been Governor of Sicily (73–71 BC). The trial, which was a simple case of alleged corruption and governing malpractice, brought by the inhabitants of Sicily, has a far higher profile than it ought, solely owing to the identity of the prosecutor; one M. Tullius Cicero, who wrote up (and dramaticised) his prosecution speeches, the *Verrines*. The survival of this highly dramaticised account has thus given it a far greater place in the surviving narrative of events than it would otherwise have. Whilst the trial itself was in 70 BC there were various efforts to get it extended into the following year (69 BC) when certain of Verres' allies would take up the Consulship. The *Verrines* also provides us with the identities of two of the Tribunes of 69 BC (Q. Cornificius and Q. Manlius), but not any mention of their actions.

Moving away from this over-sensationalised trial, the key aspect of the immediate aftermath of 70 BC is the absence of Rome's two leading men, Pompeius and Crassus. Both had refused pro-consular commands, flying in the face of custom and practice and both seem to have disappeared from our few surviving narratives for the next two years. In normal circumstances, the Consulship was the springboard into a pro-consular command of a military campaign and the chance to earn glory, and hopefully a Triumph. Yet neither man could be referred to as a 'typical' Consul, as both Pompeius and Crassus had already achieved military glory at a young age. The careers of the two men had mirrored each other, as both had already been successful generals in the First Civil War, during the Sullan invasion of Italy (83–82 BC). Pompeius had then moved on to a further civil war campaign in Spain against Sertorius, whilst Crassus had saved Rome from the threat of the slave rebellion under Spartacus. Neither man would have relished a standard pro-consulship in the provinces fighting natives; whilst the only major campaign was in the east, against Mithridates VI of Pontus and Tigranes of Armenia, and was commanded by Lucullus, who's grip on the command seemed unshakeable.

However, there is a far more compelling argument as to why both men stayed in Rome rather than leave for the provinces; namely to ensure that their political settlement was not overturned once they had stepped down from office. On this point many commentators seem to assume that the reversal of some of Sulla's key reforms was inevitable and do not consider the possibility that once Pompeius and Crassus were out of office their political opponents would seek to undo their reforms. Yet, if the previous fifty years of Roman politics have shown us anything, it is that no reform was ever permanent, and on certain subjects reforms were amended or even reversed soon afterwards. This was a natural result of the impermanency built into the Roman political system; office holders only held power for one year and their successors were not bound by their decisions. As powerful as Pompeius and Crassus were (especially when they combined their resources), in 69 BC neither man held political office and thus neither had any formal power. Although both men had considerable support in the Senate (especially after the Census of 70 BC) there would still have been considerable opposition to them, both from those who had followed Sulla and those who formed their own family factions.

In fact, the years 69 and 68 BC see the return to prominence of the Metellan family.[5] During the years 123 to 98 BC the various members of the Metellan family had dominated Roman politics with seven Consuls and four Censors during the period. This dominance had tailed off by the 90s BC due to the changing generations of the family; the older members having held office and the younger ones not being old enough to hold senior positions. This was further overshadowed by the civil war period, which disrupted the normal political process. The only notable Metellan during this period was Q. Caecilius Metellus Pius, who found himself as one of the only surviving members of the faction which opposed Cinna and Marius in 87 BC and was forced to flee to Sulla. His reward was a Consulship in 80 BC.

Yet we see Metelli as Consuls in both 69 and 68 BC (Q. Caecilius Metellus 'Creticus' and L. Caecilius Metellus), with another (M. Caecilius Metellus) holding the Praetorship of 69 BC. It would be wrong to say that the Metelli were Sullan in outlook, as first and foremost they were advocates of the Metelli and would always put their own family interests first. Whilst it is unlikely that they would have pushed to overturn the whole Pompeian-Crassan settlement, there would have been an opportunity to dilute it.

Even though neither Pompeius nor Crassus held office, they were still present in Rome and still attended the Senate and possibly the Assemblies, and thus were present to head off any revisions to their reforms by mobilising their supporters in both arenas. Had both men left Rome for their regular Proconsular commands then they would not have been able to do so. Such manoeuvrings have not been captured by our surviving sources for this period, but then we have no surviving annalistic sources, which would have recorded a year by year account of Roman politics.

Thus, we have an apparent period of calm in Roman domestic politics, with the only other notable incident being a curious one from 68 BC when one of the Consuls (Q. Marcius Rex) spent most of the year as sole Consul. His colleague, L. Caecilius Metellus, died soon after taking office and his replacement (suffect) Servilius Vatia also died. No further replacement was chosen, and Marcius spent a quiet year in office. In terms of foreign affairs, Rome had started a fresh campaign to cleanse the Mediterranean of pirates, which went disastrously wrong when two of the Praetors were themselves defeated and captured. Further afield the main military campaigns continued to be those of L. Licinius Lucullus against Mithridates VI of Pontus and Tigranes of Armenia.

3. The Bloody Return of the Tribunate (67–65 BC)

For many, the years 69 and 68 BC must have been an affirmation that the Pompeian-Crassan settlement had been successful and that a peaceful Republic had been restored. The normal business of the Republic carried on, with no violence and no bloodshed. However, if people did begin to believe that a peaceful Republic had been restored, then unfortunately the years that followed shattered that illusion as the familiar cycle of reform, violence and bloodshed returned, centred once more on the office of the Tribunate of the Plebs.

Whilst we aren't aware of the activities of the Tribunes of 69 or 68 BC, the same cannot be said of those of the year 67 BC, which saw several Tribunes using their newly restored powers to the full and the return of Tribunician clashes and the passing of legislation with violence. For 67 BC we know the identities of five of the ten Tribunes (with one additional possible identity – see Appendix Two). Central to the events of this year were two Tribunes, C. Cornelius and A. Gabinius, who both proposed several pieces of reforming legislation. We do not know to what extent the two men collaborated, but both men had connections to Cn. Pompeius. Of the two, Cornelius' primary focus seemed to be domestic affairs whilst Gabinius focussed more on overseas matters.[6]

We are aware of four reform bills which Cornelius proposed: a law to ban loans to envoys of foreign states; a law restating the recent *lex Calpurnia* on banning bribery at elections; a law forcing Praetors to adhere to their own rules; and most importantly a law which affirmed that the People (in the Assemblies) were the sole body who could pass exemptions from the law. We have a great deal of detail about Cornelius' proposals, mostly thanks to the survival of one of Cicero's defence speeches (defending Cornelius – see below) which survives in Asconius.

Initially it seems that Cornelius proposed a law regulating the practice of loans being given (most likely by Senators) to the envoys of foreign powers, which were accompanied by apparently extortionate levels of interest. Interestingly Cornelius made this proposal first to the Senate (in accordance with custom and practice), but unsurprisingly the Senate rejected his proposal.[7] Cornelius' rationale for this measure is given (by Cicero/Asconius) as defending the provincials from rapacious Roman elites. We do not know if there was a specific case which prompted this, or specific representations made to him or a patron, but Asconius does point out that Cornelius was previously a Questor of Cn. Pompeius and we can perhaps see his hand behind this, perhaps looking after the interests of a group of provincial elites.

Faced with the opposition of the Senate, Cornelius seems to have dropped this proposal, but in its place, he presented a measure to the People which curbed the Senate's power to pass exemptions to the law:

> *'He promulgated a law by which he reduced the authority of the Senate,*
> *whereby no one should be exempted from the laws except by vote of the*
> *People.' This safeguard had been incorporated in ancient law too, and*
> *thus in all Senatorial, decrees ... But gradually the practice of referral*
> *(to the People) had been abandoned.*[8]

Thus, within just two years of the Pompeian-Crassan constitutional settlement a (possibly Pompeian backed) Tribune was returning further powers from the Senate to the Assemblies of the People and thus reinforcing the power of laws passed by the Assemblies (and the Tribunes). Again, unsurprisingly the Senate opposed such a move and again were able to gain the support of one of Cornelius' Tribunician colleagues (P. Servilius Globulus) to interpose his veto (*intercessio*). Thus, just two years after the restoration of the full powers of the Tribunate Rome once again saw a Tribune vetoing another Tribune's proposals on behalf of a faction of the Senate. On this particular occasion, we are told that Globulus blocked the Tribunician officials (*scribae*) from reading the text of the proposal to the People. However Cornelius neatly side stepped this obstruction by reading the text to the People himself.

At this point, the Consul L. Calpurnius Piso intervened on the stated belief that 'the Tribunician right of veto (*intercessio*) was being subverted'.[9] Thus, we have a Consul publicly defending the Tribunician right of veto (when it suited his needs). According to Asconius / Cicero, this led to a violent clash between a (pro-Cornelian) section of the People in the Assembly and the Consul's lictors (officials) resulting in the lictors being assaulted and stones thrown at the Consul, though no serious blood seems to have been shed.

On the one hand, it seems therefore that the Republic had soon lapsed into 'business as usual' with violence in the Assemblies and clashes between Tribunes and between Tribunes and Consuls. Yet on the other hand, the violence did not turn unduly bloody and, following the suspension of the Assembly, Cornelius presented a watered-down version of his bill. This allowed the Senate to retain the power of exempting people from the laws, but only if two hundred Senators were present. Thus, a compromise was reached, something which had been sorely lacking in political reform proposals of the previous seventy years.

Following on from this, Cornelius continued with his reform proposals, meeting with mixed success. A law was passed enforcing the Praetors to *'dispense justice in accord with their own standing edicts:*[10] i.e. forcing them to follow the rules set down for the office, in an apparent attempt to stamp out favouritism when the Praetors were trying cases in the courts. Less successful was a proposal strengthening the safeguards against electoral bribery, but again a compromise was reached when the Consul Calpurnius Piso passed a watered-down version of this law himself. Cornelius, it seems, did not attempt to re-propose his law regulating loans of foreign envoys, but one was passed by his colleague A. Gabinius. Cicero sums up the rest of Cornelius' Tribunate thus:

> *Cornelius promulgated several other laws too, against most of which his colleagues interposed their vetoes* (intercessio), *and over these dissensions the whole period of his Tribunate was spent.*[11]

Of course, the great question regarding Cornelius' Tribunate is how much of this reform programme was his own work and what if any was that of Pompeius? There is no direct evidence that Pompeius was supporting him or the originator of these proposals. A comparison to Ti. Gracchus is both inevitable and perhaps instructive. Both men had reform programmes, both met opposition from the Senate and Consuls and their fellow Tribunes. What is noticeable is that Ti. Gracchus pushed on regardless, in the face of this opposition with the violence spiralling into murder, whilst Cornelius pulled back following the violence and moderated his proposals. Clearly the violence and bloodshed of the previous seventy years must have been in his mind, as they would have been to any Roman who had survived the First Civil War period. It is also possible that, unlike Ti. Gracchus, Cornelius' patron was in Rome and there to extend a restraining hand on the activities of his agent, unlike P. Cornelius Scipio Aemilianus in 133 BC.

However, Cornelius was not the only Tribune this year with a legislative programme of reforms; the other was A. Gabinius. We know of three laws he proposed and / or passed. One was possibly a restatement of Cornelius' law on regulating loans to foreign envoys. We know of a Gabinian law from this period which banned loans to foreign envoys, though there is no certain attestation to this Gabinius during his Tribunate. However, it is for his laws on overseas commands that his Tribunate is most famous. The first law was a simple enough affair and harked back to Tribunician laws of the pre-Civil War period, when he assigned the province of Bithynia and Pontus to the Consul M. Acilius Glabrio. The issue here being that those provinces were being held by L. Licinius Lucullus, who had overall command of the war in the east, held under a long pro-consulship confirmed by the Senate. The law also assigned a portion of Lucullus' army to Glabrio. Thus, once again we have a Tribune riding roughshod over Senatorial privilege, allocating military commands by popular law and removing commands from a serving pro-consul.

Though we know what Gabinius accomplished with this law, as in many cases we do not know why he did it. Lucullus was left with a sizeable army still and overall command of the war in the east. Thus, it is not comparable to the time C. Marius had a Tribune transfer the command of the Numidian War outright to himself from a serving commander. Cicero states that Gabinius was motivated due to the length of time Lucullus had been in that command (since 74 BC) and that the war was now expanding beyond its original remit (the defeat of Mithridates).[12] Plutarch even quotes a Praetor who apparently made a speech before the People accusing Lucullus of having too much power.[13]

As we shall see below, as Gabinius clearly was working on behalf of Pompeius on another law, there is always the suspicion that this was the first step of reducing the power of Lucullus and preparing the way for Pompeius to take command. It was Gabinius' second law on overseas command which is the most famous however, and it concerned the perennial problem of Mediterranean piracy.[14]

With the Roman reduction of a number of the Mediterranean powers, such as Rhodes, the policing of the Mediterranean fell into abeyance, allowing piracy to flourish. Over the years these pirate forces had become stronger and begun disrupting Roman trade routes and even attacking Italian ports. Perhaps their most famous captive was C. Iulius Caesar himself, who was captured by a pirate attack at sea and had to be ransomed for his release. Throughout the 70s BC, a number of Roman Praetors were sent to deal with the pirates, in response to an escalation in the attacks.

Most either failed to deal with the pirates or were openly defeated in battle. In 74 BC in response to this growing threat the Senate created a special command with *imperium infinitum* and appointed the Praetor M. Antonius (father of the future Triumvir). Despite the extraordinary amount of power invested in this command, Antonius met with little success and was soundly defeated off Crete in 71 BC. With the pirates still a growing threat to Roman trade and power, Gabinius proposed to create an even greater extraordinary command against the pirates:

> [*Gabinius*] *drew up a law which gave him, not an admiralty, but an out-and-out monarchy and irresponsible power over all men. For the law gave him dominion over the sea this side of the Pillars of Hercules, over the entire mainland to the distance of four hundred furlongs from the sea. These limits included almost all places in the Roman world, and the greatest nations and most powerful kings were comprised within them. Besides this, he was empowered to choose fifteen legates from the Senate for the several principalities, and to take from the public treasuries and the tax-collectors as much money as he wished, and to have two hundred ships, with full power over the number and levying of soldiers and oarsmen.*[15]
>
> *And that in all the provinces he should have a power equal to that of the Proconsular governors to a distance of fifty miles from the sea. By this decree the command of almost the entire world was being entrusted to one man.*[16]

There were three key differences between the command of 74 BC and the command of 67 BC.[17] Firstly, its power seems to have been greater, especially in terms of extending it fifty miles inland. Secondly it was created by Tribunician law, not Senatorial decree, and thirdly it was proposed (and passed) that the command would be given to Cn. Pompeius 'Magnus' himself. Thus, only three years after restoring the Tribunate's power, here was a Tribune (and a known adherent of Pompeius himself) proposing to grant Pompeius more military power than any other commander had wielded outside of either a civil war or the appointment of a Dictator. Naturally enough there was a faction of the Senate which opposed this:

But that body (the Senate) *preferred to suffer anything whatever at the hands of the pirates rather than put so great command into Pompeius' hands; in fact, they came near slaying Gabinius in the very Senate-House, but he eluded them somehow. When the People learned the feeling of the Senators, they raised an uproar, even going so far as to rush upon them as they sat assembled; and if the Senators had not gotten out of the way, they would certainly have killed them. So they all scattered and secreted themselves, except Caius Piso the Consul, for it was in the year of Piso and Acilius that these events took place; he was arrested and was about to perish for the others when Gabinius begged him off.*[18]

Following this violence, the opposing factions in the Senate turned to the Tribunate itself and its fully restored power of veto (*ius intercessio*):

After this the optimates themselves held their peace, happy if only they might be allowed to live, but tried to persuade the nine Tribunes to oppose Gabinius. None of these, however, except one Lucius Trebellius and Lucius Roscius, would say a word in opposition, through fear of the multitude; and those two men, who had the courage, were unable to fulfil any of their promises by either word or deed.[19]

Once again however just as Cornelius had overcome his colleague's veto on his proposal, so did Gabinius. In fact, Gabinius went one step further and employed the same stratagem of Ti. Gracchus and proposed a new law; that Trebellius be deposed from his Tribunate; and thus Tribunician history repeated itself:

When this man (Trebellius) *persisted in his veto, as he had promised the Senate that he would die before it was carried through, Gabinius began to call the Tribes to vote in order to annul Trebellius' office, just as one-time Ti. Gracchus as Tribune annulled the office of his colleague M. Octavius. And for some time Trebellius stood there unafraid and persisted in his veto, because he insisted that Gabinius was merely threatening it rather than intending to see it through. But after seventeen tribes accepted that proposal, and only one remained, Trebellius withdrew his veto.*[20]

Thus, Gabinius copied Ti. Gracchus and proposed, and had the Assembly vote on, the deposition of one of his Tribunician colleagues; just as had occurred seventy years before. On this occasion however, and perhaps with the previous example in mind, Trebellius withdrew his veto before it was too late. Thus, the law was passed and Pompeius was given command over the entire Mediterranean.

Therefore, within just three years the newly restored Tribunate had been used by one of Rome's leading generals to secure for himself an extraordinary command, placing the entire resources of the Mediterranean at his disposal. This had been passed with accompanying violence (though no deaths are reported) and yet again seen a Tribune ride roughshod over the constitutional safeguards imposed upon the office.

This was a theme which continued the following year (66 BC) and again saw another Tribune (C. Manilius) propose controversial legislation on both domestic and foreign matters. His first proposal was a highly symbolic one, as he seems to have resurrected P. Sulpicius' proposal to distribute all freedmen (former slaves) throughout all thirty-five voting tribes. Sulpicius' original proposal in 88 BC (see Chapter One) concerned both newly enfranchised Italians as well as freedmen, but nevertheless the proposal was a highly symbolic one, especially given that Sulpicius' Tribunate had ended with the Consuls marching their army on Rome and opening up a fresh, and deadly, chapter in the First Roman Civil War.

However, there were key differences between Sulpicius' and Manilius' proposals, based on the circumstances at the time. In 88 BC, the civil war against the rebel Italians was still being fought, making a fair constitutional settlement a priority. By 67 BC however, the Italians had theoretically gained political parity (albeit recently) and the freedmen were hardly a strategic threat. Yet nonetheless, making further amendments to the constitutional settlement was bound to be resisted by many in the Senate and possibly many within the existing Roman People. Crucially we do not have much detail of Manilius' background or patronage (if any). Naturally many at the time, and ever since, have tried to detect either the hand of Pompeius or Crassus being behind this law, but it may just as well have been Manilius' own push for political power. Certainly, whoever succeeded in giving the freedmen an equal vote should have been able to count on their support, at least in the short term.

Another possibility is that Sulla had freed a significant number of slaves just fifteen years before and so there would have been a significant pro-Sullan body of freedmen, which perhaps Manilius was trying to tap into. Though we have no details of Manilius' immediate family, the Manilii seem to have been an old Roman Senatorial family, with a Manilius holding office as far back as 449 BC, though they did not attain the Consulship until 149 BC.

In any event, it seems that Manilius used familiar tactics to push the proposal through the Assembly, including using a body of freedmen with accompanying violence. Inevitably there was a backlash, led by a Questor (L. Domitius Ahenobarbus), which resulted in bloodshed:

> *C. Manilius, as Tribune of the Plebs, supported by a gang of freedmen and slaves, was passing an utterly immoral law to allow freedmen the vote in all of the Tribes, and was pursuing this aim with rioting, and was blockading the climb to the Capitol. Domitius (a Quaestor) scattered and broke through the gathering so violently that many of Manilius' men were killed.[21]*

Thus, we can see the escalation of events which had been so familiar to the post-Gracchan period of Roman politics. In 70 BC, the powers of the Tribunate had been restored, in 67 BC a Tribune had proposed a motion to depose one of his colleagues, and now men were killed in the Assembly whilst voting on a contentious law aimed at altering the franchise. Even though Manilius' men were apparently scattered, this proposal did become law, though we are not informed of any Tribunician vetoes being used (or attempting to be used) against it. On this occasion, however the Senate had the law swiftly overturned, though we are not told by what instrument they did this.[22]

It was in the aftermath of this clash (between Tribune and Senate) that Manilius proposed and passed a second law, which again had echoes of the year 88 BC and the Tribunate of Sulpicius. This law transferred the command of the provinces of Bithynia and Pontus from the Proconsul Glabrio (who had only obtained them the year previously by the law of the Tribune Gabinius, mentioned above), the province of Cilicia from the Proconsul Q. Marcius Rex (Cos. 68 BC) and most importantly the command of the Mithridatic war from L. Licinius Lucullus. All three commands were then given to none other than Cn. Pompeius Magnus, who received his second extraordinary command by Tribunician law in two years. Pompeius had wasted no time in quickly and efficiently defeating the Mediterranean pirates in under a year (despite them having dogged Rome for more than a generation).

In fact, it seems that the Gabinian command against the pirates was for a three-year term (which was how long it was estimated to take), and so Pompeius seems to have held both commands simultaneously. This left Pompeius with command over the entire Mediterranean and all the Roman provinces of the east, making him the most powerful Roman General in a non-Civil War period (to date).

As always, the key question is why did Manilius pass this law; was it simply that he had been an agent of Pompeius all along, or was it (as Dio asserts)[23] that Manilius was trying to gain Pompeius' support and that of his allies in the Senate) in order to further his domestic agenda and overturn the ban on his freedmen law? This mirrors the debate about Sulpicius' proposal in 88 BC to transfer the Mithridatic command from Sulla to Marius, the obvious difference on this occasion being that Lucullus was in the east and in no position to change events in Rome (unlike Sulla). In this respect, the situation more closely resembled that of 107 BC, when Marius had a Tribune transfer the Numidian command from Metellus to himself.

In either respect and whatever his motivation, Manilius did not benefit from it. Not only was he not able to pass his freedmen distribution proposal into law, but as soon as he had stood down from his Tribunate his enemies put him immediately on trial.[24] Thus, we can see the one clear power left to those who were opposing a Tribune; wait until their year in office had expired and then prosecute them for their actions. This was a fate that several Tribunes had tried to avoid by standing for immediate re-election, though there is no evidence that Manilius attempted this. Manilius was not alone in this respect as the former Tribune of 67 BC, C. Cornelius, was put on trial this year as well. Famously Cicero was called to defend Cornelius, a task which he accomplished, with Cornelius being acquitted.[25]

Cicero was also called to defend Manilius; a task he attempted to get out of (unsurprising given the chance of a successful defence). Manilius' trial took place in 65 BC and sensing that he needed more than a good lawyer to secure his acquittal, Manilius turned to familiar tactics and had a mob disrupt the court proceedings. Having secured a temporary respite, Manilius, fearing a conviction, fled Rome and was convicted in absentia.

Thus, these two years of 67–66 BC saw a number of familiar patterns of behaviour emerging. Tribunes were proposing laws to reform the Roman constitution (just three years after the Pompeian-Crassan Settlement) on critical topics such as the powers of the Senate and the voting rights of freedmen. Tribunician vetoes had been overridden, sometimes with violence, whilst a Tribune had proposed (and started voting on) the deposition of one of his colleagues. The familiar pattern of escalation had occurred, with mobs of supporters being used to push legislation through the Assembly which in turn had led to violence and large scale public political murder (though we have no figures). Interestingly Asconius quotes Cicero on the roles of Pompeius and Crassus:

> *That of those who restored that power* (the Tribunate*), the one can do nothing in the face of so many and the other is too far away.*[26]

Clearly (and perhaps with hindsight) he is alluding to the roles (and responsibility) that Pompeius and Crassus bore in defending their constitutional settlement. Both men certainly had the support, in both the Assembly and the Senate, to exert more influence on these events; yet neither man had the remit to do so. Crassus was a private citizen and Pompeius had been given pro-consular commands overseas. Furthermore, Pompeius benefited greatly from both Gabinius' and Manilius' laws, legally amassing more power than any non-civil war general.

4. Pompeius' Shadow: Crassus and the Censorship (65 BC)

Yet Crassus too had not been idle in this period, and whilst Pompeius had always taken the more unorthodox route to power, he preferred to work within the Roman system and thus stood for (and won) election to the Censorship for 65/64 BC, where he unveiled his own reforms and attempted to expand the powers of that office considerably. The Censorship was the highest of the regular Roman offices; held for up to eighteen months once every five years, with powers to revise the membership of the Senate and hold the Census of all Roman citizens eligible for military service (the office's primary function).

Given the contentious nature of the citizenship issue during the civil war period, the office had lapsed under the Sullan constitution, though we are never explicitly told it was abolished. It had been revived in the Pompeian-Crassan settlement of 70 BC, and the new Censors of that year were a pair of highly undistinguished former Consuls (from 72 BC), yet were men whom the pairing of Pompeius and Crassus could rely on. Yet the next Censors (for 65/64 BC) were of a different calibre; Q. Lutatius Catulus, who had defended Rome from the attack of his colleague Lepidus in 77 BC, during the First Civil War, and none other than M. Licinius Crassus himself. Thus, we can see that both Pompeius and Crassus made extensive use of the offices they had restored; Pompeius using the Tribunate and Crassus the Censorship.

Whilst Pompeius was fighting in the east, intent on expanding Rome's empire and gaining military glory, Crassus it seems had similar aims but using completely different methods. Utilising the power of the Censorship to determine who could be enrolled as a Roman citizen, he proposed the radical step of the wholesale extension of Roman citizenship to an entire region, in this case Transalpine Gaul (Northern Italy above the River Po).[27] At the time, this region (between the Alps and the River Po) was not considered to be part of Italy, but Gaul, occupied by Gallic tribes that had migrated over the Alps from the fifth century onwards. The region had been subdued by Rome in the late-third century but had been excluded from the general grant of Roman citizenship during the First Civil War (which only applied to all Italian peoples).

As we have seen (Chapter One) the whole issue of extending Roman citizenship was one of the key drivers behind the collapse of the Republic into the First Civil War and had not fully been resolved until the Censorship of 70 BC. Here was one of the key architects of that resolution at a stroke proposing to extend citizenship to all inhabitants of the Italian peninsula up to the Alps. Previously, extending the citizenship franchise

had been a matter for Consular or Tribunician legislation. We hear of
no burning pressure from the inhabitants of that region for such a move
and it is hard to assess whether they would have considered themselves
unfairly excluded from the previous extension of citizenship across Italy.

In any case, the key issue here was the manner in which Crassus
was proposing to accomplish this extension; by Censorial power rather
than popular legislation, and it again shows how an ambitious Roman
politician could extend the theoretical powers of an office into areas that
it had never gone before or was designed to go. In this event Crassus'
designs were thwarted by the only constitutional safeguard there was; his
colleague (Lutatius Catulus) who blocked the move.

Seemingly undeterred, Crassus proposed an even bolder use of
Censorial power when he next proposed the de facto annexation of
the independent Hellenistic kingdom of Egypt, the wealthiest in the
Mediterranean world. Whilst Egypt had once been the strongest of
the successor kingdoms to Alexander the Great, its power had declined
steadily over the centuries, to such a point that it had needed Rome to
defend it from being annexed by the Seleucid Empire in 168 BC. This
decline had been exacerbated by recurring bouts of civil war or coups
between the various members of the ruling Ptolemaic family. Yet despite
this decline in military power, Egypt itself remained fabulously wealthy
and was the breadbasket of the Mediterranean. This naturally made it a
tempting target for Rome's expanding empire.

Whilst no Roman army had ventured into the Middle East at this point,
Rome's power was fast encroaching. One of Egypt's rulers, Ptolemy Apion,
had bequeathed the Kingdom of Cyrene (between Roman North Africa
and Egypt) to Rome in 96 BC. It had finally been converted into a Roman
province in 74 BC, which brought Rome's empire right to Egypt's borders.
Rome's interest in the east had naturally lulled during the chaos of the First
Civil War but had been rekindled by the renewed war against Mithridates
(the King of Pontus), which had spread to include the growing Armenian
Empire.[28] Thus, Roman commanders willingly expanded their campaigns
farther into the east. Furthermore, Roman fleets had been clearing the
eastern Mediterranean of pirates and the island of Crete (itself technically
a Ptolemaic possession) had been annexed by Rome (and Q. Caecilius
Metellus 'Creticus') only the year previously.

With Pompeius and his armies expanding further eastwards, Crassus clearly felt that he could accomplish the annexation of Egypt through administrative means rather than military ones. Naturally whichever commander or official was placed in charge of the organisation of Egypt into a province would gain a significant amount of wealth as well as glory, neither of which Crassus would have objected to, especially at the expense of his contemporary Pompeius. Thus, we can see both the power of Rome and the potential power of Roman political offices. Here a Roman official, seated in Rome itself, seriously proposed the annexation of one of the major states of the Mediterranean world. Again, on this occasion, Crassus was blocked by his colleague Catulus and the two men abdicated their office having accomplished nothing of note, with neither the revision of the Senate lists nor the Census having been completed.

Thus, it seems that Crassus' bold plans to use the Censorship to expand both Rome's empire and his own power, patronage and wealth came to nothing, but this example demonstrates perfectly both the potential power of Rome's offices when used by ambitious politicians and the precarious nature of the safeguards on them. The Censorship started life as a senior (and honorary) administrative post in Rome, to regulate the membership of the Senate and refresh the register of citizens but was now being used to enfranchise whole regions and attempt to annex far away foreign powers. Crassus was only stopped by his colleague of equal power; and here Crassus clearly failed to ensure that a compliant colleague was elected. The other important aspect to note is that the two men clashed, but Crassus chose not to pursue the matter further, or use violence and let the matter drop. Again, this was his choice, but the key question we must ask is whether this individual choice was a sufficient safeguard? Another person with a different personality might easily use violence, leading to renewed political clashes and further bloodshed.

5. The Rise and Fall of Sulla

Whilst the Censorship was one of the key flashpoints of the year, the other was a controversy over the Consulship. The Consuls elected for 65 BC were P. Autronius Paetus and none other than a certain P. Cornelius Sulla. Sulla was the nephew of the former Dictator and the eldest of the next generation of the Sullan family. The Dictator also had a son (Faustus), who was pursuing his own political career, but was decades younger. Thus P. Cornelius Sulla could tap into the famous name without being too closely associated with the mixed legacy Sulla had left behind (see below). Yet no sooner had both men been elected then they were both put on trial for bribery and corruption in the election. Furthermore, both men were found guilty and stripped of their Consulships, a unique occurrence in Consular elections (as far as we are aware).

This certainly seems too much of a coincidence, that the first time a Sulla reached high office after the civil war he was removed before he could take power, but with the sources we have left we will never know who was involved behind the scenes. One aspect to note is that their replacements as Consuls were L. Aurelius Cotta and L. Manlius Torquatus. Cotta had been a Praetor in 70 BC (under Pompeius and Crassus) and was the man responsible for the reforms of the judiciary.

Thus, history had repeated itself, and we have a second example of P. Cornelius Sulla being stripped of power, this time before he had even taken office.[29] Whilst his uncle had responded with his army, there was little this Sulla could practically do and both men had to accept this utter humiliation. Rumours soon began to circulate that there was a plot against the two replacement Consuls, though as we shall see (in the next chapter) these rumours were entangled in the dramatic events of the year 63 BC and the Second Roman Civil War.

Given the drama involving the Consuls and the Censors of the year, it is hardly surprising that the sources do not focus on the Tribunes of the year, and given the high-profile reforms and backlash encountered by the Tribunes of 67 and 66 BC it is not surprising that 65 BC and 64 BC were quieter years in terms of Tribunician activity. Yet we do know the identity and actions of one of the Tribunes of 65 BC; C. Papius. He too seems to have tapped into traditional Tribunician legislation when he passed a law expelling from Rome all inhabitants from outside of Italy who may have been claiming citizenship. Similar laws had been seen in the pre-civil war period, and most notoriously the Consular law of 95 BC. In many ways this was a logical extension. In these earlier laws it was Italians living in Rome who were claiming the benefits of citizenship. Now that all of Italy had citizenship, then it was the non-Italians who were seemingly claiming citizen rights. As with all laws of this type, it is always suspected that it was more aimed at making a political (and racial) point rather than responding to any actual issue. Furthermore, Rome lacked the infrastructure to enforce such a law (with no identity papers nor a police force).

Nevertheless, the fact that such a measure was passed does bring home that the issue of citizenship was still a topical on, even though the 'Italian question' had been resolved. Furthermore, it cannot be a coincidence that such a law was passed in the same year that Crassus proposed extending Roman citizenship to Transalpine Gaul. Unfortunately, we do not know whether this proposal was done to oppose Crassus' move, or to support it as a safeguard so that no others from outside of Italy could claim it.

6. Politics by Proxy? Tribunes and Censors (64 BC)

The following year also saw a political clash centred on the Censorship. Due to the failure of Crassus and Catulus to conduct a Census and their subsequent abdication, replacement Censors were elected. We only know the identity of one of them and again it is L. Aurelius Cotta, the man who was Praetor under Pompeius and Crassus and who had been a replacement Consul the previous year, when Sulla and his colleague were stripped of their Consulship. Not only do we see Cotta being elected as a replacement magistrate, but it is almost unheard of to be Censor the year following a Consulship. It would be interesting to know whether Cotta had a patron responsible for such a swift elevation. Nevertheless, despite this elevation he too (along with his colleague) was forced to abdicate their office following a clash with an unknown number of anonymous Tribunes:

> *And for the same reason their successors, too, did nothing in the following year, inasmuch as the Tribunes hindered them in regard to the Senatorial list, fearing that they themselves might be expelled from that body.*[30]

Thus, we can see the Tribunes prevented the Censors from undertaking one of their key duties. It is tempting to see a political battle being waged by proxy here, but we lack sufficient details to get behind the few events we have described and see who else was involved. It is all too easy to see the figures of Pompeius (albeit in his absence) and Crassus lurking behind each major or minor event of this period and we must stop ourselves from seeing them everywhere. As always there were a number of other powerful individuals and factions / families active in Roman politics.

The Consuls of the year, by contrast, seem to have had a quieter year, but the identity of one of them is of particular interest: L. Iulius Caesar (cousin of the most famous Caesar). The Iulii Caesares were an old Patrician family but had not reached the heights of the Consulship until 157 BC. It was only after a certain C. Marius married into the family that we find regular instances of Caesars holding high office, most notably in the 90s BC, though they suffered several high-profile murders in the various purges that took place during the First Civil War. Nevertheless, with this particular Caesar being elected to the Consulship in 64 BC we can see that the family was again seeing political success.

Aside from the clash with the Censors, we only have one other confirmed instance of Tribunician activity this year and only one confirmed identity: Q. Mucius Orestinus.[31] Orestinus is recorded as vetoing a bribery law of one of his colleagues and attacking the consular candidacy of a certain M. Tullius Cicero.

Again, with no further detail we cannot read too much into the vetoing of the bribery law other than it shows that Tribunes were still actively legislating (even if we do not retain a record of it in our surviving sources), that there were still continuing instances of vetoing of colleagues, and that the veto was still being respected as the norm. The other major area of interest of this year were the elections for the Consuls of 63 BC, which saw the candidacy of the noted Italian jurist (and outsider) M. Tullius Cicero, along with one of the most infamous of Sulla's lesser lieutenants, L. Sergius Catilina. The full details on this race and its consequences are covered in the next chapter.

7. Popular Politics, Caesar and the Legacy of Marius

Whilst L. Iulius Caeser had been elected Consul in 64 BC, it was C. Iulius Caesar who was the more noted, given his prominent anti-Sullan heritage. Not only was he the nephew of C. Marius himself (the latter having married Caesar's aunt) but he was also the son-in-law of Sulla's other main opponent; L. Cornelius Cinna (Cos. 87–84 BC). Despite this anti-Sullan heritage, he notably survived the Sullan purges of the late 80s despite having openly defied the Dictator over his marriage.[32] Whilst Cinna had a son (L. Cornelius Cinna) who could inherit his family glory, the same could not be said for that of the family Marius. Whilst we are aware of a number of surviving Marii in the late Republic, none had a close link to the great general due to the losses suffered in the First Civil War.[33]

We don't know how many children C. Marius had for certain and there are some anomalies in the sources. What we do know is that Marius' eldest son became one of the leaders of the post-Cinnan regime in Rome with a Consulship in 82 BC (at an age far younger than was allowed), but died during the siege of Praeneste, seemingly without issue. Another prominent Marian of the 80s BC was M. Marius Gratidianus, the son of one of Marius' brothers (again we don't know how many he had), who had become popular with the people for his economic reforms. However, whilst he survived the fighting of the 80s BC he was one of the most notable casualties of the subsequent Sullan proscriptions, being publicly murdered by his own brother-in-law, L. Sergius Catilina. A third prominent Marius was the mysterious M. Marius who led the Marian forces in the east (under the patronage of Mithridates) during the wars of the 70s.[34] He too however had been murdered (this time by Lucullus).

Thus C. Iulius Caesar found himself as the closest living relative of C. Marius and set about tapping into his uncle's legacy. Naturally enough this involved playing up the aspects of Marius as the saviour of Rome, and her greatest general, as opposed to the Marius who was an enemy of the state responsible for the massacres of 87 BC. His first opportunity came with the death of his aunt Iulia (Marius' wife). Traditionally, a funeral was an opportunity for the family to show off the lineage and achievements of the deceased. There were two issues here; firstly, it was the funeral of a Roman matron and secondly Marius himself had been outlawed. The exact year of this funeral is not certain but was c.70–69 BC (either during or just before his Quaestorship of 69 BC):[35]

When, as nephew of Iulia the deceased wife of Marius, he pronounced a splendid encomium upon her in the Forum, and in her funeral procession ventured to display images of Marius, which were then seen for the first time since the administration of Sulla, because Marius and his friends had been pronounced public enemies. When, namely, some cried out against Caesar for this procedure, the People answered them with loud shouts, received Caesar with applause, and admired him for bringing back after so long a time, as it were from Hades, the honours of Marius into the city.[36]

Thus, Caesar very publicly started the rehabilitation of Marius in the minds of the Roman People and tapped into the fame and glory of the great man. Caesar, however, continued to seek fresh opportunities and again delivered a very public eulogy when his own wife (Cinna's daughter) died, again breaking with tradition:

Now, in the case of elderly women, it was ancient Roman usage to pronounce funeral orations over them; but it was not customary in the case of young women, and Caesar was the first to do so when his own wife died. This also brought him much favour, and worked upon the sympathies of the multitude, so that they were fond of him, as a man who was gentle and full of feeling.[37]

We must also assume that his wife's father (Cinna) was mentioned during this funeral, thus publicly summoning up his connection to the two leading figures in the anti-Sullan movement, which seemed to be popular with the People, but would not have gone down well with many in the Senate. Caesar followed this up by remarrying and again the issue of legacies was prominent, as his new wife was the daughter of Q. Pompeius Rufus, son of the Consul of 88 BC and the man who had been murdered in the riots of 88 BC. Furthermore, Caesar's new wife's mother was none other than Sulla's daughter and Caesar now found himself connected (by marriage) to Sulla himself, adding to his connections to both Marius and Cinna.

Yet it was to Marius' legacy he returned (being the closest living relative). Even with such a rich heritage Caesar still had to pursue the traditional *cursus honorum*. Having served his Quaestorship in 69 BC, he could not stand as Tribune, owing to his Patrician status. Thus, he had to wait for election to the (Curule) Aedileship in 65 BC. Again, Caesar wasted no time in gaining popularity by throwing lavish games (presumably bankrolled by a patron). However, the most notable talking point of his Aedileship came when he secretly restored the victory monuments of Marius on the Capitol (which had been destroyed by Sulla):

> *When the ambitious efforts of his Aedileship were at their height, he had images of Marius secretly made, together with trophy-bearing victories, and these he ordered to be carried by night and set up on the Capitol. At day-break those who beheld all these objects glittering with gold and fashioned with the most exquisite art (and they bore inscriptions setting forth the Cimbrian successes of Marius) were amazed at the daring of the man who had set them up (for it was evident who had done it), and the report of it quickly spreading brought everybody together for the sight.*
>
> *The partisans of Marius, however, encouraged one another and showed themselves on a sudden in amazing numbers, and filled the Capitol with their applause. Many, too, were moved to tears of joy when they beheld the features of Marius, and Caesar was highly extolled by them, and regarded as above all others worthy of his kinship with Marius.*[38]

Thus, Caesar had very publicly, and with a great degree of theatricality, restored Marius as a hero of Rome and gained popular acclaim for it. Nevertheless, this would have hardened the attitudes of many in the Senate against him. What is important to stress is that this famous association would only take him so far; what a Roman politician needed to succeed (in normal times) was money, and the Iulii Caesares were not noted for being a rich family, especially given that they were on the losing side of the First Civil War. Every aspiring Roman politician needed a patron and Caesar found one in the form of M. Licinius Crassus.

We don't know when Caesar first formed a relationship with Crassus, but the Aedileship of 65 BC is the first public demonstration of a connection. Both the lavish games and the restoration of Marius' monuments would have required considerable amounts of money, and the other action Caesar is noted for during his Aedileship was a very public support of Crassus' plan (as Censor) to annex the kingdom of Egypt (see above). Thus, it seems Caesar could count on Crassus' financial support and Crassus on Caesar's popular touch. Both factors paid off handsomely in 63 BC, when Caesar won election to the high office of Pontifex Maximus (Rome's chief priest) despite his young age. This election itself was a highly symbolic one as the previous Pontifex was none other than Q. Caecilius Metellus Pius; a long-standing opponent of Marius and staunch ally of Sulla. Furthermore, Caesar's own Pontifical career had been impacted by the Civil War:

> *Indeed, while still little more than a boy he had already been made priest of Iupiter by Marius and Cinna, but all their acts had been annulled in consequence of Sulla's victory, and Caesar had thus lost this priesthood.*[39]

Thus, Caesar had once again used the legacy of Marius for his own political gain and had clearly marked himself out as one of the rising stars of the new Republic. Yet the legacy of Marius was a symbolic one; and there were few tangible signs of Marius' impact on the new Republic. The same could not be said of Sulla, who's legacy had a more immediate impact on current Roman politics and the desire for reform and which came to play an increasing role in the political life of the new Republic. This formed the background to the first major existential crisis the New Republic faced, during the year 63 BC.

Summary

Thus, we can see that the first six years of the new Republic were somewhat of a mixed bag. Two quiet years were followed by a return of political violence and bloodshed, which were in turn followed by several years of robust but non-violent political activity. In short, this period contained both positive and negative signs for political stability. The two architects of the new Republic, Pompeius and Crassus, had both made bids to use the restored political offices for their own benefit, Pompeius being the more successful of the two. He was able to use the legislative powers of the Tribunate to secure an extraordinary Mediterranean-wide command, followed by command of a major war of expansion in the east. In Pompeius' absence Crassus attempted the unprecedented move to annex the Ptolemaic Empire by administration.

Therefore, we can see that there is evidence for both sides of the argument. Yes, we can see key elements that brought down the previous Republic in this period; expansion of the Tribunate's powers, inter-Tribunician clashes and use of force in the Assembly leading to political murder. Yet at the same time we can see that politicians were mostly acting with restraint. The one outbreak of bloodshed was limited and not on a par with the massacres that had accompanied political violence in the previous decades and had not escalated into a cycle of revenge or into wider military action.

Overall, we can see that this period contained both positive and negative elements for the stability of this new Republic. The end of the First Civil War period had clearly drawn a line under it and all sides went back to 'normal' Republican politics. Unfortunately, this restoration of the Republic, whilst it had brought about peace from civil war, had clearly not eliminated the factors that had led to political bloodshed and murder.

Chapter Three

The Sullan Legacy and the Second Civil War (64–62 BC)

Whilst the first few years following the Pompeian-Crassan settlement seemed to indicate that it had indeed brought peace and stability back to Roman politics, the year 63 BC saw the New Republic facing its gravest challenge, which culminated in an attempted coup in Rome and the outbreak of a Second Civil War (albeit temporary) in Italy. Yet even though we have two contemporaneous sources for the events that took place in 63 and 62 BC, they tend to focus on the individuals and their characters rather than the underlying causes and tensions which brought these matters to a head. To fully understand the challenges that the Republic faced in these years we must turn our attention to the legacy of Sulla, both in Roman politics and in Italy itself, to understand what brought the Republic once more to the brink of collapse.

1. The Sullan Legacy on Roman Politics

In contrast to his two contemporaries, Marius and Cinna, P. Cornelius Sulla had a far greater impact on the Roman Republic and left a far greater and more tangible legacy on domestic politics. Sulla's aims were far more than simply ruling the Republic. When he came to power in 82 BC he aimed to reshape Republican politics, the ruling oligarchy, and Italy as a whole. To these ends he introduced a new constitutional settlement for Rome, placing all power in the hands of the ruling oligarchy of Roman aristocratic families, which he thoroughly purged of any who would oppose him and his reforms. This purge extended beyond the ruling oligarchy, with whole communities who had opposed him being punished (most notably the Samnites) and wholesale land confiscations to create his new veteran colonies, planted to watch over an Italy which had had to be subdued by force during the war of 83–82 BC. Individuals were murdered, their family's wealth confiscated, and their children and grandchildren stripped of their citizen rights. However, for all the losers of the Sullan settlement there were numerous winners; those promoted to the oligarchy, the new landowners, and the new communities.

Thus, all levels of society in Rome and Italy felt this dramatic change in a remarkably short time period. Unfortunately for Sulla and perhaps Roman society as a whole, these changes lacked someone to enforce them and allow them to bed in, due to the death of Sulla himself and the fact that there was no one to defend his legacy. Although Sulla abdicated his Dictatorship and retired as a private citizen, it was surely his intention to sit in the background and ensure that no one challenged his new Roman order. Unfortunately for him he died soon after abdicating (in 78 BC) and thus removed the 'guardian' of these changes, so leaving the way open for them to be challenged.

He had clearly hoped that the newly-purged Senatorial oligarchy would defend this new order, as it placed them at the centre of the Republic. Yet even whilst he was alive there were Senators willing to challenge the changes he had made, either openly, such as Lepidus, or behind the scenes, such as Pompeius. One of Sulla's key problems was that he had purged his enemies, but not his allies. There were two key groups of men in the Sullan faction, those loyal to Sulla himself and who shared his vision, such as Metellus Pius and Lucullus, and those who attached themselves to him to ensure their survival and reap the rewards of being on the 'winning side', most notably men such as Pompeius and Crassus.

Thus, despite the proscriptions, the Senatorial oligarchy was as riven and divided as ever and soon broke apart into new factions, such as those supporters of Pompeius, whilst some older factions were revived, such as the Valerii Flacci and the Metelli. Therefore, it is not a surprise that the most visible political legacy of Sulla, his constitutional settlement, was soon overturned, a process that started in 75 BC with the Tribunate and ended in 70 BC with the Pompeian-Crassan settlement which overturned many of Sulla's changes (whilst keeping others). Furthermore, the revived Censorship purged many (sixty-four) of Sulla's new Senators, including the Consul of 71 BC, P. Cornelius Lentulus Sura.

Yet there were still two very visible legacies of Sulla that were left in place, both relating to the programme of mass murder known as the proscriptions: the murderers and the victims' families. Throughout the 70s these issues seemed to go untouched (though we are lacking detailed sources for the period), and the same can be said of the first few years that followed the end of the First Civil War. This is hardly a surprise: throughout the 70s the civil war was still raging on in Spain and the East whilst the majority of the Senate were either directly involved in the murders (men such as Catilina), had benefited from them (men such as Crassus), or were complicit through their inaction. Yet by the 60s BC there was a new generation of Roman politicians emerging who were not so complicit and who equally saw a political opportunity for themselves in challenging this tacit veil of silence over the mass murders.

Three of the most notable figures were Caesar, Cato and Cicero. The first sign of this anti-Sullan backlash (at least in our surviving sources) seems to have been in 66 BC when the Tribune Memmius prosecuted M. Licinius Lucullus:

> *Marcus (Licinius Lucullus) was under prosecution by Caius Memmius for his acts as Quaestor under the administration of Sulla. Marcus, indeed, was acquitted.*[1]

We do not know whether this was a genuine attempt to attack Sulla's junior officers or part of an ongoing feud between Memmius and Marcus' brother L. Licinius Lucullus (Cos. 74 BC). In any event M. Lucullus was acquitted; but then Sulla had been granted formal pardon for all acts committed during the civil war, which presumably extended to those of his officers who had followed his orders. Nevertheless, the charge is an interesting one and does perhaps indicate that the general mood of the People was favourable to reopening these recent wounds, even if the Senate was not.

Matters seem to have come to a head in 64 BC, when we hear of two separate prosecutions of men who had served under Sulla for acts committed whilst following his orders. We do not know if they were connected or were the culmination of a longer process. What we do know are the identities of the two men leading the prosecutions; one was

C. Iulius Caesar, the other was M. Porcius Cato, and interestingly both men were acting in an official capacity.

M. Porcius Cato came from a distinguished Consular family. The first M. Porcius Cato (to enter Roman politics) was of Italian stock but became a Consul of 195 BC and a staunch advocate of Roman values, opposing the influx of Greek culture and clashing with the Scipio brothers (Africanus and Asiaticus). The family had regularly held the Consulship ever since, though they had seemingly kept a low profile in the First Civil War. Cato was only a young man, and had just been elected to his first office, the Quaestorship, which was traditionally responsible for managing the state's finances. Although a minor political office Cato used his role as guardian of the state's finances to launch a high-profile campaign to recover monies owed to the state by a number of different men:

> *While he brought the Quaestorship into greater respect than the senate, so that all men said and thought that Cato had invested the Quaestorship with the dignity of the Consulship.[2]*

One of the measures he pursued was recovering money from those who had been rewarded under the Sullan proscriptions (for murdering Sulla's enemies):

> *Again, there were many persons whom the famous Sulla had rewarded for killing men under proscription, at the rate of twelve thousand drachmas. All men hated them as accursed and polluted wretches, but no one had the courage to punish them. Cato, however, called each one of these to account for having public money in his possession by unjust means, and made him give it up, at the same time rebuking him with passionate eloquence for his illegal and unholy act. After this experience, they were at once charged with murder, were brought before their judges condemned beforehand, one might say, and were punished. At this all men were delighted and thought that with their deaths the tyranny of that former time was extinguished, and that Sulla himself was punished before men's eyes.[3]*
>
> *Marcus Cato, in his Quaestorship, had demanded back from those who had murdered anyone in the time of Sulla all that they had received for their work.[4]*

Thus, Cato launched a high-profile attack on the Sullan profiteers, despite the act being legal at the time, recovered monies they had been paid out, and then handed them over to be tried for murder. This will have undoubtedly made him a number of enemies from within the ranks of Sullan veterans, not to mention those in the Senate who had also profited (though there is no word on whether senior Senators were called to account, M. Licinius Crassus being the most prominent Sullan profiteer). Yet such moves allowed him to gain a reputation as a staunch defender of the state finances and a man of the utmost probity, not to mention someone who was not afraid to tackle an obvious (though legal) injustice.

Interestingly, these references do not elaborate on how these men, whom Cato had handed over to be tried, were prosecuted. Yet coincidentally (or not) we hear of another young politician setting up a special court to oversee cases of men who had murdered victims of Sulla's proscriptions; none other than C. Iulius Caesar. Again, we only have a handful of references to this court and all lack any background detail. Interestingly all of these references also omit any mention of Cato (the two men later becoming famous enemies). Caesar seems to have been appointed to head up a special court to try those who had murdered Roman citizens during the Sullan proscriptions:[5]

> *For the man who had slain Lucretius at the instance of Sulla, and another who had slain many of the persons proscribed by him, were tried for the murders and punished, Iulius Caesar being most instrumental in bringing this about. Thus, changing circumstances often render very weak even those exceedingly powerful. This matter, then, turned out contrary to most people's expectation.*[6]
>
> *Furthermore, in conducting prosecutions for murder, he included in the number of murderers even those who had received moneys from the public treasury during the proscriptions for bringing in the heads of Roman citizens, although they were expressly exempted by the Cornelian laws.*[7]

We are not clear how many were convicted by this special court, but Asconius names two of the most notorious men convicted:

L. Luscius, a notorious centurion of Sulla's, who made rich pickings from his victory…. he was charged with murder of three of the proscribed. … L. Bellienus too was convicted…. This man, on the orders of Sulla, who was Dictator at this time, had killed Lucretius Afella, who was standing for the Consulship against the wishes of Sulla.[8]

It is interesting therefore that we see two (perhaps cooperative) processes being pursued by young Roman politicians to bring to justice the murderers of the Sullan proscriptions, despite the fact that they were acting on the orders of the legally-appointed Roman Dictator. Thus, we can see a younger generation of Roman politicians emerging who were not afraid to reopen the old wounds caused by Sulla's actions, not to mention making names for themselves and enhancing their own reputations.

It is unfortunate that none of our surviving sources provide any background to these events, especially any connection between Caesar and Cato perhaps working together on this. With our few remaining sources, these two events appear out of the blue with no context as to what brought them about. What is clear though is that both Cato and Caesar represented a new generation of emerging Roman politicians who were untainted by their actions in the First Civil War and were quite happy to attack the legacy of Sulla and tap into the popular support for such actions.

As always, however, we must sound a note of caution as it seems that these prosecutions did not affect the highest echelons of the 'Sullan' Senate. The most notorious profiteer from the Sullan proscriptions was M. Licinius Crassus himself, who amongst other things was Caesar's patron. We hear nothing of him being made to repay monies, though there was never an accusation that he personally murdered anyone during the proscriptions. We also hear nothing of his attitude to these proceedings. Thus, it may be another case of the Roman oligarchy being happy to allow justice to be seen to be done, providing that the upper echelons of the Roman oligarchy were not themselves affected. The victims named all seemed to be notorious in their own right, but not senior members of the Senate. Perhaps the accused with the highest profile was a certain L. Sergius Catilina.

Catilina provides us with a wonderful case study of a minor Roman aristocrat during the First Civil War. In terms of background, Sergius

Catilina superficially resembled Sulla himself. The Sergii were a long-standing but obscure Patrician family, with their earliest Consulship dating back to 478 BC, but they had not occupied the highest office since 429 BC and had spent the intervening four centuries amongst the lower ranks of the Senatorial oligarchy. We know little of his background, other than that he was a young man when the First Civil War broke out and seems to have successfully navigated life in Rome during this bloody period.

We know that he ingratiated himself with the ruling Cinnan order by marrying the sister of the elder Marius' nephew (M. Marius Gratidianus; Pr. 85 BC), though the date is unknown. His skill in navigating the changing fortunes of the many sides during the First Civil War can be seen during his next appearance in the sources, in 82 BC, as a legate of Sulla himself in the latter's army during the invasion of Italy (83/82 BC). Thus, he seems to have overcome his close Marian ties and successfully joined Sulla, deciding like many others that this was the most likely winning side. In this he was in good company, following in the footsteps of both Pompeius and Crassus.

He next appears in our surviving records during the Sullan proscriptions, where he gained notoriety for his role as an enthusiastic participant in the slaughter of Sulla's enemies. In fact, he was responsible for perhaps the highest profile of the murders committed in this period, when, presumably to prove his loyalty to the new regime, he brutally murdered none other than M. Marius Gratidianus (his own brother-in-law), and the highest-profile living Marian:

> *Marcus Marius, to whom the People erected a statue in every street, to whom they made offerings of incense and wine, had, by the command of Lucius Sulla, his legs broken, his eyes pulled out, his hands cut off, and his whole body gradually torn to pieces limb by limb, as if Sulla killed him as many times as he wounded him. Who was it who carried out Sulla's orders? who but Catilina, already practising his hands in every sort of wickedness? He tore him to pieces before the tomb of Quintus Catulus, an unwelcome burden to the ashes of that gentlest of men.*[9]

Naturally enough it was not long before Catilina (perpetrator of perhaps the most infamous proscription) was brought before Caesar's special court:

Also, the case of Catilina, who, although charged with the same crimes as the others (for he, too, had killed many of the proscribed), was acquitted.[10]

Surprisingly, given the notoriety and the openness of Catilina's murder of Marius Gratidianus, he was acquitted, and perhaps we again see that political witch hunts of this nature had a better chance of convicting those of the lesser ranks than wealthy Senators. So once again it is clear that those of the lower orders became scapegoats whilst the Senatorial oligarchy remained unscathed. Given this very high-profile reminder of Catilina's role in the Sullan proscriptions and his murder of, not just a prominent Marian, but one who had been incredibly popular with the people in the 80s BC, it is perhaps surprising that Catilina once again set his sights on the Consulship, this time for 63 BC.

2. The Sullan Legacy and the Consular Elections for 65 & 63 BC

We have already seen the Sullan legacy being challenged and defended in the courtroom, and it appears that it was increasingly being raised in elections; the two most notable being those for the Consulships of 65 and 63 BC, both of which were linked through the figure of Catilina, but also due to the issue of confronting the Sullan legacy. The year 66 BC saw the first major electoral test of a member of Sulla's family. Whilst Sulla's son Faustus was still too young to hold high office, Sulla's nephew (of the same name), P. Cornelius Sulla, was eligible to stand as Consul, having worked his way steadily through the *cursus honorum* (though his years in office are undated). Thus, Sulla's nephew, carrying the same name as the former Dictator, stood for and was unanimously elected as Consul, along with a running mate, P. Autronius Paetus, thus securing a major electoral Triumph for the Sullan faction.

However, both men were accused of bribery by their opponents, L. Aurelius Cotta and L. Manlius Torquatus, which was a common occurrence in Republican politics. Yet what was uncommon was that both men were convicted, disqualified from holding public office, and stripped of their Senatorial membership, an almost unheard-of occurrence in the Republic and one which must strike us as suspicious. We must ask ourselves whether it was mere random chance that the only

Consul Designates to be stripped of their office in this period included the leading member of the Sullan family, or was there a move amongst their opponents to ensure that another Sulla was not elected, one who would surely have defended the Sullan legacy. If so, then it ties in with the moves to prosecute lower level Sullan supporters.

Having been stripped of the Consulships, their electoral rivals and accusers (Cotta and Torquatus) were elected in their place (adding insult to injury). Thus, for the second time, a Cornelius Sulla had been robbed of his crowning achievement. This had happened to his uncle in 88 BC when as Consul he was stripped of the command against Mithridates. The elder Sulla responded by marching his army on Rome and sparking another bout of civil war. His nephew however had no such military resources, but there were rumours of his involvement in a plot or coup. Here we must be incredibly careful, as, for many of our sources, what happened in 63 BC simply confirms rumours of the alleged plot in 65 BC, As always, Dio presents the most level-headed details:

> *Publius Paetus and Cornelius Sulla, a nephew of the great Sulla, who had been elected consuls and then convicted of bribery, had plotted to kill their accusers, Lucius Cotta and Lucius Torquatus, especially after the latter had also been convicted. Among others who had been suborned were Cnaeus Piso and also Lucius Catilina, a man of great audacity, who had sought the office himself and was angry on this account. They were unable, however, to accomplish anything because the plot was revealed beforehand, and a bodyguard given to Cotta and Torquatus by the Senate. Indeed, a decree would have been passed against them, had not one of the Tribunes opposed it. And when Piso even then continued to display his audacity, the Senate, fearing he would cause some riot, sent him at once to Spain, ostensibly to hold some command or other; there he met his death at the hands of the natives whom he had wronged.*[11]

The problem we have is that all accounts of this were written after the events of 63 BC, when a real attempted coup occurred. Furthermore, it is clear that Cicero, in the elections in 64 BC, not only voiced this rumour but embellished it greatly to tar his electoral opponent, Catilina. Certainly, there are unusual elements to this case, in the fact that the Senate granted the Consuls a bodyguard (as far as we are aware) and that Cn. Calpurnius Piso was given an unusual command in Spain by decree of the Senate: *questor pro-praetore.*

Suetonius presents the most outrageous version of events, which has Crassus as the mastermind behind the whole plot, aiming to engineer a crisis in order to be elected Dictator and save the Republic again.[12] For good measure Iulius Caesar was at the heart of the plot too (despite his pro–Marian and anti–Sullan career). What is clear is that even if there was a plot by a disgruntled group of Sullans, it came to nought and that Sulla was at the centre of it, not Catilina.[13] For good measure, Catilina was suffering his own misfortune, having been charged with corruption during his propraetorship in Africa, rendering him ineligible to stand for Consul.[14]

Thus, we have the background to the elections (in 64 BC) for the Consulships of 63 BC. Thanks to the involvement of Cicero, we know that there were seven candidates for the two Consulships, but the leading individuals were Catilina, Cicero and C. Antonius. The three all represent different strands of the Republic. Antonius was the son of a Consul (M. Antonius Cos. 99 BC) and hailed from an old (though not leading) Plebeian Senatorial family. Catilina represented an old Patrician family, which had not reached high office since the early Republic but whose fortunes had been revived by backing the Sullan regime. Cicero represented the 'new men', one of Italian stock who had just entered Roman politics. It also seems that Antonius and Catilina paired up as a joint electoral ticket (as was common in the era).

Whilst Antonius turned to throwing lavish games for the People, Cicero deployed his key talent, his oratory, and gave what has become a famous speech (written down in later years and most likely significantly embellished by Cicero himself); the '*oratio in toga candidia*'. The speech itself no longer survives but a commentary on it by Asconius does, in which he detailed the shortcomings of his two opponents: Antonius' corruption and Catilina's murders during the proscriptions.[15] Furthermore, he laid out the alleged plot in 65 BC, with Catilina as the ringleader (not Sulla), and Crassus and Caesar as the shadowy puppet masters behind it all.

He [Catilina] *besmirched himself with all manner of sexual misconduct and disgraceful acts, bloodied himself in criminal slaughter, despoiled our allies, did violence to our laws, the courts, the judiciary.*[16]

As always, we must be careful when ascribing too much importance to Cicero's speeches (he himself suffered no such problem). If we consider his background alone, then Cicero had significant advantages over his two rivals; he was an outsider (although a Senator) and had a clean record as far as his participation in the civil wars was concerned. Catilina, however, was forever tainted with the murders he had committed, and Antonius was no doubt 'guilty by association' with the Sullan regime in many people's eyes. He had also been expelled from the Senate during the Pompeian-Crassan purge of 70 BC. Given that, as we have seen, there was a growing anti-Sullan backlash it is perhaps not surprising that Cicero was elected as Consul, along with C. Antonius.

It is equally unsurprising that, with his background, Catilina was not elected as Consul. He had now stood for election on two occasions and been unsuccessful on both. Under normal circumstances Catilina would have joined a long list of Praetors who failed to reach the highest office and be consigned to a footnote in the history of the Republic.

3. The Tribunician Reform Programme of 63 BC[17]

With the elections concluded, these issues seemed to be forgotten and Roman politics swiftly moved on, with the domestic agenda becoming dominated by the various Tribunician proposals, many of which are revealing:

For the Tribunes united with Antonius, the Consul, who was very much like themselves in character, and one of them supported for office the sons of those exiled by Sulla, while a second wished to grant to Publius Paetus and to Cornelius Sulla, who had been convicted with him, the right to be members of the Senate and to hold office; another made a motion for a cancelling of debts, and yet another for allotments of land to be made both in Italy and in the subject territory.[18]

Thus, we can see that the Tribunician programme contained 'classic' proposals for land distribution and debt alleviation, but also measures to tackle the legacy of the Sullan proscriptions (the families of the proscribed) and one to pardon Sulla and Autronius. Of all the Tribunes it was P. Servilius Rullus who seemed to be the most dominant, proposing a full-blooded piece of agrarian legislation aimed at distributing public land in Italy, and thus reviving the image of Ti. Sempronius Gracchus.[19] Rullus hailed from a long-standing noble family, the Servilii, but his branch had never achieved high office.[20] Rullus wasted no time and immediately proposed the establishment of a new Agrarian Commission of ten, who would have sweeping legal powers to seize and distribute public land both in Italy and the provinces, including the newly-annexed Seleucid Kingdom of Syria, along with sweeping financial powers to fund the measure. Thus, once again, Tribunician proposals would encroach on Senatorial prerogatives, including foreign policy with regard to the freshly-conquered kingdom of Syria, an act which had not yet been formally ratified by the Senate.

The Consuls were split on the matter, but Antonius was in favour (apparently being guaranteed one of the ten positions on the Commission), and Cicero was vehemently opposed. Cicero later wrote up an account of the matter (*de lege agraria*) which ran to two books and still survives. Interestingly he notes that he heard of the proposal prior to the Tribunes taking office and that Rullus, though its spokesman, was not the only Tribune supporting it. The whole work is highly interesting for anyone with an interest in the Tribunate and Cicero's view of it. In the end, though, he was able to successfully block the proposal aided by one of Rullus' colleagues, L. Caecilius Rufus, and a threatened veto (*ius intercessio*). Again, this proposal shows that once more the Tribunes were proposing sweeping pieces of empire-wide legislation and that they could be successfully and peacefully opposed.

Cicero, it seems, took the lead domestically, with Antonius seemingly happy for him to do so, and in particular he seemed to take the lead in opposing the various Tribunician measures, with an almost Patrician attitude:

These motions were taken in hand betimes by Cicero and those who were of the same mind as he, and were suppressed before any action resulted from them.[21]

Another measure he strenuously opposed on political and moral grounds was the proposed debt cancellation:

> *We must, therefore, take measures that there shall be no indebtedness of a nature to endanger the public safety. It is a menace that can be averted in many ways; but should a serious debt be incurred, we are not to allow the rich to lose their property, while the debtors profit by what is their neighbour's. For there is nothing that upholds a government more powerfully than its credit; and it can have no credit, unless the payment of debts is enforced by law. Never were measures for the repudiation of debts more strenuously agitated than in my Consulship.*[22]

It seems that Cicero also made a speech in the Senate concerning the sons of the proscribed; though we only have a passing reference to it.[23] Once again, it seems that Cicero opposed this 'populist' measure on the grounds that a lawful decision should be upheld:

> *You entreat, and the sons of proscribed men blush at having canvassed for public honour.*[24]
> *The invalidation of condemned.*[25]

On the matter of the Tribunician proposal for the reinstatement of Sulla and Autronius, Cicero did speak in favour of the matter, arguing that the decision was legal and lawful, but that clemency should be shown:

> *When a man is complaining of a penalty, it is not the decision with which he is finding fault but the law. For the conviction is the act of judges, and that is let stand; the penalty is the act of the law, and that may be lightened ... The law was proposed only a few days; it was never begun to be put in train to be carried; it was laid on the table in the Senate. On the first of January, when we had summoned the Senate to meet in the Capitol, nothing took precedence of it; and Quintus Metellus the Praetor said, that what he was saying was by the command of Sulla; that Sulla did not wish such a motion to be brought forward respecting his case.*[26]

It is interesting that it seems that the proposal was withdrawn on the request of Sulla himself and delivered via a member of the Metellan family, which had been closely allied to the Sullan faction. If we are to believe this (and it comes from a later Ciceronian defence speech on behalf of Sulla) then it seems that Sulla had accepted his punishment, or wanted to look like he had, which may argue against there being a conspiracy in 65 BC. Alternatively, it could have been a piece of political grandstanding from Sulla to show his contriteness and respect for the *res publica*. Ultimately, we can argue both ways, though it does seem unlikely that Sulla had become humble and contrite in the face of such a reversal.

One proposal that did make it through was the restoration of elections for the various priesthoods. This had been established in 104 BC by the Tribune Cn. Domitius Ahenobarbus, but abolished by Sulla, who naturally put selection back in the hands of the Senate. Thus, another Sullan measure had been overturned by a Tribune and returned to the People. Cicero also united with his colleague Antonius to pass through the Senate another anti-bribery law, perhaps with the Sullan incident of 66/65 BC in mind.

Furthermore, the Tribunes clashed with the Senate over a very unusual prosecution, one which dredged up memories of a previous period of bloodshed and asked some interesting political questions:

> *Titus Labienus, however, by indicting Caius Rabirius for the murder of Saturninus caused the greatest disorder. Saturninus had been killed some thirty-six years earlier, and the fight waged against him by the Consuls of the period had been at the direction of the senate. Hence, as a result of the proposed trial, the senate would lose the authority to enforce its decrees. In consequence the whole order of the state was being disturbed; for Rabirius did not even admit the murder but denied it. The Tribunes, however, were eager to overthrow completely the power and the dignity of the Senate and were first preparing for themselves authority to do whatever they pleased. For the investigation of acts which had received the approval of the senate and had been committed so many years before tended to give immunity to those who might attempt to imitate Saturninus' conduct, and to render ineffective the punishments for such deeds.*[27]

Thus, Labienus and some of his colleagues were attempting to prosecute for treason one of the murderers of L. Appuleius Saturninus, the Tribune killed in 100 BC, all of which was conducted under the command of C. Marius operating under the *senatus consultum ultimum*. By dredging up such an ancient case, the Tribunes were once again questioning the legality of the SCU with regard to it seeming to allow magistrates to execute Roman citizens without trial, which given what happened later in the year makes this very relevant and interesting in its timings.

Just as interesting was the choice of judges for the case, C. Iulius Caesar himself and his kinsman, L. Iulius Caesar. Given that Caesar had styled himself as the heir to Marius and that it was under Marius' command that Saturninus was murdered this is an interesting choice. It seems however that the Caesars were eager for Rabirius to be convicted, partially exonerating Marius in the process.[28] Rabirius was convicted but saved by procedural wrangling and finally the intervention of one of the Praetors, Q. Caecilius Metellus Celer, who was also an Augur who cancelled the Assembly. A renewed prosecution was not followed up and the matter was dropped. Once again Cicero states that he opposed the Tribunes and this prosecution.[29]

Thus, the year had seemingly passed without major incident; there had been a full programme of wide ranging Tribunician measures including the raising of the issue of the children of the proscribed and a major agrarian bill. The majority of these proposals had been opposed by the Consul Cicero, and all business was conducted with the absence of any violence or bloodshed. Yet from this high point matters in Rome and wider afield (in Italy and Gaul) soon spiralled out of all control and plunged the Republic into a Second Civil War.

4. The Sullan Legacy and the Consular Elections for 62 BC

Attention soon turned to the elections for 62 BC, which saw a number of notable persons standing for office; Caesar was elected as one of the Praetors and Cato elected as a Tribune, along with an unknown L. Marius. Amazingly, Catilina stood for the Consulship for a third time (his first being prevented due to a bribery charge and his second losing to Cicero and Antonius). Whilst there was nothing in the constitution to stop a bid for the Consulship, being rejected so clearly the year before usually signalled the end of a political career. Yet Catilina persisted.

Clearly thinking over his previous rejections, Catilina latched on to the various political reforms which had been frustrated by Cicero this year, again showing the dangers of the Senate not taking a lead in dealing with issues. Dio mentions both land distribution and the cancellation of debts, both of which had been Tribunician proposals blocked by Cicero:

> *He* [Catilina] *assembled from Rome itself the lowest characters and such as were always eager for a revolution and as many as possible of the allies, by promising them the cancelling of debts, distribution of lands, and everything else by which he was most likely to tempt them.*[30]
>
> *Surrounded, too, with a numerous body of colonists from Arretium and Faesulae, a crowd made conspicuous by the presence of men of a very different sort in it, men who had been ruined by the disasters in the time of Sulla.*[31]

The bulk of these supporters seemed to be veterans from Sulla's new colonies, many of which had become impoverished in the intervening years and resentful, given their role in putting Sulla and his supporters in power. Thus, the previous debt relief proposal may well have been aimed at Sullan veterans. Therefore, we can see that, as happened in the run up to the First Civil War, there were social and economic problems fermenting in Italy, which the politicians at Rome were aware of, as we can see through the Tribunician proposals, but which the Senatorial oligarchy as a whole preferred to do nothing about.

As it turns out, championing these constituencies did Catilina himself no good and for the second year in a row he was rejected at the ballot box. The new Consuls were D. Iunius Silenus and L. Licinius Murena, both solid and undistinguished men from the old Senatorial oligarchy. Under normal circumstances this would have been the end of Catilina's political career, one of many men who had achieved the Praetorship but not the Consulship and who was resigned to spend his remaining years as a 'backbench' Senator.

5. The 'Sullan' Coup of 63 BC

Determining what happened next is a perfect example of the frustration of having a contemporary source (for a change) written by one of the key men involved, but which presents us with a completely biased picture of what actually happened and why. Even the very name of this event is a red herring; the so-called 'Conspiracy of Catiline' placed everything at the feet of a man who has become one of the late Republic's pantomime villains. Yet Catilina was a convenient scapegoat for events which showed just how flawed the new Republic really was and his swift elimination could re-assure the Senatorial oligarchy that the problem had been dealt with. However, as is clear, Catilina was not the cause of the issues which faced the New Republic but merely a symptom.

It is certain that a group of the Senatorial nobility, all with affiliations to the Sullan faction, organised a coup in Rome and an uprising in Italy. Frustratingly, what is uncertain is who organised it and why? Cicero would like us to believe that Catilina was its mastermind, whilst others saw the shadowy hand of Crassus in the background. What is clear is that there were a few key ringleaders of this attempted coup: P. Cornelius Lentulus Sura, C. Manlius and Catilina himself.

Cornelius Lentulus is an interesting character and one who has fallen behind the shadow of Catilina in this matter, yet was of senior rank to him. Lentulus hailed from one of Rome's oldest and most noble families, the Cornelli, and his branch of the family had been one of the most successful, with the family first achieving the Consulship in 324 BC and holding it virtually every generation since. In his youth Lentulus had followed Sulla and held the Questorship in 81 BC when Sulla himself was Consul:

> *In Sulla's time he was Quaestor and lost and wasted large amounts of the public moneys. Sulla was angry at this and demanded an accounting from him in the Senate, whereupon Lentulus came forward with a very careless and contemptuous air and said that he would not give an account, but would offer his leg, as boys were accustomed to do when they were playing ball and made a miss.*[32]

Thus, Lentulus was part of the Sullan oligarchy which ruled the Republic in the aftermath of Sulla's victory, a point confirmed when he was elected to the Consulship of 71 BC. Yet he had clearly fallen foul of either Pompeius or Crassus, as he was immediately purged from the Senate during the Censorship of 70 BC, as was the current Consul (C. Antonius). It is unsurprising that a man of his character did not take this humiliation lying down, and he stood for and won one of the Praetorships for 63 BC and thus was a serving Praetor this year. Furthermore, it is reported, though with what accuracy we will never know, that Lentulus firmly believed in the purported Sibylline Oracle:

> *These recited forged oracles in verse purporting to come from the Sibylline books, which set forth that three Cornelii were fated to be monarchs in Rome, two of whom had already fulfilled their destiny, namely, Cinna and Sulla, and that now to him, the third and remaining Cornelius, the heavenly powers were come with a proffer of the monarchy, which he must by all means accept, and not ruin his opportunities by delay, like Catilina.*[33]

C. Manlius by contrast was a different character altogether. We are told that he was a Sullan veteran, who became leader of the Sullan veterans in Etruria. The main surviving sources portray him as nothing more than an agent of Catilina, yet he seems to have been a power in his own right:

> *These men, I say, with Manlius for a leader, one of the men who had served with distinction under Sulla, associated themselves with Catilina and came to Rome to take part in the consular elections.*[34]

Thus, we can see Manlius, rather than an agent of Catilina, as a power in his own right, and the leader of a group of Sullan veterans looking for allies amongst the Roman oligarchy.

The key question still remains as to what this disparate group of men was hoping to achieve? Clearly as late as mid-63 BC Catilina and Manlius were hoping to achieve the election of Catilina to the Consulship, no doubt followed by legislation to alleviate the plight of the Sullan veterans, with fresh measures on land distribution and debt relief. When this electoral route failed then they began to think of extra-constitutional means. Here we must remember that all of the key men involved had been part of the winning side of the First Civil War, yet all had (for different reasons) not been able to reap the rewards they felt they were due (though in most cases they had and then squandered them). As was common throughout the period that preceded the First Civil War, when men found the constitutional route blocked they turned to violence, and here all the men had seen first-hand the rewards that violence could bring, which was perhaps Sulla's greatest and most lasting legacy.

To those ends this new faction planned to seize power in the Republic both via a coup in Rome, supported by levied armies of veterans in Italy, and even uprisings in Gaul (which would most likely have been suppressed by the new regime anyway). The new Consuls were to be murdered, as was Cicero, whilst Antonius (the other Consul) was believed (at least by them) to be sympathetic to their cause. Sallust sums it up thus:

> *Relying upon such friends and accomplices as these, Catilina formed the plan of overthrowing the government, both because his own debt was enormous in all parts of the world and because the greater number of Sulla's veterans, who had squandered their property and now thought with longing of their former pillage and victories, were eager for civil war. There was no army in Italy; Cnaeus Pompeius was waging war in distant parts of the world.*[35]

Thus, with Pompeius absent and no armed forces in Italy, this faction would seize power in Rome and enact a coup along the lines of those of 88 and 87 BC. With both Consuls elect dead, no doubt Lentulus and Catilina would be appointed as new Consuls, who would then use their forces to intimidate a freshly-purged Senate to legitimise their seizure of power, as had been done in 88, 87, 82 and 70 BC. We get the sense that once in power this faction would then attempt to turn the clock back to the Sullan Republic as it had been in 82–80 BC, with the hardcore Sullan faction (as they saw themselves) in power and benefiting from power. The Sullan veterans would no doubt be handsomely rewarded again (which would merely re-start the cycle of reward and impoverishment).

Thus, we also get the feeling that this was a Sullan backlash against the way this new, post-civil war Republic was being run, which had seen the hardcore Sullan faction lose their monopoly on power and gradually find themselves losing the victory they had fought so hard to earn. Yet the great irony is that Sulla, for all his faults, did not fight the First Civil War to simply ensure that his followers would be rich and powerful. Furthermore, this coup went against everything that Sulla had wanted for the New Republic, namely an end to the political violence and bloodshed, and unified Senatorial oligarchy.

It is also worth noting the absence of any of the leading members of the Sullan family or faction in this attempted coup. Lucullus had returned from the East and finally was able to celebrate his Triumph (along with his brother for his own campaign), which was followed by retirement from public life. The sources are quiet about the role of P. Cornelius Sulla, whose deposition had been the source of proposed Tribunician legislation and a very public act of contrition. There was no clear evidence of his involvement, and an attempt to connect him to the coup was thwarted by a robust defence conducted by none other than Cicero himself. Faustus Sulla, Sulla's only surviving son, was serving, with distinction, in the armies of Pompeius in the east, who was now his father-in-law (Faustus having married Pompeius' daughter).[36] Thus, this faction lacked a clear figurehead and was seemingly nothing more than group of lower ranking Sullans embittered by their own failures but willing to exploit the tensions that existed in both Rome and Italy as a whole; the social and economic consequences of the First Civil War, which Rome's ruling oligarchy had failed to deal with.

Another interesting aspect concerns this coup and the two most prominent 'Sullans', Crassus and Pompeius, the architects of this New Republic which these men so vigorously opposed. Pompeius was obviously in the east, now engaged in a war of conquest, having disposed of Mithridates. Not only would he not support this coup, but he would have viewed it as a splendid opportunity to return from the east, with his armies, overthrow the newly installed coup leaders and save the Republic, and put himself back in charge of the Republic. The same could apply for Crassus, who was in Rome throughout. Various attempts were made to implicate him (and Caesar) but we must challenge the assumption that he was the shadowy mastermind behind the whole coup. Not only was it incompetently organised but the men involved, Sullan loyalists, had little in common with him and seemed to want to overturn the Republic that he and Pompeius had fashioned. This does not rule out Crassus becoming aware of the plot or even giving the plotters his tacit approval in the belief that he could exploit another crisis facing the Republic, as he had done so successfully in the late 70s BC. Thus, had the coup succeeded in the short term, the new ruling faction would still have to contend with the two architects of the 'New Republic'; Crassus and Pompeius, men vastly more experienced and powerful than they were.

7. The Bloody Failure of the Coup of 63 BC

Unfortunately for the coup plotters, however, their planning was shambolic. Whilst Manlius fulfilled his part and raised an army of Sullan veterans and the disaffected (see below), the plot in Rome ended in dismal failure. In a closely interconnected oligarchy, word of the plot soon leaked, brought about by a failure to act swiftly and a desire to include an ever-growing range of figures, many of whom were only lukewarm in their support for the coup; they supported its aims but did not want to risk active involvement.

Once Catilina had failed in his attempt to gain power via election to the Consulship he should have acted; yet they made a crucial mistake. The plot called for co-ordinated action between the insurrections in Italy and the coup in Rome. What happened in fact was that news of Manlius' raising of his army reached the Senate, along with reports of revolts in other parts of Italy:

A few days later, in a meeting of the Senate, Lucius Saenius, one of its members, read a letter which he said had been brought to him from Faesulae, stating that Caius Manlius had taken the field with a large force on the twenty-seventh day of October. At the same time, as is usual in such a crisis, omens and portents were reported by some, while others told of the holding of meetings, of the transportation of arms, and of insurrections of the slaves at Capua and in Apulia.[37]

Thus, the Senate was fully warned and was allowed time to act, raising forces and dispatching commanders to deal with the Italian elements of the plot (see below). The SCU was passed and the Consuls (both of them) were ordered to defend the Republic. Antonius was assigned the task of defeating the rebel army whilst Cicero (with his total lack of military experience) stayed in Rome to deal with the coup threat.[38]

In response, the coup plotters could only make a feeble attempt to assassinate Cicero, who was tipped off and the plot came to nought. Thus, Cicero and the Senate had ample time to prepare a response to the outbreak of a Second Civil War in Italy and the moment was lost. Furthermore, many in the Senate were now aware that the rebels in Italy had allies amongst the Senatorial oligarchy who were planning a coup, and Catilina soon came under suspicion. Cicero naturally wasted no time in making a series of speeches to the Senate (the Catilinarians) condemning his old rival; but as yet there was no hard evidence.

This evidence was soon provided by none other than Lentulus himself, who in seemingly a last throw of the dice attempted to involve the Gallic tribe of the Allobroges in the plot. The Allobroges were a tribe who lived to the very north of Rome's Province of Transalpine Gaul and who had been defeated by Rome during a war in the 120s BC. Lentulus gambled that they would want to rebel from Roman rule and thus aid the coup in Rome and the rebellion in Italy. That they were considering rebelling can hardly be in doubt, but that they would throw in their lot with a group of Roman aristocrats, whose plot was looking decidedly shaky and who, even if they took power, were hardly likely to grant them their independence, was highly unlikely. Thus to throw suspicion off themselves they betrayed the plot and the Senate had the evidence they needed.

Catilina had by this point wisely left Rome to join with Manlius and his army, whilst the others were rounded up in Rome; and thus the coup failed miserably. Cicero and the Senate were now left with the thorny issue of what to do with the plotters. Though the coup had failed, Italy was now in the throes of another civil war (its second) with the Senate understandably concerned about the dangers of Manlius' rebel army and a number of other uprisings in Italy, and its own lack of military resources. Furthermore Catilina, one of the key plotters, was now the de-facto leader of the rebellion or at least its figurehead, though Manlius seems to have been the more militarily qualified. Under Roman law, the plotters would have to be tried for treason, though it was known that they had many sympathizers within the oligarchy who had not been formally implicated, the Tribune elect L. Calpurnius Bestia for one. Thus, a conviction could not be guaranteed.

What followed was one of the most notorious debates in Senatorial history, whose details can be found in both Cicero and Sallust, about the fate of the plotters. Again, we have the problem that although we have contemporary accounts of the debate, they seem to have been amended, with the benefit of hindsight, to emphasise the contrasting roles and views of Caesar and Cato. Caesar is said to have called for leniency and to have the men stripped of their possessions and exiled to towns in Italy, whilst Cato called for their (illegal) execution. In the end, and with the civil war in Italy looming, the majority of the Senate agreed with Cato and Cicero was instructed to arrange the execution/murder of the prisoners. Thus, on 5th December, a serving Praetor (though he was compelled to abdicate the office first) was murdered on the orders of the Senate along with four of his noble colleagues (see Appendix One), with a number of others condemned in absentia (including Catilina).[39]

Dio reports that the search for others who may have been involved in the plot continued, which led to further unsanctioned murders:

> *The Consuls conducted most of the investigations, but Aulus Fulvius, a Senator, was slain by his own father; and the latter was not the only private individual, as some think, who acted thus. There were many others, that is to say, not only Consuls, but private individuals as well, who slew their sons.*[40]

8. The Sullan Legacy and the Second Civil War in Italy (63–62 BC)

Whilst the attempted coup in Rome receives the bulk of the coverage in our surviving sources (especially Cicero), the real threat to the Republic came from the rebellion which these Roman noblemen had started. Rebellions sprang up throughout Italy and we must ask ourselves what motivated these men to rise up and take arms against Rome, in what must surely be considered the Second Civil War (see Appendix Three). One thing we can be certain of, is that they did not do so to support a failed Roman politician, or his colleague spurred on by oracles from the gods. The majority of these men took up arms against their own state as they saw it as the only way to resolve their grievances and thus we can clearly see that the faults of the Republic which had brought about the First Civil War were still present in the New Republic. Sallust identified three key groups:

> *Meanwhile Manlius in Etruria was working upon the populace, who were already ripe for revolution because of penury and resentment at their wrongs; for during Sulla's supremacy they had lost their lands and all their property. He also approached brigands of various nationalities, who were numerous in that part of the country, and some members of Sulla's colonies who had been stripped by prodigal and luxurious living of the last of their great booty.*[41]

Thus, we can see impoverished Sullan veterans from the new colonies; those dispossessed by either the Sullan proscriptions or the creation of the Sullan colonies; and those who had taken to banditry and could see the spoils that could be accumulated by being on the victorious side in a civil war. Aside from opportunists, the first two groups were both dealing with the aftermath of the Sullan victory in the First Civil War, both victors and defeated, finally united in an impoverished aftermath. We must not forget that Italy had been badly affected by the Sullan invasion of 83 BC and subsequent peninsula–wide war (83–82 BC). Both the social and economic patterns of Italy were further disputed by the Sullan colonies being created and the changes to landholding brought about by the proscriptions. This was then followed by the demands of the continuing civil wars in Spain and the east, followed by the disruption and devastation caused by the Spartacan Slave Rebellion.

It is not as though those in Rome did not realise the state that certain parts of Italy were in, as we have seen with the proposed Tribunician legislation of this year on land distribution and debt relief, but the Senatorial oligarchy as a whole, enthusiastically supported by Cicero, chose to maintain the status quo. The similarities with the situation in 91 BC are striking, with those in Italy feeling that their legitimate grievances were being visibly ignored by those in the Senate. Thus, when the banner of rebellion was raised, there were many who felt that they had nothing to lose by taking up arms; the true failure of the New Republic.

The sources preserve what purports to be a letter from Manlius to the Roman commander sent to face him, setting out their grievances:

> *We call gods and men to witness, general, that we have taken up arms, not against our fatherland nor to bring danger upon others, but to protect our own persons from outrage; for we are wretched and destitute, many of us have been driven from our country by the violence and cruelty of the moneylenders, while all have lost repute and fortune. None of us has been allowed, in accordance with the usage of our forefathers, to enjoy the protection of the law and retain our personal liberty after being stripped of our patrimony, such was the inhumanity of the moneylenders and the Praetor.*[42]

The scale of the rebellions can be seen from the sources:

> *Thereupon by decree of the Senate Quintus Marcius Rex was sent to Faesulae and Quintus Metellus Creticus to Apulia and its neighbourhood. Both these generals were at the gates in command of their armies, being prevented from celebrating a Triumph by the intrigues of a few men, whose habit it was to make everything, honourable and dishonourable, a matter of barter. Of the Praetors, Quintus Pompeius Rufus was sent to Capua and Quintus Metellus Celer to the district of Pisa, with permission to raise an army suited to the emergency and the danger ... further, that the troops of gladiators should be quartered on Capua and the other free towns according to the resources of each place.*[43]
>
> *At about this time there were disturbances in both Transalpine and Cisalpine Gaul, as well as in the Picene and Bruttian districts and in Apulia; for those whom Catilina had sent on ahead were doing everything at once, acting imprudently and almost insanely. By their meetings at night, by their transportation of arms and weapons, and by their bustle and general activity they caused more apprehension than actual danger.*[44]

By far the biggest threat came from C. Manlius, who was able to raise an army of at least ten thousand men from Etruria. Despite these various uprisings, the Senate found itself in a better position than it should have been. Outside Rome were several returning armies, with their commanders awaiting Triumphs. This gave the Senate sufficient forces to immediately counter the largest threat, C. Manlius, and soon Catilina himself, in Etruria, whilst still being able to send another four commanders to various parts of Italy: Faesulae, Apulia, Capua and Pisa. The Consul C. Antonius was suspected of having sympathies with the coup himself.

The second advantage the Senate had was the disorganised nature of their opposition. Whilst Manlius was able to put an army into the field to possibly march on Rome in support of the coup, the other regions seemed uncoordinated and unfocussed, more intent on local rebellions than a knock-out attack on Rome itself. This allowed the Senate to focus on the clearest danger: the army of Manlius and Catilina.

This disorganised nature of the rebellion played another crucial role in the Senate's eventual victory. As discussed earlier, the rebellions in Italy should have coordinated their actions with the coup in Rome, but whilst Manlius fulfilled his part, Catilina and Lentulus squandered their opportunity. Further damage was done to their cause, as it seems that they had informed their army that they were to support a coup in Rome. When that failed, and the plotters were executed, their forces realised that the prospect of a quick win had disappeared and that they would have to face the full force of the Roman state. We are told that this resulted in mass desertions.

Nevertheless, Catilina and Manlius preserved the nucleus of an army. Yet whilst they still had numbers, their quality was poor:

> *Only about a fourth part of the entire force was provided with regular arms. The others carried whatever weapons chance had given them; namely, javelins or lances, or in some cases pointed stakes.*[45]

Thus, this seems to have been an army in name only, more a rag-tag collection of poorly-armed citizens. Facing them were the armies of Q. Metellus Celer and the Consul C. Antonius, both with large armies of veteran soldiers. We are told that Celer had three legions of his own and Antonius an equally large army. Thus, the army of Catilina and Manlius was seriously outnumbered both in terms of numbers and quality of soldiers.

Realising the forlorn state of this situation, Catilina and Manlius gave up on the idea of a march on Rome and apparently tried to march their army into Transalpine Gaul, and possibly over the Alps, no doubt hoping to stir up further rebellion as they went. Unfortunately, they were trapped when Metellus marched ahead of their route and blocked their path, with Antonius trailing them. Faced with being caught between two opposing armies, Catilina and Manlius chose to attack Antonius' army, presumably to force an escape route. The result was the Battle of Pistoria in January 62 BC.

Given the disparity between the two sides, both in terms of numbers and quality, the result was a foregone conclusion and the rebel army was annihilated, with both Catilina and Manlius being killed in the fighting (Antonius sent Catilina's head to Rome as proof). Yet whilst the largest threat had been crushed, the war did not end there and military operations in Italy continued throughout 62 BC:

> *A rebellion in Paelignia engineered by the Marcelli, father and son, was betrayed by Lucius Vettius. It was, as it were ripped up by the roots after Catilina's conspiracy had been uncovered, being suppressed by Bibulus in Paelignia and by Cicero in Bruttium.*[46]

We see that a number of the newly-elected Praetors were fighting in Italy; M. Calpurnius Bibulus in central Italy against the Paeligni, and Q. Tullius Cicero (the younger brother of the Consul) in southern Italy in Bruttium. Though we have insufficient information, it would be worth speculating on connections between those regions that rebelled during this war and those that had during the First Civil War, to see if again it was unfinished business for them.

9. Rebellion in Gaul (63–61 BC)

As is common, whilst the surviving sources focus in great detail on the events in Rome, those taking place within Italy and Gaul receive far less attention. The sources tell us that both Gallic provinces saw rebellions, though not the extent. We do know that the Praetor, Q. Caecilius Metellus Celer arrested and imprisoned a number of ringleaders who had been sent from Rome, as did L. Licinius Murena, the legate commanding in Transalpine Gaul.[47]

Similarly, with the deaths of Catilina and Manlius, the sources seem to lose interest in the whole affair.[48] Yet the sources report that during 62 BC the Allobroges did indeed rebel against Roman rule, requiring a major campaign to subdue them once more. Even though they had betrayed the coup being organised in Rome to the Senate, we can see that it was not out of loyalty to Rome, but self-interest. Having earned the thanks of the Senate and with Roman forces fully occupied in Italy they chose this time to rebel. Thus, we can see the continuing effects of the Second Civil War on Rome's territories. The campaign details fall outside the remit of this present work, but Dio preserves an account. C. Pomptinus (Pr. 63 BC) was dispatched as Governor of Transalpine Gaul and spent the next eighteen months fighting the war against them. Amongst his legates was a certain L. Marius (relationship unknown). It was not until 61 BC that the Allobroges were subdued and brought back under Roman domination.

Summary

Any analysis of these events has to contend with the bias in the surviving sources. Firstly, their focus on the events in Rome at the cost of those in Italy and Gaul, and secondly the desire to focus on Catilina at the cost of the wider issues being raised. Whilst we can understand Catilina's motivations and those of Lentulus, the focus must be on those others, both in Rome and Italy, who joined the plot. The very fact that a number of the Roman oligarchy joined the plot shows the tensions that were still present in the Republic, caused by the First Civil War, which seem to be glossed over in the sources that survive (though they may have not recognised them). This helps skew the picture towards it being all the work of one dissolute individual, Catilina, as cause rather than symptom. Harrison presents the best modern analysis of the factors that seem to have been present in this period.[49]

Yet for all those in Rome and Italy who took part in either the coup or the armed uprising, it must be said that the New Republic withstood this shock remarkably well. The key to the failure of both the plot and the uprising was the absence of any of the leading figures of the day. During the First Civil War, it was the Consuls and senior generals who were leading the armies, whereas here it was the lower ranks of the oligarchy. Had Crassus genuinely been behind this plot then it would have succeeded (at least until Pompeius returned). In many ways the war was a reaction by those who had lost out under the Pompeian–Crassan settlement: both Cornelius Lentulus and Antonius (strongly suspected of sympathising) had been expelled from the Senate in 70 BC, and Catilina was forever tainted with his actions under Sulla.

Ultimately therefore, this Second Civil War had the potential to be a serious threat to the Republic but this did not materialise due to the majority of the Senatorial oligarchy, especially the leading members, choosing to work within the system, and likewise the majority of Italian cities and regions making a similar choice. Thus, whilst this period showed that there were still major issues facing the Republic, it seemed (for now at least) that this New Republic was strong enough to withstand them.

Chapter Four

A Stronger Republic? The Shadow
of the Triumvirate (62–59 BC)

A
s we have seen, just seven years after the Pompeian-Crassan
Settlement, which brought an end to the First Civil War, the
Republic collapsed once more into a Second Civil War. Unlike
the first war, this conflict was soon confined to tumult in Rome, fighting
in Italy, rebellion in Gaul. The tumult in Rome was swiftly (and bloodily)
brought to a conclusion, thanks to a series of extra judicial murders,
and the fighting in Italy culminated with just the one set piece battle,
followed by a number of minor pacification campaigns. Thus, within a
few months Rome had successfully contained the fighting and prevented
it spreading empire wide (though the rebellions of the Allobroges took
several years to pacify). Though the military aspect of this new civil war
had been brought to a fairly swift conclusion, the true test of the strength
of the restored Republic would be the years that followed this outbreak of
violence and bloodshed.

1. The Aftermath of the Second Civil War

Away from the fighting in Italy and Gaul, we can see further repercussions
in Rome itself. Naturally enough, even though the various rebellions in
Italy had been defeated militarily the presence of so many supporters of
the planned coup at Rome, especially amongst the Senatorial oligarchy,
led to a degree of paranoia and questions over who else was involved.
Thanks to a passage of Suetonius we know that a special commission was
established to uncover any further coup plotters, headed by L. Novius
Niger. The commission initially benefited from those supporters of the
coup who wished to inform on their colleagues to save their own skins:

> *Others who had been avoiding observation were convicted and condemned
> on information furnished by Lucius Vettius, a knight, who had taken*

part in the conspiracy but now on promise of immunity revealed the participants.[1]

Dio goes onto state that Vettius was suspected by the Senate of adding names to the list of those conspirators in order to settle scores or make personal gain, and that he was exposed. Interestingly he omits the names of those (unjustly?) accused. Had we only Dio's account, a very interestingly nugget of information would have been lost forever, Suetonius by contrast names Caesar as being at the centre of this political scandal:

He [Caesar] again fell into danger by being named among the accomplices of Catilina, both before the commissioner Novius Niger by an informer called Lucius Vettius and in the Senate by Quintus Curius, who had been voted a sum of money from the public funds as the first to disclose the plans of the conspirators. Curius alleged that his information came directly from Catilina, while Vettius actually offered to produce a letter to Catilina in Caesar's handwriting. But Caesar, thinking that such an indignity could in no wise be endured, showed by appealing to Cicero's testimony that he had of his own accord reported to the Consul certain details of the plot, and thus prevented Curius from getting the reward. As for Vettius, after his bond was declared forfeit and his goods seized, he was roughly handled by the populace assembled before the Rostra, and all but torn to pieces. Caesar then put him in prison, and Novius the commissioner went there too, for allowing an official of superior rank to be arraigned before his tribunal.[2]

Thus, Vettius was disgraced and jailed (and beaten) and the magistrate in charge of the commission was thrown into jail himself; it is not known whether the work of the commission continued under another magistrate. As discussed previously we will never know who was or was not involved (those at the time could not be certain) and clearly both Caesar, and earlier Crassus, were implicated.[3] Both men naturally used their considerable resources to ensure public exoneration, continuing the proud Roman tradition of ensuring that no senior members of the Senatorial oligarchy were implicated in political scandals of this magnitude.[4]

The two former Consuls met with differing reactions. Antonius seemingly did not return to Rome (and thus avoided any fallout) but proceeded to his allocated Proconsular province of Macedonia, whose borders he had to defend from native tribes (the Dardani and Bastarni). Over the next two years he was defeated on several occasions and returned to Rome in disgrace, whereupon he was promptly tried, convicted and exiled for treason and extortion (but in reality, for military incompetence and perhaps his role in the civil war).

With Antonius' absence it was Cicero who was left to face the political fallout. The earliest signs of what form this would take came at the end of Cicero's Consulship when he attempted to make a traditional speech summarising his achievements:

> *However, there were those who were ready to abuse Cicero for what he had done, and to do him harm, and they had as leaders among the magistrates elect, Caesar as Praetor, and Metellus and Bestia as Tribunes. When these assumed office, Cicero having still a few days of Consular authority, they would not permit him to harangue the People, but placing their benches so as to command the Rostra, would not suffer or allow him to speak; instead, they ordered him, if he wished, merely to pronounce the oath usual on giving up office, and then come down. Cicero accepted these terms and came forward to pronounce his oath; and when he had obtained silence, he pronounced, not the usual oath, but one of his own and a new one, swearing that in very truth he had saved his country and maintained her supremacy. And all the People confirmed his oath for him.*[5]

Thus, Cicero was prevented by at least two Tribunes, Q. Caecilius Metellus Nepos and L. Calpurnius Bestia, from addressing the People, but still managed (with his customary modesty) to claim the sole credit for 'saving the Roman state'. This is confirmed by Asconius, who quotes Cicero directly:

> *I swore that the state and the city had attained its salvation by my efforts and mine alone.*[6]

Plutarch in his biography of Cicero goes further:

> *So, at this time Cicero had the greatest power in the state, but he made himself generally odious, not by any base action, but by continually praising and magnifying himself, which made him hateful to many. For*

there could be no session either of Senate or Assembly or court of justice in which one was not obliged to hear Catilina and Lentulus endlessly talked about. Nay, he even went so far as to fill his books and writings with these praises of himself; and he made his oratory, which was naturally very pleasant and had the greatest charm, irksome and tedious to his hearers, since this unpleasant practice clung to him like a fatality.[7]

Such an attitude was hardly likely to endear him to his opponents or the supporters of the commanders who took to the field against Catilina and Manlius's forces. However, it was not his arrogance that brought him so much trouble, but the charge of murdering Roman citizens without a trial (in clear breach of the law). This conundrum had been present in Roman politics since the first political murder, that of Ti. Sempronius Gracchus, in 133 BC. None of his attackers, nor their ringleader P. Cornelius Scipio Nasica were brought to trial. The subsequent use of the *senatus consultum ultimum* further complicated matters. Though it may have been the ultimate decree of the Senate (a de-facto declaration of a state of emergency) it could not circumnavigate the issue that Senatorial decrees were not laws but learned opinions; they could not suspend the most basic Roman law that no Roman citizen could be put to death without a trial by his peers.

Thus, the Consul charged with eliminating C. Sempronius Gracchus and M. Fulvius Flaccus in 121 BC (L. Opimius) was subsequently charged with murder, though acquitted. C. Marius too used the SCU to eliminate L. Appuleius Saturninus and C. Servilius Glaucia in 100 BC but was not charged at all, more due to his political power rather than any legal exemption. Cicero therefore had lain himself open to charges of executing Roman citizens without trial, and the Tribune Metellus Nepos looked to bring such charges:

Cicero, on his side, came near being tried then and there for the killing of Lentulus and the other prisoners. This charge, though technically brought against him, was really directed against the Senate. For its members were violently denounced before the populace, especially by Metellus Nepos, on the ground that they had no right to condemn any citizen to death without the consent of the People. Nevertheless, Cicero escaped on this occasion. For the Senate granted immunity to all those

who had administered affairs during that period, and further proclaimed
that if anyone should dare to call one of them to account later, he should
be regarded as a personal and public enemy; so that Nepos was afraid
and made no further trouble.[8]

Thus, for now, Cicero was saved from prosecution, but again, a grant of
Senatorial immunity was not legally binding without an accompanying
law, which was not passed. Cicero received strong support from the new
Consul L. Licinius Murena, whom Cicero had defended from a charge
of corruption in his election as Consul. What this also shows is that even
with fighting still taking place in Italy, back in Rome a Tribune from
one of Rome's leading Senatorial families was seemingly siding with the
People against the Senate and accusing them of being murderers, with all
the parallels to previous bouts of political bloodshed and infighting this
summoned up.

2. Political Reforms, Violence and the Shadow of Pompeius

The fallout from the Second Civil War of 63/62 BC continued, with a
number of proposed pieces of legislation. We know for certain the
identities of five of the Tribunes for this year, (and possibly one other
– see Appendix Three), but centre-stage were three men; Q. Caecilius
Metellus Nepos, M. Porcius Cato and L. Marius. Marius is perhaps
the easiest to begin with, owing to what seems to have been a relatively
quiet year (based on our few surviving sources). Together with Cato he
proposed and passed a minor law, amending the criteria for commanders
claiming a Triumph (who would now have to include figures for the
numbers of the enemy forces killed and their own losses). Yet it was far
more what Marius represented than what he did. We do not know the
exact relation he was to the (in)famous Marius, but here was a relative
of the general (from the same family; unlike Caesar who was related by
marriage), holding office in Rome once more.

Yet it was his two colleagues, Cato and Metellus, who dominated the
domestic agenda in this year and between them plunged Rome back into
political violence and bloodshed. Cato had started the year by playing a
prominent role in the Senatorial debate on the fate of the coup plotters
arrested in Rome (see Chapter Three) and continued when he accused

one of the Consuls, L. Licinius Murena, of achieving his election through bribery, thus, harking back to the annulled Sullan election of 65 BC. It was perhaps a high-risk strategy for an incoming Tribune to accuse an incoming Consul of corruption, but merely cemented his status as an opponent of corruption and the Sullan faction. He was also building on the enhanced reputation of his illustrious ancestor of the same name (Cos. 195 BC). Murena was successfully defended by none other than Cicero himself (an outgoing Consul defending an incoming one). Nevertheless, Cato cemented his populist standing even further when he proposed that the Senate extend those eligible for the corn dole (the subsidised grain distribution to Roman citizens introduced by C. Sempronius Gracchus himself).

Whilst the measure itself was always a popular one with the People, the way he went about it (as reported by our surviving sources) also shows a deft political touch. Plutarch stresses that he proposed this measure to the Senate rather than bypass them, so that it seemed their idea and he is reported as proposing the measure to cut off a '*feared revolution of the poorer classes*' and thus it was a measure to bring stability to the state.[9] Thus, Cato seems to have proposed a popular reform with the Senate's blessing, which would earn him supporters from both camps.

By contrast, Cato's colleague Q. Caecilius Metellus Nepos showed far less political subtlety, but then hailing from Rome's leading political dynasty he perhaps felt that he did not need it. He exploited the opportunities offered, not only by the ongoing crisis in Italy and Gaul caused by the civil war, but also the impending return of Cn. Pompeius. Pompeius had recently completed Rome's most successful war in the east to date and annexed not only the kingdoms of Bithynia and Pontus, but also the remnants of the Seleucid Empire (in Syria) and extended Rome's empire in the east, as far as Judaea.[10] Pompeius was still in the east when the Second Civil War erupted, but with the fighting ended he was dealing with administrative matters and was due to return to Italy at some point this year.

Metellus proposed two bills. One was that Pompeius (and his army) be recalled to Italy to secure the Republic from the supporters of the coup and the various groups in rebellion. A second was that Pompeius should be elected Consul in absentia (for the following year) due to the serious nature of the crisis, much as Marius had been in the 100s BC.[11] These proposals received much support from many sections of the People and also a certain Praetor, none other than C. Iulius Caesar himself. Naturally enough the Senate was split on the matter, with the supporters of Pompeius welcoming the move and his opponents worried over the potential consequences; especially given Pompeius' record of using armies to gain political advancement (81, 77 and 70 BC).

The most vocal opponent was none other than M. Porcius Cato, one of Metellus' Tribunician colleagues, which thus raised the prospect of an intra-Tribunician clash, the source of so much political violence in the pre-civil war period. The few surviving sources confirm that events did indeed take a turn for the worst and violence broke out:

> *Nevertheless, when Caecilius Metellus, Tribune of the Plebs, brought forward some bills of a highly seditious nature in spite of the veto of his colleagues, Caesar abetted him and espoused his cause in the stubbornest fashion, until at last both were suspended from the exercise of their public functions by a decree of the Senate.*[12]
>
> *When the People were about to vote on the law, in favour of Metellus there were armed strangers and gladiators and servants drawn up in the Forum, and that part of the people which longed for Pompeius in their hope of a change was present in large numbers.*[13]
>
> *In the first place, Cato and Quintus Minucius, the Tribunes, vetoed the proposition and stopped the scribe who was reading the motion. Then when Nepos took the document to read it himself, they took it away, and when even then he undertook to speak extempore, they stopped his mouth. The result was that a battle waged with clubs and stones and even swords took place between them, in which some others joined, assisting one side or the other. Therefore, the Senators met in the Senate House that very day, changed their raiment and gave the Consuls charge of the city, that it might suffer no harm. Then Nepos once more became afraid and immediately retired from their midst; subsequently, after publishing some piece of writing against the Senate, he set out to join Pompeius, although he had no right to be absent from the city for a single night.*[14]
>
> *Accordingly, when Cato paused in the Forum and saw the temple of Castor and Pollux surrounded by armed men and its steps guarded by gladiators, and Metellus himself sitting at the top with Caesar, he turned*

to his friends and said: 'What a bold man, and what a coward, to levy
such an army against a single unarmed and defenceless person!'[15]

Thus, once again a clash between Tribunes led to violence and bloodshed
in the Forum, with the Senate asking the Consuls to defend the city,
though the SCU does not seem to have been passed. This was followed
by one of the key Tribunes fleeing the city (and deserting his post) to join
one of Rome's generals in the east. Apparently, it was Cato himself who
prevented the Senate from deposing Metellus (though only the People
had the power to do so):

But he won still more esteem by not allowing the Senate to carry out its
purpose of degrading Metellus and deposing him from his office, which
course Cato opposed, and brought the Senate over to his views.[16]

Thus, we can see that although Rome's generals had secured Italy and
the provinces against rebellions encouraged by members of the Roman
oligarchy, political arguments were once again being settled with
bloodshed and violence within Rome itself. The flaws that had plunged
the Republic into the First Civil War were still present, despite the
Sullan and Pompeian-Crassan settlements. Unusually, we hear little of
Crassus' role in this political violence. Caesar was clearly in favour of
Pompeius returning with an army, and Crassus was his sometime patron,
but this does not automatically mean that Crassus himself would be in
favour of his long-term rival returning at the head of an army to 'save the
Republic'.

Whilst Crassus was anonymous in these events (as we have them
reported), Caesar was in the thick of them, but clearly had a year in office
to forget. Not only did he back Metellus in his Pompeian proposal (which
was defeated) but pushed Pompeius' cause in a second and more bizarre
affair when he prosecuted Q. Lutatius Catulus, who was responsible for
rebuilding the Temple of Iupiter Capitolinus. He advocated the removal
of Catulus' name and that Pompeius be given responsibility to finish the
building, despite his being overseas.

He was also involved in a domestic scandal when a male intruder
secretly obtained entrance to a female-only religious ceremony (the *Bona*

Dea) being held in Caesar's house. The man in question was P. Claudius Pulcher and the outcome of this scandal was that Caesar divorced his wife. Given that he had also been linked to the coup and been suspended from office for his part in the Metellan violence, it all added up to a somewhat disastrous year in politics for Caesar and not the springboard for a successful run at the Consulship. He left Rome the following year to take up his Propraetorian command in Spain.

Yet throughout the year all the domestic events were overshadowed by the presence of Cn. Pompeius, undeniably now Rome's leading general and being famed as a new Alexander for his eastern conquests (though they hardly compare). He had now been absent from Rome for five years; firstly, clearing the Mediterranean of the pirate problem (in under a year) and then taking command of Rome's eastern campaign, ostensibly to defeat the Pontic king Mithridates. Yet this war had seen a number of major Roman milestones, such as the capture of Jerusalem, an expedition to the Caucasus, the humbling of the Parthian Empire and the annexation of the Seleucid Empire.[17] Yet for all his glory, at the heart of the legend lay the protégé of Sulla: the man who had created his own private army and supported an invasion of Italy, the man who had three times used his army to gain political advantage (81, 77 and 71 BC). He was now returning to Italy from the east (just as Sulla had done) with a battle-hardened army and to a Republic which had suffered (and survived) not only a civil war in Italy and Gaul, but a possible uprising in Rome itself, and now bloodshed in the Forum and political chaos in Rome.

It seems that it was towards the end of the year that Pompeius crossed from Greece to Brundisium with his army. Prior to his arrival he sent word to the Senate requesting that the Consular elections be postponed in order to allow him to appear in Rome in person to canvas on behalf of one of his legates (M. Pupius Piso Frugi Calpurnianus) who was a candidate. Once more it seems that the main opponent to this was none other than Cato, who was able to overcome Pompeius' considerable powers of patronage and persuade the Senate not to grant Pompeius' request. Thus, whilst most Romans were trying to ingratiate themselves with this 'new Alexander' Cato either genuinely thought Pompeius a danger to the stability of the Republic, or that there was more political capital to be gained from such a 'principled stance'. Clearly, he was tapping into the image of his famous ancestor, but this is something that (as far as we are aware) none of his immediate forbears had done.

Pompeius was apparently so impressed with Cato's political ability that he proposed a marriage alliance between the two families (Pompeius himself had just divorced his third wife).[18] Once again Cato played up to his 'incorruptible' image and refused Pompeius' offer. As it was, despite Cato's opposition and his absence, Pompeius' candidate (Piso) was able to be successfully elected as one of the Consuls of the following year (61 BC), giving Pompeius one of the two Consuls for his first year back in Rome. It was against this background that Pompeius landed his army at Brundisium in late 62 BC.

3. The Calm Between Storms (61–60 BC)

Given his role in the First Roman Civil War, Pompeius must have been well aware of the worries back in Rome (and Italy) about his return and the possibility of a repeated civil war, and therefore he made a very grand and obvious show of discharging his army upon arrival in Italy. Ever the consummate showman, he followed this with perhaps Rome's grandest ever Triumph, it being a triple Triumph with victories over the pirates of the Mediterranean, Mithridates of Pontus and Tigranes of Armenia.

It is clear that Pompeius not only wanted to return to his pre-eminent position in the domestic life of Roman politics but had a clear agenda of measures he needed to be pushed through. Central to this was the Senate's (or the Peoples') ratification of his settlement of the eastern provinces and allies in the wake of his victory.[19] There was also the matter of securing land for his landless veterans. He clearly hoped that having one of his legates as Consul would facilitate this, but unfortunately it was not to be the case. Piso became embroiled in the *Bona Dea* scandal, clashing with his Consular colleague (M. Valerius Messalla Niger).

Eventually a special court (for a charge of sacrilege) was convened under a law passed by a Tribune (Q. Fufius Calenus). The accused, P. Claudius Pulcher, was found not guilty and was able to take up his post of Quaestor in Sicily.

In fact, aside from this incident, we have very little surviving detail of the domestic events of this year, which makes it somewhat of an anti-climax, considering the two previous years and the worries about Pompeius' return. Further proof is that we know that a Census took place this year, but we have no surviving record of who the Censors were or what they did. The only other Tribunician activity we know about comes from a M. Aufidius Lurco, who proposed but did not pass a bribery law, and even this is only mentioned in passing in a letter of Cicero.

As always, we will probably never know if this 'calm after the storm' was down to a genuine lack of political activity or the random survival of material in our sources. It is odd that given the effort Pompeius went to, to get his man elected as Consul, that so little was achieved. It is possible that all sides were trying for a period of calm after the violence and bloodshed of the previous two years, but given the personalities involved this seems unlikely. What is more likely is that Pompeius' Consul (Piso) was ineffective, but the clashes were kept from escalating into violence. It is also possible that whilst Pompeius (in his absence) was able to arrange for one of his supporters to be elected as Consul, he was unable to arrange the same for the Tribunate.

If 61 BC had been an unexpectedly quiet year, the same could not be said of the following year (60 BC). Keeping to his policy, Pompeius had another of his former legates (L. Afranius) elected as one of the Consuls and secured the election of none other than Q. Metellus Nepos (Tr. 62 BC) as Praetor.[20] He was also able to secure at least one supporter as Tribune; L. Flavius. Having secured men in these key magistracies, Pompeius pushed for his programme of measures to be introduced, namely the ratification of his eastern settlement and land for his veterans.

To those ends, L. Flavius proposed a fresh agrarian law, which would distribute public land (*ager publicus*) to Pompeius' discharged veterans, along with fresh purchases of land. This measure was ably supported by none other than Cicero himself, but soon ran into opposition in form of the other Consul; Q. Caecilius Metellus Celer. Celer's opposition is interesting given the staunch support that Pompeius received from another Metellus (Q. Caecilius Metellus Nepos – Tr. 62 BC) and is a wonderful example of the clear danger of assuming that all members of the same political family followed a coherent policy.[21] Therefore, once again we can see a clash between a Consul and a Tribune over an agrarian law (some seventy years after Gracchus in 133 BC).

This clash resulted in the Tribune ordering the Consul to be sent to prison and stripping him of his assigned Proconsular province (Transalpine Gaul). The key difference here is that on this occasion, the check and balances of the Roman system worked, and the measure was prevented, with neither side resorting to violence or extra-constitutional means. Nevertheless, the parallels from recent Roman history were manifold, including the dangers of blocking a Roman commander from passing a land distribution law for his veterans (as had been seen with Marius). Thus, unlike the years 63–62 BC, although there were clashes in Roman politics they were held within the system and did not escalate into violence.

The other major domestic topic for this year again involved P. Claudius Pulcher. On his return from his Questorship he proposed a most extraordinary move. Claudius hailed from one of the most distinguished of Republican families, and as such held Patrician status. Whilst this was the highest mark of esteem in the Republican oligarchy, in practice it meant that Claudius was barred from holding the Tribunate (a Plebeian office), and thus would have to wait several years for his next office (the Praetorship).

Whilst every other Patrician had accepted this limitation, Claudius seemingly thought differently. To that end he persuaded a Tribune (C. Herennius) to propose a law transferring him from the Patrician order to the Plebeian one, thus overturning over five hundred years of bloodlines and precedent. Clearly Claudius was very publicly acknowledging a political truth; namely that the Republic had evolved and that the Tribunate was more valuable to a politician than Patrician status. Whilst in reality the Patrician/Plebeian distinction had long been lost, with the merging of the rich Plebeian families into the Senatorial oligarchy, in terms of a society based on ancestral (and divine) sanction it would have been seen as a scandalous step to renounce one's birth right amongst the Republican oligarchy.

Naturally enough, there was significant opposition to such a precedent being established and again leading the opposition was the Consul Metellus Celer, even though he was actually Claudius' brother-in-law and a member of the leading Plebeian political family:

That which, the year before, his brother Metellus and the Senate, which
even then was unanimous, had refused, and in the most rigorous manner
rejected with one voice and one mind.[22]

Therefore, we can see that, on the face of it, the year ended well in
constitutional terms; two controversial measures had been proposed by
Tribunes and opposed by their colleagues and one of the Consuls. Vetoes
had been used and upheld and both measures had been dropped (for
now). This is exactly what hadn't happened in the previous generations
of the Republic, where lawful opposition was not respected and extra-
constitutional (and mostly violent) measures were taken. In both cases
however it did not mean that both matters would not be raised in the
following year.

Aside from these two high profile domestic issues a third emerged;
which at first seemed far less explosive. As was common (having been
introduced by C. Gracchus) the contract for the collection of the taxes of
the Roman province of Asia had been auctioned off by the (anonymous)
Censors of 61 BC. Whilst this had been a long-established practice,
it seems that, in their eagerness, the winning cartel had bid far more
than they found themselves able to collect and thus stood to lose money.
Naturally enough they petitioned the Consuls to dissolve their contracts;
though unsurprisingly one of the Consuls (Metellus again) refused the
request. Again, nothing further came of this matter in this year, but the
cartel, faced with a large loss, would not let the matter rest once the
individual magistrates had stepped down. It is also possible that none
other than M. Licinius Crassus was advancing their cause, though his
name is not linked to it this year. On a lesser note, whilst Pompeius'
high profile proposals were blocked, Metellus Nepos was able to pass an
interesting law, abolishing all custom duties in Italian ports, which was
clearly of benefit to the trading community.

4. Senatorial Opposition and an Alliance of Convenience

In many ways, we can see that the years 60–61 BC saw the Republican
system working well. Throughput its history whenever one Roman
politician/general had become pre-eminent, then the rest of the

Senatorial oligarchy rallied together to ensure that his pre-eminence was not translated into political dominance and used to subvert the nature of the oligarchy. Generals such as Scipio Africanus, Scipio Aemilianus and Marius had all achieved military glory and been the most dominant figures of their period, yet none had been able to translate it into lasting political dominance, and all saw their subsequent political careers dwindle and, if anything, tarnish their previous military reputation. Naturally the collapse of the Republican system into civil war saw the rise of a series of military dynasts, who clearly controlled the Republic, most notably Cinna and Sulla. Yet they too were unwilling, or unable, to translate this into more than fleeting control.

Thus, we can see Pompeius as the latest in a long line of military figures whose battlefield exploits did not translate into political power at home. Despite his popularity, wealth and powers of patronage, he was unable to secure the domestic legislation he needed. Certainly he was able to use his power and wealth to secure a Consulship for one of his subordinates two years running, and in 60 BC also secure at least one Praetor and one Tribune (that we know of), but they proved powerless in the face of a combined and effective opposition. The Republican system seemed to be working as it should, with no one person being able to dominate the domestic agenda or turn to violence and bloodshed.

It is clear that Pompeius was well aware of the limitations of using violence to achieve his goals: short term success would come at too high a cost. He must also have been equally aware of how fragile the restored Republic was, especially given his own role in the First Civil War, and the recent outbreak of the Second. Yet the failure of 'his' magistrates in pushing through his domestic legislation must have caused him to rethink, if not the method, then the personnel. Clearly the two men he had secured for the Consulship had been chosen more for their loyalty (both his former legates) than their political acumen. If he was to continue this tactic he clearly needed a more adept political operator. Of the 'younger' (in experience if not in age) generation of Roman politicians two men stood out; M. Porcius Cato and C. Iulius Caesar. Of the two, Cato had proved himself unwilling to be an ally of Pompeius, but fortunately Caesar was wanting to stand as Consul.

Having had an extremely frustrating year as Praetor (see above), Caesar had taken up his Propraetorian governorship of one of the Spanish provinces (Farther Spain), where, as was custom, he fought wars (colonial policing actions) against the native tribes. Naturally, Caesar's thoughts turned to resurrecting his political career and thus he returned to Rome (before his replacement had arrived) in time for the Consular elections for 59 BC. To enhance his chances, he also submitted a request for a Triumph; a very public statement of his military powers and thus Consular suitability. Unfortunately for him he faced a constitutional problem:

> *Caesar, on returning from his Praetorship in Spain, desired to be a candidate for the Consulship, and at the same time asked for a Triumph. But since by law candidates for a magistracy must be present in the city, while those who are going to celebrate a Triumph must remain outside the walls, he asked permission from the Senate to solicit the office by means of others. Many were willing to grant the request, but Cato opposed it; and when he saw that the Senators were ready to gratify Caesar, he consumed the whole day in speaking and thus frustrated their desires. Accordingly, Caesar gave up his Triumph, entered the city.*[23]

Thus, Caesar met with another setback, again at the hands of Cato and this must have raised doubts as to both the certainty of his election and (if elected) how he would spend his year in office. Thus, we see that at the time of the Consular elections we have a powerful figure looking for a suitable candidate to back, and a suitable candidate in need of a patron. Furthermore, Caesar had backed Pompeius' interests during his Praetorship and was no friend of Cato. Thus, as often happened in the Republic, an alliance of convenience was formed, though the exact details will forever remain a mystery, known only to the participants behind closed doors. It seems that this alliance was cemented with the promise of a marriage alliance, with Pompeius marrying Caesar's daughter (which happened after the elections). Unsurprisingly, Caesar was duly elected as one of the two Consuls for 59 BC. Naturally both Pompeius and Caesar had an interest in securing a pliant colleague for Caesar, especially given Metellus' opposition to Afranius that year:

Of the two other candidates for this office, Lucius Lucceius and Marcus Bibulus, Caesar joined forces with the former, making a bargain with him that since Lucceius had less influence but more funds, he should in their common name promise largess to the electors from his own pocket. When this became known, the aristocracy authorized Bibulus to promise the same amount, being seized with fear that Caesar would stick at nothing when he became chief magistrate, if he had a colleague who was heart and soul with him. Many of them contributed to the fund, and even Cato did not deny that bribery under such circumstances was for the good of the Republic. Thus, Caesar was chosen Consul with Bibulus.[24]

Even with Pompeius' resources, he could only secure one of the Consuls of this year and had an opponent as the other. It was probably at this point that Pompeius and Caesar brought a third man into this alliance of convenience; none other than M. Licinius Crassus.[25] As we have seen (Chapters Two and Three), Crassus' domestic position had been on the wane for a number of years; his Censorship of 65 BC had seen his schemes for enfranchising Transalpine Gaul and for annexing Egypt blocked and he had narrowly avoided being officially implicated in the insurrection of 63/62 BC. The sources make much of the supposed enmity between Pompeius and Crassus, yet both had followed similar paths, and both had successfully combined to secure the Consulship for themselves in 70 BC and introduced their constitutional settlement, which had modified the Sullan Republic in to its present form.

We remain unclear as to what exactly Crassus got out of reforming his alliance with both Pompeius and Caesar. Certainly, he seems to have been acting on behalf of the Asian tax consortium (see above), and it is possible that he was acting on behalf of the Egyptian king Ptolemy XII (see below). However, aside from specific pieces of legislation he may have wanted passing, this alliance gave Crassus a chance to place himself at the heart of power in Rome once more. For these reasons, Crassus accepted the offer of an alliance and Caesar, as Consul, was now backed (albeit temporarily) by the two most powerful men in Roman politics. The Duumvirate of 70 BC had become the Triumvirate of 59 BC.[26]

5. Political Reform and the Triumvirate (59 BC)

There are two aspects of this alliance that we must be clear on. Firstly, even though today this alliance is now known as the Triumvirate, it was not an alliance of equals. Pompeius and Crassus were the two dominant partners and Caesar their junior. This is not only important in our understanding of the events of 59 BC but also the events of the following decade. Secondly, this alliance, like most in Roman politics, was one of temporary convenience. Recent Roman history had seen its like before, notably in 101–100 BC when the duo of L. Appuleius Saturninus and C. Servilius Glaucia, allied with the more powerful C. Marius, pooled their political strengths in an alliance to temporarily overwhelm their political opponents. Once their short-term aims had been achieved, then the three men would go their separate ways again.

Yet despite this backing, it is clear that the same constitutional safeguards which had blocked Pompeius' Consuls of 61 and 60 BC were still in place, namely the other Consuls and the Tribunes, not to mention opposition in the Senate. It is clear that (as usual) Pompeius (and Crassus) secured the support of a number of Tribunes this year, notably P. Vatinius and C. Alfius Flavus. It is also apparent that their opponents did likewise, with at least three Tribunes opposing them throughout the year.

It is clear that the Triumvirs mapped out a programme of laws and reforms that should be passed this year. Interestingly Caesar's initial legislation was centred on the passing of an agrarian law, once again distributing the *ager publicus*, a staple of political reform since the time of Ti. Gracchus. At its heart lay the fact that Pompeius needed an agrarian law passed to provide land to his discharged soldiers from his eastern campaigns, but Caesar (and Pompeius and Crassus) took this one stage further and widened the scope to include the wider landless citizens:

> *The best part of this land especially round Capua, which was leased for the public benefit, he proposed to bestow upon those who were the fathers of at least three children, by which means he bought for himself the favour of a multitude of men, for twenty thousand, being those only who had three children each, came forward at once.*[27]

Furthermore, Dio preserves several passages which seem to set the tone for the legislation and may well have come from the justification which Caesar himself presented:

> *The swollen population of the city, which was chiefly responsible for the frequent rioting, would thus be turned toward labour and agriculture; and the great part of Italy, now desolate, would be colonized afresh, so that not only those who had toiled in the campaigns, but all the rest as well, would have ample subsistence ... For they had a great deal of surplus money, he asserted, as a result of the booty which Pompeius had captured, as well as from the new tributes and taxes just established, and they ought, inasmuch as it had been provided by the dangers that citizens had incurred, to expend it upon those same persons.*[28]

Thus, the Triumvirs presented a narrative that this was a public safety measure, coming so soon after the renewed civil war in Italy, and that it would refresh Italy anew. Furthermore, it was the Roman state returning something to its citizens for all their years of sacrifice and that it was affordable thanks to the victories of Pompeius in the east. On the face of it, it seemed a perfectly reasonable reform; a distribution of land to the landless citizens after years of hardship, paid for by the funds from a foreign campaign, which is probably exactly how Caesar (and Pompeius and Crassus) wanted it to be viewed. Such a reform would get the People on their side and make them more amenable to some of the other legislation that the trio had in mind, not to mention greatly bolster the standing of the man who proposed it (Caesar) and the man who ultimately made it possible (Pompeius).

Naturally enough their opponents in the Senate did not see it in such amenable terms but would have been presented with something of a quandary, namely how to oppose a popular (with the People) piece of legislation. Caesar made their discomfort all the more acute by presenting the bill to the Senate first (as custom dictated) to allow their approval before it went to the Assembly:

> *For he had read it beforehand in the Senate, and calling upon each one of the Senators by name, had inquired whether he had any criticism to*

offer; and he promised to alter or even to strike out entirely any clause which might displease anybody.[29]

Thus, Caesar bent over backwards (or at least he seemed to) to accommodate his opponents, whilst in reality putting them in an awkward position. Dio reports that no public opposition was made to the bill by the Senators, aside from one man, one who made a career out of being steadfast, namely M. Porcius Cato. Cato opposed the measure in the Senate, which led to a confrontation between him and Caesar, with some sources reporting that Caesar apparently threatened Cato with imprisonment but relented. Nevertheless, whilst the Senators did not oppose the bill in the Senate, they did not approve it either.

Ultimately Senatorial approval was not constitutionally necessary, and Caesar had observed the formal rights of going to the Senate first. The real challenge lay in passing the law in the Assembly and here Caesar met with strong opposition in the form of his Consular colleague Bibulus and three Tribunes; Q. Ancharius, Cn. Domitius Calvinus and C. Fannius. Despite the supposed popularity of the proposed reform Bibulus stood fast and is quoted as stating; '*You shall not have this law this year, not even if you all wish it.*'[30]

Nevertheless, Caesar presented the bill to the People and had both Pompeius and Crassus publicly speak in its favour. Dio preserves what are apparently Pompeius' words:

> *It is not I alone, who approve this measure, but the whole Senate as well, inasmuch as it has voted for land to be given not only to my soldiers but to those also who once fought with Metellus. On the former occasion, to be sure, since the treasury had no great means, the granting of the land was naturally postponed; but at present, since it has become exceedingly rich through my efforts, it is but right that the promise made to the soldiers be fulfilled and that the rest also reap the fruit of the common toils.*[31]

Nevertheless, the bill was faced with three Tribunician vetoes (*ius intercessio*) and the Consul Bibulus, who took his opposition a stage further by invoking the religious powers of the Consulate and declaring that all the remaining days were sacred and thus no public assemblies could be held.

However, as the Consulate was a dual body, and one Consul's opinions could not outweigh another, Caesar simply declared a set day not to be sacred and arranged for the Assembly to gather for a vote.

On the day of the vote, Bibulus and the three Tribunes arrived at the Forum, along with their supporters, and attempted to stop Caesar from speaking. As happened frequently in such circumstances, violence erupted between the two sets of supporters and Bibulus and the three Tribunes were beaten up and ejected from the Forum. Thus, using a precedent set by Saturninus, some forty year earlier, with no Tribunes present to use their veto, the bill was passed into law and the largest agrarian distribution programme since the Gracchi began. Once again, we see that constitutional opposition had been overcome by the use of brute force in the Assembly and a major reform was passed into law using violence. Furthermore, both Crassus and Pompeius were selected to be on the Agrarian Commission (with full judicial powers), along with a number of other supporters, giving them a prestigious and influential domestic position.

Given the contentious methods used, Caesar went one step further and added a clause to the law which meant that all Senators had to swear to uphold the law on pain of exile; a tactic again copied from Saturninus (the erstwhile ally of Caesar's own uncle, C. Marius). Aside from attempting to ensure that the law was not overturned after his year of office, this oath was also a clear trap for his political enemy, M. Porcius Cato. In 100 BC Saturninus had used this tactic to trap his (and Marius') political enemy Q. Caecilius Metellus Numidicus, who chose exile rather than swear to a measure he had publicly opposed. Thus, whilst Metellus had retained his integrity, a clear obstacle to Marius and Saturninus had been removed from Rome. Clearly Caesar (and his backers) hoped to remove another equally troublesome opponent from Rome, or at least embarrass him politically. The surviving sources do depict Cato as wanting to stick to his principles and not to swear the oath, but relenting in the end. Plutarch puts this down to a last minute intervention from Cicero, but Cato made a show of taking the oath next to last and having made his point was able to remain in Rome to pursue his own ongoing career (Metellus having reached both the Consulship and Censorship before indulging in his defiant stand).

Not only had the Triumvirs succeeded in passing this major policy, but apparently Bibulus and the three Tribunes were so cowed by the violence that they withdrew from public life for the rest for the year. Bibulus famously withdrew to his house and regularly issued notices whenever Caesar passed a measure that the day was inauspicious and thus no public business could be conducted. Thus, Caesar was effectively sole Consul for the rest of the year and there was apparently no more opposition from amongst the Tribunician College (effectively down to seven). This made the enactment of the rest of the Triumvirate's legislative programme all the easier. It seems that Caesar had also made his point in his dealings with the Senate:

> *After that he* [Caesar] *communicated nothing further to the Senate during his year of office but brought directly before the People whatever he desired.*[32]

The surviving sources confirm that following this contentious law, Caesar was able to pass laws changing the contracts for the collection of Asian taxes, which benefited the Equestrian cartels that had secured the contract (and Crassus) and more importantly had the People ratify Pompeius' eastern settlement. Thus, the re-structuring of the east, which Pompeius had conducted in the wake of the eastern war, was finally passed into law, including the Roman annexation of the rump of the Seleucid Empire. Clearly Caesar had handsomely paid off Pompeius for his investment, which soon translated into Caesar securing his reward (see below).

Yet despite having delivered on the central issues for his patrons, the three men seemingly used their position to push ahead with a number of other laws. Following on from his agrarian legislation came a second agrarian bill which added lands in Campania to the original distribution programme. Some sources report that it was on this occasion that Cato objected so strongly that he was threatened with imprisonment, but the sources cannot agree on this:

> *Elated by this success, Caesar introduced another law, which provided that almost the whole of Campania be divided among the poor and needy. No one spoke against the law except Cato, and him Caesar ordered to be dragged from the Rostra to prison.*[33]

This law was complemented by the Tribune P. Vatinius, who proposed a colony to be founded in Italy at Novum Comum (modern Como).[34] There were three other areas of legislation. Firstly, in terms of domestic politics, Caesar passed an important reform stating that:

> *The proceedings both of the Senate and of the People should day by day be compiled and published. He also revived a bygone custom, that during the months when he did not have the fasces an orderly should walk before him, while the lictors followed him.*[35]

Whilst one was the restatement of an obscure custom, possibly made necessary by the disappearance from public life of the other Consul, the compilation and publication of the acts of the Senate and People did open up the working of the Roman government to a wider audience.

Caesar also had a law passed which was another attempt at curbing corruption by Roman governors, perhaps as a supplement to the ratification of the eastern settlement, which brought a number of the Mediterranean's richest states more closely into Rome's orbit (either directly or indirectly). Eastern affairs were affected by another of Caesar's laws when he proposed to the People that Ptolemy XII be recognised as the rightful ruler of Ptolemaic Egypt, albeit in return for a large donation. It is tempting to see the hand of Crassus behind this, having been thwarted in his attempts to annex Egypt (in 65 BC – see Chapter Two). Equally interesting is that Caesar also had the Assembly pass a law recognising Ariovistus, a German tribal leader, as a Roman ally, with Caesar perhaps having one eye one a future campaign in the north.

Another area of reform was connected to the vexed question of jury composition, which had plagued Roman politics since the Tribunate of C. Gracchus. On this occasion it was a Praetor (Q. Fufius Calenus) who proposed the reform, namely that each of the three groups which composed Roman juries (Senators, Equestrians and Tribuni Aerarii) cast their votes separately, supposedly in a bid for greater transparency. This is an interesting reform for several reasons. Firstly, it touched on a subject that had been a highly contentious one, namely jury composition. Secondly it is perhaps not a coincidence that the current nature of jury composition, split evenly between three groups – the traditionally hostile Senators and Equestrians (though this is often overplayed) and a balancing group of Tribuni Aerarii – had been introduced by a Praetor in the Consulship of Pompeius and Crassus. Thus, once again we have a Praetor introducing reforming law (a highly unusual act in itself) in a year when Pompeius and Crassus (though not in office themselves) were dictating the domestic agenda.

Therefore, we can see that Caesar and his powerful patrons passed a large number of reforms this year: perhaps the most in any one year since the restoration of normal Republican government following Sulla. The relationship between the three men had been a complete success, with Caesar not only being able to deliver on the proposals his patrons had wanted but able to use their support to push through a range of other measures. Clearly for all sides the alliance had paid off: Pompeius saw his eastern settlement ratified after nearly three years, which cemented his position as Rome's leading general; Crassus got his proposals through, which re-affirmed his role as patron to his Equestrian clients and got himself back into the centre of power; and most of all Caesar had recovered the political capital which he had lost during his unsuccessful Praetorship.

He had pushed through an agrarian distribution programme, which would reap political rewards from the People who benefited from it and the men who occupied the Agrarian Commission, and had cemented his position as being a friend to the People. However, all this had been accomplished at the expense of his relationship with the Senate, having used force to push his agrarian bill through the Assembly, sidelined his Consular colleague, and ridden roughshod over the Senate. Although his relationship with the Senate had never been a harmonious one (see Chapters Two and Three), this year in office had cemented his reputation as being someone who would circumnavigate the Senate when it suited him.

Under normal circumstances this would have presented an issue, as all pro-Consular commands were at the behest of the Senate, which could arrange for him to have an uninspiring command for only one year before it being terminated. Yet it was here that Caesar's gamble had paid off. Whilst his relationship with the Senate might have been damaged, his relationship with the Assembly was stronger, as was that with his two patrons. It was thanks to these relationships that Caesar got his reward for his successful year in office when the Tribune P. Vatinius, prominently supported by Pompeius in the Assembly, proposed an extraordinary command for Caesar, a move which Pompeius himself had utilised to great success twice in the preceding decade (see Chapter Two).

However, unlike the decade before, on this occasion there clearly was no need for an extraordinary command. When Pompeius had utilised this tactic in 68 and 67 BC Rome had faced the twin threats of a Mediterranean being overrun by pirates and a war in the east against the expanding empires of Pontus and Armenia. Yet by now both threats had been neutralised by Pompeius (and Lucullus) and for the first time in a generation the near east was not actively threatening Roman interests and under (temporary) Roman control. The main eastern threat remained the Parthian Empire, but they themselves were recovering from a civil war and their defeat at the hands of the emerging Armenian Empire. Likewise, there were no threats from Africa and nothing from Spain other than the routine policing actions against the tribes.

This left the northern frontier; Gaul and Macedon, where Rome's empire bordered the (almost) endless tribes of mainland Europe. Again, there were no obvious threats to Rome's security, other than skirmishes with the bordering tribes. Yet it was against the northern tribes that Caesar's uncle Marius had cemented his reputation, defeating the invading tribes of the Cimbri, Teutones and Ambrones.[36] Under Pompeius, Roman armies had recently expanded Rome's dominance right across the near east; Caesar now undertook to do the same in Gaul.

Thus Vatinius, with Pompeius' backing, proposed that Caesar receive the provinces of Cisalpine Gaul and Illyricum for a period of five years and be granted four legions. Shortly afterwards the province of Transalpine Gaul was added to his command. Thus, Caesar was effectively made commander of Rome's northern provinces for a period of five years. Though perfectly legal (as it was passed by the Assembly) such an extraordinary command (and in peacetime) was a clear breach of the Sullan constitution, which, as it ultimately turned out, was a wise prohibition. Nevertheless, faced with the support of the Assembly and Pompeius and Crassus, and with compliant Tribunes, the law was passed and Caesar got his command, though many in the Senate would have been happy to see him packed off to Gaul for five years. For Caesar the key issue here was the stability of command in terms of the five years. Most commanders only had a year or two to conduct their military operations, which (deliberately) limited the scope and scale of their campaigns. Caesar now had a secure tenure, provided that the command wasn't overturned in the Assembly.

6. The So-Called Vettian Plot

The sources do preserve details of a highly bizarre incident of opposition to the Triumvirs which came in the reappearance of L. Vettius, the Equestrian who had been part of the coup plot of 63 BC but who had saved his life by turning informer (see Chapter Three). His record in that incident had rendered him a totally untrustworthy character, yet he appears to have been involved in a supposed plot to assassinate Pompeius and Caesar, though the accounts range wildly:

> As these proceedings were resented by the nobles, the partisans of Pompeius produced a certain Vettius, whom, as they declared, they had caught plotting against the life of Pompeius. So, the man was examined in the Senate, where he accused sundry persons, but before the People he named Lucullus as the man who had engaged him to kill Pompeius. However, no one believed his story, nay, it was at once clear that the fellow had been put forward by the partisans of Pompeius to make false and malicious charges, and the fraud was made all the plainer when, a few days afterwards, his dead body was cast out of the prison. It was said, indeed, that he had died a natural death, but he bore the marks of throttling and violence, and the opinion was that he had been taken off by the very men who had engaged his services.[37]
>
> And now Vettius, a Plebeian, ran into the Forum with a drawn dagger and said that he had been sent by Bibulus, Cicero, and Cato to kill Caesar and Pompeius, and that the dagger had been given to him by Postumius, the lictor of Bibulus. Although this affair was open to suspicion from either point of view, Caesar made use of it to inflame the multitude and postponed till the morrow the examination of the assailant. Vettius was thrown into prison and killed the same night.[38]

We also find an account in Cicero, from which Plutarch seems to have based his version and thus differs from the one found in Appian.[39] Commentators at the time rightly poured scorn on the validity of this assassination plot, which has divided opinion ever since.[40] Whatever his involvement, it earned Vettius a swift and unceremonious murder, showing the stakes that were involved whether the plot was real or not.

7. Securing the Triumviral Reforms

With Caesar having secured his own personal future, the Triumvir's attention turned to securing the future of the reforms they had introduced. As always in Roman politics, a seemingly unassailable position one year could evaporate the next. Although the Senate had all sworn to uphold the agrarian legislation, this was hardly a fool-proof mechanism, as even if the legislation were not overturned, it could be undermined by a lack of funding, changes to the agrarian commission's remit or composition, or amendments made to the available pool of land. Furthermore, the Triumviral alliance would be splitting up with Caesar leaving Rome for Gaul for up to five years with Pompeius and Crassus going their separate ways once more and thus having to rely on further elected agents, as both men had already served in high office.

Therefore, the Triumvirs fell back on the tried and tested method of securing the key magistracies for the following year (Consulship and Tribunate). Perhaps showing just how much control and power the Triumvirs had this year, they were able to secure both Consulships for their supporters, L. Calpurnius Piso Caesoninus (Caesar's new father-in-law) and A. Gabinius:

> *For Consuls, too, they secured the election of Calpurnius Piso, who was Caesar's father-in-law, and Aulus Gabinius, a man from the lap of Pompeius, as those say who knew his ways of life.*[41]

It is interesting to note that Pompeius on his own had only ever been able to secure one Consulship, and the Triumvirs combined had not been able to elect someone as Caesar's colleague who would be an ally. Thus, we can see that the Triumvirs were able to translate the control they had over the Assembly this year into securing their legacy, albeit only for a year.

As well as the Consulships, the Triumvirs would need to secure allies in the Tribunate for the following year, and here they seemed to have met with mixed success. We know the names of six of the men elected as Tribunes for 58 BC and at least one of them, L. Antistius, used his Tribunate to attack Caesar's year in office. Of the others, the most notable was a man known as P. Clodius Pulcher, who would go on to be one of the most (in)famous Tribunes of the late Republic.[42]

Clodius could hardly be called the follower of any of the Triumvirs, but up to this point was an undistinguished Roman nobleman from one of Rome's most distinguished families; the Claudii Pulchri. As such he was a Patrician by birth and thus ineligible to stand for the Tribunate, it technically still being an office of the Plebeian Order, not the Roman state. However, Claudius was an ambitious, and most would say unscrupulous, young politician (though most successful Roman politicians were) and saw a way around this prohibition. Throughout the Republic, it had been common practice for the sons of various noble families to be adopted into other noble families, to ensure that the adopted family did not die out when they lacked a male heir. The adopted son thus took on the name of the adopted family and continued its lineage. Claudius took this one stage further and sought to be adopted into a Plebeian family and thus adopt Plebeian status, and thus eligibility to the Tribunate. To date we are not aware of this Patrician-Plebeian religious divide being crossed in this manner, and certainly never for the short term aims that Claudius was intending. He seems to have been prevented from doing this during previous years (see above). During 59 BC however this adoption was arranged and pushed through by the Triumvirs;

> *Caesar transferred the orator's* [Cicero's] *enemy Publius Clodius that very same day from the Patricians to the Plebeians, a thing for which Clodius had for a long time been vainly striving.*[43]
>
> [Pompeius] *acted as augur at the adoption of Publius Clodius.*[44]
>
> *In the first place, in order that he might be lawfully excluded from the Patricians, he transferred him with Pompeius' cooperation to the Plebeian status once more, and then immediately had him appointed Tribune.*[45]

Clodius, as he now was, immediately sought and was elected to the Tribunate. The Triumvirs now had what they wanted, a prominent ally in the Tribunician college for the following year who would protect their interests (or so they thought). In the short term this strategy appeared to have paid off as one of Clodius' first acts as Tribune was to prevent Caesar's colleague M. Calpurnius Bibulus from delivering his usual end of office address (having finally emerged from his self-appointed exile).

Thus, the three Triumvirs could end the year on a high note. Caesar had restored his political career, gaining popularity amongst the People and powerful allies (Pompeius and Crassus), plus a long-term military command (albeit in the unglamorous theatre of Gaul). Pompeius had his eastern victories and settlement ratified, securing his position as Rome's greatest living general. Crassus had secured his clients' wishes and more than likely been paid handsomely for the privilege, and had found himself on equal footing (albeit temporarily) with his old rival Pompeius once more.

Summary

In terms of the wider issues though, the two men who had done so much to shape this Republic (Pompeius and Crassus) had ridden roughshod over the restored Republic, using violence in the Forum to drive off a Consul and effectively institute sole Consular rule in Rome (albeit their agent). Interestingly in the pre-civil war Republic, powerful men had used the Tribunate to push through reforms, now Pompeius and Crassus had used the Consulship to do the same. Yet both men would have perhaps argued that what they had done was not so damaging to the new Republic. Certainly, violence had been used in the Forum, but no one had been killed and the military had not been involved. If anything, it had shown once again the benefit of co-operation between Rome's leading men rather than confrontation.

On two occasions now Pompeius and Crassus had co-operated and pooled their resources (71/70 and 60/59 BC) to temporarily get what they wanted. If anything, the new Republic was strong enough to resist any one powerful individual, forcing them to temporarily co-operate. As long as this co-operation was temporary then the Republic could resist these years of disruption and return to normal the following year.

Part III

The Crisis of the New Republic (58–49 BC)

Chapter Five

Bloody Chaos: The Tribunates of Clodius and Milo (58–56 BC)

1. The Tribunate of Clodius (58 BC)

Despite the dominance of the Triumvirate in 59 BC, the political agenda of the following years was dominated by another individual, namely one P. Clodius Pulcher. We will never know exactly what bargain the Triumvirs struck with Clodius in return for their aid in his transfer to the Plebeian order and his election to the Tribunate, though clearly he would have promised to uphold Caesar's legislation with the use of his veto (*ius intercessio*).[1] It is equally clear that he had no intentions of simply serving his year of office in a passive manner, especially considering the lengths he had gone to in order to be elected. Clodius had a full programme of reforming legislation in mind, more akin to the Gracchi, rather than merely serving as someone else's agent. He also benefitted greatly from having, at least in the beginning, the full support of the Triumvirs and more importantly both Consuls of 58 BC (a feat the Gracchi never managed).

The year 58 BC began in a predictable manner, with the opponents of the Triumvirs going on the offensive against both Caesar and his legislation. The surviving sources tell us of attacks on his legislation by two of the Praetors, L. Domitius Ahenobarbus and C. Memmius. Caesar also faced an attempt by one of the Tribunes, L. Antistius to try him for his actions as Consul:

When at the close of his Consulship the Praetors Caius Memmius and Lucius Domitius moved an inquiry into his conduct during the previous year, Caesar laid the matter before the senate; and when they failed to take it up, and three days had been wasted in fruitless wrangling, went off to his province. Whereupon his Quaestor was at once arraigned on several counts, as a preliminary to his own impeachment. Presently he himself too was prosecuted by Lucius Antistius, Tribune of the Plebs and it was only by appealing to the whole college that he contrived not to be brought to trial, on the grounds that he was absent on public service.[2]

The Praetor Memmius, having no success attacking Caesar, then turned his attention to the former Tribune Vatinius, who was also an agent of the Triumvirs. On the day of the trial, though, Vatinius turned to a tried and trusted technique, and he and his supporters attacked the judges and drove them from the Forum:

Has any criminal ever mounted up to the tribunal of the president of the court which tried him and driven him down from thence by violence? and upset all the benches? and overturned all the balloting urns? and in short, in disturbing the court of justice committed all those crimes on account of which courts of justice were instituted? Are you aware that Memmius fled at that time? that your accusers were with difficulty saved from your hands and those of your friends? that the judges were even driven away out of the tribunals which were near? that in the Forum, in broad daylight in the sight of the Roman People, the investigation was put an end to.[3]

Once again violence had been used in the Forum, this time to disrupt a judicial proceeding. Vatinius then avoided any fall out from this affair by taking up a legateship in none other than Caesar's army in Gaul, this protecting him from further prosecution for the duration. Cicero, in a later prosecution speech against Vatinius, pointed out that this appointment was none other than a blind to protect him from Caesar's enemies in the Senate, though Caesar was well within his rights as commander to appoint his own legates. Vatinius prospered under Caesar's patronage, reaching the heights of the Consulship in 47 BC.

With these initial attacks losing pace, attention turned to the legislative programme for this year, which was to be dominated by the Tribune Clodius. Whilst he may have had influential backing, it is clear from the start that he had no intention of merely passing his year in office passively defending the Triumviral legislation of Caesar. In fact, he launched into the most ambitious legislative programme of any Tribune since the First Civil War and one on a par with C. Gracchus himself.

One of his first and most notable reforms had more than passing reference to C. Gracchus, and that was the issue of subsidised grain for the urban populace. Since the time of Gracchus, the grain supply had been a highly politicised issue, with Gracchus being the first to pass reforms forcing the Roman state to sell grain to its populace at a fixed rate and thus secure the basic food supply of the urban populace. Since its introduction the measure had become a political football, with restrictions being passed and subsequently removed. The most recent had been by M. Porcius Cato himself, when as Tribune in 62 BC he persuaded the Senate to lower the price the state sold the grain for, and thus increasing the subsidy. Clodius however went one stage further and proposed (and had passed) legislation which provided for grain to be distributed to the urban populace free of charge. Thus, the Roman state would now pay for, and supply, the most basic staple of the average Roman city dweller's diet.

Not only did the expenditure of the Roman state increase drastically, but so did the importance of securing the grain supply to Rome, both of which would have a shorter-term impact the following year (see below) and longer-term impacts for the future of the *res publica*. Whoever controlled the grain supply of Rome would control the urban populace (and as some would say the urban mob). We cannot also overlook that in the short term Clodius would also reap a large political following amongst the urban populace of Rome, who could be used in the Assemblies either as voters or armed support.

Clodius soon introduced a second popular measure when he restored the Collegia of Rome: urban guilds of the various trades and professions. These had been banned by the Senate in 64 BC. The full role of the Collegia and their political aspects are not well understood in Roman history, passing little-mentioned in the surviving sources. Yet throughout European history there have been examples of powerful urban guilds, of tradesmen and merchants, who wielded great political power in urban settings. What is also unclear are the connections between these Collegia and the elections to the Tribunate. If a Collegia wanted some lesser legislation passing, such as guarding the rights of a certain profession, then the easiest way would be to use their collective voting power and influence to elect a Tribune. This leads into the wholly-underdeveloped field of lesser Roman legislation, that which affected everyday matters in Rome.[4] In overturning the Senatorial ban, these various Collegia, both old and new, would have owed Clodius a debt, which could be called upon should he need it in the Assembly.

The surviving sources refer to a further ten reforms Clodius passed during his year in office, which can be grouped into three areas of interest; constitutional powers, judicial matters and foreign policy. The first of these topics, constitutional powers, contained three laws. First came a minor law banning treasury clerks (working for the Quaestors) from engaging in business.[5] More importantly came laws removing restrictions on the powers of the Tribunes, amending a group of old laws known as the *leges Aelia-Fufia*. Unfortunately, we do not know when these original laws were passed, but they are most commonly ascribed to the period when we are missing the books of Livy (either 292–218 or post 167 BC). Cicero provides the best description of the laws, though much scholarship has been written on them:[6]

> *When a Tribune of the People* [Clodius] *procured a law to be passed that no regard should be had to the auspices, that no one should on that account be allowed to interrupt the Assembly or the Comitia, or to put his veto on the passing of a law; and that the Aelian and Fufian laws should have no validity, which our ancestors had enacted, intending them to be the firmest protection of the Republic against the insanity of the Tribunes.*[7]

Thus, the original laws had laid down that legislative assemblies could be interrupted, and legislation blocked if bad omens were detected. We do not have to look far to see where this law originated, as Caesar's consular colleague (M. Calpurnius Bibulus) had spent the majority of his Consulate declaring bad omens (*inauspicia*) and trying to prevent or invalidate Caesar's' legislation. Furthermore, it seems that the *leges Aelia-Fufia* also touched on use of the Tribunician veto. Thus, Clodius made sure that no objections could be raised to his laws on religious grounds. Next came a law restricting the powers of the Censors in regard to their selection of men for the Senate and their ability to exclude anyone from any of the citizenship lists:

To prevent the Censors in selecting the Senate from passing over or
branding with any mark of ill repute any man who had not been charged
before them and condemned by the declared verdict of both Censors.[8]

Again, the origins of this law are easy to determine. As we have seen, throughout recent Roman history there had been clashes between Censors and Tribunes, and in particular Censors had the ability to expel former Tribunes from the Senate, perhaps the most obvious example being the attempted expulsion of the former Tribune L. Appuleius Saturninus in 102 BC. Clodius was clearly planning ahead for life after the Tribunate and ensuring that he could not be expelled from the Senate by the next Censors. However, whilst his motives may have been short term and personal, this reform did curb the arbitrary powers of the Censorship, which was prone to being used to settle political scores and was a logical extension to the Roman concept of no punishment without trial and conviction (as long as you were a Roman citizen).

It is perhaps Clodius' defence of this principle which led to his most notorious laws, the first of which laid down a punishment of exile (the prevention of the condemned receiving fire and water whilst in Italy) for anyone who put to death Roman citizens without trial (and conviction). On the face of it this law merely re-affirmed one of the key foundations of Roman citizenship, namely the rule of law and the protection from arbitrary punishment.

However, this law also had a more obvious and immediate objective, namely re-opening the issue of the execution of Roman citizens by the then Consul. M. Tullius Cicero in 63 BC: namely the aristocratic supporters of L. Sergius Catilina, caught up in the coup plot in Rome during the Second Civil War (see Chapter Three). It was Cicero, as Consul, who had ordered the execution of the noblemen caught up in the apparent conspiracy. He argued that he was acting under the umbrella of the *senatus consultum ultimum*, the so-called final decree of the Senate. However, *senatus consulta* were not law, merely the considered opinion of the Senate (albeit one with significant religious and political weight). Thus, Cicero was still technically liable for murdering Roman citizens without trial.

There were two previous precedents for this: in 121 BC with the murders of C. Sempronius Gracchus and M. Fulvius Flaccus, and in 100 BC with those of L. Appuleius Saturninus and C. Servilius Glaucia. The first example (of 121 BC) was a near-identical case, with the Senate passing the SCU and ordering the Consul L. Opimius to defend the state (from Gracchus and Flaccus). As always, the Senate kept their hands clean by not expressly stating that the men threatening the 'security of the Republic' should be killed, but both were (along with a number of their supporters) and Opimius actually stood trial for his actions and was acquitted. In 100 BC it was the Consul Marius who was duly instructed under the SCU., which also led to the deaths of those deemed 'enemies of the state' (Saturninus, Glaucia and a number of their supporters).

On this occasion however, Marius was never brought to trial but then he had considerably more power and influence than either Opimius or Cicero. On far from clear legal ground and facing an Assembly controlled by Clodius, Cicero chose to exile himself from Rome and Italy and thus play the martyr, rather than be convicted by a partisan court.[9] Following his departure, Clodius proposed (and had passed) a second law exiling Cicero by name, seizing his possessions, demolishing his house, and erecting a Temple to Liberty on its site as the ultimate insult. The surviving sources state that there was opposition to this attack on Cicero from elements within both the Senate and the Equestrian order, but Cicero had no real powerbase with which to defend himself and drew this criticism from Dio:

> *As a result of this and because he was the greatest boaster alive and regarded no one as equal to himself, but in his words and life alike looked down upon everybody and would not live as anyone else did, he was wearisome and burdensome, and was consequently both disliked and hated even by those very persons whom he otherwise pleased.*[10]

With these laws, Clodius achieved several aims. Firstly, it was a public declaration that the People (and their Tribunes) were the supreme source of legislation and that the Senate followed their rules. Secondly there must have been some support from the families of the murdered men, who came from noble (and in some case Consular) families (see

Appendix One). Their kinsmen's deaths were now publicly stated to be illegal and their kinsmen's names partially repudiated. As with Clodius' previous laws limiting Censorial power, there must have been a degree of this being a preventative measure. Aside from 63 BC, the two previous occasions the SCU had been deployed had been by factions within the Senate who were opposed to 'seditious' Tribunes. Clearly Clodius wished to ensure that the SCU was not passed with him named as an 'enemy of the Republic'. Finally, we must never overlook the personal aspect, as Plutarch reports that the two men fell out during 63 BC in relation to the Catilina situation:

> *Now, Cicero was a friend of Clodius, and in the affair of Catilina had found him a most eager co-worker and guardian of his person; but when Clodius replied to the charge against him by insisting that he had not even been in Rome at the time but had been staying in places at the farthest remove from there, Cicero testified against him, declaring that Clodius had come to his house and consulted him on certain matters; which was true. However, it was thought that Cicero did not give his testimony for the truth's sake, but by way of defence against the charges of his own wife Terentia.*[11]

Thus, Clodius seized on the chance for personal revenge, made all the sweeter by not just exiling Cicero from Rome but turning his 'greatest' victory, the defeat of the attempted coup in Rome, into a criminal act. Clodius' last grouping of laws concerned matters of foreign policy; again, traditionally a matter for the Senate but one which had become increasingly in the remit of the Tribunate. The greatest of these laws was the annexation of the island of Cyprus. This in many ways was an extraordinary piece of legislation. Cyprus was a province of the ailing Ptolemaic Empire (though had its own Ptolemaic king) but was of critical strategic value in the eastern Mediterranean. The recent wars of conquest of Lucullus and Pompeius had massively expanded Rome's empire in the east. As an ally of Rome, Ptolemaic territory had not been subject to annexation, but in a decisive act of imperialism Clodius, showing the power of Rome, annexed the province of a Roman ally with a law passed in Rome: empire by legislation. The King of Cyprus, Ptolemy, the younger brother of the Ptolemaic ruler of Egypt (Ptolemy XII) was deposed and committed suicide.

Furthermore, as well as gaining the personal reputation for this conquest by legislation, Clodius effectively exiled one of his (and the Triumvirs) chief domestic opponents, M. Porcius Cato. Clodius' legislation named him as a *quaestor pro praetore* (a Questor with a Praetors' powers) in charge of organising the annexation of Cyprus to Rome's empire, thus effectively removing him from Rome (and Clodius' path) for several years.[12] Thoroughly outmanoeuvred, Cato could hardly refuse a clear command from the Assembly and duly left Rome (following Cicero). The law also called for the restoration of a group of exiles from the city of Byzantium.

Further lesser laws on foreign affairs were passed by the Assembly under Clodius' guidance, including naming a new king of the allied Kingdom of Galatia and appointing a new Chief Priest in the city of Pessinus. These laws, though inconsequential in the grand scheme of Roman politics in themselves, show both the breadth of Clodius' ambition in passing legislation and the continuing expansion of power of the Tribunate, in becoming the main legislative body of Rome's growing empire at the expense of the Senate. A further trampling of Senatorial prerogative came when Clodius passed legislation allocating the Consular provinces for the following year: Macedon and Cilicia (later amended to Syria). That the Consuls were given their provinces by Tribunician law rather than Senatorial decree was a demonstration of the level of support that the Triumvirs had granted him. Both Consuls (L. Calpurnius Piso Caesoninus and A. Gabinius) had been elected using the combined patronage of the Triumvirs.

We can see from the sources that Clodius used many familiar Tribunician tactics, such as using violence in the Forum to drive away his opponents, particularly amongst the Tribunate. Surprisingly there were a number of Tribunes this year who were opposed to Clodius; most notably L. Ninnius Quadratus. The sources (Cicero himself) states that no less than eight Tribunes, led by Ninnius, passed a motion in the Senate for the recall of Cicero. It is notable that they were able to pass this in the Senate, but not the Assembly, which appears to have been securely under the control of Clodius. Nevertheless, despite this being nothing more than the Senate's opinion, it was vetoed nonetheless by Clodius' colleague L. Aelius. Another of his Tribunician colleagues, Q. Terentius Culleo, proposed a law annulling the one which exiled Cicero but was unable to pass it.

Thus, it seems on the matter of Cicero's exile at least the Tribunician college was split 8:2 against Clodius. Yet despite this numerical inferiority, the use of violence in the Assembly meant that Clodius and Aelius were able to pass their legislation and use their vetoes successfully, whilst the other eight were not, again highlighting the difference between the theoretical application of constitutional power in Rome and the practical. Furthermore, Clodius had the support of both Consuls (something no other reforming Tribune had managed), which not only provided him with allies in the Senate but removed one of the major constitutional sources of opposition.

Yet towards the end of the year, Clodius seems to have set out his plans for his political career after his year in office had expired. Constitutionally he was unable to immediately seek a higher office, nor did he try to overturn this obstacle. He did however ensure that his brother (Ap. Claudius Pulcher) was elected as a Praetor for the following year. However, Clodius himself seems to have worked on the principle that whoever controlled the streets controlled Rome itself. During his year in office he had already removed both Cato and Cicero from Italy; whilst of the Triumvirs, Caesar had begun his campaigns in Gaul, against the migrating Helvetii tribes. This left the two most powerful men in Rome as Pompeius and Crassus. We are far from clear about Crassus' relationship with Clodius, but it certainly seemed closer than Pompeius'. Thus, Clodius turned his sights on Pompeius, one of the men who had sponsored him, but the most powerful Roman politician still in Rome itself.

Here we see Clodius' clear understanding of the realities of power in the Republic. Pompeius, for all his military prowess, string of victories and offices held, had no active power in Rome itself, and had no soldiers to protect him. Thus, a man with a far less distinguished career could gain the upper hand simply through using armed supporters to physically intimidate his opponents, and at one point he had Pompeius under virtual siege in his own house. Pompeius would have difficulty in bringing his political patronage to bear if he could not appear in the Senate or the Assembly safely. Crassus, it seems, remained unmolested and equally unenthusiastic to help his occasional ally and long-time rival. Thus, Clodius set out his plan to maintain his position even out of office through controlling the streets of Rome and thus the organs of power.

2. A Bloody Rivalry: Milo and Clodius (57 BC)[13]

Whilst Clodius may have gained a temporary superiority over his opponents, it was a situation that was not likely to last long, especially now that he had made an enemy of one his sponsors, Cn. Pompeius. Although apparently caught by surprise at the attacks by Clodius, he seems to have soon come up with a strategy to deal with him and eliminate the weakness of his position on Rome, both practically and constitutionally.

In terms of the practical, Pompeius stuck with the tried and tested technique of securing the services of a Tribune. Whilst this had ultimately backfired for him with Clodius, this was down to the individual he had chosen, rather than it being a flawed tactic. Furthermore, Pompeius seems to have been determined to fight fire with fire and selected a man from the same mould as Clodius, in terms of the practical application of power: T. Annius Milo. No sooner had Milo been elected to the Tribunate then he copied Clodius' tactics and gathered together his own armed force and thus was able to challenge Clodius' control of the streets and the Assembly. This coupled with him holding a Tribunate, as opposed to Clodius, who was officeless, would tip the balance in Milo's favour.

Unusually, we know the identities of all ten tribunes for 57 BC and their actions give us an insight into the political balance of this year. Aside from Milo, perhaps the most prominent was a P. Sestius, who was a close ally of Milo and jointly helped him organise street gangs to rival Clodius'. The pair of them could count on the active support of three colleagues; C. Cestilius, Q. Fabricius and C. Messius. Of the other five Tribunes, two were allies of Clodius: Sex. Atilius Serranus Gavianus and Q. Numerius Rufus, whilst the other three seemed to steer clear of close involvement in the politics of this year, though they did support the bill of Fabricius (see below). Aside from the Tribunes, we know that five of the Praetors were working against Clodius, but they were opposed by none other than

Clodius' brother; Ap. Claudius Pulcher. Of the Consuls, P. Cornelius Lentulus Spinther was an opponent of Clodius, but Q. Caecilius Metellus Nepos was an ally.

Thus, we can see that Clodius still had allies amongst the elected magistrates of this year, but that they were outnumbered by his opponents. It seems that there were two key political issues this year; neutralising the power of Clodius and a growing crisis in Rome's grain supply. It was naturally the first that seemed to dominate Roman politics this year and there were three key strands: prosecuting Clodius for his actions as Tribune; overturning his exile; and neutralising Clodius' power on the streets of Rome and in the Assembly.

Naturally enough, given the volume of Cicero's own writings which survive, the ancient sources are dominated by the attempt to overturn the exile of Cicero. Yet the man himself was far from important. What was important was what Cicero's recall represented, namely the visible overturning of Clodian legislation and the ability to break his control of the Assembly. The matter was raised in the Senate by L. Aurelius Cotta, who interestingly argued that Clodius' law was illegal as it had been passed by the *Comitia Tributa* (the Tribal Assembly) not the *Comitia Centuriata* (the older and unwieldy Centuriate Assembly).

However, despite strong support in the Senate, the matter was vetoed by the Tribune Sex. Atilius Serranus. With the Senatorial route stymied, the Tribune Q. Fabricius, supported by seven of his colleagues, proposed a bill to the Tribal Assembly recalling Cicero. Faced with such opposition and having no formal office of his own, Clodius returned to his tried and trusted technique of using violence to prevent a vote. On this occasion he introduced a new element and used trained gladiators in the Assembly.

Clodius, knowing that the multitude would be on Cicero's side, took the gladiators that his brother held in readiness for the funeral games in honour of Marcus, his relative, and rushing into the assemblage, wounded many and killed many others. Consequently, the measure was not passed, and Clodius, both as the companion of those armed champions and otherwise, was dreaded by all.[14]

Despite all the sources we have for this outbreak of bloodshed we are not given any figures for casualties, though notable victims were the Tribune

Sestius and Cicero's own brother Quintus, who were both injured. It is difficult to estimate how large an outbreak of bloodshed this was: certainly there were no notable deaths and we are not helped by Cicero's own works which naturally overemphasize the scale of the bloodshed:

> *You recollect, judges, that on that day the Tiber was filled with the corpses of the citizens, that the sewers were choked up; that blood was wiped up out of the Forum with sponges.*[15]

With the Assembly prevented from voting on the bill, the matter was dropped for now as attention turned to the fallout of the violence in the Assembly. Milo was able to bring a prosecution against Clodius for the bloodshed, but the matter never came to trial as the Consul Metellus ordered the Praetors not to try the case and so this approach also failed. Having exhausted all legal means, Milo turned to matching Clodius' tactics and along with Sestius fought a series of running battles through the streets of Rome, with both sides deploying gladiators in their forces. Dio describes it: '*So that bloodshed occurred throughout practically the whole city.*'[16]

Thus, we have the strange situation, with Rome enforcing its will in Gaul, the Mediterranean and the near east, yet facing daily bloodshed on the streets of the capital itself. Rome had no standing police force and armed forces were not allowed to be deployed for fear of a tyranny. Roman politics had descended to armed groups fighting through the streets as all concepts of the unity which held the Roman oligarchy together had been shattered. Thus, we can see that Clodius represents the evolution of the Republican politician. The most notable occurrences of bloodshed had been in 121 and 100 BC, when Tribunes/former Tribunes had turned to force to protect their legislation from being overturned, and Clodius seemed to have learnt this lesson well and used force, not only to pass legislation, but to protect his position when he was out of office.

This was a key challenge to the 'New' Republic and a far greater threat than seen in 63 BC. Catilina and his allies had been dealt with efficiently and swiftly and thus validated the strength of the new Republic, whereas here the Republic was being made to look weak and impotent by a junior Senator and a gang of gladiators. This must have made many begin to wonder whether a new solution was needed.

Despite this violence, Pompeius seems to have made a fresh push to break Clodius' constitutional power at least. Here he used four tactics. The first was to persuade the Consul Metellus to abandon his support for Clodius (at least on this matter). Thus, with both Consuls united, they proposed a bill to restore Cicero. The second tactic was an unusual constitutional one: to bypass the Tribal Assembly (run by the Tribunes) and summon the older Centuriate Assembly, which voted not by the thirty-five Tribes of the Roman People, but by hundreds of Centuries (an older division of the Roman Populace). As Cotta had argued earlier, the Centuriate Assembly certainly had more *auctoritas* when it came to legislation, if not greater legal force in practice. Thirdly, the Senate issued a summons for large numbers of citizens from Italy to travel to Rome for this vote, diluting the influence of the urban population. The fourth and final tactic was to ensure that Milo's and Sestius' armed forces were present to guard the Assembly to fight off any disruption by Clodius. Plutarch sums the situation up:

> *Many joined themselves to Pompeius both from the People and from the surrounding cities. With these Pompeius came forth, drove Clodius from the Forum, and summoned the citizens to the vote. And it is said that the People never passed any vote with such unanimity. The Senate, too, vying with the People, wrote letters of thanks to all the cities which had ministered to Cicero during his exile, and decreed that his house and his villas, which Clodius had destroyed, should be restored at the public cost.*[17]

Cicero was therefore recalled from exile and had his house rebuilt and property restored by the state. However, although this was a personal triumph for Cicero and a blow to Clodius, it was hardly a major victory. Certainly, a way had been found to pass legislation that Clodius opposed, though this could not be used on a more regular basis. Clodius himself was undiminished and the street battles continued. Furthermore, Clodius was able to successfully run for the Aedileship for the following year and thus was back in office.

Yet aside from the violence of the street battles and the issues surrounding Cicero and Clodius, it seems that there was another major issue occupying the People of Rome – and a far more practical one. Whilst the Roman oligarchy had been preoccupied with matters of high politics it seems that Rome was again affected by grain shortages. The reasons behind this are not well documented, but these shortages usually began with a poor harvest. It is far from clear whether Clodius' measure the year before, for the state to provide free grain for the urban citizens, actually exacerbated the matter. Whatever the cause, in mid-57 BC the matter exploded into violence:

> *Whilst he* [L. Caecilius Rufus; the Urban Praetor] *was holding the Games of Apollo, a mob of the lower orders gathered and rioted so violently at the high price of corn that all who had taken their seats in the theatre to watch were driven off.*[18]
>
> *A severe famine had arisen in the city and the entire populace rushed into the theatre (they were then still using a temporary theatre for public games) and afterwards to the Capitol where the senators were in session, threatening at first to slay them with their own hands, and later to burn them alive, temples and all.*[19]

Thus, the Urban Praetor was attacked in broad daylight by a mob, supposedly complaining about the corn prices. Asconius is the main source for this violence and we don't know how (if at all) this riot fitted in with the clashes between Clodius and his opponents. We do have one of Cicero's letters on the matter, which stated that this issue was being used by Clodius to stir up a mob.[20] Furthermore Cicero also states that at some point during the year a Clodian mob attacked Caecilius' house.[21] What is clear is that this grain crisis was affecting the population of Rome and most likely other urban centres and was becoming a major political topic; one which was ripe for exploitation. Whilst it seems that Clodius was attempting to exploit this situation for his own gain, there was another who also saw the opportunity this crisis provided; namely, Pompeius himself.

Some ten years earlier, Pompeius had been granted an extraordinary command across the whole Mediterranean to deal with the pirate problem which had been plaguing Rome (and its food supply – see Chapter Two). Having been granted this extraordinary power, Pompeius had swiftly and skilfully resolved the issue. Thus, some ten years later, he seemed to be the ideal man (at least according to the pro-Pompeian propaganda) to resolve this current food crisis. As stated earlier, Pompeius had found himself on the back foot when being attacked by Clodius, as despite all his accomplishments, officially he was now nothing more than a private citizen. He had already held two Consulships and an overseas command would take him away from the centre of Roman political life. This crisis presented him with the ideal opportunity. Thus, when the Senate debated the matter, none other than the man of the moment (Cicero himself) proposed that Pompeius be given a special command; an empire-wide command over Rome's grain supply, which was duly passed into law by the Consuls. This law was soon followed by a second at the proposal of the Tribune Messius, which further extended Pompeius' powers. At first this seems an odd command for Rome's greatest living general, with there being no military aspect. Yet, if we look at the details below, we can see the genius of this reform:

The Consuls drew up a law by which complete control over the corn-supply for five years throughout the whole world was given to Pompeius. A second law was drawn up by Messius, granting him power over all money, and adding a fleet and army, and an imperium in the provinces superior to that of their governors.[22]

By his advocacy of the corn law he in a manner once more made Pompeius master of all the land and sea across Rome's dominions. For under his direction were placed harbours, trading-places, distributions of crops, in a word, navigation and agriculture. Clodius alleged that the law had not been proposed on account of the scarcity of grain, but the scarcity of grain had arisen in order that the law might be proposed, a law whereby the power of Pompeius, which was withering away, as it were, in consequence of his failing spirits, might be rekindled again and recovered in a new office.[23]

As the Romans were suffering from scarcity, they appointed Pompeius the sole manager of the grain supply and gave him, as in his operations against the pirates, twenty assistants from the Senate. These he distributed in like manner among the provinces while he superintended the whole,

and thus Rome was very soon provided with abundant supplies, by which
means Pompeius again gained great reputation and power.[24]

So now in the case of the grain supply, as previously in the case of the
pirates, he was once more to hold sway over the entire world then under
Roman power.[25]

Thus, we can see the scale of the power which Pompeius had been granted. A standard provincial command only came with power in the magistrate's appointed province. This command however, as with the previous pirate one, was an empire-wide grant of power for a period of five years, and as his remit was to secure Rome's food supply, which was nebulous enough that most activities could be brought under this banner. His legates were sent across Rome's empire and in representing him had greater power than the local governors. This also meant that all the time Pompeius had this power, he could remain in Rome, at the heart of the political scene and, if the problems were cured (which they were), then it would ensure that he gained the glory for saving the populace from famine and the Senate from revolution.

On what seems at first a minor issue of food supply, Pompeius was able to gain a command which placed him as the supreme magistrate across all of Rome's empire (in civilian matters).[26] Whilst in practical terms this command was a sound move, placing someone who had already proven themselves to be a superb organiser and giving them the power they needed to deal with this matter as a whole (on an empire-wide basis), in political terms set a dangerous message. In a Republic which was already showing signs of not being able to deal with the violence on the streets, admitting that they needed to turn to one man and giving him a superior (*maius*) imperium to deal with the Republic's problems was a dangerous precedent.

It is interesting to note the role that the supply of grain was having on Roman politics. Though food supply had always been a political issue in Rome, stretching back to the fifth century BC, it was C. Gracchus who had first truly politicised it by introducing state intervention in the form of a subsidised grain dole. Other Tribunes had picked up on this issue of state intervention, culminating in Clodius making the grain dole free. Yet the Tribunes had always done this in defiance of the Senate. On this occasion it was the Senate themselves, perhaps fearful of a popular Tribune exploiting this crisis, who escalated state intervention, so that the Roman state now became responsible for the whole of the grain supply to Rome and food security. Yet it was not the faceless Roman state or some bureaucracy responsible for the food supply of the Republic, but one man.

The grain crisis was not the only foreign matter which became a political issue in mid- to late-57 BC, there were two others; one in Gaul, one in Egypt. Throughout the whole of the political crisis engulfing Rome during 58 and 57 BC Caesar had been in Gaul and had been far from idle. Traditionally, Gallic commands had involved nothing more than policing actions, ensuring that the local tribes respected the territorial integrity of the southern coast of Gaul, which Rome had annexed in the 120s BC (to safeguard the route between Spain and Italy). The greatest campaign in this region had been by none other than Caesar's illustrious uncle, C. Marius, who had fought and defeated the invading tribes of the Cimbri and Teutones. The region had also been the scene of one of Rome's greatest ever defeats when these aforementioned tribes destroyed two Roman armies at the Battle of Arausio (105 BC), with the surviving sources putting the numbers of Romans killed as on a par with, or even exceeding, the defeat at Cannae in 216 BC (100,000 plus).

Clearly Caesar had more than the usual policing action in mind when he embarked upon his Proconsular command, having secured a tenure of five years. Wanting to match Pompeius' conquests in the east, Caesar had launched into an ambitious war of expansion, exploiting the ever-shifting patterns of local tribal conflicts to defeat a swathe of local tribes and bring large areas of Gaul under Roman control. Such a sudden and unexpected series of victories went down well with the somewhat beleaguered Roman Senate and People (especially given defeats in Macedonia to the local tribes) and Caesar was not slow to exploit these politically. Thus, towards the end of the year, the Senate and People voted Caesar fifteen days of public celebrations for his victories. Therefore Caesar, though absent from the daily politicking of Rome, was still an ever-present factor and perhaps a further spur to Pompeius, and, as it turned out, to Crassus too.

The second area of concern was Egypt, and the ailing Ptolemaic Empire; now reduced to just Egypt itself, with Rome having annexed

Cyrene and most recently Cyprus. The Ptolemaic Empire was the last of the great Hellenistic monarchies which had succeeded Alexander the Great, but by now was the 'sick man' of the Mediterranean. The only reason that it had survived Roman annexation was the simple fact that no Roman trusted one of his colleagues to accomplish the task, for fear of them seizing Egypt's fabulous wealth for themselves. No less a figure than Crassus had proposed such a scheme in 65 BC (as Censor) and had been soundly blocked. Yet by 57 BC, the Ptolemaic family had descended into another familial civil war and Ptolemy XII came to Rome seeking the restoration of his throne. Although reticent to get involved in Egypt, for the aforementioned reasons, Egypt was Rome's most valuable client kingdom and Rome required a stable and pliant government. Therefore, one of the outgoing Consuls, P. Cornelius Lentulus Spinther, was chosen to lead an expedition to Egypt and restore Ptolemy XII to his throne (and nothing else). Naturally there were many others who coveted this command.[27]

There was also an interesting religious matter which occurred this year, also involving the Consul Lentulus Spinther, with echoes of Clodius' methods. A place in the College of Augurs became available (upon the death of a member) and Spinther wanted to ensure his son took the prestigious position. Unfortunately for them both, there was an ancient limitation which stated that no more than one member of a Roman Gens (the extended Roman family) could hold an Augurate. Spinther and his son belonged to the Cornelian Gens but a certain Faustus Cornelius Sulla (son of the Dictator) was already an Augur. Therefore, Spinther had his son adopted into another family (the Manlii Torquati) to overcome this limitation and have him selected. Thus, we can see a second Roman politician, the son of a Consul no less, being adopted into another family to overcome an ancient limitation on office holding, all with the approval of a Consul, and therefore another example of a Roman nobleman placing office-holding above religious tradition and circumnavigating ancient restrictions.

The elections for the following year saw an interesting set of results, despite all the interference from the rival gangs. Clodius was elected to the Aedileship, not a major office in itself, but it put him back in elected office. However, another brother (Caius) was elected Praetor, and thus could use that office to support his brother. Milo naturally was out of office and unable to stand for another this year. In terms of the Tribunate, one of the most notable candidates was C. Porcius Cato, a kinsman of the more famous M. Porcius Cato, but a staunch ally of none other than Clodius himself.

Thus, a year of bloodshed and turmoil ended with few issues resolved. Cicero had been recalled, but Clodius was still an active political force and had now been elected to the Aedileship for the following year, with his brother Caius elected as Praetor. Clodius' seeming monopoly on legislative power had been broken, but only at the cost of running street battles between the rival armed factions (including the use of gladiators). The antagonism between Clodius and Milo seemed unlikely to abate and Rome's growing grain crisis had seen Pompeius stage an audacious power-grab to secure an empire-wide command. The shadow of Caesar, though physically absent from Rome, continued to cast a growing presence on Roman politics and the issue of Egypt had arisen once more.

3. A Violent Stalemate (56 BC)

Being back in elected office once more, Clodius wasted little time in using this office to attack Milo, prosecuting him for his role in the violence of the previous year (a new level of hypocrisy, even for Rome). Yet according to Dio, Clodius' aim was to embarrass Pompeius, who had to turn up in person to speak in Milo's defence, thus giving Clodius and his supporters the chance to embarrass the great man in public:

> *He immediately instituted proceedings against Milo for providing himself with gladiators, actually charging him with the very thing he was doing himself and for which he was likely to be brought to trial. He did this, not in the expectation of convicting Milo, inasmuch as the latter had many strong champions, among them Cicero and Pompeius, but in order that under this pretext he might not only carry on a campaign against Milo but also insult his backers.*[28]

Almost inevitably, given that the two men involved both commanded factions of armed men, the trial broke down into violence:

About three o'clock, as though at a given signal, the Clodians began spitting at our men. There was an outburst of rage. They began a movement for forcing us from our ground. Our men charged: his men turned tail. Clodius was pushed off the Rostra: and then we too made our escape for fear of mischief in the riot. The Senate was summoned into the Curia, Pompeius went home.[29]

Cicero's eye witness account continues:

On the 8th the Senate met in the Temple of Apollo, that Pompeius might attend. Pompeius made an impressive speech. That day nothing was concluded. On the 9th in the Temple of Apollo a decree passed the Senate 'that what had taken place on the 7th of February was treasonable'. On this day Cato warmly inveighed against Pompeius, and throughout his speech arraigned him as though he were at the bar. He said a great deal about me, to my disgust, though it was in very laudatory terms. When he attacked Pompeius' perfidy to me, he was listened to in profound silence on the part of my enemies. Pompeius answered him boldly with a palpable allusion to Crassus and said outright that 'he would take better precautions to protect his life than Africanus had done, whom C. Carbo had assassinated'.[30]

Thus, we first see the charge that Pompeius believed that it was Crassus who was behind the attacks on himself and Cicero, a belief later confirmed between the two men:

For Pompeius understands what is going on, and imparts to me that plots are being formed against his life, that Caius Cato is being supported by Crassus, that money is being supplied to Clodius, that both are backed by Crassus and Curio, as well as by Bibulus and his other detractors: that he must take extraordinary precautions to prevent being overpowered by that demagogue with a people all but wholly alienated, a nobility hostile, a Senate ill-affected, and the younger men corrupt.[31]

Therefore, it seems that Pompeius at least believed that Crassus was bankrolling both Clodius and C. Cato, forming an interesting Triumvirate

(Crassus, Clodius and C. Cato), and thus, was orchestrating the attacks on him and his plans.[32] This may well have been true, as Crassus always seems to have preferred working behind the scenes in Roman politics, rather than taking the fore (his last office being the Censorship of 65 BC). If this is to be believed, we therefore have Pompeius, Cicero and Milo on one side and Crassus, Clodius and C. Cato on the other, not to mention Caesar in Gaul, and the various other factions within the Senate, including M. Porcius Cato. It is interesting that Pompeius brought up the possible assassination of Scipio Africanus Aemilianus by the Gracchan supporter C. Papirius Carbo (Cos. 120 BC).[33] Here, Pompeius was publicly stating that he believed he would be assassinated (an interesting piece of hyperbole and a very interesting comparison between the situation in the 130s/120s BC and his present day). Cicero goes on to note what Pompeius' plans were to counter this attack:

> *So he* [Pompeius] *is making his preparations and summoning men from the country. On his part, Clodius is rallying his gangs: a body of men is being got together for the Quirinalia. For that occasion, we are considerably in a majority, owing to the forces brought up by Pompeius himself: and a large contingent is expected from Picenum and Gallia, to enable us to throw out Cato's bills also about Milo and Lentulus.*[34]

Thus, Pompeius was planning on flooding Rome (and the Assembly) with his supporters from his own estates in Italy to counteract the influence of Clodius and C. Cato. Given the levels of violence used, and Milo's powerful backers, the trial seems to have fizzled out, with Milo acquitted. The next clash seems to have developed over the exiling of Cicero by Clodius:

> *Finally, taking with him Milo and some Tribunes, he ascended the Capitol and took down the tablets set up by Clodius to commemorate his exile. This time Clodius came up with his brother Caius, a Praetor, and took them away from him, but later he watched for a time when Clodius was out of town, and going up to the Capitol again, took them and carried them home.*[35]

Cicero therefore attempted a very public act of exonerating his own name and overturning his exile but was initially prevented by Clodius' brother (who was a Praetor). Nevertheless, it seems that the hostility between the two men continued, with Cicero going on the attack, and questioning the legitimacy of Clodius' transfer to the Plebeian order and thus his whole Tribunate:

After this occurrence no quarter was shown on either side, but they abused and slandered each other as much as they could, without refraining from the basest means. The one declared that the tribuneship of Clodius had been contrary to the laws and that therefore his official acts were invalid, and the other that Cicero's exile had been justly decreed, and his return unlawfully voted.[36]

But Cicero had now come back from the exile into which he was driven by Clodius, and, relying on his great influence in the Senate, had forcibly taken away and destroyed, in the absence of Clodius, the records of his Tribunate which Clodius had deposited on the Capitol. When the Senate was convened to consider the matter, and Clodius made his denunciation, Cicero made a speech in which he said that, since Clodius had been made Tribune illegally, all that had been done or recorded during his Tribunate ought to be void and invalid.[37]

It was at this point that we see the unlikely alliance between M. Porcius Cato, a staunch traditionalist (at least in his public utterances) and P. Clodius Pulcher, the apparent antithesis of traditionalist Republican values. In what is a wonderful example of the ever-shifting temporary alliances in Roman politics, Cato found himself having to defend Clodius' Tribunate. Taking Cicero's' line of attack, if Clodius' Tribunate was invalid then so were Cato's whole command in Cyprus, and all his subsequent actions, placing a black mark against his own political career. Thus, however distasteful it may have been, Cato had to defend the legality of Clodius' Tribunate, if not his actions.

Cato contradicted Cicero while he was speaking, and finally rose and said that, although he was wholly of the opinion that there was nothing sound or good in the administration of Clodius, still, if everything which

Roman Forum.

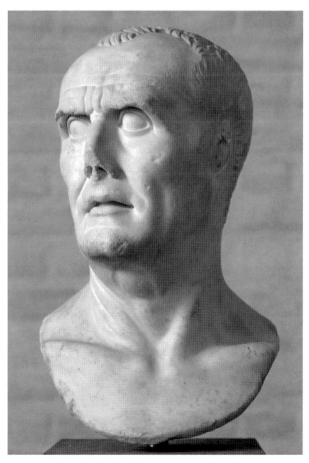

Possible bust of C. Marius.

L. Cornelius Sulla.

Cn. Pompeius Magnus.

Possible bust of
L. Licinius Crassus.

M. Tullius Cicero.

C. Iulius Caesar.

M. Antonius.

Augustus.

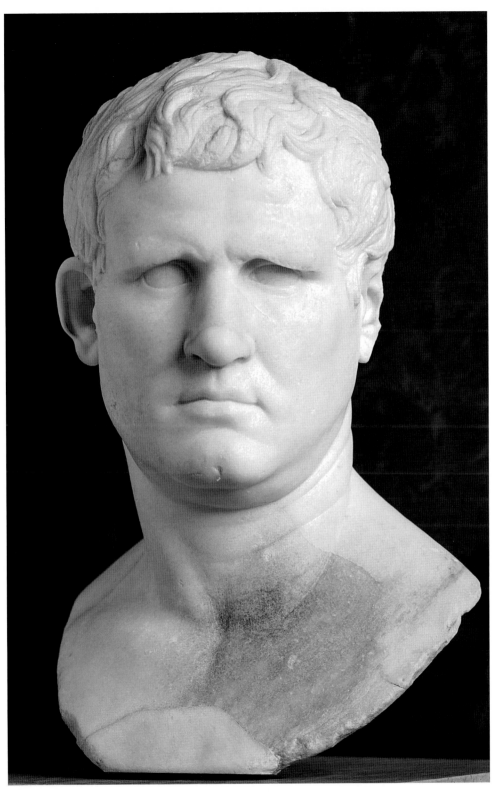

Agrippa.

Tiberius.

Clodius had done while Tribune were to be rescinded, then all his own proceedings in Cyprus would be rescinded, and his mission there had not been legal, since an illegal magistrate had obtained it for him; but it had not been illegal, he maintained, for Clodius to be elected Tribune after a transfer from Patrician to Plebeian rank which the law allowed, and if he had been a bad magistrate, like others, it was fitting to call to an account the man who had done wrong, and not to vitiate the office which had suffered from his wrong doing. In consequence of this speech Cicero was angry with Cato, and for a long time ceased friendly interactions with him.[38]

Thus, we can see that Roman politics in this period was not some neat clash between two well-defined sides, but an ever-changing mix of temporary political alliances, with each politician balancing the good of the Republic and his own political progression. Pompeius had not been idle this year either. Aside from his involvement in the trial of Milo, he was both working in his new role as Proconsul in charge of Rome's grain supply whilst also planning to expand his overseas remit. In terms of his role as Proconsul he undertook a special census of Rome' freedmen, the first not to be carried out by the Censor. He also undertook many short trips overseas to ensure Rome's grain supply was secure:

Having thus been set over the administration and management of the grain trade, Pompeius sent out his agents and friends in various directions, while he himself sailed to Sicily, Sardinia and Africa, and collected grain ... By this exercise of zeal and courage attended by good fortune, he filled the sea with ships and the markets with grain, so that the excess of what he had provided sufficed also for foreign peoples, and there was an abundant overflow, as from a spring, for all.[39]

Once again, Pompeius had proved his administrative skills and alleviated Rome's grain shortage, thus raising his profile once more. With that in mind, he seems to have been planning ahead for his next major command and again the situation in Egypt came to the fore. Despite the former Consul Lentulus Spinther being appointed to restore the deposed King Ptolemy XII, he had been prevented from doing so by a combination of political opposition, including the Tribune C. Cato proposing a law to recall Lentulus, and religious sanction; a Sibylline oracle had been interpreted (as they always were) as a warning against Spinther undertaking this restoration. Sensing an opportunity, Pompeius had a Tribune (L. Caninius Gallus) propose that none other than Pompeius himself be placed in command of the restoration of Ptolemy XII.

> *However, Caninius, as Tribune of the People, brought in a law providing that Pompeius, without an army, and with two lictors only, should go out as a mediator between the king and the people of Alexandria. Pompeius was thought to regard the law with no disfavour, but the Senate rejected it, on the plausible pretence that it feared for his safety. Besides, writings were to be found scattered about the Forum and near the Senate House, stating that it was Ptolemy's wish to have Pompeius given to him as a commander instead of Spinther.*[40]

Thus, we can see that the proposal came to nought, but it shows that Pompeius was still eager for a formal command (in addition to his current Proconsulship). Of his rivals, we can see that Caesar was in the ascendancy, having subdued a significant portion of Gaul, and was eager to both seek the public acclamation of this feat and have his conquests formally recognised, by having Gaul converted into a new Roman province. On the downside however, Caesar's prolonged absence from Rome weakened his political position and his two major accomplishments from his Consulship, the agrarian legislation and his Gallic command, both came under attack from opponents hoping to overturn both. Caesar's agrarian legislation came under attack from both Cicero himself and the Tribune P. Rutilius Lupus, whilst L. Domitius Ahenobarbus campaigned for the Consulship on a platform of ending Caesar's Gallic command.

As usual it is difficult to determine the actions of Crassus, who, as always, seems to have shunned public demonstrations of his political actions. As mentioned above, Pompeius (if we are to believe Cicero) believed that Crassus was funding Clodius and C. Cato, and thus the attacks on both him personally and his proposals, but as in much of Crassus' political activity there are no hard facts to go on.

Summary

In many ways, it seemed that it was in this year that a balance was achieved in the Republic, and a stalemate had been reached. The two previous years had seen the turbulent Tribunates of first Clodius and then Milo. The Roman Assembly, and seemingly much of the city of Rome itself, had been wracked with violence and battles between the armed supporters of the two men (and their sponsors). Yet this violence, although more protracted, was of a different level of magnitude than that of previous generations. In the generation between 133–100 BC the violence had been state sponsored (or at least tacitly approved) and had been short, sharp uses of force by factions within the Senate against each other and their supporters, who were deemed to be 'enemies of the state'. The violence had been far bloodier but had been more focused and time limited. This escalated in the period 91–70 BC, when Roman politicians engaged their opponents using Roman armies, plunging the Republic into an existential crisis and bloody civil war, as again seen in 63–62 BC.

Yet, although it may not have seemed it at the time, this third phase of violence was of a lesser degree. We have no reports of notable deaths amongst the nobility nor significant casualties amongst their supporters. If anything, the two sides seem to have neutralised one another. Once the key men had vacated the Tribunate, events seemed to have calmed down (relatively). In many ways, this period showed the Republican system working; no one man or faction held dominance and the ambitions of powerful men were held in check by their peers. Interestingly, we know the identities of all ten Tribunes this year, but none seem to have proposed any new reforms. If anything, their actions were dominated by fighting old battles, whether it be the Egyptian question or the previous actions of Clodius, Milo or even Caesar.

Thus, we can see that there is an argument for stating that the evolution of violence in the Republic was cyclical rather than linear. Short bursts of bloody violence had escalated into full-scale civil war but had been followed by more protracted low-level violence. No one side held a monopoly on power and thus was not able to pass the *senatus consultum ultimum* against their opponents and seize the moral high ground as being defenders of the state (and thus brand their opponents as 'enemies of the state'). In point of fact, it is clear that none of the key participants in these events gave their opponents the excuse to call for the SCU. It is notable that unlike many of their 'illustrious' predecessors, and for all their faults, both Clodius and Milo left the Tribunate after their year of office and continued their political careers, balancing a legitimate pursuit of the *cursus honorum,* along with using powerful patrons and applied violence when called for. There were no grandstanding attempts to hold multiple Tribunates or breach the *cursus honorum* by seeking office early. Thus, an apparent stalemate had been reached in Roman politics allowing the Republican system to continue, though this is not to say that the situation was ideal, especially with the frequent outbreaks of low-level violence.

Yet whilst this situation may have benefited the Republican system as a whole and many non-affiliated members of the Senate, for the key men involved such a stalemate clearly did not meet any of their ambitions. It was against this background that later in the year 56 BC, one of the most important meetings in Republican history took place in the town of Luca, in northern Italy. The meeting was a large one, with apparently over two hundred Senators in attendance (the largest non-military Senatorial gathering outside of Rome), not to mention various provincial governors and Roman officials (such as Praetors). Despite the numbers involved in this largest political gathering outside of Rome though, at the heart of this meeting lay three men: Cn. Pompeius 'Magnus', M. Licinius Crassus, and C. Iulius Caesar, and its outcome shaped Roman politics for evermore.

Chapter Six

The Rise and Fall of the 'Triumviral Republic' (55–52 BC)

1. The Conference at Luca

It would be melodramatic to say that the meeting between the three men, now commonly referred to as the Conference of Luca, marked the beginning of the end of the Roman Republic; however, it was certainly a significant milestone in the short history of the post-civil war Republic.[1] We will never know for certain who initiated this meeting or the proposed alliance, yet all of Plutarch's works have the catalyst as being Caesar, as best seen here:

> *Now when Caesar came back from his province and prepared to seek the Consulate, he saw that Pompeius and Crassus were once more at odds with each other. He therefore did not wish to make one of them an enemy by asking the aid of the other, nor did he have any hope of success if neither of them helped him. Accordingly, he tried to reconcile them by persistently showing them that their mutual ruin would only increase the power of such men as Cicero, Catulus, and Cato, men whose influence would be nothing if Crassus and Pompeius would only unite their friends and adherents, and with one might and one purpose direct the affairs of the city.*[2]

Brushing aside Plutarch's usual hyperbole, there does seem to be more than a grain of truth in these statements. However, Caesar didn't need another Consulate, he needed official recognition of his annexation of Gaul, much as Pompeius did (of the east) some five years earlier when the three men last forged an alliance. He also needed an extension to his Gallic command, or face the prospect of someone else (possibly even Pompeius himself) being appointed to finish the job and take all the credit.

Yet there were significant differences between the alliance of 60/59 BC and what was proposed at Luca. Firstly, the alliance of 60/59 BC was not one of equals; it was a reformation of the Duumvirate of Pompeius and Crassus (which had been so influential in 70 BC – see Chapter One), with Caesar acting as their agent (in the Consulship). Now, whilst Caesar was far from being an equal to Pompeius or Crassus, especially whilst he was away from Rome, he was the man of the moment. He had defeated or subdued virtually all of the tribes of Gaul and was attempting to annex the whole Gallic region west of the Rhine. The Gallic tribes had been Rome's traditional enemies, and a highly symbolic one, ever since the Gallic Sack of c.390 BC. Furthermore, Caesar was attempting to add a huge swathe of territory to Rome's empire, unlike any which had gone before it (which would take Rome's empire from the Mediterranean to the Channel and the heart of Europe).

These conquests had brought him popularity and wealth, and it had also left him in command of a large army, something the other two men lacked; a situation they would understand, given their previous uses of their armies for political ends. We must also not forget the close family ties between the men; Pompeius was still married to Caesar's daughter, Iulia, whilst Crassus' eldest son (Publius) served as a legate under Caesar in Gaul. However, aside from the relationship between the three men, the main difference was the nature of their alliance. Earlier, in 60/59 BC, each man had had short term aims and the alliance was a temporary one, with Caesar leaving for Gaul, and Pompeius and Crassus re-engaging each other in a political struggle, albeit one conducted via proxies. Thus, this was a typical Roman political alliance; a short-term attempt at domination to achieve certain specific ends. What was proposed at Luca was far wider ranging, with a far greater impact on the governance of the Republic:

> *But between himself* [Caesar], *Pompeius, and Crassus the following compact was made: these two were to stand for the Consulate, and Caesar was to assist their candidacy by sending large numbers of his soldiers home to vote for them; as soon as they were elected, they were to secure for themselves commands of provinces and armies, and to confirm Caesar's present provinces to him for another term of five years.*[3]

Thus, rather than working through agents, as they had been doing since 69 BC, both Pompeius and Crassus sought the Consulate themselves, some fifteen years after their previous one, which was a highly unusual gap in this period of the Republic. Furthermore, they agreed to secure themselves five-year Proconsular commands; Pompeius in Spain, and Crassus in the East. Along with renewing Caesar's Gallic command for another five years, this gave the three of them control over the majority of Rome's military resources for five years, and the power to shape Rome's immediate future for that period. It is also clear that the three men had a clear vision of how they would use this power. Pompeius was to stay in Rome and regulate domestic politics, Caesar was to continue his Gallic campaigns and annex Gaul to Rome's empire, whilst Crassus was to head east and command the campaigns to defeat (and annex) the supposedly weakened Parthian Empire.

Thus, what was proposed at Luca was nothing short of the takeover of the Roman Republic by three of its leading men, who would guide its destiny (both political and military) for at least the next five years, foreshadowing the later official role of Triumvir (see Chapter Nine). This was a clear revision to the Republic as envisaged in 70 BC by Pompeius and Crassus; temporary stewardship by its leading men. We will never know if these men intended their stewardship to last beyond the initial five-year period but given what had occurred in Roman politics since 70 BC (with Catilina, Clodius and Milo); it is not hard to see how these men (and their supporters) could believe that the Republic would benefit from stable leadership and domestic peace and no-one else had the resources to match this alliance.

Yet, in terms of domestic politics, this was not a Triumvirate, but rule by one man; Cn. Pompeius. With both of his partners in the provinces and his ruling of his provinces via legates, it was Pompeius who was now the de-facto guardian, or *Princeps*, of Roman domestic politics, a vision more akin to that which Sulla perhaps saw himself taking up in the 70s BC, if ill heath had not cut him short.

2. The Violent Implementation of the Triumviral Vision

Thus, Pompeius and Crassus returned to Rome with their supporters, soon followed by a large contingent of Caesar's veterans; men who could do more than just vote in the Assembly. Naturally, given the size of the meeting at Luca, both the People of Rome and the other Senators would have been aware that something major was in the offing:

When all this was publicly known, it gave displeasure to the chief men of the state, and Marcellinus [the Consul] *rose in the Assembly and asked Pompeius and Crassus whether they were going to be candidates for the Consulate. As the majority of the People bade them answer, Pompeius did so first, and said that perhaps he would be a candidate, and perhaps he would not; but Crassus gave a more politic answer, for he said he would take whichever course he thought would be for the advantage of the Republic.*[4]

Naturally enough there were many of the Senate who opposed this power grab:

For this reason, diverse persons were emboldened to stand for the consulate, one of whom was Domitius. When, however, Pompeius and Crassus openly announced their candidature, the rest took fright and withdrew from the contest; but Cato encouraged Domitius, who was a kinsman and friend of his, to proceed, urging and inciting him to cling to his hopes, assured that he would do battle for the common freedom. For it was not the consulate, he said, which Crassus and Pompeius wanted, but a tyranny, nor did their course of action mean simply a canvass for office, but rather a seizure of provinces and armies.[5]

Even if these weren't Cato's own actual words, then it would certainly have been the sentiment of many of the Senate; one man's stewardship is another man's tyranny, and many would have seen it as Rome having three masters (albeit with two absent). Certainly, the two Consuls of 56 BC, Cn. Cornelius Lentulus Marcellinus and L. Marcius Philippus, attempted to prevent Pompeius and Crassus from standing as Consuls. Yet there were no constitutional barriers preventing either man from standing for Consul, it being fifteen years since their previous one.

It seems that there were few practical barriers either, with Rome's two largest street gangs – those of Milo and those of Clodius – now under Triumviral control. In fact, the argument for Crassus being the paymaster of Clodius became stronger when Clodius turned up in the Assembly and made a very public declaration of support for his former enemy (Pompeius):

> *But Clodius had meanwhile leaped over to the side of Pompeius and espoused his cause again, in the hope that if he should give him any help in securing his present objects, he would make him thoroughly his friend. So, he came before the populace in his ordinary garb, without having made any change as the decree required, and went to inveighing against Marcellinus and the rest. As great indignation was shown by the Senators at this, he left the People in the midst of his speech and rushed to the Senate House, where he came near perishing. For the Senate confronted him and prevented his going in, while at that moment he was surrounded by the Equestrians and would have been torn limb from limb, had he not raised an outcry, calling upon the People for aid; whereupon many ran to the scene bringing fire and threatening to burn his oppressors along with the Senate House if they should do him any violence. Thus, Clodius was saved after coming so near to being killed.*[6]

With the Triumviral control of the armed gangs in the streets of Rome, and thus the Assembly, preventing their opponents from successfully disrupting the elections, all that could be done was to prevent the elections themselves being held in the first place. This is the tactic which C. Porcius Cato took, and here it weakens the argument that he was in Crassus' pay, or that there were some matters he would not be acquiescent on.

> *When they (Pompeius and Crassus) began to canvass for the office outside of the period specified by law, and, among others the consuls themselves (for Marcellinus had some little influence) made it plain that they would not allow them to be elected, they tried to bring it about, through the agency of Caius Cato and others, that the elections should not be held that year, in order that an interrex might be chosen and they might then seek and secure the office in accordance with the laws.*[7]

Thus, the Consuls of Rome worked with one of the Tribunes to prevent lawful elections from being held. It seems therefore that there was a delay in all the elections (an interregnum), which meant that the Republic had no elected officials for a short period. Yet this could not last and at best was a delaying tactic, especially when the Triumvirs' opponents were out of office themselves. Therefore, elections were eventually scheduled, with those for the Consulate being first, and Pompeius and Crassus ensured that they would be elected unopposed.

> *Later Crassus and Pompeius were elected Consuls after an interregnum, as no one else of the earlier candidates opposed them. To be sure, Lucius Domitius, who canvassed for the office up to the very last day of the year, set out from his house for the Assembly just after dark, but when the slave who carried the torch in front of him was slain, he became frightened and went no farther. Hence, since no one at all opposed them, and furthermore since Publius Crassus, who was a son of Marcus and at that time lieutenant under Caesar, brought soldiers to Rome for this very purpose, they were easily chosen.*[8]

Thus, despite some delays, Pompeius and Crassus had achieved their first goal-election to the Consulate.

3. The Rule of the Three (55 BC)

Having secured their own election to the highest office, the next stage of their plan was to ensure that the other magistracies were filled, if not by their allies, then at least by men who weren't opposed to them. In terms of opponents, Cato emerges (at least in the surviving sources) as a key opponent they wanted to ensure was not elected to office. To these ends, Pompeius and Crassus used a combination of procedural changes and electoral sharp practice. Thus, the Senate passed a vote at their behest that the Praetors should enter office earlier than normal and not be subject to a period between their election and taking up of office, when charges of bribery could be brought, and then attempted to 'encourage' the electorate into voting for their candidates. When this policy did not seem to work, and the first tribe had voted, Pompeius (as Consul) declared that he had heard thunder; and thus, the gathering was declared 'inauspicious' and thus could be dissolved mid-election. The Assembly was then reconvened, with a number of citizens excluded, which then voted P. Vatinius, the Tribune of 59 BC, as a Praetor instead of Cato. A Tribune managed to call an Assembly to discuss this manoeuvre, but it came to nought.

Dio provides an overview of the process of the elections for the other magistracies:

> *The election of the Praetors, now, was made in peace, for Cato did not see fit to offer any violence; in the matter of the Curule Aediles, however, there was some bloodshed, so that even Pompeius was much bespattered with blood. Nevertheless, in the case of both these and the other officials elected by the People, they made appointments to please themselves, since they personally held the elections, and they made friends with the other Aediles and most of the Tribunes; but two Tribunes, Caius Ateius Capito and Publius Aquilius Gallus, did not come to terms with them.*[9]

Thus, we can see that the Triumvirs (or Duumvirs in Rome) ensured, by both bribery and violence, that the majority of the other magistracies were filled by their supporters. Although it was normal practice for all political factions to try to secure as many allies amongst the other magistracies as possible, it had not been done on this scale since the civil war period and the quiescent governments secured by Cinna, Carbo and then Sulla.

Certainly, it appears no coincidence that this period was overseen by Sulla's two most prominent protégés. Yet, logically, a unified group of magistrates would lead to a less fractious political environment in Rome. We have few details for the violence which broke out at the Aedile elections, other than there were fatalities:

> *It once happened that at an election of Aediles people came to blows, and many were killed in the vicinity of Pompeius and he was covered with their blood, so that he changed his garments.*[10]

Thus, the Triumvirs, as well as holding the two Consulships, secured the election of allies to the vast majority of the other elected offices in order to implement their legislative programme, with just two Tribunes opposing them. This certainly gave them a practical mandate far greater than any other politicians since the resignation of Sulla. Having secured this power, it seems that the first stage of the Triumviral programme was to secure their military position for the next five years. To give this seizure of military power a greater veneer of due process, it was a Tribune (C. Trebonius) who proposed the measure:

> *Caius Trebonius, however, a Tribune, presented a measure, that to the one Syria and the neighbouring lands should be given as a province for five years, and to the other the Two Spains, where there had recently been disturbances, for the same period; they should employ as many soldiers as they wished, both citizens and allies, and should make peace and war with whomsoever they pleased.*[11]

As we can see, this is an extraordinary grant of military power, giving the two men carte blanche for five years, including unlimited numbers of men and the ability to wage war as they saw fit. Thus, the Senate, the traditional arbiter of all military matters would be made redundant in these key provinces. We can see the continued evolution of the Tribunate on military matters, here giving the two Consuls extraordinary commands in terms of length and degree of autonomy from the Senate. Thus, Rome's military power was handed over to two individuals by legal means.

Naturally enough the Assembly at which this proposal would be voted on became a focal point for opposition, violence and eventually bloodshed. Cato, although a private citizen and one of junior office, was apparently given two hours to speak on the proposal in the Assembly but was eventually hauled way and then imprisoned on his attempted return.

> *Hence, when bidden to be silent, he did not stop immediately, but had to be pushed and dragged from the assembly, whereupon he came back, and though finally ordered to be taken to prison, he did not moderate his behaviour.*[12]

Naturally the two Tribunes opposed to the Triumviral measure attempted to use their vetoes (*ius intercessio*) to block the proposal, but were prevented from attending the Assembly and thus were unable to use them. Almost inevitably these clashes led to bloodshed and on this occasion murders:

> *Others occupied the meeting place of the Assembly by night and barred out Ateius, Cato, Favonius, and the others with them. When Favonius and Ninnius got in somehow unobserved, and Cato and Ateius climbed upon the shoulders of some of those standing around, the attendants of the Tribunes drove them both out, wounded the rest who were with them, and actually killed a few.*[13]

Thus, the Tribunician *viatores* (attendants) of the eight pro-Triumviral Tribunes attacked and killed the supporters of the other two Tribunes, and actually injured one of the two Tribunes, P. Aquilius Gallus. Thus, the *lex Trebonia* on Proconsular provinces was passed and vast military power was transferred to Pompeius and Crassus. Both men capitalised on this victory by immediately calling a fresh Assembly and passing a measure extending Caesar's Gallic command for a further five years, though it does not seem to have been an explicit grant of five years, merely that it banned discussion on a successor to the Gallic command until five years' time (March 50 BC). Caesar was able to use this power not only to consolidate his Gallic campaigns but widen the war to include an invasion of the island of Albion/Britannia and across the Rhine into Germania, with punitive raids against invading Germanic tribes.

The Triumviral control of Rome's empire was now complete. For the next five years Pompeius controlled the armies of Spain, Caesar those of Gaul and Crassus those of Syria and the east. The only other provinces with significant armies were Macedonia, under L. Calpurnius Piso Caesoninus, and the armies of the Proconsul A. Gabinius, also in the East. Not only was Gabinius a supporter of Pompeius, thus placing another army under Triumviral control, but the Triumvirs staged a de-facto seizure of the Ptolemaic Kingdom of Egypt. As we have seen (Chapter Five), for several years now domestic opposition had held up the Roman reinstatement of the deposed King of Egypt, Ptolemy XII. With a clear control of domestic policy, the Triumvirs (as Consuls) formally instructed Gabinius to invade Egypt and reinstall Ptolemy XII. Egypt was duly invaded by a Roman army for the first time, and the ruler Berenice IV's forces were defeated.[14] Ptolemy was then reinstalled as Pharaoh; a de-facto puppet ruler for Rome (and the Triumvirs). Having reinstated Ptolemy, Gabinius withdrew but left behind a contingent of Roman soldiers to support the new Pharaoh, placing the Mediterranean's richest kingdom squarely as a Roman (and Triumviral) client.

Having secured both political and military control of Rome, Pompeius and Crassus turned their attention to domestic reforms, with several proposals. The first two measures were both unusual ones in terms of the levels of hypocrisy involved; a measure creating harsher punishments for electoral bribery and a sumptuary measure, trying to curb personal expenditure (by Rome's two richest men). The measure on bribery was passed into law; that of expenditure was dropped in the face of opposition. If we put aside the obvious hypocrisy here, it is unusual to see both men using their control of the Roman domestic agenda to push policies such as this. Here perhaps we can see shades of Sulla, who believed he was strengthening the Republic by preventing anyone else doing as he had done.

The next proposals from the Consuls were two separate laws on the composition of juries, which again had been a perennial topic for reform ever since the Tribunate of C. Sempronius Gracchus in 124–122 BC. Pompeius proposed, and passed, a law restricting juries to men from the highest census class and thus making it more exclusive. Crassus carried a law restricting jurors to a choice of five Tribes. Thus, in both cases, the Triumvirs had restricted the choice of jurors to the upper echelons of Roman society, again demonstrating a two-handed approach. In terms of selfish interests, it seems that the two men tried to ensure that any trials faced by their supporters (or even themselves) would have a far narrower range of jurors and men more likely to support them. In terms of the interests of the Republic, jury service and trials in general had increasingly been a politicised issue and thus, in their minds at least, by narrowing down the jurors to Rome's upper echelons they may have been trying to return control of the courts to the oligarchy. The clear flaw being that it was the lack of cohesion within Rome's ruling oligarchy which caused the bulk of the political dissensions and bloodshed over the past eighty years.

The whole Triumviral programme was crowned by Pompeius' opening of a grand new theatre accompanied by lavish games and entertainment for the People. Here was a public demonstration of the power and majesty of the new 'temporary' ruling group of Rome, both in stone and in the entertainment of the Roman People. With their power secure, Crassus left Rome for his eastern campaigns against the Parthian Empire, an event in itself which turned into political discord, when one of the opposing Tribunes, Ateius Capito, attempted to prevent Crassus from leaving Rome to take up his province in the east:

> *But Ateius, on meeting Crassus, at first tried to stop him with words, and protested against his advance; then he bade his attendant seize the person of Crassus and detain him. And when the other Tribunes would not permit this, the attendant released Crassus.*[15]

Thus, Crassus left Rome to start what he hoped would be a glorious eastern campaign, expanding Rome's empire in the east and adding glory to both himself and the ruling faction he was part of. Pompeius, by contrast, stayed in Rome after his year in office and ruled his provinces and their armies by legates, allowing him to try to exert some measure of control over the domestic agenda.

Given the combination of wealth, popularity and political power that the alliance of Rome's three leading men brought together, we can ask ourselves what impact it had? Certainly, they seized control of Rome's military forces and were able to direct foreign policy, but domestically, at best they oversaw nothing more than a respite. Despite having control of both Consulships, the Praetors, the Aediles and eight of the ten Tribunes, not to mention a sizeable chunk of the Senate, Rome was still plagued by violence, bloodshed and murder in the Assemblies. Certainly, the running street battles between the rival gangs of Clodius and Milo had been checked, but the Triumvirs still found themselves opposed at every turn, be it electoral or legislative, and had to resort to violence to get many of their measures passed. In many ways it was a testament to the resilience of the Republic that such an alliance was still opposed so successfully. Yet the violence and bloodshed continued, and such a combination of political power was not able to check it.

4. The Decline of the Triumvirate and a Republic in Crisis (54–53 BC)

In 55 BC, the Triumvirs had managed to achieve a near monopoly on legitimate political power (backed up by violence), yet the transitory nature of their power was shown in the elections for 54 BC when they were unable to repeat their control over the elections for the magistracies. The two most obvious setbacks for them were the elections of L. Domitius Ahenobarbus to the Consulship and M. Porcius Cato to the Praetorship, both of whom had been blocked by the Triumvirs the year before. This, more than anything else, showed the weakness of the Triumvirs' political position when they were not holding active office, and the robustness of one of the fundamental aspects of the Republic: annual magistracies. Pompeius and Crassus may have dominated whilst holding high office themselves, much as Marius had done before them, but once out of office they struggled to assert any control over the Republic. Therefore, it seemed that trying to dominate Roman politics without holding political office proved to be ineffective.

Thus, the Triumvirs could expect opposition from the Consulship, the Praetorship and as it turns out the Tribunate, in the form of the Tribune C. Memmius. The opponents of the Triumvirs refrained from attacking either Pompeius or Crassus directly, but concentrated on their agents, most notably through persecutions of P. Vatinius, C. Porcius Cato and especially A. Gabinius. All three men were able to be acquitted, perhaps reflecting the success of Pompeius and Crassus' changes to the composition of juries the year before. In Vatinius' case, he was aided by a defence speech by none other than Cicero himself. However, both Cato and Gabinius were prosecuted on a second occasion. In Gabinius' case the second prosecution was by the Tribune C. Memmius on a charge of corruption, and on this occasion he was convicted.[16]

If anything, aside from a slew of prosecutions this year,[17] the other notable political activity came from the Consul L. Domitius Ahenobarbus, a committed opponent of them (the other Consul being Ap. Claudius Pulcher, who seemed sympathetic towards the Triumvirs). Whilst the Triumvirs' other opponents attacked their agents, Domitius focused his attention on Caesar himself and most notably his Gallic command, an issue he had raised in 56 BC when campaigning for the Consulship (see Chapter Five). However, we only have a passing reference to his attempts to overturn it this year and no further detail as to his method, or its failure: *Afterwards in his own Consulship he tried to deprive Caesar of the command of the armies in Gaul.*[18]

Overshadowing the domestic agenda, at least in our surviving sources, were the actions of the two other Triumvirs, Caesar and Crassus, both of whom were engaged in notable invasions; of Britannia and Mesopotamia respectively, though neither was successful. Another notable event this year was the death (in childbirth) of Pompeius' wife, Iulia. Even this death became a political issue; with both sides (Pompeius and Domitius) using the burial to make political points:

> *They caught up the body, as soon as she had received proper eulogies in the Forum and buried it in the Campus Martius. It was in vain that Domitius opposed them and declared among other things that it was sacrilegious for her to be buried in the sacred spot without a special decree.*[19]

Whilst death in childbirth was a common (though tragic) occurrence in this period, this marriage (and death) had far wider significance, as Iulia was the daughter of Caesar and the marriage had been part of the alliance between the two men since 59 BC. With Iulia's death, this personal link was now broken. The last major political controversy of the year centred on the elections for the following year (53 BC), when M. Porcius Cato and his allies in the Senate attempted to pass electoral reform legislation aimed at stamping out corruption. Here we have a first-hand account of the matter in Cicero's latter to his friend Atticus:

> *Our friend* [Valerius] *Messalla and his fellow candidate, Domitius Calvinus, have been very generous to the People. Nothing can exceed their popularity. They are certain to be Consuls. But the Senate has passed a decree that a 'trial with closed doors' should be held before the elections in respect to each of the candidates severally, by the panels already allotted to them all. The candidates are in a great fright. The Comitia are postponed by a decree of the Senate until such time as the*

law for the 'trial with closed doors' is carried. The day for passing the law arrived. Terentius vetoed it. The Consuls, having all along conducted this business in a half-hearted kind of way, referred the matter back to the senate. Hereupon Bedlam! ... Forgive me: I can hardly restrain myself. But, nevertheless, was there ever such a farce? The Senate had voted that the elections should not be held till the law was passed: that, in case of a Tribunician veto, the whole question should be referred to them afresh. The law is introduced in a perfunctory manner: is vetoed, to the great relief of the proposers: the matter is referred to the Senate. Upon that the Senate voted that it was for the interest of the state that the elections should be held at the earliest possible time![20]

Thus, it seems that there was a bribery scandal surrounding all the candidates for the Consulship which the Senate got involved in, calling for a special court to try these accusations. This proposal was in turn vetoed (using the power of *ius intercessio*) by the Tribune Terentius and thus deadlock, though we have Cicero's contemporary judgement on the farce that ensued. Interestingly, Cicero does not mention Cato in relation to these events, but by the time of Plutarch Cato has taken centre stage, using his Praetorship to propose the following:

Therefore [he] persuaded the senate to make a decree that magistrates elect, in case they had no accuser, should be compelled of themselves to come before a sworn court and submit accounts of their election.[21]

In Plutarch's account violence breaks out during an Assembly when the motion is being discussed; presumably the one that Terentius used his veto during:

Early in the morning, therefore, when Cato had gone forth to his tribunal, crowds assailed him with shouts, abuse, and missiles, so that everybody fled from the tribunal, and Cato himself was pushed away from it and borne along by the throng.[22]

The net effect was that the Consular elections at least were postponed, and most likely all other curule elections too, with just the Plebeian

Tribunes and Aediles being the only elected officials in Rome at the start of the year; and a very visible sign of the chaos into which the Republic was descending once more.[23] Yet even in the chaos there was opportunity, as Cicero himself describes: *Matters are drifting on to an interregnum; and there is a Dictatorship in the air, in fact a good deal of talk about it.*[24]

Thus, the year ended with no Consuls being elected due to a bribery scandal and procedural deadlock, and a Dictatorship was being discussed; with naturally only one name in the frame; Cn. Pompeius. Furthermore, the question must have been asked whether the Republic, in its current form, was governable?

With no Consuls or Praetors elected, the year opened with the Tribunes, in practice, being the most senior magistrates in Rome. It must have come as no surprise that two of their number, M. Coelius Vinicianus and C. Lucilius Hirrus, proposed that a Dictator be appointed to deal with the chaos:

> *There was much talk in favour of a Dictator, which Lucilius the popular Tribune first ventured to make public, when he advised the people to elect Pompeius dictator. But Cato attacked him, and Lucilius came near losing his Tribunate, and many of Pompeius' friends came forward in defence of him, declaring that he neither asked nor desired that office.*[25]
>
> *Because of the dictatorship of Pompeius there was a considerable uprising in the city.*[26]

Thus, it seems the proposal was made and roundly opposed, perhaps even violently so. Interestingly though, Cicero seems to dismiss the whole affair without marking it out as anything major:

> *And the promulgation of a law for the appointment of a Dictator, brought M. Coelius Vinicianus suddenly to the ground, and caused him to be loudly hooted when down.*[27]

This incident does seem to indicate two things; the first was that Pompeius was testing the water using a proxy Tribune (as was his custom) to see what the reaction would be to the proposal, and secondly that his opponents were strong enough to easily defeat such a proposal. Thus, it seems that a formal office of Dictator, as had been held by his old mentor and father-in-law Sulla, was out of the question. Nevertheless, the chaos in Rome continued and it was not until July[28] that Consuls (Cn. Domitius Calvinus and M. Valerius Messalla Rufus) were elected. It is interesting to note that the men who were elected were two of the frontrunners, as mentioned by Cicero, with both having been accused of bribery.

Dio preserves an account, which is somewhat garbled, that places Pompeius at the heart of affairs and does perhaps preserve some detail of the chaos that seems to have been present:

> *All the Tribunes offered various objections, and proposed, among other things, that Consular Tribunes should replace the Consuls, so that more magistrates might be elected, as formerly. And when no one would heed them, they declared that in any case Pompeius must be chosen Dictator. By this pretext they secured a very long delay; for he was out of town, and of those on the spot there was no one who would venture to vote for the demand, since in remembrance of Sulla's cruelty they all hated that institution, nor yet would venture to refuse to choose Pompeius, on account of their fear for him. At last, very late, he came himself, refused the Dictatorship offered to him, and took measures to have the Consuls named.[29]*

In this account, written many centuries later, it is Pompeius who was offered the Dictatorship and declined in a display of Republican virtue. He then arranged for fresh Consuls to be elected. This contrasts nicely with Cicero's contemporary account which had the measure being laughed out of the Assembly. It is interesting to note that according to Dio the Tribunes were the main stumbling block and, in an echo of the role of the Tribunes in the constitutional crisis of the 370s and 360 BC, prevented the elections of other magistrates in order to effectively be Rome's chief magistrate themselves. There may be some measure of truth in this accusation that the Tribunes exploited the absence of other elected magistrates to expropriate some of their power and privileges.

It is more likely though that Tribunician vetoes were being used by the various factions to prevent one particular set of candidates from being elected and there must have been many who saw an opportunity to exploit this continued chaos, most notably Pompeius himself. It is worth speculating that Dio (or his source) has made the accurate connection between Pompeius being denied the Dictatorship (rather than refusing it) and the eventual election of the Consuls. Whilst there is no evidence to say that Pompeius caused the chaos, if there was an opportunity then there would be no rush to use his power and influence to bring the chaos to an end. Once this opportunity passed then he could use this power to try and force a resolution and allow elections to be held.

5. The Deaths of Crassus and Clodius and the Rise of Pompeius (53–52 BC)

Events at Rome however were soon overshadowed by news from the East. Whilst these events were taking place in Rome, Pompeius' fellow Triumvir M. Licinius Crassus had led the first Roman invasion of the Parthian Empire, Rome's main rival in the east. Despite being an astute general and backed up with the might of the Roman army, the first major battle of the war was the decisive one; at the Battle of Carrhae, a Roman army of seven legions was annihilated by an army of Parthian mounted archers led by the Parthian general Surenas.[30] The defeat stands as the greatest Roman defeat since the Battle of Arausio (105 BC) and one of the greatest ever. In imperial terms, Rome's seemingly inexorable push eastwards, as masterminded by Lucullus and Pompeius, ground to a halt and Rome's eastern provinces now lay vulnerable to a renewed westward push by the Parthian Empire (whose own seemingly inexorable westward expansion had only been stalled by its own civil wars).

It was not just in imperial terms that the Battle of Carrhae had such a dramatic effect on Rome; its effect on Rome's domestic politics was just as great, though nowhere nearly as obvious. Though he had survived the battle itself, M. Licinius Crassus had been killed in the aftermath, during the long retreat back to Roman Syria, and his head carried to the Parthian court. Thus, Pompeius' long term rival (and sometime partner) for over thirty years had been killed, along with one of his sons, Publius (the second time in a row that this had happened to this branch of the Licinii Crassi).[31] Crassus had maintained a formidable network of patronage in Rome, using his immense wealth to buy political power and favours from behind the scenes, including, it seems, Clodius himself at one time. Yet suddenly this patronage vanished, leaving a void in the heart of Roman politics. Crassus' only surviving son, the younger Marcus, although he inherited his father's vast wealth, seems not to have inherited his father's appetite for frontline politics.

Thus, the Triumvirate was no more and Pompeius' long term ally/rival was no more, leaving his political patronage up for grabs. Although Caesar was still in Gaul, he was not of the stature of Pompeius and Crassus and had been their agent just a few years previously, although his star was ascendant, at least in military terms. We have few other details about events at Rome, overshadowed by the chaos of the non-election of magistrates at the start of the year and the major defeat in Mesopotamia. We hear of no other activities from either Consul or Tribunes until we come to the elections for the following year (52 BC). There must have been many in Rome, especially in the Senate, who were hoping that the chaos of the previous year was a one-off, brought about by a unique set of circumstances. Yet they were to be disappointed. For a second year in a row, the election of the magistrates turned into a battleground and brought the Republic to a standstill.

If anything, the chaos surrounding the elections for the magistrates of 52 BC were worse and bloodier than the year before. Whilst the year before there had been procedural deadlock and widespread accusations of bribery, this year was made worse by the presence of two key figures; Clodius and Milo. Under the alliance of their respective patrons the violence between the two men had died down; but both now stood for election at the same time, though interestingly for different offices. Though Clodius had held the Tribunate a year before Milo (58 BC), his subsequent career had stalled. He was elected as an Aedile in 56 BC but had achieved no further electoral success since. We are told that he had postponed a bid for the Praetorship of 53 BC due to the chaos of the postponed elections. Milo by contrast, had prospered, no doubt thanks to his patron Pompeius, and he had jumped from a Tribunate in 57 BC to a Praetorship on 55 BC. This now made Milo eligible for a Consulship in 52 BC, whilst Clodius could only stand for the Praetorship. Naturally, these two rivals would each try to ensure that the other did not succeed, though the pressure was especially on Clodius, given that his rival was aiming for a superior office: *It occurred to him that his Praetorship would be crippled and powerless, if Milo was Consul.*[32]

Thus, Clodius did all that he could to keep disrupting the Consular elections to ensure Milo did not succeed, with frequent outbreaks of violence:

> *They struck both of the Consuls with stones. The Consuls were Cn. Domitius Calvinus and M. Valerius Messalla. The main reason that the meeting of the Senate had been summoned, was that P. Clodius had sent a gang of ruffians, to disrupt the elections for new Consuls, in which Milo was a candidate.*[33]

Clodius however did not always seem to have the upper hand and was himself apparently the subject of a violent and potentially murderous attack by none other than a young M. Antonius (if we are to believe Cicero):

> *What would men have thought if he* [Clodius] *had been slain at the time when you* [Antonius] *pursued him in the Forum with a drawn sword, in the sight of all the Roman People; and when you would have settled his business if he had not thrown himself up the stairs of a bookseller's shop, and, shutting them against you, checked your attack by that means?*[34]

Yet to make matters worse, the violence was not just limited to Clodius and Milo, but broke out between the three main candidates for the Consulship (of which Milo was one):

> *T. Annius Milo, P. Plautius Hypsaeus and Q. Metellus Scipio sought the Consulship not only by openly lavished bribery but also surrounded by gangs of armed men.*[35]

Furthermore, Asconius preserves details of a battle fought between the supporters of Milo and Plautius, forces which resulted in a number of deaths:

There was a battle on the Via Sacra between the supporters of the candidates Hypsaeus and Milo and many Milonians were surprised and killed.[36]

Both Dio and Plutarch sum up the situation well:

For there was no moderation and no decency at all being observed, but they vied with one another in expending great sums and, going still further, in fighting, so that once even the Consul Calvinus was wounded. Hence no Consul or prefect of the city had any successor, but at the beginning of the year the Romans were absolutely without a government in these branches.[37]

But presently Scipio, Hypsaeus, and Milo sought the Consulship. They not only used those illegal means which were now a familiar feature in political life, namely, the giving of gifts and bribes, but were openly pressing on, by the use of arms and murder, into civil war, with daring and madness.[38]

We can see that the Republic had descended into chaos for the second year running and that there were armed battles breaking out frequently in Rome and its environs, with at least four armed bands roaming the city. Rome had no formal police force or militia to restore order and the Consuls themselves had proved to be ineffective (especially having been central to the chaos the year before). It is interesting to note the absence of Pompeius in all this chaos, but again the sources report that there were calls for him to take charge, but, as the previous year had proved, despite the chaos there was no appetite for appointing a Dictator (not after Sulla). Thus, it seems Pompeius kept to the background and allowed the violence to continue, as it suited his purposes, especially as one of the main protagonists was one of his clients (Milo).

The year ended without any senior magistrates being elected (for the second year running), though we presume that the Plebeian elections for the Tribunate ran as normal, and the violence continued. Matters soon came to a head on 18 January when a chance encounter between two groups occurred on the Via Appia near the town of Bovillae (near Rome). The two groups in question were none other than the supporters of Clodius and Milo. Clodius was returning from Africa to Rome and Milo heading from Rome to his home town of Lanuvium. Neither was apparently looking for the other; Clodius had three friends with him and an entourage of thirty armed slaves, whilst Milo had a far larger force of slaves, along with a number of gladiators, but also had his wife with him in a carriage (his wife being none other than Sulla's daughter). Thus, after over five years of armed clashes in Rome, the decisive and final encounter occurred by chance on a road leading out of Rome. Asconius provides the most detailed description of the clash which followed:

> *Clodius had turned to look at this brawl, when Birria (one of Milo's gladiators) struck his shoulder with a hunting spear. Then as a battle developed, more of Milo's men arrived on the scene. The wounded Clodius was carried off to a nearby tavern in the territory of Bovillae. When Milo learnt that Clodius was wounded, he took the view that his survival would be a continued danger to himself; whereas his death would be a great benefit, even if he had to pay the penalty for it, and so ordered him to be brought out of the tavern. ... And so Clodius was dragged out from hiding and killed with many wounds. Since Clodius' slaves had either been killed or had hidden with severe injuries, the body was left on the road.*[39]

Thus, one of the main protagonists of the violence that had dogged the last decade of the Republic met with his end at a roadside tavern; murdered in cold blood by one of his political rivals. However, rather than calm the situation down, this murder inflamed the situation to new heights of chaos and disorder. With hindsight it is clear that Milo should not have left the body of his fallen rival in the open as it soon became a very public symbol of the violence that had engulfed Rome. The body was carried back to Rome, where it soon attracted a large crowd of his supporters from the People at his house. This tense situation was then deliberately inflamed by his widow and two Tribunes; Q. Pompeius Rufus (a grandson of Sulla) and T. Munatius Plancus Byrsa, both allies of Clodius.

At their instigation, the next day, Clodius' body was carried into the Forum for public display, where the Tribunes whipped up the crowds of Clodius' supporters into a frenzy, at the height of which the body was taken into the temple being used as the Senate House and cremated there and then, inside the building.[40] The fire from the funeral pyre soon spread and the whole Senate House caught fire and was burnt down. The crowd then attacked Milo's house but were driven off by a barrage of arrows from Milo's men, and also laid siege to the house of M. Aemilius Lepidus, the *Interrex* (a temporary senior magistrate appointed in the absence of Consuls). The crowd then apparently visited the houses of Plautius and Metellus, calling for them to be elected as Consuls, and then to the house of Pompeius calling for him to be made Consul or Dictator.

To make matters worse, rather than allow this chaos to die down, Milo returned to Rome to continue to canvass for the Consulship, even being invited by another Tribune (M. Caelius Rufus) to address the People, where he claimed that he had been attacked by Clodius (despite having a smaller force of men). Naturally the two Tribunes who had been allies of Clodius called for his prosecution for the murder. Whilst many in the Senate would not have shed a tear at the murder of Clodius, the burning down of the Senate House and the escalating violence and disorder had reached a new level and order clearly needed to be restored. Unfortunately for them there was only one man they could turn to Cn. Pompeius Magnus.

The Senators, indeed, did at once assemble on the Palatine for this very purpose, and they voted that an Interrex should be chosen, and that he and the Tribunes and Pompeius should look after the guarding of the city, so that it should suffer no harm.[41]

And so, a decree of the Senate was passed that the Interrex, the Tribunes of the Plebs and Cn. Pompeius, who as Proconsul was close by the city, should 'see to it that the Republic come to no harm' and that Pompeius should recruit troops all over Italy.[42]

Thus, the Senate once again passed the *senatus consultum ultimum*, last passed during the Second Civil War in 63 BC and named Pompeius, along with the Interrex and the Tribunes (the only elected magistrates in office)[43] to restore order. Although that amounted to naming twelve men in total, the Interrex was a ceremonial position and the Tribunes had no practical power and were split between the supporters of Milo and those of Clodius (along with some neutrals). In effect the Senate nominated Pompeius to restore order, yet he was only empowered by the *senatus consultum ultimum*, which had no legal force and was of limited tenure. They did grant him the power to levy an army in Italy, something that the Sullan constitution had attempted to prevent.

Yet despite this nomination, this was not the position that Pompeius had sought for several years (since the departure of Crassus for the east). Pompeius therefore met the Senate, in his new Theatre outside the Pomerium, guarded by a force of his men, where he seemingly pushed to be appointed to a more formalised office; the Dictatorship being the obvious constitutional choice. What happened next surprised everyone, when Cato, a staunch advocate of the traditional, at least in public, had his kinsman M. Calpurnius Bibulus make a counter offer: that of Pompeius being appointed to a sole Consulship, along with an extension of his commands in Spain, command of the province of Africa and a thousand talents a year from the public coffers to maintain his commands.

> *And when even Pompeius, although in words he affected to decline the honour, in fact did more than anyone else to affect his appointment as Dictator, Cato saw through his design and persuaded the Senate to appoint him Sole Consul, solacing him with a more legal monarchy that he might not force his way to the Dictatorship. They also voted him additional time in which to hold his provinces; and he had two, Spain, and all Africa, which he managed by sending legates thither and maintaining armies there, for which he received from the public treasury a thousand talents annually.*[44]

Summary

It was in these crucial few years that the tensions which had been bubbling under the surface in the Republic finally broke free. The period began with an attempt by a cabal of Rome's leading men to seize control of the Republic (through legitimate means) and attempt to bring calm to domestic politics in Rome whilst shaping her imperial ambitions. Yet even though it was a rule of three, in effect Rome itself was to be dominated by Pompeius, mastering the resources of all three Triumvirs, whilst his two colleagues fought overseas. Yet despite this attempt to modify the nature of the Republic, and despite all their combined wealth and influence, their control of Roman political life did not last beyond their year in office and was followed by political paralysis and then the total breakdown of republican government, as best exemplified by the symbolism of the Senate House burning as Clodius' funeral pyre.

Yet throughout this chaos the position of Pompeius became even stronger. The Roman defeat at Carrhae removed his long-time rival and associated network of patronage and allowed Pompeius to cement his dominant position in Rome. The murder of Clodius brought matters to a head and plunged the Republic into a crisis so grave that even Pompeius' opponents in the Senate felt they had no choice but to appoint a Dictator in all but name.

Thus, we can see a period of experimentation in the Republic, first with a Triumvirate of Rome's most powerful men and then with a sole figure to act as guardian of the Republic. The first experiment proved to be short lived, though one of the great 'what ifs' of history concerns the ramifications for the Republic of the victorious return of Crassus from the First Romano-Parthian War. Aside from such speculation, even Rome's most powerful men could not control Roman politics, once they had no formal office, a lesson which all who came after were to learn. The key aspect though would be the success of the second experiment in Republican government: the (temporary) appointment of one man to restore peace and act as guardian of the Republic, and what consequences that would bring.

Chapter Seven

The Rise and Fall of the 'Pompeian Republic' (52–49 BC)

1. The Principate of Pompeius (52 BC)

At the beginning of 52 BC, Cn. Pompeius Magnus found himself in a unique position: specially appointed as sole Consul of Rome (totally against the spirit of the Republican *mos maiorum*) by the Senate, backed by a *senatus consultum ultimum*, and with control over the bulk of Rome's western empire and the ability to raise troops in Italy. He was now truly the first man of the Republic, or *Princeps*, albeit temporarily. Before him lay the task of restoring peace and stability to a Republic wracked by political violence and bloodshed, a system which seemed to once again be on the brink of collapse; albeit a collapse he had helped to create.

Armed with this unprecedented power and backing, Pompeius set to work eliminating the key sources of the disorder, namely the individuals involved. Despite the power he had been granted, Pompeius was determined to be seen to be working within a legal framework, rather than using arbitrary power, especially given the weak legal powers of the *senatus consultum ultimum*. Furthermore, by choosing to work through the Senate, as its appointee, he would temporarily have its full support (however grudgingly). Thus, the Senate passed two decrees: the first tackling violence, with specific mention of the murder of Clodius, and the second on bribery. In both cases Pompeius introduced new shorter trials with harsher punishments and thus increased the effectiveness of the judicial process (despite having previously introduced laws in 59 BC altering the composition of juries to ensure a more compliant result):

> *For each law prescribed first the production of the witnesses, and then on the same day completion of the cases both for the prosecution and defence, with two hours granted for the accuser, three for the defendant.*[1]

Thus, Pompeius put a stop to the long drawn out trials lasting several days and curtailed the time for prosecution and defence speeches (which would have much annoyed Cicero). This also had the benefit of reducing the amount of time for disruption as well. Furthermore, the second law had an interesting aspect to it; namely that it was to be applied retrospectively, as far back as Pompeius' first Consulship (70 BC), thus covering the previous twenty years.

> *He brought forward a law, that any citizen who chose to do so might call for an account from anybody who had held office from the time of his own first Consulship to the present. This embraced a period of a little less than twenty years, during which Caesar also had been Consul.*[2]

This measure would have had both practical and symbolic aspects to it. Firstly, the timescale would cover the earlier activities of all the key current figures of the period, bringing them all within scope of this law. Secondly it publicly stated a clear link to his first Consulship when he (and a now dead colleague) 'restored' the Republic. The clear message here being that he had restored the Republic once and he would do so again. Furthermore, according to Dio, Pompeius also ensured that he had control of the juries in these trials: *He himself selected the entire list of names from which drawings for jurors must be made.*[3]

Naturally enough, despite Pompeius' power and remit, there was a Tribune (M. Caelius Rufus) willing to oppose these measures, and not surprisingly (given his role in the murder of Clodius) it was one who was an ally of Milo:

> *And when Caelius became too persistent in attacking these laws, Pompeius' fury reached the point where he declared that, if compelled he would defend the Republic by force of arms.*[4]

It seems though that Caelius took the hint and withdrew any Tribunician veto or threat of veto (*intercessio*) and the Senatorial decrees were passed into law. We can see that Pompeius backed up the rule of law with the threat of force, and many sources comment on the presence of armed troops in Rome; ostensibly to defend the Senate against the threat of

Milo, a point which Cicero makes in his famous, and ultimately doomed, defence of Milo:

> *If you are afraid of Milo, if you believe that he either now cherishes wicked designs against your life, or that he ever has entertained such; if the levying of troops throughout Italy, as some of your recruiting sergeants pretend, if these arms, if these cohorts in the Capitol, if these watchmen, these sentinels, if this picked body of youths, which is the guard of your person and your house, is all armed against an attack on the part of Milo; and if all these measures have been arranged, and prepared, and aimed against him alone, then certainly he must be a man of great power, of incredible courage; surely it must be more than the power and resources of one single man which are attributed to him, if the most eminent of our generals is invested with a command, and all Italy is armed against this one man.*[5]

Cicero's point is a clear one; namely that Pompeius' forces now guarded Rome; a guarantor that no further gang violence would break out, but also a guarantor that Pompeius' orders would be carried out. Thirty years earlier Rome had been ruled by Sulla, elected to the Dictatorship but holding power via his army. Now Pompeius (Sulla's protege) was holding power, but in a more nuanced manner chosen by the Senate to a sole Consulship and with troops on the street to enforce law and order. Thus, Pompeius' two weapons in his attempt to 'restore order' to Rome were judicial power backed up by armed force. Trials would be swift and would not be able to be disrupted by armed supporters of the men involved:

> *Moreover, although he presided over the suits for corruption and bribery, and introduced laws for the conduct of the trials, and in all other cases acted as arbiter with dignity and fairness, making the court-rooms safe, orderly, and quiet by his presence there with an armed force.*[6]
>
> *He passed his law, and straightway there ensued a great number and variety of prosecutions. In order that the jurors might act without fear Pompeius superintended them in person, and stationed soldiers around them.*[7]

Armed with these two weapons, Pompeius went on the offensive, and there followed a judicial blitz against nearly all the key men involved in the disruptions and violence of the last few months. The two most notable victims were two of the three men standing for the Consulship; T. Annius Milo, and P. Plautius Hypsaeus. Milo was naturally the most high-profile target: convicted by one of Pompeius' new courts for ordering the murder of Clodius, though he had not struck the blow himself.[8] For good measure he was indicted and convicted on a further two counts; once for bribery and another for further violent acts. Neither a defence speech from Cicero, nor his former association with Pompeius could save him. His property was confiscated, and he was sent into exile.[9] Following Milo, a number of other men were convicted, including Plautius Hypsaeus on a charge of bribery:

> *The first defendants convicted were absentees: Milo for the murder of Clodius; Gabinius both for violation of law and for impiety, because he had invaded Egypt without a decree of the Senate and contrary to the Sibylline books; Hypsaeus, Memmius, Sextius, and many others for taking bribes and for corrupting the populace. The People interceded for Scaurus, but Pompeius made proclamation that they should submit to the decision of the court. When the crowd again interrupted the accusers, Pompeius' soldiers made a charge and killed several. Then the People held their tongues and Scaurus was convicted. All the accused were banished, and Gabinius was fined in addition.[10]*

Pompeius' courts cleared from Rome almost everyone involved in the chaos of the last year, including his old lieutenant Milo, as well as Gabinius, both of whom were now surplus to his requirements. Alongside Milo and his supporters, a number of Clodius' supporters were convicted and exiled as well, such as Sex. Cloelius, who had instigated the moving of Clodius' body into the Senate House. It is interesting to note that all the convicted, even Milo, were exiled from Rome rather than executed, despite the *senatus consultum ultimum* having been passed. Each of the previous occasions the SCU had been passed had been followed by extra-judicial murders, as most recently seen in 63 BC Now, Pompeius was clearly keeping his hands clean of Roman blood and being seen to do so.

The obvious exception to this was the incident at Scaurus' trail where Pompeius' troops attacked the crowds, killing an unknown number. If anything, this merely emphasised the point that the law would be upheld, even with deadly force, and that the disruption which had marred trials and elections for the previous few years would not be tolerated in Pompeius' Rome. However, this did raise the point that even with the new law trials could only be upheld by military force, raising questions about the Republic's long-term stability once this crisis had passed.

Thus, Pompeius purged Rome of all the men involved in the previous years' violence and disorder. There were however two exceptions; one minor and one major. The minor exception was M. Saufeius, a friend of Milo who had actually led the attack on the tavern at Bovillae in which Clodius had been killed and who was probably a prime suspect for delivering the killing blow. He was obviously brought before a Pompeian court for his role in the murder but was defended again by Cicero and the Tribune Caelius. On this occasion he was acquitted by one vote. Brought to trial a few days later on a more general charge of violence, he was acquitted again, this time by a bigger margin; proving that juries, no matter what the encouragement, could never be relied upon to deliver the expected verdict.

The second figure was a far more important one: the third of the three men who were standing for the Consulship of 52 BC; Q. Caecilius Metellus Pius Scipio Nasica. Born P. Cornelius Scipio Nasica, he was the scion of one of Rome's most noble and Patrician families; the Cornelii Scipiones. He then united two of Rome's greatest families when he was adopted as the son and heir of Q. Caecilius Metellus Pius, the Consul of 80 BC (and close ally of Sulla) who had no surviving son. Although inter-family adoption was common amongst the Roman oligarchy, uniting Rome's leading Patrician and Plebeian families was unusual. Despite this heritage though he too had taken a full part in the bribery and violence that had dogged the elections for 52 BC, and under normal circumstances could have expected to be convicted under the Pompeian courts. Unlike both Milo and Plautius though, Metellus Scipio had two things that they did not; an impeccable Republican ancestry and a newly-widowed young (and attractive) daughter, Cornelia.

Pompeius had been single since the death of his fourth wife Iulia (Caesar's daughter) in 54 BC.[11] Clearly a man of his standing, who had always married for political gain, was on the lookout for a new bride and it is said that Caesar offered him another relative from the Iulian family; an offer he refused. Metellus Scipio's daughter, however, had distinct advantages, aside from her personal qualities. Not only was her father uniting two of Rome's greatest Republican families, but until the previous year she had been the wife of P. Licinius Crassus, the son of Pompeius' old ally/rival M. Licinius Crassus, who had died (before his father) during the Battle of Carrhae. Whilst Crassus had another surviving son, Marcus, who would inherit the family fortune, Pompeius could also tap into some of the supporters of the Crassan family, especially given Marcus' subsequent (and perhaps understandable) low profile in Roman politics. Thus, Pompeius married Cornelia, making Metellus Scipio, who was younger, his new father-in-law. When Metellus Scipio was charged under the new Pompeian laws for his role in the violence and bribery of the previous year, his new son-in-law came to the rescue:

> *When Scipio, his father-in-law, was put on trial, he* [Pompeius] *summoned the three hundred and sixty jurors to his house and solicited their support, and the prosecutor abandoned the case when he saw Scipio conducted from the Forum by the jurors.*[12]

Pompeius therefore used his position to defend his new father-in-law from prosecution and secured himself a firm alliance with two of Rome's most aristocratic families, whilst shocking nobody with his blatant double standards. Nevertheless, it is clear that, through his judicial purges, he had succeeded in restoring peace and stability to Rome. All of those involved in the chaos of the previous years were either dead, exiled, or allied to him and Rome now had a functioning and efficient judicial system (albeit backed up by Pompeius' forces). He had thus succeeded in his aims to restore peace and order to Rome and allow the Republic to function, albeit under his guidance.

Having achieved this short-term restoration of order, he turned his mind to longer-term reforms. Pompeius enacted two laws in this respect, neither original (both being re-statements of earlier laws):

Pompeius revived the law about elections that commanded those who seek an office to present themselves without fail before the Assembly, so that no one who was absent might be chosen; this law had somehow fallen into disuse. He also confirmed the decree, passed a short time previously, that those who had held office in the city should not be assigned to command abroad until five years had passed.[13]

Both measures were therefore aimed at separating the twin functions of the Roman magistrates, military and political. The first law meant that no one holding active imperium could stand for election, as they were prevented from crossing the Pomerium (the sacred boundary of Rome) whilst holding imperium and thus could not present themselves. This had occurred frequently in the past, and the most notable cases involved both Pompeius and Caesar themselves. Nevertheless, in theory this would stop military commanders from demanding elected office with the implicit threat of force. Unfortunately, such a law, without someone to enforce it, had not stopped either man in the past. The second law created a gap between the holding of a political office in Rome and the subsequent taking up of a military command, which had most prominently been an issue in 88 BC, when Sulla was denied the Mithridatic command and had retaliated by attacking his own city.

Naturally, though, these laws could be suspended, or exceptions could be granted by the Assembly, usually at the behest of a Tribune. Indeed, that is what immediately happened, as the Tribunes, apparently at Pompeius' behest, passed a law granting Pompeius' former colleague Caesar such an exemption, giving him the right to stand for election in absentia. In the short term this was of little use to Caesar, who was in the middle of a full-scale Gallic war with the chieftain Vercingetorix.

However, this grant seems to have been a concession to Caesar on Pompeius' behalf; a consolation prize if you will. Caesar was clearly falling further behind his Triumviral colleague due to his prolonged absence from Rome, during which time Pompeius had capitalised on the crisis and been placed in temporary charge of the Republic. Whilst this may have been diplomatic, it did show the ease with which these laws could be circumnavigated without someone to police them – as Dio rightly points out:

For he [Pompeius] *had amended the law to read that only those should be permitted to do it who were granted the privilege by name and without disguise; but this was no different from its not having been prohibited at all, for men who had any influence were certainly going to manage to get the right voted to them.*[14]

With these measures passed and the emergency which Rome faced now clearly over (at least in the short term), thoughts turned to selecting a colleague for Pompeius, his sole tenure having been an extraordinary one due to the nature of the crisis. Unsurprisingly Pompeius acquiesced in this (having passed the measures he wanted) and he would have seen the dangers in remaining sole Consul for too long; it being so obviously a breach of the Roman unwritten constitution and *mos maiorum*, leaving him open to accusations of tyranny, a lesson perhaps learnt from his former mentor (and father-in-law) Sulla.

Yet although in theory a consular colleague would be his equal, Pompeius clearly had no desire to brook a rival and so he was apparently allowed to nominate his own colleague. Unsurprisingly he nominated his new father-in-law, Q. Caecilius Metellus Pius Scipio Nasica, a man whose pursuit of the Consulship for this year had helped cause the very chaos that Pompeius was chosen to end, an irony surely lost on no-one. Thus Pompeius' sole Consulship ended, whilst allowing him to retain the dominant position in Rome.

Metellus Scipio used his Consulship to pass one reform (no doubt at the behest of Pompeius); namely overturning Clodius' law removing powers from the Censorship. Thus, the Censorship was restored its traditional powers of selecting and excluding Senatorial members and its role as guardian of the Senate; yet another potential check on members of the oligarchy. Pompeius himself (along with Crassus) had restored the Censorship once before (in 70 BC) and had immediately used it to his own benefit.

We can see therefore that Pompeius' and Metellus' reforms had a traditional feel about them, perhaps channelling Sulla's desire to restore the Republican constitution to an older version (and the myth of a golden age). The Censorship was restored and elections in absentia prevented (except in named cases). The only innovation was re-stating a recent law of a gap of five years between a political office and a military command. At their heart lay the desire to regulate the Roman oligarchy, in terms of stating the clear lines between the military and the political fields and their personal conduct. The fact that these reforms were introduced by one of Rome's most notorious breakers of established practice would have been lost on no-one and ultimately these reforms would have been as effective as those of Sulla. In other words, without someone (or a group) to enforce them, they were fairly empty gestures.

Perhaps with that in mind Pompeius looked to his own future when the Senate extended his Proconsular imperium in the two Spanish provinces for a further five years, along with one thousand talents a year from public funds to support him. Thus, Pompeius had control of half of the military forces of Rome's western empire; the other half was in Gaul with Caesar, who we should note did not receive a similar extension. Pompeius therefore would have military forces at his command (to match those of Caesar), whilst remaining in Rome. Furthermore, his command outlasted that of Caesar, who only had two more years (to 50 BC) as it stood. By contrast, Rome's eastern empire was in disarray, with Crassus' seven legions being destroyed at the Battle of Carrhae and the subsequent chaotic retreat from Mesopotamia. In fact, whilst these events were occurring in Rome, the Parthians had invaded the Roman province of Syria, albeit with a lesser force, but had been beaten back by Crassus' Quaestor, C. Cassius Longinus.

Thus, with his own future secured, Pompeius prepared to leave office, but again ensured that this time his loss of office would not mean a loss of control, as he oversaw the elections for the Consuls of the following year. These were the first peaceful elections in three years and unsurprisingly saw Pompeius' allies elected to office. The Consuls were Ser. Sulpicius Rufus and M. Claudius Marcellus who were both undistinguished, Sulpicius having been a Praetor as far back as 65 BC. In fact, the most distinguished man to run for the Consulship was none other than M. Porcius Cato himself, who failed to be elected. Whilst at first glance this may have seemed surprising – a distinguished man such as Cato being beaten by two non-entities – Cato as Consul would not have been as compliant for Pompeius as the other two. Cato, for all his oratory and brandished Republican credentials, had far less of a powerbase in

Rome than Pompeius. Appian goes too far when he describes Pompeius' control, yet the point is well made:

> *At the expiration of his term, however, although others were invested with the Consulship, he was none the less the supervisor, and ruler, and everything in Rome.*[15]

Even though he was no longer sole Consul, Pompeius was now once more '*primus inter pares*' or first amongst equals. Of all his political opponents of the last few years; Clodius was dead and Milo had been exiled, and both of their street gangs had been disbanded. Crassus lay dead in ignominy in the east, whilst Cato had been complicit in arranging for Pompeius' sole Consulship to 'save the Republic'. Only one rival remained and that was Caesar, who had been absent from Rome for six years at this point and was embroiled in a seemingly never-ending war in Gaul and whose command was due to expire shortly.

2. Waiting for Caesar (51–50 BC)

Even though the immediate crisis had passed, judicial purges continued the following year, the most notable casualties being the two prominent Clodian-supporting former Tribunes, T. Munatius Plancus Byrsa and Q. Pompeius Rufus (the latter being a grandson of Sulla). No sooner had both men left office than they were charged before Pompeius' special courts for violence (their involvement in the riots which had burnt down the Senate House) and exiled. The conviction of Munatius actually came despite Pompeius' efforts to defend him, with Cato being on the jury that convicted him. In many ways this was unfinished business as both men had been prominent in the violent Clodian backlash in Rome, but neither could be prosecuted during 52 BC as they held the Tribunate. These prosecutions also sent a message to the Tribunes, that these new courts could also be used to hold them to account once their year in office had expired.

With peace restored in Rome, the main political topic for the year was the issue of Caesar and his Gallic command. In 55 BC Pompeius and Crassus (as Consuls) had passed a motion which stated that no successor to Caesar could be appointed for five years; a timescale which was swiftly approaching. Although Caesar had achieved a great deal, with the defeat of numerous Gallic tribes west of the Rhine, the whole campaign had suffered from repeated rebellions, such as that of Vercingetorix, and from being drawn further into mainland Europe, as can be seen from his campaigns against the Britons and Germans. Thus, despite all his victories, the outcome of the war was far from certain and his political position was becoming precarious.

The last time Caesar had needed to extend his command had been in 56 BC and he had been able to call upon his rivals/allies Pompeius and Crassus, who had drawn together in a fresh alliance to allow the three men to dominate the Republic. However, much had changed in the last five years; Crassus lay dead in Mesopotamia, with his head being used as a dramatic prop in the Parthian court, and Pompeius was in the ascendancy in Rome and needed no ally. Naturally, Pompeius was scrupulous in his public utterances about being fair to Caesar. Yet whilst he had granted Caesar the right to stand for election in absentia he had noticeably not included him in the extension of his own commands by a further five years. Thus, Caesar could expect no help from that quarter and was paying the price for his prolonged absence in Gaul.

It was not long before the first political assault came on his position and it was led by the Consul Marcellus, a convenient stalking horse for Pompeius:

> *Marcellus at once directed all his efforts towards compassing the downfall of Caesar, inasmuch as he was of Pompeius' supporters; among the many measures against him that he proposed was one to the effect that a successor to him should be sent out even before the appointed time. He was resisted by Sulpicius and some of the Tribunes; the latter acted out of good-will toward Caesar, and Sulpicius made common cause with them and with the multitude, because he did not like the idea of a magistrate who had done no wrong being removed in the middle of his term.*[16]

Thus, Marcellus' proposals came to nothing, blocked by his consular colleague and at least four of the Tribunes. Cicero's letters record the motions presented in the Senate and that Tribunician vetoes were used on at least three separate motions; four Tribunes at first and then two Tribunes on the second and third motions.[17] Thus Marcellus' proposals were blocked, and Caesar's command was not curtailed, but nor was it extended. Once again Pompeius used the opportunity to demonstrate his even-handedness, but again his lack of actions spoke louder than any words; Caesar was being outmanoeuvred, whilst Pompeius was playing a waiting game. Dio summed it up thus:

> *Now when he heard how things were going, he pretended that the plan of having Caesar relieved of his command did not please him, either, but he arranged matters so that when Caesar should have served out the time allowed him, an event not of the distant future, but due to occur the very next year, he should lay down his arms and return home to private life.[18]*

It is also worth noting that the violence which had marred the previous years of Roman political clashes was absent from these. Consuls opposed each other in the Senate, Tribunician vetoes were used and respected. Thus Pompeius' interventions the previous year appeared to have paid off and the Republic, albeit under his watchful eye, returned to a peaceful political cut-and-thrust, though whether this was due to the threat of the new and efficient courts or to Pompeius and his now demobilised forces in Italy was another matter. Pompeius also made a very public display of leaving the city, but not going too far:

> *Pompeius had set out from the city as if he were going to make an expedition into Spain, but he did not even at this time leave the bounds of Italy; instead, he assigned the entire business in Spain to his legates and himself kept close watch on the city.[19]*

Thus, the Republic now had an individual in the role that perhaps Sulla had intended to play, until ill health cut him short; an unofficial arbiter, or guarantor, of Republican peace, not directly holding office but keeping a high enough profile and armed with enough military power to ensure that everyone else in Rome kept to peaceful political activity. Therefore, under Pompeius' watchful eye, the Republic experienced its first peaceful year in nearly a decade.

The elections for the following year were held and again passed peacefully. Again, we must assume that both successful consular candidates were agreeable to Pompeius: L. Aemilius Lepidus Paullus and C. Claudius Marcellus (a kinsman of the outgoing Consul).

> *It was in pursuance of this object that he caused Caius Marcellus, a cousin of Marcus, or a brother (both traditions are current), to obtain the Consulship, because, although allied to Caesar by marriage, he was hostile to him; and he caused Caius Curio, who was also an old-time foe of his rival, to become Tribune.*[20]
>
> *For this reason, the bitterest enemies of Caesar were chosen Consuls for the ensuing year: Aemilius Paullus and Claudius Marcellus, cousin of the Marcellus before mentioned. Curio, who was also a bitter enemy of Caesar, but extremely popular with the masses and a most accomplished speaker, was chosen Tribune. Caesar was not able to influence Claudius with money, but he bought the neutrality of Paullus for 1500 talents and the assistance of Curio with a still larger sum, because he knew that the latter was heavily burdened with debt.*[21]

As the year drew to a close, Rome received better news from the provinces. In the west Caesar had been victorious against the Gallic tribes and Gaul was seemingly pacified and under Roman control. In the east, the Parthians had invaded Roman Syria in force, intent on exploiting the destruction of Rome's eastern legions at Carrhae and annexing Syria to their empire, but had been defeated by C. Cassius Longinus, leading the remnants of Crassus' seven legions.

In many ways the politics of the year 50 BC saw a full return to normalised Republican political life, albeit without the bloodshed and disorder. Of the two Consuls, Marcellus continued his kinsman's policy of attacking Caesar's Gallic command and met with an equal lack of success:

> *Marcellus had brought before the Senate prematurely, and in violation of a law of Pompeius and Crassus, a motion touching the provinces of Caesar. Opinions were expressed, and when Marcellus, who coveted for himself any position to be secured from the feeling against Caesar, tried to divide the House, a crowded Senate passed over in support of the general negative.*[22]

Thus, we can see that although Pompeius (via his agents) kept probing at this issue, Caesar was still covered by the Triumviral law of 55 BC (banning any successor for the Gallic command for five years) so was secure in his tenure; but not beyond it. It seems that the accusations that Aemilius Lepidus took Caesar's money were well founded, as he continued throughout the year to advocate Caesar's cause and oppose his colleague, though not in an aggressive manner.

If anything, the Consuls passed a quiet year in office, but attention soon turned once more to the Tribunate and C. Scribonius Curio. The Tribunes had had a relatively quiet few years since the Tribunates of Clodius and Milo, but Curio clearly had a desire to turn the clock back and introduced a range of proposed reforms (both domestic and foreign), many of which had echoes of the more famous Tribunician proposals of past generations. We have few details for any of them and most are only known from passing references, mostly by Cicero. In terms of domestic reforms, there seems to have been a proposal for an agrarian law in Campania, a grain law connected to the Aediles, a law taxing luxurious travelling, a law on road construction (with himself as a special commissioner), and a law to recall C. Memmius from exile. In terms of foreign affairs, he seems to have proposed the annexation of the allied African kingdom of Numidia. Certainly, none of these proposals seem to have caused a major stir in Rome and few became law. Yet it is an indication that Roman politics was returning to normal, with the Tribunate once again being the primary source of legislation.

One area that Curio had a greater impact upon was the issue of Caesar's Gallic command, whose expiration date was fast approaching. In many ways, Caesar's position was actually improving, in so much that Gaul finally appeared to have been pacified after nearly a decade of fighting. This meant that he did not need a further extension of his command to finish the conquest. Thus, under normal circumstances, the expiry date of Caesar's Gallic command should not have been an issue. He could have returned to Rome, having conquered Gaul, an unprecedented achievement in such a short space of time (especially compared with the centuries-long annexation of Spain), celebrated a Triumph and tried to convert this military glory into political power. Furthermore, he would return to Rome as a major figure in his own right, as opposed to being an agent of Pompeius and Crassus; the position he had held during his first Consulship in 59 BC.

Yet, we can question just what Caesar had to look forward to, when the adulation of his Triumph had died down? For Caesar, another Consulship would have been an anti-climax, as would the Censorship and indeed retirement into private life. The obvious solution would have been another important military command, with the continuation of the First Romano-Parthian War being an obvious choice. However again we must question whether Caesar would have had enough power in Rome to secure such a command if Pompeius chose to oppose him. Regardless of the future, a Roman commander, even one with a victorious conquest behind him, would have been expected to lay down his command and return to Rome, much as Pompeius himself had done in 62 BC, and return to the political fray.

Yet, it is clear that Caesar's role was far from a normal one; not only had he been given ten years in command of the Roman conquest of Gaul, but his political position had been elevated beyond that of a normal general by his participation in the Triumvirate. Whilst he held no new political position (unlike his two colleagues) he had clearly been a part of the group determined to oversee the Republic. Crassus' untimely (and undignified) death in 53 BC had reduced that ruling cabal to two. Unfortunately for Caesar, his magnificent Gallic conquest had been overshadowed by the rise of Pompeius, from Triumvir to Princeps. The removal of Crassus had left Pompeius with no serious rival in Rome, a position he cemented with the judicial exiling of any remaining threats to his position. Thus Pompeius' rise had overshadowed Caesar politically and left him isolated in terms of more than just geography.

Unless Pompeius agreed to a new alliance; perhaps backing Caesar's bid to take over command of the Parthian War, his only real bargaining chip was the command of his legions. Once he gave this up and returned to the political fray as a private individual, he would have to either come to an accommodation with Pompeius, retire, or fight him politically. Under normal circumstances any other general would have accepted this, as Pompeius had himself in 62 BC. Yet the formation of the Triumvirate in 56 BC had elevated all three men to a higher position in the state, in practice if not in theory, both in his own eyes and in the eyes of many in the Senate and the People. This, coupled with his unprecedented military success in Gaul, would have given him an elevated sense of entitlement and an unwillingness to return to being just a 'backbench' Senator. Thus, we can see the dangers of Rome's leading men elevating themselves above their contemporaries.

3. Escalation and the Elevation of Pompeius

With this in mind Caesar opened negotiations about his future, having no opportunity, or probably desire, to remain in Gaul. The first tactic was to bargain for a new Consulship:

> *So, he directed his friends to make an agreement in his behalf, that he should deliver up all his provinces and soldiers, except that he should retain two legions and Illyria with Cisalpine Gaul until he should be elected Consul. This was satisfactory to Pompeius, but the Consuls refused.*[23]

Thus, Caesar would give up the bulk of his forces but retain a military command until he could arrange for his election as Consul (with Pompeius' tacit approval) and then most likely a further command. The idea that the two Consuls, neither of whom had much of a powerbase themselves, could have prevented Pompeius' and Caesar's combined political might does not bear entertaining and so we must look to Pompeius for not supporting this proposal.

This was followed by a compromised proposal from the Tribune Curio; namely that both Pompeius and Caesar should lay down their commands simultaneously. In many ways this was cunning politics. With Pompeius having opposed a proposal that both men have parity in terms of holding military commands, Caesar was proposing the opposite; that neither man hold a military command and thus together be reduced in status. Thus, he widened the issue from being about his command to being about Pompeius' command also (which still had several years to run). Furthermore, this proposal would have appealed to Pompeius' many enemies in the Senate and offered them the opportunity to reduce Pompeius' power and his grip on the Republic. However, the language that Caesar used (if we are to believe the surviving sources) saw a dangerous escalation:

> *A proposal that he would lay down his command at the same time with Pompeius, but that if Pompeius should retain his command he would not lay down his own but would come quickly and avenge his country's wrongs and his own.*[24]

Thus, Caesar gave a voice to the fear that many must have been harbouring; namely that this political dispute between Caesar and Pompeius would escalate into another civil war. Thus, we can see that the Triumvirate had come full circle: being formed by Rome's most powerful men to stabilise the Republic, but now threatening to tear it apart. Yet Caesar was in effect doing nothing more than using Pompeius' own weapons against him, namely threatening to use his army to gain political leverage, as Pompeius had himself done on three occasions (81, 77 and 71 BC).

Thus, Pompeius found himself politically outmanoeuvred, having gone from blocking any extension to Caesars' command to having the prospect of his own being taken away and both men being reduced once more to the status of private citizen, thus evening the field out for Caesar. Perhaps surprisingly given Pompeius' political power, the Senate voted overwhelmingly to back Curio's (Caesar's) proposal:

> *Then Curio put the question whether both should lay down their commands, and 22 Senators voted in the negative while 370 went back to the opinion of Curio in order to avoid civil discord.*[25]

This should have been the signal for the two men to negotiate a new settlement; a formation of a new Duumvirate, with Caesar being allowed to keep his command until his election to Consul, followed by another prestigious military command (against the Parthians). In return Pompeius would undoubtedly keep his Spanish command and happily wave Caesar off to the east hoping that he met a similar fate to Crassus. Throughout his career Pompeius had always chosen political compromise over confrontation; most famously in 71/70 BC with Crassus, bringing an end to the First Civil War. Yet on this occasion it was not to be the case and thus the inherent weakness of the new Republican system was shown; dependent upon the personalities of the strongest of the oligarchs.

Whilst we will never know Pompeius' mind; the situation in the late-50s had seen the pinnacle of his political career; selected by the Senate for a sole Consulship and ordered to save the state from ruin, which he had done. He had now established a quiet dominance over the Republic (which he had helped shape since its reconstruction in 70 BC) and was now unofficial Princeps of the Republic. Yet having achieved this position he was now being forced to compromise with a man who was not an equal (or contemporary, like Crassus) but had until recently been a clear political inferior and a former agent.

Thus, despite the Senate's vote (which had no legal force), it seems that Pompeius went on the offensive and attacked the man (Curio), not the proposal. We should not be surprised to read that one of the Censors, Ap. Claudius Pulcher, proposed that Curio be expelled from the Senate (though he would retain his Tribunate). When this move was blocked by his colleague (L. Calpurnius Piso Caesoninus) he then attacked Piso in the Senate, but this came to naught. With the attacks coming to nothing, Pompeius seems to have switched to his favourite tactic: escalate the tension in Rome until it presented him with another opportunity to 'save' the Republic and thus we hear of rumours being spread that Caesar had already invaded Italy.

Suddenly a false rumour came that Caesar had crossed the Alps and was marching on the city, whereupon there was a great tumult and consternation on all sides. Claudius moved that the army at Capua be turned against Caesar as a public enemy. When Curio opposed him on the ground that the rumour was false he exclaimed, 'If I am prevented by the vote of the Senate from taking steps for the public safety, I will take such steps on my own responsibility as Consul.' After saying this he darted out of the Senate and proceeded to the environs with his colleague, where he presented a sword to Pompeius, and said, 'I and my colleague command you to march against Caesar in behalf of your country, and we give you for this purpose the army now at Capua, or in any other part of Italy, and whatever additional forces you yourself choose to levy.'[26]

And rushing out of the Senate, he [Marcellus] came to Pompeius, who was in the suburbs, and on his own responsibility, without the formality of a vote, entrusted him with the protection of the city and likewise with two legions of citizens.[27]

These legions, therefore, were apparently made ready to be sent against the Parthians, but when there proved to be no need of them, there being really no use to which they could be put, Marcellus, fearing that they might be restored to Caesar, at first declared that they must remain in Italy, and then, as I have said, gave them into Pompeius' charge.[28]

Though this Consular endorsement did not have the same force as the *senatus consultum ultimum*, for Pompeius it was a step in the right direction and he could again claim to be lawfully defending the Republic. With the crisis escalating, both sides turned to the elections for the next year, which would be a crucial battleground. Pompeius it seems was able to secure both Consuls, who even before they had entered office confirmed Marcellus' arrangements:

Accordingly, he won over to Pompeius's side Cornelius Lentulus and Caius Claudius, who were to hold the Consulship the next year, and caused them to issue the same commands. For since magistrates elect were still allowed to issue proclamations and to perform some other functions pertaining to their office even before they entered upon it, they believed that they had authority also in this matter. And Pompeius, although he was very scrupulous in all other matters, nevertheless on account of his need of soldiers did not either enquire at all from what sources he was getting them, or in what way, but accepted them very gratefully.[29]

Caesar it seems was able to secure at least two of the Tribunes for the following year; M. Antonius and Q. Cassius Longinus.[30] Thus, the year ended with a heightened state of tension and the threat of a new civil war.

4. Escalation and the Eclipse of Pompeius (49 BC)

As it was, events soon spiralled out of control. As soon as the new Consuls had taken office, C. Scribonius Curio, who had left Rome upon the end of his Tribunate, returned with a letter to the Senate from Caesar himself. The letter was delivered to the Consuls, who were compelled by two Tribunes (Antonius and Cassius) to read it to the Senate:

As to the letter, it contained a list of all the benefits which Caesar had ever conferred upon the state and a defence of the charges which were brought against him. He promised to disband his legions and give up his office if Pompeius would also do the same; for while the latter bore arms it was not right, he claimed, that he should be compelled to give up his and so be exposed to his enemies. The vote on this proposition was not taken individually, lest the Senators through some sense of shame or fear should vote contrary to their true opinions; but it was done by their taking their stand on this or on that side of the Senate chamber. No one voted that Pompeius should give up his arms, since he had his troops in the suburbs; but all, except one Marcus Caelius and Curio, who had brought his letter, voted that Caesar must do so.[31]

On the face of it, Caesar was offering to disband his troops, but again not until Pompeius did likewise. Yet constitutionally, Pompeius held a legitimate command, whilst Caesar's was close to expiring and was here treating all of Rome's military forces as though they were the property of the two oligarchs, rather than forces of the Republic. Here we can see the legacy of the decision taken in 56 BC by the Triumvirs to carve up Rome's military forces between them. Here was a Roman commander bargaining to keep his forces to protect him from his 'enemies', despite the fact that Pompeius had given no indication of a threat to Caesar himself, nor would he have done so.

Thus, Caesar's own inflated sense of importance came before the stability of the Republic. Certainly, he had been outmanoeuvred politically, but he was at the height of his career, had led a ten-year conquest of Gaul and could look to a glorious Triumph on his return and the accompanying adulation of the People. Granted, he would have had to return to the rough and tumble of Roman politics, as all generals did on their return, including both Marius and Pompeius himself. Although Pompeius temporarily held a greater position, as recent history had shown, this could have been fleeting had Caesar chosen to contest him in the political arena.

The presence of Pompeius' troops in the environs of Rome, on the dubious authorisation of the outgoing and incoming Consuls, clearly ensured that the Senate and Assembly would vote the way he wanted them to. Clearly Pompeius had chosen to leave behind a lifetime of political compromise and force Caesar to make a choice; back down and leave Pompeius with the upper hand, or risk rebellion and an attempted civil war in which he would be declared an 'enemy of the Republic'. Thus, we can see that both men contributed to the collapse which followed, Caesar for refusing to disband his forces and Pompeius for not offering him a compromise or face-saving way out.

Naturally the Tribunes Antonius and Cassius attempted to veto this decision but were expelled from the Senate House by the Consul Cornelius Lentulus. They then took the highly unusual decision to leave the city (breaking one of the clear oaths of the office), along with Curio and went to join Caesar. It is not known if Suffect Tribunes were elected to replace them. With this obstacle removed and in the presence of Pompeius' forces, the Senate reconvened outside the sacred Pomerium and went a stage further. The *senatus consultum ultimum* was passed, for the second time in three years, and the Consuls and other magistrates, including Pompeius, were charged with defending the security of the Republic.[32] Furthermore, Caesar was given a specific ultimatum to disband his army or be declared an enemy of the state.

Thus, Pompeius got what he wanted, and for the second time in three years he was being asked to defend the Republic. Furthermore, Pompeius was given command of Italy, ordered to raise an army, and provided with all the funds he needed:

> *But the Senate, thinking that Caesar's army would be slow in arriving from Gaul and that he would not rush into so great an adventure with a small force, directed Pompeius to assemble 130,000 Italian soldiers, chiefly veterans who had had experience in war, and to recruit as many able-bodied men as possible from the neighbouring provinces. They voted him for the war all the money in the public treasury at once, and their own private fortunes in addition if they should be needed for the pay of the soldiers. With the fury of party rage, they levied additional contributions on the allied cities, which they collected with the greatest possible haste.[33]*

Once again, the Republic turned to Pompeius as its protector, confirming his unofficial position as the Princeps of the Republic. However, it was from this lofty height that Pompeius soon fell to earth with a speed which no one, least of all himself, could have anticipated. Despite the passing of *senatus consultum ultimum*, it must be pointed out that Caesar had not yet been named as an enemy of the Republic, merely that he would be if he did not disband his army. He had as yet committed no infringement of Roman law and still had allies in the Senate, the magistrates and amongst the People.

Thus, Caesar still had the option to defuse the situation and even take some of the credit for ensuring a peaceful resolution to this crisis. What he did next took everyone by surprise. Not only did he not disband his forces, but with only a relatively small force he invaded Italy itself, crossing the river Rubicon (the boundary between his province of Cisalpine Gaul and Italy itself), thus triggering the Third Civil War.[34]

Here we can see that what Caesar lacked in political acumen, he more than made up for in military tactics. Had he allowed Pompeius time to raise his army in Italy and draw reinforcements from Rome's empire (notably Spain and Africa) then his position would have been a weak one; caught between Pompeius' armies in Spain and in Italy. Yet Pompeius had not yet had the time to draw this Italian army together and there were relatively few forces between Caesar and Rome itself. By seizing the initiative he had put his enemies on the back foot at the risk of declaring himself to be an 'enemy of the Republic'. Pompeius immediately saw the danger and that he had been outmanoeuvred and attempted to buy time:

Pompeius, because of what was told to him about Caesar and because he had not yet prepared a force sufficient to cope with him, changed his plans; for he saw that the people in the city, in fact the very members of his party, even more than the rest, shrank from the war through remembrance of the deeds of Marius and Sulla and wished to be delivered from it. Therefore, he sent to Caesar, as envoys, Lucius Iulius Caesar, a relative of his, and Lucius Roscius, a Praetor, both of whom volunteered for the service, to see if he could avoid his attack in some way and then reach an agreement with him on reasonable terms.[35]

With Caesar reiterating that both he and Pompeius should disband their armies and become private citizens, it was Pompeius' turn to face a dilemma. He could accede to Caesar's demands and ensure there was no civil war, but lose his dominant position in the Republic, or he could fight another civil war, but from a weakened position. The key factor here was Rome itself. As the First Civil War had shown, possession of Rome was a key factor in any conflict, not from a military position, it not being very defensible, but from a political one. Whoever controlled Rome, controlled the Senate and the Assembly and thus became the voice of the Roman Republic. Whoever had control of Rome could cloak themselves in constitutional power and declare their enemies to be those of the whole Republic and its empire. They could issue legitimate commands to Rome's territories and allies and draw upon the full religious and ceremonial power of Rome.

Thus, Pompeius' calculation was a simple one: could his forces block Caesar's approach to Rome and if they couldn't, could he hold Rome? As the First Civil War had seen, Rome was easily captured in 88 and 82 BC and fell in 87 to a very bloody siege. As events unfolded, however, the resistance Caesar faced soon crumbled and in fact defected to his cause. Thus, Pompeius and his allies in the Senate gambled that they could fight Caesar more effectively outside of Italy and gain the time they needed to assemble their own forces. Therefore, Pompeius and his allies, including the two Consuls, Cato, Metellus Scipio, Faustus Sulla and L. Iulius Caesar, all quit Rome, with the majority of them heading to Greece. Thus, Caesar had his first prize, Rome itself, having fought no more than a few skirmishes.

On reaching Rome he summoned what remained of the Senate to meet outside the Pomerium and issued assurances to the People that there would be no tyranny or bloodshed; an easy promise to make in the short term given that his declared enemies had already left the city. This however did not stop him from seizing the Treasury, which he did in spite of the opposition of one of the Tribunes (L. Caecilius Metellus) whom he threatened to kill. He did this despite his later assertion that one of his motivations in invading Italy had been to uphold the power and dignity of the Tribunes (namely M. Antonius and Q. Cassius Longinus).[36]

Given the state of chaos which the Republic was in, and the fact that he had not yet secured military control of Italy, Caesar did not stay long in Rome. Furthermore, he himself held no power in Rome, only possessing a Proconsular provincial command. To resolve this problem, he turned to his remaining allies who held office. The most senior of these was M. Aemilius Lepidus; son of the Consul Lepidus who had attacked Rome itself during the First Civil War and who had been defeated by Pompeius (77 BC). Lepidus was one of the Praetors this year, but with the two Consuls having fled, they now became the senior magistrates in Rome. We do not know how many of his colleagues remained in the city, but we must suppose that a number had retreated along with the Consuls and Pompeius. Thus, Caesar informally appointed him to rule Rome in his absence, no doubt backed up by a body of troops outside the city.

Caesar had two more allies holding office this year: the Tribunes M. Antonius and Q. Cassius Longinus. They returned to Rome to resume their role as Tribunes of the People. It is not known if they had been replaced when they left the city to join Caesar or were formally stripped of their Tribunates, but it is most likely that there had not been time to do either. Yet both men were to receive unique additional powers as Caesar gave each man a military command, on top of his Tribunician powers. Cicero refers to this as *tribunis plebis pro praetore*, or Praetorian Tribunes. Both men then left Rome (again), in command of military forces; Cassius going to Spain and Antonius remaining within Italy. We are not told how this was achieved, the Tribunate having the restriction of its powers not being valid beyond the sacred boundary of Rome (the Pomerium) and Tribunes themselves not being able to spend the night outside of Rome. There may well not have been any constitutional niceties observed here, merely Caesar combining both roles (Tribune and military leader) in two of his closest allies. Nevertheless, Caesar had set a precedent for combining Tribunician powers with military commands.

Thus, with his allies holding the Praetorship and the Tribunate, and all of his declared opponents having evacuated Rome, Caesar had a secure grip on the remnants of the Senate and the Assembly, no doubt backed up by a body of troops outside the city. With Rome itself secure politically, Caesar then left Italy to head to Gaul and then Spain to try and counter the expected Pompeian thrust from Spain. Here again Caesar's swiftness appears to have caught his opponents off balance, and, despite Pompeius' legates (L. Afranius and M. Petreius) having ruled Spain for over five years, he was able to defeat them and he appointed Q. Cassius Longinus as his Governor in the Spanish provinces. He then returned to Italy, via a siege of Massilia.

Having secured military control of the bulk of Rome's western empire (Spain, Gaul, Italy and Sicily, though not Africa), Caesar returned to Rome just before the end of the year to secure his political position. Despite this military success his political position was a precarious one, as his only constitutional power came from his Proconsular command in Gaul, power which he had clearly exceeded. Thus, Caesar secured himself an appointment as Dictator, the emergency position held in times of crisis. It is interesting that the surviving sources vary on whether he was appointed by law, the Senate or simply by decree, obviously reflecting the competing traditions in Roman historiography depending on their pro or anti-Caesarian stance.[37] Both Cicero, and later Dio, state that it was contrary to custom (but not illegal in itself) that a Praetor should propose the appointment of a Dictator as opposed to an Interrex (the method Sulla had used).[38] Regardless of the method of appointment, Caesar now held the supreme office in Rome (albeit temporarily, the Dictatorship being limited to six months under normal circumstances).

It is interesting to contrast Caesar's and Pompeius' stance on the office of Dictator. Traditionally, the office was an emergency one, which bestowed supreme power on one individual, but only for up to six months to deal with a crisis. However, the office had fallen out of usage, the last traditional one being held in 202 BC during the latter stages of the Second Punic War. Yet the office had been revived under Sulla, who abandoned the six-month limit to hold it as long as the 'crisis' continued (as defined by him). Though he did indeed step down, the office had been contaminated with the taint of tyranny and the bloodshed of Sulla's tenure. Certainly, during the crisis of the late 50s BC, whenever someone had suggested Pompeius hold the office, the idea was comprehensively rejected and Pompeius and the Senate opted for a sole Consulship for the duration of the crisis.[39] Caesar however immediately opted for this choice, despite the Sullan associations, though he too seemingly only held it for less than six months.

Summary

Thus, the year 49 BC saw a startling change in the balance of Roman politics. The year had started with Rome securely under the grip of Pompeius, and Caesar on the back foot in Gaul. It ended with Rome securely under the grip of Caesar and Pompeius on the back foot in Greece. The year ably demonstrates the two facets of Roman society – warfare and politics. Pompeius had the upper hand politically, but Caesar chose to counter this by a military thrust at Rome itself, which was achieved so swiftly that Rome fell without a shot fired; one of the most successful gambles in military history. After three years effectively in charge of the Republic, Pompeius now found himself as an exile in Greece and no longer the voice of the Republic.

Yet as well as showing us just how quickly fortunes could change, these few years show us the fragility of the New Republic. Under Pompeius' 'guidance' the Republic was brought out of the chaos of political violence and bloodshed and restored to some semblance of stability. Yet a dispute between its two most powerful oligarchs, ostensibly over the tenure of military commands, shattered this stability and plunged the Republic into its third civil war in forty years (91–70 BC and 63–62 BC – see Appendix Three). As we have seen, the timing of the war was strictly down to the two participants and their refusal to co-operate (unlike 70 BC). Yet Caesar's soldiers found nothing untoward about marching on their own city to fight his political opponents. Roman armies had become used to fighting political opponents as well as imperial wars and were well aware of the rewards such a campaign could bring. All that was needed was to cloak the whole campaign in the rhetoric of saving the Republic and restoring peace and stability.

Thus, we have the whole twenty years between 70 and 49 BC encapsulated in two decisions. In 70 BC Pompeius and Crassus chose to co-operate rather than fight. In 49 BC Pompeius and Caesar chose to fight rather than co-operate. Thus, was laid bare the fundamental weakness of the Republican system: that peace and stability relied upon the decisions of such men.

Part IV

The Fall of the New Republic (49–30 BC)

Chapter Eight

A New Model: The Rise and Fall of the Caesarian Republic (49–44 BC)

1. The Iulian Reform Programme (49 BC)

As it turns out, Caesar held the Dictatorship for just eleven days, passing a raft of measures which secured not only his immediate political position, but also contained a number of longer-term measures. Thus, Caesar used his temporary ascendancy in Rome to pass measures which mapped out his longer-term vision for how the Republic should be run, and thus took his first steps to assuming the mantle of Princeps which had been vacated (at least in Rome) by Pompeius. Key to securing his short term political position was the appointment of provincial governors and his oversight of the elections for 48 BC. This gave him the power not only to place his lieutenants formally in control of the provinces he controlled militarily (Spain, Gaul, Italy, Sicily and Sardinia), but to make formal appointments to the provinces under the control of Pompeius and thus de-legitimise the existing governors. This did not automatically bring them under his control, but did go some way to undermining them, especially in the eyes of the provincials and Roman allies. Thus, if Rome's allies fought for Pompeius, they now fought against the legitimate Roman appointments.

Yet whilst this measure formalised his control of the western provinces, the most important issue was to secure his own position and to do this he chose the expedient method of ensuring his own election to a Consulship (for 48 BC), with the bonus that this was within the constitution, it being more than ten years since his first Consulship (in 59 BC). As his fellow Consul he ensured the election of a pliant colleague (P. Servilius Isauricus). We must also assume that he secured the election of his allies to the Praetorship and Tribunate, though no Tribune for 48 BC can be securely attested (see Appendix Two).

Yet with his constitutional position secure and political and military control of the bulk of Rome's western empire, Caesar went a stage further and passed a series of popular reforms on debt reduction, corn distribution, and the return of exiles – familiar topics for Tribunician legislation. Thus, the People received a distribution of corn at the state's expense, and the burden of debt was eased, measures that brought immediate benefit to the mass of the populace:

> *When he was asked to decree an abolition of debts, on the ground that the wars and seditions had caused a fall of prices, he refused it, but appointed appraisers of saleable goods which debtors might give to their creditors instead of money.*[1]

Furthermore, he overturned the results of Pompeius' judicial purge brought about by the reformed court system (see Chapter Seven), allowing all those exiled by Pompeius' courts to return to Rome, with the notable exception of Milo himself. This last measure ensured that Caesar did not stir up trouble in Rome by pardoning Clodius' murderer or leave a dangerous opponent behind him in Rome. Thus far all his measures had been short-term ones brought about by circumstances. Yet Caesar also used this power to bring about one of his longer-term goals:

> *So, having been made Dictator by the Senate, he brought home exiles, restored to civic rights the children of those who had suffered in the time of Sulla.*[2]

Thus, after thirty years, Caesar overturned one of the most enduring legacies of the Sullan regime and restored full citizenship to the descendants of those men proscribed by Sulla in his purges.[3] Here Caesar achieved three things. Firstly, in the short term he would gain the support of these men and their families. Secondly, he was attempting to draw a clear distinction between his Dictatorship and the last one (Sulla). Thirdly, he was restating his association with the Marian cause (he being Marius' nephew by marriage and heir) and in some ways drawing parallels between this Third Civil War and the first one. If he was Marius (glossing over the Sack of Rome in 87 BC), then Pompeius was clearly Sulla (his former father-in-law).

We can see that Caesar accomplished much with his eleven-day Dictatorship, but continued in his policy of acting swiftly by leaving Rome before the new year had started in order to pursue the civil war with Pompeius and his allies. Whilst his policy of attacking his enemies before they were fully prepared had worked in Italy, Spain, and Sicily (which had been taken from Cato, who retreated without a fight), elsewhere he was not so fortunate, and he suffered two defeats. The most serious defeat was that of Caesar's commander in North Africa (C. Scribonius Curio), who was defeated and killed in battle, along with the loss of two legions, by the Numidian King Juba, who was allied to Pompeius. A lesser defeat occurred in Illyria when C. Antonius (one of three brothers fighting for Caesar) was also defeated by Pompeian forces.

Consequently, although Caesar had control of Rome and the western provinces, those to the south and the east lay firmly in the grip of Pompeius and the exiled Senate, again mirroring the east/west split of the First Civil War. Furthermore, as Dio points out, once again Rome had two governments (or two Republics as it were): Caesar's in Rome and Pompeius' in the east.

The ensuing year the Romans had two sets of magistrates, contrary to custom, and a mighty battle was fought. The People of the city had chosen as Consuls Caesar and Publius Servius [Servilius], along with Praetors and all the other officers required by law. Those in Thessalonica had made no such appointments, although they had by some accounts about two hundred of the Senate and also the Consuls with them and had appropriated a small piece of land for the auguries, in order that these might seem to take place under some form of law, so that they regarded the People and the whole city as present there. They had not appointed new magistrates for the reason that the Consuls had not proposed the lex curiata; but instead they employed the same officials as before, merely changing their names and calling some Proconsuls, others Propraetors, and others Proquaestors. For they were very careful about precedents, even though they had taken up arms against their country and abandoned it, and they were anxious that the acts rendered necessary by the exigencies of the situation should not all be in violation of the strict requirement of the ordinances.[4]

With the Roman Republic and its empire once again split in half and two governments in power, Caesar set off from Rome to once more take the offensive, rather than sit back and try to defend Italy; a tactic that had failed in the First Civil War, as Caesar himself had seen first-hand as a young man.

2. Rome without Caesar – Caelius, Milo and Economic Reforms (48 BC)

With Caesar out of Italy, pursing the civil war against Pompeius in Greece, control of Rome and Italy fell to his fellow Consul, P. Servilius Isauricus. Yet for all of his military successes, Caesar's control of Rome was at best tenuous. Whilst his obvious enemies (the close followers of Pompeius) had retreated to Greece – most obviously some two hundred Senators – this did not mean that all those that remained were supporters of Caesar. There would have been many who were supporters of neither man, including those former allies of Crassus and Clodius, not to mention the still exiled Milo. Furthermore, Caesar had brought back to Rome all those men exiled by Pompeius (done to stabilise Rome by ridding it of the most notorious disruptive element) and who now had a free hand with neither Pompeius nor Caesar in Rome to control them.

Ironically, Caesar found himself in the same position that Sulla had done in 88 BC, during his military control of Rome. Whilst he could ensure that his enemies weren't elected he could not guarantee the loyalty of those men who were elected once he was absent from Rome himself. Just as violence had erupted in Sulla's absence in 87 BC, the same thing happened in 48 BC, this time centred on the clash between Caesar's colleague Servilius and one of the Praetors (M. Caelius Rufus).

Caelius hailed from a long-established Tribunician family (stretching back to just after the Second Punic War) and had been a Tribune in 52 BC during the sole Consulship of Pompeius, where he had been a staunch ally of Milo. Now elected to the Praetorship and with Caesar in Greece, he renewed that relationship. Although Caesar had not pardoned Milo or recalled him, Milo represented the last of the politicians from the chaotic period of the 50s BC not actively engaged in the civil war.

Caelius used his Praetorship to propose popular reforms aimed at alleviating the growing economic crisis caused by the outbreak of another civil war. Caesar himself had attempted to alleviate conditions during his brief Dictatorship but had pulled back from a full programme of debt relief (obviously balancing his need for support from the money lenders along with currying favour with the Roman populace). Therefore, Caesar had raised people's hopes and then let them down with a half measure, allowing for debts to be settled with goods rather than money. This naturally left an opportunity for a popular politician to step into the breach and offer the People full debt relief. Caelius though went one stage further and offered the abolition of all private rents for one year:

> *He also gave notice to such as owed anything that he would assist them against their creditors, and to all who dwelt in other people's houses that he would release them from payment of the rent. Having by this course gained a considerable following, he set upon Trebonius with their aid and would have slain him, had the other not managed to change his dress and escape in the crowd. After this failure Caelius privately issued a law in which he granted everybody the use of houses free of rent and annulled all debts.*[5]
>
> *His next step was to promulgate a law that the money owed shall be paid without accumulation of interest on that day six years. ...He cancelled his former law and promulgated two others, one whereby he made a free gift of a year's rent of houses to the hirers, another authorizing a repudiation of debts; and when the mob made a rush at C. Trebonius and some persons were wounded, Caelius drove him from his tribunal.*[6]

We can see how flimsy Caesar's control of Rome was in his absence. Caelius had offered debt relief and free accommodation and used violence to drive one of his colleagues (the Urban Praetor) from the Forum. Rome now had neither Pompeius nor Caesar exerting their control over domestic politics and thus the situation had been turned back to the late 50s. It seems that Caelius was not alone in this, as the Consul Servilius found his initial actions in the Senate being vetoed by an unknown number of anonymous Tribunes.[7] With constitutional means blocked, Servilius fell back on the use of military force and used some of Caesar's soldiers to enforce order in Rome:

When Caelius drove these men away and even involved the Consul himself in a tumult, they convened again, still protected by the soldiers, and entrusted to Servilius the guarding of the city, a procedure concerning which I have often spoken before. After this he would not permit Caelius to do anything in his capacity as Praetor, but assigned the duties pertaining to his office to another praetor, debarred him from the Senate, dragged him from the rostra while he was delivering some tirade or other, and broke his chair in pieces.[8]

Thus we have a Consul of Rome, backed by military forces, which should not have been in the city, depriving a Praetor of his duties. Finding all constitutional means blocked, Caelius left Rome and set out to join his old ally Milo, who it seems had been biding his time. With both Pompeius and Caesar out of Italy and with the debt issue being a major political topic, Milo returned to Italy from exile at the head of a force of gladiators. This force was bolstered by freed slaves and had the aim of recruiting impoverished Roman citizens with the twin appeals of debt relief and the claim that he was acting on behalf of Pompeius. Yet despite these aims he seemingly met with more resistance than support and was defeated near Capua, turning back into Campania.

There meeting with the Praetor Q. Pedius at the head of a legion, he [Milo] was struck by a stone from the wall and perished. And Caelius, setting forth, as he gave out, to Caesar, reached Thurii. There, on trying to tamper with certain inhabitants of the municipality and promising money to Caesar's Gallic and Spanish horsemen who had been sent there on garrison duty, he was killed by them.[9]

Thus, both Caelius and Milo were killed, engaged in their own civil war against the Roman (Caesarian) state. Although militarily Rome did not appear to be in danger, given the number of Caesarian forces in Italy, this incident did show the fragmentation of Roman politics in this period and the overall fragility of the Republican system. Nevertheless, the rebels were easily defeated, and Italy held for the Caesarian cause.

Yet events in Italy were nothing more than a side show as far as the main civil war was concerned. Caesar had crossed into Greece where

Pompeius and his supporters were gathered, hoping to bring this Third Civil War to a swift conclusion. Yet the war initially ebbed and flowed. Although Caesar had managed to cross into Greece, his reinforcements (commanded by M. Antonius) found themselves blocked by Pompeius' naval forces. Once Antonius had managed to safely land in Greece himself, the war turned in Caesar's favour and Pompeius withdrew into the fortified city of Dyrrachium, which was placed under siege. Caesar however had overreached himself and was driven off by Pompeius, retreating into Thessaly and finding himself on the back foot. Pompeius then advanced and the two sides met at Pharsalus in Thessaly.

The full details of this battle fall outside of this present work, but the battle was a classic confrontation between two different armies. Pompeius had the greater numbers, but Caesar the more experienced and cohesive units. Pompeius was also relying on large numbers of allied forces, from Greece and the east, whilst Caesar was using his battle-hardened Roman legionaries. In the end it was experience and Roman training which proved to be the decisive factor and Pompeius' forces were comprehensively defeated and routed. Yet although the Battle of Pharsalus is usually depicted as one of the key clashes in the history of the Republic and often as a turning point, its effects were not immediately apparent, especially given that Pompeius and virtually all of his key allies survived and fled overseas to regroup. Metellus Scipio, Faustus Sulla and Cato all retreated to Africa, held by the Numidian King and Pompeian ally Juba. Pompeius himself headed east, to Egypt, in order to tap into the financial wealth held by the Ptolemaic Dynasty to rebuild his fortunes.

Whilst militarily the Pompeian forces had been defeated and had lost the Greek mainland, they still had the stronghold of North Africa to regroup from. What was more damaging however was not the military effects of the defeat at Pharsalus but the psychological ones. Going into the battle Caesar had been the usurper, and quite frankly the outsider, facing Pompeius Magnus, Rome's leading man and the bulk of the Senate. There would have been many, Roman and allied alike, who were supporting Pompeius as he looked like the natural winner, with his military record and powerful position. This defeat reversed that position and shattered Pompeius' myth of invincibility. It was Caesar who now looked the likely winner and Roman and ally alike thus changed their calculations. Most of Pompeius' Roman allies remained loyal and opposed to Caesar. The most high-profile defection was none other than Cicero himself, who slunk back to Italy and made peace with Caesar, which was hardly a major loss militarily. The most notable defection with hindsight however was a young Roman aristocrat named M. Iunius Brutus, rumoured at the time to possibly be Caesar's bastard son. Captured at Pharsalus he too made his peace with Caesar and returned to Italy.

Yet it was amongst Rome's provincials and allies that this defeat had the most profound effect. To back the losing side in a civil war invited the wrath of the winner and Caesar now looked like the winner. To the Ptolemaic dynasty, whose control of Egypt in the face of Roman domination was precarious enough, there was only one course of action: ingratiate themselves with Caesar. The method they chose was a typically Ptolemaic one, a family wracked by civil war and bloodshed; namely the assassination of Pompeius himself as he set foot on Egyptian soil (the beach). This was ordered by the new young Pharaoh Ptolemy XIII and carried out by Roman soldiers left in Egypt after the restoration of Ptolemy XII (see Chapter Six).

Cn. Pompeius Magnus, who had dominated the Roman Republic for over thirty years and had been one of the architects of the New Republic created in 70 BC, died on an Egyptian beach, with his head being hacked off and taken as a trophy. One of the great ironies is that his fellow architect and long-time rival, M. Licinius Crassus, too met his death in the east, assassinated in the aftermath of a great defeat and he too had his head taken as a trophy. In the end it was this failure of political judgement that brought about Pompeius' death, not a military defeat; his failure to see how weak the defeat had made him in the eyes of others and his separation from the bulk of his remaining forces brought about a fatal mistake.

3. Debt and Bloodshed (48–46 BC)

Yet Pompeius' death did not bring the civil war to a conclusion, as the remaining generals regrouped in Africa along with their Numidian allies, and the two sons of Pompeius (Cnaeus and Sextus). If anything, Caesar aided their recovery by becoming entangled in another Ptolemaic civil war in Egypt. He had chased Pompeius there, only to be presented with his head. Had he been able to capture Pompeius intact then there was always the chance of a settlement and Pompeius ordering his force in Africa to stand down. Pompeius' death robbed him of that chance and thus the civil war would have to continue. Yet Caesar became entangled (in more ways than one) in the ongoing civil war in the Ptolemaic family between Ptolemy XIII and his sister Cleopatra VII. Thus, rather than press on for Africa he stayed to winter in Egypt.

Yet once again, despite his military victory and control of the bulk of Rome's empire, Caesar's political position was a matter of concern. His constitutional power came from his Consulship, shortly to expire at the end of the year, and he was hardly in a position to return to Rome to stand for/be appointed to a third Consulship. Thus, once again he turned to the office of Dictator, and had the Consul Servilius propose this to the People. However, unlike the first occasion when he held the office for just eleven days, this time it was proposed that Caesar be Dictator for a whole year, thus breaching the fundamental temporary nature of the office and drawing unenviable comparisons with Sulla.

Given a compliant Senate and People and the presence of Caesar's troops either in Rome or its environs, unsurprisingly we hear of no objections to this proposal. Another innovation was that Caesar had been appointed Dictator but was not even in Italy. It was perhaps this fact alone that may have made this year-long Dictatorship more palatable; namely that Caesar was not present in person and so would only be exercising its power outside of Rome and Italy. Yet the office of Dictator came with a deputy, the *Magister Equitum*, 'Master of the Horse', who could exercise powers on Caesar's behalf. For this role Caesar chose none other than M. Antonius, who, combined with the failure to hold Consular elections, now temporarily held power in Rome. Thus, the year ended with Caesar in military control of the bulk of Rome's empire and having been appointed Dictator for a year, and with M. Antonius controlling Rome for him.

Yet again we can see that military dominance did not automatically translate into political control in Rome itself. Neither Caesar nor Antonius apparently saw the need to hold the curule elections for 47 BC, meaning no Consuls, Praetors or Quaestors were elected. However, this did not stop the Plebeian elections and thus a fresh set of Tribunes were elected, the only other elected power to rival that of Antonius.

Even with M. Antonius overseeing Rome, as Caesar's Master of the Horse, dissension broke out amongst the Tribunes which soon spiralled out of control. Although Caelius and Milo had been killed the year before, the issue of debt and the worsening economic impact of the civil war still remained ripe to be taken up by another magistrate. The magistrate who took it up was the Tribune P. Cornelius Dolabella. We know little of Dolabella prior to his election to the Tribunate, yet Dio reports one important statement; namely that Dolabella, like Clodius before him, transferred from the Patrician class (the Gens Cornelia was a Patrician one) to a Plebeian family, via the method of adoption, so as to be eligible to stand for the Tribunate.[10] Having secured his Tribunate he took up the cause of the impoverished people and proposed a law to abolish debt and house rents (following in Caelius' footsteps).

On this occasion he was opposed by one of his Tribunician colleagues, L. Trebellius along with another man C. Asinius Pollio (who himself may possibly have been another one of the Tribunes this year).[11] Thus, a familiar pattern emerged when the two Tribunes clashed with each other and Rome fell into disorder once more. Despite holding Dictatorial power (acting in Caesar's name) Antonius proved to be ineffective:

> *This, too, naturally resulted in great turmoil and many weapons were everywhere to be seen, although the Senators had commanded that no changes should be made before Caesar's arrival, and Antonius that no private individual in the city should carry arms. As the Tribunes, however, paid no attention to these orders, but resorted to absolutely every sort of measure against each other and against the men just mentioned, a third party arose, consisting of Antonius and the Senate.*[12]

Therefore, the chaos continued and for the second year running Rome fell into political chaos. The two Tribunes and their supporters continued to clash, and Dolabella continued to push his debt relief programme and attempted to overcome his colleague's veto by the trusted technique of seizing the Forum and expelling his opponents, thus being allowed to vote without the presence of a Tribunician veto. In the end, Antonius had only one option and having been duly authorised by the Senate, brought Roman troops into the city to restore order. This inevitably led to clashes between the two and an outbreak of bloodshed:

> *For Dolabella had occupied the Forum in order to force the passage of his law; so Antonius, after the Senate had voted that arms must be employed against Dolabella, came up against him, joined battle, slew some of his men, and lost some of his own.*[13]
>
> *The Tribune of the Plebs Publius Dolabella caused unrest when he proposed a law to cancel debts, and the plebs started to revolt. However, Marcus Antonius, the Master of Horse, sent soldiers into the city and 800 people were killed.*[14]

Therefore, despite Caesar holding Dictatorial power and having military control of the bulk of Rome's empire, he and his supporters were unable to prevent Roman politics from breaking out into violence and ultimately bloodshed and the large-scale loss of life. Throughout 47 BC Caesar had been embroiled in the ongoing Egyptian Civil War, at one point finding himself besieged in Alexandria; a conflict that resulted in the destruction of the Great Library for the first time. Having been persuaded to support the cause of Cleopatra VII against her brother Ptolemy XII, Caesar was ultimately victorious and secured Egypt as his ally, placing Cleopatra VII on the throne, pregnant with his child. Nevertheless, this Egyptian excursion had allowed his opponents time to regroup in North Africa, under the command of the Proconsul Metellus Scipio (Pompeius' father-in-law). Caesar was further delayed by the need to secure Rome's Eastern possession from an invasion by Pharances II of Pontus, son of the legendary Roman enemy Mithridates VI.[15]

Despite the need to continue to take the civil war to North Africa, Caèsar found it necessary to divert to Rome, despite being based in Egypt. He had to do so for two reasons: to stabilise the situation in Rome itself and further secure his political position. In his absence the issue of debt had been used to stir up a revolt in 48 BC under Milo and now had seen troops deployed on the streets of Rome and a battle that had resulted in nearly one thousand dead, at the heart of the Republic. Thus, upon his return to Rome, he utilised the powers of his Dictatorship to address the issues of the bloodshed and the underlying political issue of debt, something he had deliberately avoided in 49 BC.

Perhaps surprisingly, despite the bloodshed in the Forum, Dolabella himself had survived and no action had been taken against him, perhaps on Caesar's orders. Upon his return Caesar chose to calm matters by pardoning all involved, including Dolabella, who was fast-tracked for advancement in the Caesarian regime (becoming Consul in 44 BC). Thus, Caesar continued his widespread policy of showing clemency to his opponents, having brought Dolabella to his side with offers of advancement. However, though the individuals involved had been dealt with, the debt issue still remained and so he used his Dictatorial powers to pass some measure of debt relief, though again not the full remittance of debts that Caelius and Dolabella had offered. Interestingly he adopted Caelius' and Dolabella's policy of rent relief as well:

> *For he made a present to the multitude of all the interest they were owing from the time he had gone to war with Pompeius, and he released them from all rent for one year, up to the sum of two thousand sesterces; furthermore he raised the valuation on the goods, in terms of which it was required by law for loans to be paid to their worth at the time the loan had been made, in view of the fact that everything had become much cheaper as a result of the great amount of confiscated property.*[16]

He also finally held elections for the Consulship (and presumably the other Curule offices) for the current year, with two lower-ranked supporters (Q. Fufius Calenus and P. Vatinius) being elected. Both men had held office with Caesar during his first Consulship (in 59 BC), Calenus as Praetor and Vatinius as Tribune.

4. Caesar's Dilemma: Holding Political Power

Having hopefully (in his eyes at least) dealt with the debt issue and the violence that it had caused, his attention turned once again to the perennial problem of his own political position. Despite the fact he was in military control of Rome's whole empire (with the exception of North Africa), his political position was still far from secure. To date, since his attack on Italy in 49 BC, he had held the Dictatorship twice (once for eleven days and the other for a year) and a Consulship in between. His dilemma was that each of these offices only granted temporary power, and with the civil war dragging on into its fourth year he still needed a legitimate grant of power to avoid looking like a tyrant holding nothing but military might.

Both Caesar's maternal uncle, C. Marius, and his former father-in-law, L. Cornelius Cinna, had dominated Rome; Marius in a legitimate military crisis and Cinna during the First Civil War, and both had used the expedient method of repeat Consulships (Marius between 104–100 BC and Cinna between 87–84 BC. Yet neither example brought long-term power; with Marius retiring into civilian life after the emergency had passed and Cinna being murdered.

The only other examples were Sulla, who had held a Dictatorship but then retired into private life, and Pompeius, who had held one sole Consulship and then left office to wield influence behind the scenes. Yet again neither example gave Caesar much hope. He clearly did not want to relinquish political control of the Republic nor reduce his power so much that he allowed a rival to emerge (as Pompeius had done with Caesar). Yet with the impending war in North Africa to prosecute, all he could do was to postpone any longer-term considerations and hold another Consulship (only two years after his last one). Caesar was duly elected as one of the Consuls for 46 BC, alongside his trusted ally M. Aemilius Lepidus (himself the son of a civil war general who had attacked Rome with his army). With his power secure for one more year, Caesar again left Rome before he formally took up office and sailed to North Africa for a showdown with the surviving Pompeian forces.

The result of this conflict was the Battle of Thapsus (46 BC) which saw another major victory for Caesar and the destruction of the Pompeian/ Numidian army. Once again, even though he was successful on the battlefield, all the key opposing commanders survived the actual battle. On this occasion, though, the aftermath of the battle saw the deaths of the majority of the opposition's leading figures, through either suicide or execution. There were a number of prominent suicides of Caesar's opponents, the most famous being that of Cato, who chose to cut his wrists rather than be taken alive and thus achieved a far greater status in death than he had held in life. Metellus Scipio also chose suicide rather than capture, as did the Numidian King Juba, whose kingdom was soon annexed to Rome's growing empire. M. Petreius, a Pompeian commander, also died in a suicide pact with Juba.

Alongside this wave of suicides came a number of prominent murders, most notably Faustus Cornelius Sulla (son of the late Dictator) and L. Iulius Caesar (a kinsman). Yet despite the wave of bloodshed, both self-inflicted and otherwise, the two most prominent survivors were Pompeius' two adult sons, Cn. Pompeius Magnus and Sex. Pompeius, who fled to Spain where they stirred up a rebellion, thus ensuring that the civil war would enter a fifth year.

5. Caesar's Solution – Rome's Princeps and the Iulian Reform Programme (46–45 BC)

Nevertheless, Thapsus had seen the destruction of the Pompeian armies and leadership and cemented Caesar's military control of the Republic and its empire. Rather than pursue the sons of Pompeius, Caesar returned to Rome in order to convert his military control into political control. Despite his still holding the Consulship for 46 BC, Caesar determined on a more permanent solution. Having weighed up the various models of rule that had gone before him (including those of his uncle and father-in-law – above) Caesar's supporters in the Senate proposed and passed the following measures:

> *Furthermore, they elected him overseer of every man's conduct (for some such name was given him, as if the title of Censor were not worthy of him) for three years, and Dictator for ten in succession. They moreover voted that he should sit in the Senate upon the curule chair with the successive Consuls, and should always state his opinion first, that he should give the signal at all the games in the Circus, and that he should have the appointment of the magistrates and whatever honours the People were previously accustomed to assign.*[17]

Caesar was voted to be Dictator for ten years and for the first three of those he was to have Censorial power (*cura morum*) without the restrictions of having to hold the office (which came with an eighteen-month limit and a colleague). Thus, Caesar stripped the powers of Censor away from the office and had it invested in himself as an individual, not an office holder. His physical position was to be sat with Consuls (the Republic's leaders) yet he was always designated the right to speak before them and had the right to appoint magistrates. These powers came in addition to the annual Consulship he held and the fact that since 63 BC he had been the Pontifex Maximus (Rome's chief priest), adding religious authority to the temporal one.

Caesar chose to follow a Sullan solution and implement a very obvious period of personal rule (both in terms of powers and ceremony), far greater than Sulla himself had chosen. Even though he held a constitutional office, he had also personally been invested with power, something that none of his predecessors had chosen. The Roman Republic now had a very obvious chief magistrate, a *Princeps* (the first amongst equals). The challenge however, as all of his predecessors had found out, was not seizing supreme power in the Republic, but holding on to it. Both Sulla and Marius had chosen to step down, Cinna had been murdered, whilst Pompeius had been overthrown by a rival.

Nevertheless, having clearly waited for this moment for a number of years Caesar seemed determined to use this extraordinary set of powers to reshape the Republic into one which fitted his own vision of how it should be, not what it had become, much as Sulla himself had done before him. Therefore, he launched into a large programme of reforms which touched on all aspects of the Republic. It seems that Caesar had two main periods of issuing reforms; 46 BC (on his return from Africa) and 45 BC (on his return from Spain). The surviving sources do not agree on which measure belongs to which year, so we shall examine them as a whole.

First came the pageantry, and Caesar celebrated an unprecedented four Triumphs at the same time for his victories in Gaul, Egypt, Pontus and North Africa, putting on banquets and shows for the People. This was also a symbolic statement that the civil wars were over, despite a growing Pompeian rebellion in Spain. It further allowed Caesar to paint himself as Rome's greatest general. In addition, he took the opportunity to parade the wealth he had captured and was able to discharge the bulk of his army and still find money to present a gift to the People of Rome:

It is said that money to the amount of 60,500 silver talents was borne in the procession and 2,822 crowns of gold weighing 20,414 pounds, from which wealth Caesar made apportionments immediately after the Triumph, paying the army all that he had promised and more. Each soldier received 5,000 Attic drachmas, each centurion double, and each tribune of infantry and prefect of cavalry fourfold that sum. To each Plebeian citizen also was given an Attic mina. He gave also various spectacles with horses and music, a combat of foot-soldiers, 1,000 on each side, and a cavalry fight of 200 on each side. There was also another combat of horse and foot together. There was a combat of elephants, twenty against twenty, and a naval engagement of 4,000 oarsmen, where 1,000 fighting men contended on each side.[18]

Caesar was clearly hoping to usher in a new period of peace and prosperity, on the back of which he could introduce his reform programme. This programme had well over a dozen key pieces of legislation, which can be collected together under themes such as judicial, political, economic, moral, infrastructure, calendar and provincial. Whilst some were truly unique (such as the reforms to the Roman calendar), others were all too familiar and had been seen in the various Tribunician reforms programmes of earlier generations. The most obvious of these was yet another reform to the composition of juries. This had been a long-standing political football since the Tribunate of C. Gracchus, some eighty years earlier.

Every generation had seen a change to the composition of juries, either for the benefit or the detriment of one section of the Roman oligarchy. Pompeius and Crassus, when they reformed the Republic in 70 BC, had split juries between Senators, Equestrians and a third 'balancing' category the *Tribuni Aerarii*. This reform was reversed by Caesar, who redistributed juries between Equestrian and Senators once more. Thus, power was restored to the two main social elements of the Roman oligarchy, but ones which had traditionally been prone to mutual antagonism and favouritism towards their own. There was also a law restating that the punishment for being convicted of violence or treason was the denial of 'fire and water' (exile).

There were a number of political reforms; both at the higher and lower levels. The most obvious ones were a large increase in the number of Senators (using his Censorial powers). Dio states that the Senate reached a figure of nine hundred members,[19] along with an increase in the numbers of magistrates; there were now to be fourteen Praetors (soon increased to sixteen), six Aediles and forty Questors. This reflected a similar expansion carried out by Sulla and recognised the need for more provincial administrators. Many of the newer Senators came from the exiles, who had been recalled by a Caesarian–sponsored Tribunician law (as had happened under Pompeius and Crassus in 70 BC) which was a public declaration of Caesar's clemency and reaching out to his former enemies. Having grown up under the Sullan regime, he was obviously trying to disassociate himself from the bloodier aspects of a Dictator ruling Rome, though the bloodbath of his leading opponents after Thapsus made this easier.

Caesar also followed Sulla's lead in extending the Pomerium, the sacred boundary of the city, Sulla having been the first man to do so since the time of the kings. In reality this meant that Rome's sacred boundary could match its physical one (Rome being an ever-expanding city), but the symbolism of such an act was a key one: setting the sacred boundaries of the city, something that only the Roman Kings could do, and harking back to the legendary Romulus.

Caesar also harked back to hallowed antiquity when he used his combined powers, including those of the Pontifex Maximus, to create new Patrician families. Patrician status was inherited from a small group of original Roman aristocratic families who had held power when the Roman Republic was created from the ashes of the overthrown monarchy. There had been no new Patrician families since the re-establishment of the Republic in 449 BC, following the overthrow of the Decemvirate. Naturally, over the centuries many of these Patrician families had died out, a trend exacerbated by the last century of political bloodletting and the last fifty years of intermittent civil wars. Again, however, the symbolism was high, and Caesar was exercising powers that had been a royal prerogative.

There were a number of lesser political reforms; Rome's collegia (associations) once again become a target, with a law abolishing the newer collegia. These collegia had long been associated (at least in the minds of the Roman oligarchy) as sources of political dissension (not helped by their connections with Clodius).[20] Another minor law stated that no Roman citizen between the ages of twenty and forty could remain outside of Italy for more than three successive years (unless on military service) and that no Senator's son could leave Italy unless as part of an official delegation. More importantly, Caesar passed a law reducing the number of recipients of the corn dole (a free issuing of grain to Rome's poorer citizens):

> *[He] reduced the number of those who received grain at public expense from three hundred and twenty thousand to one hundred and fifty thousand. And to prevent the calling of additional meetings at any future time for purposes of enrolment, he provided that the places of such as died should be filled each year by the Praetors from those who were not on the list.*[21]

In practical terms this represented a major saving for the Roman state, in terms of both expenditure and the time it took to secure sufficient grain. Throughout the 50s BC grain shortages had led to political dissension and required the Senate to appoint Pompeius to supervise Rome's grain supply. The obvious downside to this law was that there were nearly two hundred thousand Roman citizens who now no longer received free grain.

Caesar also took great pains to demonstrate his role as 'guardian of public morals' and used his Censorial power to curb what he saw as a moral decline amongst the Roman People (and the aristocracy in particular); a familiar political position. To these ends he passed sumptuary laws restricting how much could be spent on private banquets and the use of litters, and another law offering rewards for Romans who had large families. This role as guardian of public morality did not clearly extend to himself, as Cleopatra soon arrived in Rome along with Caesar's bastard son, Caesarion.

There were several economic reforms, notably the imposition of tariffs on the import of foreign goods into Italy, presumably to encourage domestic production, which was another staple of a politician wishing to make a public statement on his traditionalist views. He also passed a law in the same vein which stated that:

Those who made a business of grazing should have among their herdsmen
at least one-third who were men of free birth.[22]

Despite the obvious lack of monitoring or enforcement in the Italian
countryside, this was a populist measure which looked like he was
tackling the issue of rural unemployment and citizens having their jobs
taken away from them by slaves. Caesar also encouraged the recruitment
of medical staff and teachers by giving them citizenship if they settled
in Rome:

He conferred citizenship on all who practised medicine at Rome, and on
all teachers of the liberal arts, to make them more desirous of living in
the city and to induce others to resort to it.[23]

In terms of Rome itself, there came a major building programme, using
the city to celebrate the renewed (Caesarian) Republic, with a new Forum
(the Iulian Forum) and the Basilica Iulia. Aside from Rome itself, Italy
was to benefit from the new regime with an ambitious programme of
works, many of which would never be carried out:

To open to the public the greatest possible libraries of Greek and Latin
books, assigning to Marcus Varro the charge of procuring and classifying
them; to drain the Pomptine marshes; to let out the water from Lake
Fucinus; to make a highway from the Adriatic across the summit of the
Apennines as far as the Tiber; to cut a canal through the Isthmus.[24]

Caesar also created a vast colonisation programme, to discharge the bulk
of his forces and to create a series of Roman veteran colonies throughout
the empire. Again, this followed a tried and tested pattern set by the
previous great generals Marius, Sulla and Pompeius, but it followed
more in the Sullan mode with the need to secure his military victory in
a civil war. The sources report that over eighty thousand soldiers were
settled in new colonies, the most famous of which was a new Roman city
of Carthage.

Perhaps Caesar's most lasting domestic reform was to the Roman
calendar. The Romans had long realised that the length of their calendar

year did not match the length of the natural one; it being too short. Controlling the calendar had long been the preserve of the Pontiffs, who had needed at times to add additional (intercalary) months to balance out the Roman year, but this had been done in such a haphazard manner that the Roman calendar no longer matched the changing of the seasons:

> *He reformed the calendar, which the negligence of the Pontiffs had long since so disordered, through their privilege of adding months or days at pleasure, that the harvest festivals did not come in summer nor those of the vintage in the autumn; and he adjusted the year to the sun's course by making it consist of three hundred and sixty-five days, abolishing the intercalary month, and adding one day every fourth year. Furthermore, that the correct reckoning of seasons might begin with the next Kalends of January, he inserted two other months between those of November and December; hence the year in which these arrangements were made was one of fifteen months, including the intercalary month, which belonged to that year according to the former custom.*[25]

Caesar introduced the Iulian calendar, which was to be the basis of western countries' calendars for the next fifteen hundred years, and in some countries lasting until the 20th century.

In terms of foreign policy, Caesar expanded Rome's empire by adding Gaul in the north and annexing eastern Numidia (whose king had supported Pompeius) and turning it into the new province of Africa Nova.[26] Cleopatra's rule of Egypt was formally ratified, and she was officially recognised as a friend and ally of the Senate and People of Rome, not to mention Caesar himself. As mentioned above, Cleopatra and her son Caesarion moved to Rome and took up residence, an unhelpful reminder of Caesar's royal connections.

In terms of provincial government, as well as increasing the number of magistrates available to govern Rome's provinces, Caesar passed a law limiting the terms of provincial governors; one year for Propraetorian governors and two years for Proconsular ones. Thus, Caesar was attempting to ensure that no one could follow his own example and use a prolonged command in a province as a springboard for an attack on

Rome. The obvious problem with this was that his own example showed only too well the success of such a tactic.

We can see that Caesar used this supreme power to attempt to remould the Republic into another reformed and renewed Republic, which would reflect his vision for Roman society: an end to the political and military anarchy and a return to a 'golden age' of peace, prosperity and traditional values. This new 'golden age' would be protected by Caesar himself as Rome's wise and benevolent (as he would have liked it to be seen) guardian, the protector of the Republic, its Princeps (though that is not a term he used).

Throughout the period of Caesars' dominance of the Republic it is clear that he spent very little time actually in Rome, spending the majority of his time abroad, prosecuting the various conflicts within the civil war, not to mention becoming entangled in the Egyptian Civil War. As the year passed (46 BC) and with his reforms programme progressing, Caesar again became restless and once again decided to leave Rome to personally take up command against a growing rebellion in Spain, commanded by Pompeius' two sons, Cnaeus and Sextus. What is clear throughout this period of civil war is Caesar's reluctance to leave commanding armies to his subordinates, and he does seem to have been happiest when in command of an army – this may well account for his prolonged stay in Gaul (58–49 BC) and the periods away from Rome during the civil war.

As we have seen previously, Caesar had not excelled in Roman politics prior to the Third Civil War, with a disastrous Praetorship (being caught up in the conspiracies at the heart of the Second Civil War) and his Consulship only coming as an agent of Pompeius and Crassus. Such an attitude is the opposite of Pompeius, who spent over a decade at Rome and ruled his provinces through legates from 55–49 BC. On the one hand there may well have been political benefits to these absences, most notably not being an ever-present reminder that Rome now had a supreme magistrate with power over all others. Thus, Caesar the Dictator was an absent Dictator, one constantly fighting Rome's enemies and enlarging the empire. The obvious downside was that he relied on his subordinates to control Rome, something that had not happened in either 49 or 48 BC, leading to political bloodshed. It also meant that he was not present to control his enemies, although pardoned, amongst the Roman oligarchy.

6. Caesar's Final Elevation and Downfall (45–44 BC)

Caesar left Rome once more, this time to fight Pompeius' sons in Spain.
Yet notwithstanding all his constitutional reforms he took an odd decision
before he left. Despite being Dictator for the next ten years, along with
Censorial power he felt the need to hold another Consulship at the same
time (his fourth). The elections were supervised by M. Aemilius Lepidus;
Caesar's deputy and the Master of the Horse. Yet only the Consular
elections were held and only one Consul (Caesar) was elected. Thus,
Caesar completely ignored Republican tradition and had himself elected
as sole Consul (following a path which Pompeius had taken in 52 BC).
However, when Pompeius took this route (with the Senate's blessing)
Rome itself was facing a wave of political violence and potential collapse.
All Caesar faced was a rebellion in Spain and he was already Dictator for
a ten-year period. Thus, once again Caesar took the path which marked
him out as a breaker of tradition and Rome's obvious ruler.

This was further emphasised when he left Rome not only under the
control of the Master of the Horse (Lepidus) but also appointed a group
of City Prefects to administer the affairs of the city in the absence of
Curule magistrates. Thus, we can refer back to Suetonius who stated (see
above) that Caesar ruled by nominated magistrates, not elected ones:

> *In addition to these measures carried out that year, two of the city
> prefects took charge of the finances, since no Quaestor had been elected.
> For just as on former occasions, so now in the absence of Caesar, the
> prefects managed all the affairs of the city, in conjunction with Lepidus
> as Master of the Horse. And although they were censured for employing
> lictors and the magisterial garb and chair precisely like the Master of the
> Horse, they got off by citing a certain law which allowed all those with
> receiving any office from a Dictator to make use of such trappings.*[27]

Once again Republican tradition had been replaced by Caesarian
expediency. Caesar left the city in the control of a group of handpicked
supporters, with the only other magistrates being the Plebeian Tribunes
and Aediles. The only evidence we have of the Tribunician activity this
year was a certain Caecilius (or Pomponius in some sources)[28] who passed
a law as part of Caesar's renovation of the city.

However, for the third time in four years, Caesar's absence saw political dissension break out in Rome. On this occasion it was not from an elected magistrate but from a rabble-rouser, who claimed to be the grandson of C. Marius.

> *Some men from the city, as they seemed, brought me a message and a letter from 'Caius Marius, son of Caius, grandson of Caius,' written at great length: 'they begged me in the name of our relationship to them, in the name of the famous Marius on whom I had composed a poem, in the name of the eloquence of his grandfather L. Cassius, to undertake his defence,' he then stated his case in full detail. I wrote back to say that he had no need of counsel, as all power was in the hands of his relation Caesar, who was a most excellent and fair-minded man, but that I would support him.*[29]
>
> *Herophilus, a horse doctor, claimed C. Marius, seven times Consul as his grandfather had so aggrandised himself that a number of colonies of veterans and distinguished municipalities and almost all collegia adopted him as their patron.*[30]
>
> *One Chamiates, a man of the lowest rank, pretending to be the son of Caius Marius, caused disturbances among the credulous plebs.*[31]
>
> *There was a certain pseudo-Marius in Rome named Amatius. He pretended to be a grandson of Marius, and for this reason was very popular with the masses.*[32]
>
> *Octavius asked permission to go home to see his mother, and when it was granted, he set out. When he reached the Janiculan Hill near Rome, a man who claimed to be the son of Caius Marius came with a large crowd of people to meet him. He had taken also some women who were relatives of Caesar, for he was anxious to be enrolled in the family, and they testified to his descent.*[33]

In reality, Marius's only son Caius (Cos. 82 BC) had been killed in the First Civil War and had left no issue.[34] It was this fact which allowed Caesar to claim to be the inheritor of Marius (Snr) and the custodian of his uncle's legacy. As was shown though, the Marius name still carried weight and any attempt to claim to be directly descended from Marius clearly undermined Caesar's own claim in this regard. The pseudo-Marius also showed that whilst Caesar had total military control of Rome, he did not enjoy the complete support of the People, and certainly not of all of the Senate. As it was, when Caesar returned to Rome from Spain, he found it necessary to banish his supposed cousin from Italy.

In military terms, Caesar met with continued success this year, with the sons of Pompeius being brought to battle in Spain at Munda. The result was another crushing defeat for the Pompeian forces, with Cn. Pompeius (the eldest son) being killed (murdered) during the retreat from the battle. The youngest son Sextus survived and attempted to raise further forces but was harried into the Spanish interior by one of Caesar's commanders, C. Carrinas, where he continued to fight into the next year.[35] Militarily therefore, the Battle of Munda marked Caesar's ultimate victory in the early years of the Third Civil War and the final extinguishing of the Pompeian forces.

Having achieved this victory, Caesar returned to Rome to even greater acclaim and further accolades. Following the celebration of another Triumph for his victory in Spain, over the natives rather than Pompeius' sons, Caesar introduced another constitutional innovation, resigning his Consulship before his annual term had been completed. Presumably he felt that as he was no longer on campaign he did not need to be holding the Consulship. Although this allowed two of his supporters to be elected (Q. Fabius Maximus and C. Trebonius) they could only hold office for a few months (his resignation coming in October). More importantly, though, was the effect of discarding Rome's highest office when he no longer needed it, thus cheapening the whole institution of the Consulate.

It seems that as well as holding the Consular elections, he finally held the other Curule elections (for Praetors, non-Plebeian Aediles and Questors), again only allowing the office holders some three months in position. No sooner had those men been elected than the office holders for 44 BC were elected/chosen. The sources talk of Caesar choosing the men for the offices of the following year, but it is not clear whether he directly appointed them or simply provided the People with a list of approved candidates and allowed them a token vote for the men he had already selected. It is more probable that it was the latter and Suetonius and Dio describe it thus:

He shared the elections with the People on this basis: that except in the case of the Consulship, half of the magistrates should be appointed by the People's choice, while the rest should be those whom he had personally nominated. And these he announced in brief notes like the following, circulated in each tribe: 'Caesar the Dictator to this or that tribe. I commend to you so and so, to hold their positions by your votes.'[36]

While the Consuls were appointed in this manner, the remaining magistrates were nominally elected by the plebs and by the whole People, in accordance with ancestral custom, since Caesar would not accept the appointment of them; yet really they were appointed by him and were sent out to the provinces without casting lots.[37]

Amongst the men selected/elected for the following year were M. Iunius Brutus and C. Cassius Longinus, whilst he selected himself for another Consulship (the fifth) alongside M. Antonius. Antonius' two brothers were also selected for office, Caius as a Praetor and Lucius as a Tribune. Yet Caesar's debasement of the Consulship continued, as he let it be known that his plan was to abdicate before leaving Rome on another campaign, and he appointed P. Cornelius Dolabella (the Tribune of 47 BC) to be Suffect Consul. Furthermore, Caesar retained his Dictatorship, appointing M. Aemilius Lepidus once more to be the Master of the Horse, though he also laid out plans for Lepidus to stand aside when he joined Caesar on campaign. He was to be replaced by Caesar's great nephew, and official Roman heir, C. Octavius (then eighteen years old).

Unlike previous years, where he could not seem to be bothered to fill the Curule posts, Caesar carefully selected the magistrates for 44 BC, though he did so in a manner which left no one in any doubt as to who was in charge. Once again, he was planning on leaving Rome to go on campaign, this time a war of conquest against the Parthian Empire; to avenge the Roman defeat at the Battle of Carrhae and the loss of the First Romano-Parthian War.[38] As his preparations for this war continued, we must presume he continued with his reform programme (outlined above), with the greater constitutional reforms (Senate and magistracies) being the most likely in this period.

Yet it was not Caesar's actions in this period that began to undermine his position, but the actions of others, which Caesar allowed. Despite already holding an unprecedented series of offices and powers (Dictator, Consul, Pontifex Maximus, Censorial power), Caesar allowed the Senate to continue with their offers of further honours. These included the permanent titles of 'Father of his Country' (*pater patriae*) and Imperator, along with a whole range of other privileges:

> *It was decreed that he should transact business on a throne of ivory and gold; that he should himself sacrifice always in triumphal costume; that each year the city should celebrate the days on which he had won his victories; that every five years priests and Vestal Virgins should offer up public prayers for his safety; and that the magistrates immediately upon their inauguration should take an oath not to oppose any of Caesar's decrees. In honour of his birth the name of the month Quintilis was changed to July. Many temples were decreed to him as to a god, and one was dedicated in common to him and the goddess Clemency.*[39]
>
> *For they offered him the magistracies, even those belonging to the plebs, and elected him consul for ten years, as they previously made him Dictator. They ordered that he alone should have soldiers, and alone administer the public funds, so that no one else should be allowed to employ either of them, save whom he permitted. And they decreed at this time that an ivory statue of him, and later that a whole chariot, should appear in the procession at the games in the Circus, together with the statues of the gods. Another likeness they set up in the temple of Quirinus with the inscription, 'To the Invincible God', and another on the Capitol beside the former Kings of Rome. Now it occurs to me to marvel at the coincidence: there were eight such statues, seven to the kings, and an eighth to the Brutus who overthrew the Tarquins, and they set up the statue of Caesar beside the last of these.*[40]

In constitutional terms the Senate offered him further offices and powers. He was granted the Censorial power for life along with a grant of Tribunician sacrosanctity[41] (more powers divorced from their offices) as well as a Consulship for ten years (to match that of his Dictatorship), which he refused, and then they offered him the title of *dictator perpetuus*, or Dictator for life, and unwisely he accepted.[42] In constitutional terms, this must have been what Caesar had wanted; a perpetual grant of political power, not just for the duration of the civil war crisis, but an acknowledgement of his permanent role as head of the Republic. Yet for all his military brilliance, Caesar did not seem to understand the position he was placing himself in or that many of these honours seem to have been a trap placed by his enemies, as Plutarch points out:

It was Cicero who proposed the first honours for him in the Senate, and their magnitude was, after all, not too great for a man; but others added excessive honours and vied with one another in proposing them, thus rendering Caesar odious and obnoxious even to the mildest citizens because of the pretension and extravagance of what was decreed for him.[43]

Caesar's enemies (Cicero amongst them) realised all too well that whilst he could not be defeated on a military battlefield, he could be defeated in the political one. Caesar now held power for life and had his statue placed with those of Rome's kings. Furthermore, he now had two heirs in the city of Rome, his legitimate one (C. Octavius), whom he was grooming for public office, and his illegitimate one (Caesarion), heir to the Ptolemaic Empire. Thus, the rule of one man was beginning to look like the start of a dynasty. This fear was further confirmed when the Senate granted him the right that his son (should he legally have one, Caesarion being illegitimate) or adopt one, would be appointed Pontifex Maximus. A surviving fragment of Nicholas of Damascus sums up the situation well:

While others treacherously included extravagant honours, and published them, so that he might become an object of envy and suspicion to all. Caesar was of guileless disposition and was unskilled in political practices by reason of his foreign campaigns, so that he was easily taken in by these people, supposing, naturally enough, that their commendations came rather from men who admired him than from men who were plotting against him.[44]

Thus, a general who could not be ambushed on the battlefield walked straight into a political trap. This lack of political acumen became obvious when he clashed with the newly elected Tribunes of 44 BC. The situation began when Caesar was watching the Lupercalia festival:

These ceremonies Caesar was witnessing, seated upon the Rostra on a golden throne, arrayed in triumphal attire. And Antonius was one of the runners in the sacred race; for he was consul. Accordingly, after he had dashed into the Forum and the crowd had made way for him, he carried a diadem, round which a wreath of laurel was tied, and held it out to Caesar. Then there was applause, not loud, but slight and preconcerted. But when Caesar pushed away the diadem, all the People applauded; and when Antonius offered it again, only a few applauded, and when Caesar declined it again, all applauded. The experiment having thus failed, Caesar rose from his seat, after ordering the wreath to be carried up to the Capitol; but then his statues were seen to have been decked with royal diadems. So two of the Tribunes, Flavius and Marullus, went up to them and pulled off the diadems, and after discovering those who had first hailed Caesar as king, led them off to prison. Moreover, the people followed the Tribunes with applause and called them Brutuses, because Brutus was the man who put an end to the royal succession and brought the power into the hands of the Senate and people instead of a sole ruler. At this, Caesar was greatly vexed, and deprived Marullus and Flavius of their office, while during his denunciation of them he at the same time insulted the People.[45]

Therefore, Caesar had two Tribunes (L. Caesetius Flavus and C. Epidius Marullus) stripped of their Tribunate, via a bill proposed by one of their colleagues (C. Helvius Cinna), and had two other men selected in their place (L. Decidius Saxa and Hostilius Saserna).[46] Yet for Caesar the damage had been done and he had publicly been associated with aspiration for a kingship, the most ancient taboo in the Republic, and had attacked the Tribunes who had prosecuted those calling for a kingship. Furthermore, Plutarch reports that the rumour was being spread about Rome, no doubt by his enemies, that '*a report that from the Sibylline books it appeared that Parthia could be taken if the Romans went up against it with a king*'.[47]

With feeling amongst many of the Senate and People running high, a group of Roman nobles, mostly men whom Caesar had pardoned, felt that the time was right to act, before Caesar left Rome for his Parthian War. On the one hand, Caesar was leaving Rome, which would remove his overbearing political presence and allow Roman politics to continue. On the other, it would mean that Caesar would be surrounded by his troops and unreachable for many years. We will never know the full extent of Caesar's intended campaigns, but he must have envisaged a conquest of the Parthian Empire, following in the footsteps of Alexander the Great. Certainly, Plutarch reports an exaggerated campaign:

> For he planned and prepared to make an expedition against the Parthians; and after subduing these and marching around the Euxine by way of Hyrcania, the Caspian Sea, and the Caucasus, to invade Scythia; and after overrunning the countries bordering on Germany and Germany itself, to come back by way of Gaul to Italy, and so to complete this circuit of his empire, which would then be bounded on all sides by the ocean.[48]

Not only would Caesar be out of reach for a number of years, but it was assumed that he would come back more powerful and successful than ever; a new Roman Alexander. If he ever returned to Rome at all. Another rumour circulating in Rome had it that he would make Alexandria the capital of a new Caesarian empire. Whatever the truth of the matter, a conspiracy was formed amongst the Roman oligarchy, with C. Cassius Longinus, the former Quaestor who had fought with Crassus in the First Parthian War, as its leader. He soon co-opted his brother-in-law and fellow-Praetor M. Iunius Brutus to be the symbolic figurehead of the plot. Brutus claimed descent from the near-mythical Brutus, the man who led the overthrow of the Roman King Tarquinius Superbus and the founder of the Roman Republic some five centuries earlier (overlooking his role as a member of the said royal household). Brutus could therefore uphold the symbolic role as tyrant slayer and defender of the Republic. Thus was formed the most famous conspiracy in history, which came to fruition in the Senate House on the Ides (15th) of March[49] with the murder of Iulius Caesar by a party of his fellow Senators, led by the man who was also rumoured to be his bastard son (Brutus himself). Caesar was fatally stabbed, some twenty-three times, his body left, in another symbolic act, at the foot of a newly-restored statue of Cn. Pompeius himself.

Summary

Thus, C. Iulius Caesar was murdered in the Senate House, some ninety years after the murder of Ti. Sempronius Gracchus in the Forum, also by a group of Roman Senators seemingly concerned by the prospect of a single Roman politician wielding too much power in the Republic. In the intervening ninety years we can see that although much had changed – Gracchus aiming for a consecutive Tribunate, Caesar Dictator for life – the fundamentals of Roman politics remained. If one man disputed the equilibrium of the Roman Republic then his fellow oligarchs would group together and bring about his downfall, as had happened (though without bloodshed) throughout the history of the Roman Republic. Despite Caesar's total military dominance of the Republic and his amassing of unprecedented constitutional powers, he was brought down by the men he had tried to reconcile to his rule, and with his death the Republic was re-set and entered a new phase, to be contested by new faces, with Caesar being the last of the great men who had contested power throughout the previous two decades of the New Republic.[50]

Chapter Nine

The Ghost of Caesar and the Bloody Rise of the Triumviral Republic (44–42 BC)

1. The Bloody Aftermath (44 BC)

The sudden murder of Caesar resulted understandably in Rome collapsing into chaos, with violence breaking out across the city:

Some Senators were wounded in the tumult and others killed. Many other citizens and strangers were murdered also, not designedly, but as such things happen in public commotions, by the mistakes of those into whose hands they fell.[1]

Once this outbreak of popular (and murderous) rage had subsided though, the Republic was finely balanced between two hostile factions; the supporters of Caesar and those of Brutus and Cassius. The former was led by the surviving Consul, M. Antonius and the Master of the Horse, M. Aemilius Lepidus; the latter by the Praetors C. Cassius Longinus and M. Iunius Brutus. Between the two antagonistic factions there must have been many neutrals who were hoping that the aftermath of this assassination could be resolved peacefully, along with a handful of ambitious politicians hoping to exploit the situation.

In the immediate aftermath of the assassination, Antonius fled the Senate (fearing for his own life) and fortified his household, leaving the Senate in the hands of Brutus and Cassius. It was Lepidus however who acted the most quickly and decisively. He was apparently in the Forum when news broke and immediately rushed to a legion of Caesar's veterans placed outside the city, took command and moved to the Field of Mars, ready to act. The conspirators, along with a group of armed gladiators secured the Capitol.

With both sides withdrawing from the Senate House and Forum, two men seemingly stepped into the field. The first was the Praetor L. Cornelius Cinna (the son of Cinna who had ruled Rome in the 80s BC and a relative of Caesar by marriage) who took the opportunity to denounce Caesar as a tyrant whilst supported by armed men.[2]

> *While they were thus engaged the Praetor Cinna, a relative of Caesar by marriage, made his appearance, advanced unexpectedly into the middle of the Forum, laid aside his Praetorian robe, as if disdaining the gift of a tyrant, and called Caesar a tyrant and his murderers tyrannicides. He extolled their deed as exactly like that of their ancestors and ordered that the men themselves should be called from the Capitol as benefactors and rewarded with public honours.*[3]

The second was none other than P. Cornelius Dolabella, the former Tribune of 47 BC, who had been named by Caesar as his successor in the Consulate. Dolabella seized this opportunity to publicly assume the robes of Consul (despite only being twenty-five) and supported Cinna. This brought Brutus and Cassius back to the Forum to support the new Consul and their fellow Praetor. Amongst the promises they issued were the restoration of the two deposed Tribunes and the recall of Sex. Pompeius, still fighting in Spain.

Yet this power grab was cut short by the arrival of Lepidus and his troops, who swiftly occupied the Forum and forced the conspirators back to the Capitol. Once there they sent emissaries to both Antonius and Lepidus. Despite Lepidus having the only military force in Rome, Antonius and Lepidus chose to defuse the situation, fearful of collapsing the Republic into renewed civil war in Italy (Sex. Pompeius was still fighting in Spain). Appian states that both men were worried concerning D. Iunius Brutus who commanded the armies of Cisalpine Gaul (much as Caesar himself had done in 49 BC), whilst Dio stated that the two men distrusted each other, with both seeing themselves as heirs to Caesar. Thus, both sides agreed to a compromise to defuse the situation (albeit temporarily) and organised a meeting of the Senate the next day. Naturally enough Cicero was present and made a speech decrying the tense situation:

Do you not see what is taking place; that the people are again being divided and torn asunder and that, with some choosing this side and some that, they have already fallen into two parties and two camps, and that the one side seized the Capitol as if they feared the Gauls or somebody, while the others with headquarters in the Forum are preparing, as if they were so many Carthaginians and not Romans, to besiege them?[4]

In the debate that followed, and with communications being made to those on the Capitol, a truce was brokered to the effect that the Caesarians would not seek vengeance on the conspirators, whilst the conspirators would not reverse any of Caesar's reforms or appointments. Thus, all sides stepped back from the brink of further bloodshed and a staged reconciliation between all parties was held:

So, they came to an agreement on the terms that had been voted, but those on the Capitol would not come down till they had secured the son of Lepidus and the son of Antonius as hostages; then Brutus descended to Lepidus, to whom he was related, and Cassius to Antonius, under promise of safety. And while they were dining together they naturally, at such a juncture, discussed a variety of topics.[5]

With all sides temporary reconciled, peace returned to Rome, albeit one punctuated by a murderous outbreak of violence following the funeral of Caesar, where his body was burned in the Forum (much akin to that of Clodius, some years earlier). The most notable victim was ironically none other than the pro-Caesarian Tribune C. Helvius Cinna, who was murdered by a mob apparently mistaking him for his kinsman; the Praetor L. Cornelius Cinna (above).[6]

They burned the Senate chamber where Caesar was slain, and ran hither and thither searching for the murderers, who had fled some time previously. They were so mad with rage and grief that meeting the Tribune Cinna, on account of his similarity of name to the Praetor Cinna who had made a speech against Caesar, not waiting to hear any explanation about the similarity of name, they tore him to pieces like wild beasts so that no part of him was ever found for burial. They carried fire to the houses of the

other murderers, but the domestics besought them to desist. So, the People
abstained from the use of fire, but they threatened to come back with arms
on the following day.[7]

With Lepidus still occupying Rome with his veterans and a pro-Caesarian
mob rampaging through the city, the conspirators took the opportunity
to leave Rome, with Brutus and Cassius spending some months in Italy.
Both men were then given a legitimate excuse to leave Italy when they
were appointed on a special commission to oversee Italy's grain supply.
Both men later received (as was their due) Propraetorian provincial
commands, but neither was a significant one; Cassius received Cyrene
and Brutus Crete. Both men were therefore sent to the east where neither
would command significant military forces.

2. The Rise of the Duumvirate (44 BC)

This left Rome under the control of the Caesarians, notably Antonius
and Lepidus. Antonius held one of the Consulships, whilst Dolabella was
confirmed in the other. Lepidus naturally had to abdicate his position
as Master of the Horse (there being no Dictator), but received the
consolation of being named as Caesar's successor as Pontifex Maximus.
Whilst Caesar's assassins had left Rome and soon Italy, the two men faced
a number of issues, not the least of which was that neither fully trusted the
other, with both wanting to be seen as the successor to Caesar. A further
complication arose when Caesar's will was read out and it was discovered
that Caesar's great nephew, C. Octavius, had been posthumously adopted
as Caesar's son, though he had as yet no powerbase of his own.

Furthermore, there were challenges both at home and abroad. At
home, there was the other Consul, P. Cornelius Dolabella; hardly a
staunch Caesarian supporter, with a history of political agitation. To
make matters worse, the pseudo–Marius returned to Rome from exile
to resume his agitation. Overseas, Sex. Pompeius had defeated the latest
Caesarian commander sent to face him in Spain (C. Asinius Pollio),
whilst D. Iunius Brutus held Cisalpine Gaul. This Brutus had been a
close ally of Caesar and had been named as a second heir in his will yet
had been one of the assassins in the Senate House. He too left Rome

soon afterwards, but unlike the others had a significant province to go to – Cisalpine Gaul (having been Praetor in 45 BC). This not only gave him a sizeable army, but also placed him on Italy's doorstep, much as Caesar had been in 49 BC.

Of the many problems the two men faced, the easiest turned out to be P. Cornelius Dolabella, who worked with Antonius and helped him to govern Rome. The two Consuls together passed a law establishing an agrarian commission to distribute land to Caesar's veterans, whilst Antonius also passed laws ratifying Caesar's acts, extended Roman citizenship to Sicily and recalled exiles. Yet at the same time there were several laws which modified or reversed those passed by Caesar and one which made a very public statement about Caesar's method of dominating the Republic.

The first law made yet another modification of jury composition, where the Senatorial-Equestrian split was diluted by the addition of a third element; one composed of former centurions. Another law saw the right of appeal added to those convicted of violence or treason, again modifying another law of Caesar's. Perhaps Antonius' most obvious public statements disassociating himself from the legacy of Caesar was a law abolishing the office of Dictator.

Antonius took a Pompeian route and ensured that no one else would be able to take up the office of Dictator and obviously dominate the Republic as Sulla and Caesar had done. Whilst there was no obvious criticism of Caesar, Antonius was clearly pointing out that he did not agree with Caesar holding the Dictatorship and that no one else should be able to, himself included. There was further action against the memory of Caesar when the Consul Dolabella destroyed an altar to the memory of Caesar in his family tomb and removed a column which marked the spot where Caesar's body had been burnt:

> *But the Consuls overthrew this altar and punished some who showed displeasure at the act, at the same time publishing a law that no one should ever again be Dictator and invoking curses and proclaiming death as the penalty upon any man who should propose or support such a measure, besides openly setting a price upon the heads of any such.*[8]

Whilst Dolabella openly took this action some sources report that Antonius was away from Rome in his role as agrarian commissioner, thus giving him a degree of deniability in these actions. Thus, we can see that even Caesar's close allies were having to exercise a degree of caution when it came to the memory of Caesar, with the Senate and People of Rome so divided on the man and what he represented. Certain aspects of Caesar's reputation were to be cherished, others (such as the hint of tyranny/kingship) to be strenuously avoided. Antonius also passed several laws on foreign affairs; one minor one restoring the King of Galatia, and another affecting the status of Crete (then assigned to Brutus). For the next year both Antonius and Dolabella secured major provinces for themselves; Dolabella receiving Syria and Antonius Macedonia, thus securing the bulk of the Republic's military forces in the east.

Antonius used his position as Consul to pass a large programme of legislation touching on citizenship, judicial proceedings and foreign affairs, and cemented his position as the leading Caesarian figure. This is not to mention the fact that he was ably supported by his two brothers, who both held important offices this year, Caius as Praetor and Lucius as Tribune. Thus, the three Antonii brothers had a firm grip on domestic legislation. Lepidus by contrast found himself somewhat outmanoeuvred, holding no formal political power (having had to resign as Master of the Horse). He soon left for Spain to deal with Sex. Pompeius. Antonius, now holding the upper hand in Rome, turned his attention to the third major domestic problem: the pseudo-Marius. Here Antonius had no need for subtlety as a rumour was circulated that this pseudo-Marius was planning on seizing control of the Republic and murdering the Senate:[9]

> *On this rumour, Antonius, making capital out of the plot, and using his consular authority, arrested Amatius and boldly put him to death without a trial. The Senators were astonished at this deed as an act of violence and contrary to law, but they readily condoned its expediency.*[10]

Thus, the pseudo-Marius was put to death, possibly an illegal act, but given the uncertainty of the man's true origins, that would have been unclear. Yet despite the boldness of this action the situation soon descended into chaos and violence when the followers of this pseudo-Marius retaliated:

> *The followers of Amatius* [Marius], *and the Plebeians generally, missing Amatius* [Marius] *and feeling indignation at the deed, and especially because it had been done by Antonius, whom the people had honoured, determined that they would not be scorned in that way. With shouts they took possession of the Forum, exclaiming violently against Antonius, and called on the magistrates to dedicate the altar in place of Amatius* [Marius], *and to offer the first sacrifices on it to Caesar. Having been driven out of the Forum by soldiers sent by Antonius, they became still more indignant, and vociferated more loudly, and some of them showed places where Caesar's statues had been torn from their pedestals. One man told them that he could show the shop where the statues were being broken up. The others followed, and having witnessed the fact, they set fire to the place. Finally, Antonius sent more soldiers and some of those who resisted were killed, others were captured, and of these the slaves were crucified and the freemen thrown over the Tarpeian rock.*[11]

Thus, Rome saw another armed sedition which could only be ended by the Consul sending troops in to kill the protestors, these acts becoming so common that the *senatus consultum ultimum* was no longer even being used to justify the force used. Having dealt with Marius, Antonius and Lepidus then dealt with Sex. Pompeius. Having successfully defeated the Caesarian commanders sent against him in Spain, Antonius and Lepidus chose to neutralise him through politics rather than military force (again a break from Caesar's methods). To those ends Lepidus was sent to Spain to negotiate with Pompeius:

> *Antonius also moved that Sextus Pompeius (the son of Pompeius Magnus, who was still much beloved by all) should be recalled from Spain, where he was still attacked by Caesar's lieutenants, and that he should be paid 50 million of Attic drachmas out of the public treasury for his father's confiscated property and be appointed commander of the sea, as his father had been, with charge of all the Roman ships, wherever situated, which were needed for immediate service. The astonished Senate accepted each of these decrees with alacrity and applauded Antonius the whole day.*[12]

We can see that Antonius and Lepidus achieved through negotiation what Caesar could not through bloodshed, and the civil war in Spain was neutralised for now and Lepidus returned to Rome. It was from this high point of having secured control of Italy and Spain however that the Duumvirs found their position undermined both at home and abroad, as the Republic collapsed once again into renewed civil war.

3. The Fall of the Duumvirate (44–43 BC)

On the face of it, the Duumvirate of Antonius and Lepidus was faced with just one major threat: D. Iunius Brutus, one of Caesar's assassins, Governor of Cisalpine Gaul and a man with a battle-hardened army a few days march from Italy proper. Yet the situation was not a repeat of the one which Pompeius had found himself in in 49 BC. Whilst the Duumvirs may well have been expecting an aggressive move from Brutus, he had a far smaller army than Caesar had, and they had significant military resources in Italy already.

There is nothing to say that Brutus was intending an invasion of Italy, but his thoughts must have been turning to the impending end of his military command. With Antonius and Lepidus controlling the Senate there would have been no opportunity for an extension and the atmosphere in Rome was still not favourable to Caesar's killers. Furthermore, having seen Antonius dispose of the pseudo-Marius, he must have been fearful for his life should he have returned to Rome in 43 BC. In the end it was Antonius and Lepidus however who made the first move. Clearly wanting to remove all threats to their new regime they had the Senate pass a decree transferring the command of Cisalpine Gaul from Brutus to Antonius himself for a period of five years. Furthermore, in anticipation of this transfer, he transferred the legions from Macedonia to Italy, under the command of his brother Caius, giving him a large army stationed in Italy.

Here it seems however that Antonius had overplayed his hand. Brutus had made no overtly aggressive moves and the Senate now faced the prospect of Antonius dominating Italy from Cisalpine Gaul for a period of five years, contrary to the laws Caesar had just passed on the length of provincial commands. Appian reports that there were many in the Senate who had no wish to see Antonius dominating the Republic any more than Caesar and so sent word to Brutus not to accept this transfer of command (though Brutus may well have been planning to do just that anyway).[13]

Thus, the Duumvirs forced Brutus to defend his province making the renewal of the civil war more likely.

Prior to setting off for Gaul to dislodge Brutus, Antonius and Lepidus faced the same problem that all men who sought to dominate the Republic had faced: how to secure their political control of the Republic once out of annual office themselves. Clearly neither Antonius nor Lepidus had the power and control of Caesar; the Senate could not be relied upon to allow a repeated Consulship, and the Dictatorship had been abolished. Furthermore, both of Antonius' brothers were out of office at the end of 44 BC as well. Antonius and Lepidus clearly calculated that as long as they had control of Rome's military power, then the political power could be left in the hands of sympathetic but powerless allies.

The Consulship for 43 BC fell to two junior Caesarian officers, C. Vibius Pansa Caetronianus and A. Hirtius, whilst Antonius, his brother Caius, and Lepidus all received major military commands. M. Antonius had received both Cisalpine and Transalpine Gaul for a period of five years and took his youngest brother (Lucius) with him as a legate. Caius Antonius replaced his brother as Governor of Macedonia, securing Italy's eastern flank, whilst Lepidus received Nearer Spain and Norbonensis Gaul. Thus, on paper, the Duumvirs had control of the majority of the Republic's military assets, Spain, Gaul, and Macedonia, along with Dolabella taking up command in the east. Seemingly all that was required was to remove Brutus from Gaul. Unfortunately for them however, whilst all their attention was on Brutus, two new challenges arose, one predictable, one not so.

The first challenge came from the other leaders of the anti-Caesarian faction, namely M. Iunius Brutus and C. Cassius Longinus. Although both had been given minor provinces to command (Cyrene and Crete respectively) with no military assets, Antonius and Lepidus's attack on D. Brutus clearly sent a signal that the Duumvirs were not looking for a compromise with their opponents but sought to dominate the Republic. Again, their thoughts must equally have turned to what fate would befall them after their year in office.

However, they noticed one critical fact – that Antonius and Lepidus had focused all their attention on D. Brutus in the west. leaving an opportunity to consolidate power in the east, especially as C. Antonius was in control only of Macedonia and Dolabella had not yet taken up his command in Syria.

Thus, both men determined to seize control of the Roman east and build up a rival powerbase. Cassius was to seize control of the Middle East, which he knew well from his time in the First Romano-Parthian War and his successful defence of Syria from the Parthian invasion following the Battle of Carrhae. Brutus was tasked with seizing control of Macedonia and Greece. Thus, whilst Antonius and Lepidus focussed all their efforts to secure control of the Western Republic, the Eastern Republic began to slip away from them.

Worse was to come, however, when they faced an unexpected challenge from within Rome and Italy itself. Throughout the various phases of civil war in the last fifty years, one aspect had been crucial, namely control of Rome itself and with it the political legitimatisation of that control. Antonius and Lepidus had assumed that their control of Rome was secure, especially with the co-option of Dolabella and the elimination of the pseudo-Marius. However, they faced an unexpected challenge from the newly adopted eighteen-year-old son of their former mentor, C. Octavius.

Octavius had been Caesar's great nephew, born to a mid-ranking Consular Plebeian family, and had slowly been groomed as Caesar's Roman successor, Caesar's natural son (Caesarion) not being legitimate under Roman law. Yet Caesar's will saw Octavius legally adopted (post-mortem) making him Caesar's legitimate son and heir. Given his young age and political inexperience neither Antonius nor Lepidus took this young man seriously and both saw themselves as the political heirs of Caesar. Ironically this dismissal had echoes of the past when the Dictator Sulla had dismissed a young Caesar as not being worth the trouble, despite his being the last remaining heir of Marius.[14] For Antonius and Lepidus, however, this dismissal brought a more immediate impact.

Whilst Antonius and Lepidus may have dismissed this nineteen-year-old as an irrelevance, it seems that the young Octavius took himself and his new role as the heir to Caesar very seriously and set about building his own powerbase.[15] Here he found a natural constituency to build on; the opponents of Antonius and Lepidus within Rome and Italy. These opponents ranged from Caesarian supporters to neutrals, most of whom would not support Brutus and Cassius due to their assassination of Caesar. Yet Octavius had impeccable Caesarian credentials, but apparently none of his father's (and his father's lieutenants') obvious desire to dominate the Republic (as far as they could tell).

Antonius thus seemingly both underestimated Octavius and acted in a high-handed manner towards him. The two men clashed over the issue of Caesar's money, his will having specified each citizen to be paid a cash lump sum out of Caesar's fortune, which Antonius opposed. They next clashed over the issue of the Tribunate, for which there was now a vacancy following the murder of C. Helvius Cinna (see above). Here the sources are split. Appian reports that Octavius backed a candidate (Flaminius) for the role whilst Dio and Plutarch state that Octavius himself wanted to secure the position (despite legally being adopted into a Patrician family, via Caesar's will).[16]

In any event, Antonius used his power to block this and apparently even had Octavius dragged away by his (Antonius') Lictors. They then publicly clashed once more over the placing of a golden chair in the Theatre, in his father's honour, as decreed by the Senate. On each occasion Octavius was able to speak to the People, and his father's veterans, painting himself as a loyal and devoted son of a great man, treacherously cut down, whilst painting Antonius as a disloyal follower of Caesar who dishonoured his memory and let his murderers escape justice. Thus, Antonius found himself being undermined politically and found the need to stage-manage a public reconciliation.

Yet even then Antonius seemed not to give the matter too much importance, focusing on gaining military control of the Republic by defeating D. Iunius Brutus and securing Gaul. Yet Antonius seemed to share his late mentor's inability to understand the crucial importance of appearances in the Republic. Caesar had held military dominance over Rome but was undermined when he translated this into an obvious political dominance. Antonius was seemingly heading down the same path, but without having the overarching military dominance to support it. Octavius, however, was building a broader coalition of both Caesarian veterans and Antonius' opponents, including Cicero.

Clearly still not sensing the political danger, Antonius focused on the upcoming campaign in Cisalpine Gaul against Brutus and left

Rome for Brundisium to meet his army, which had been transferred from Macedonia, thus leaving Rome to Octavius. In Antonius' absence, Octavius had one of the Tribunes (Ti. Cannutius) denounce Antonius before the People:

> *Having learned his intentions Cannutius addressed the people, saying that Octavius was advancing with real hostility to Antonius and that those who were afraid that Antonius was aiming at tyranny should side with Octavius as they had no other army at present. After speaking thus, he brought in Octavius, who was encamped before the city at the temple of Mars, fifteen stades distant. When the latter arrived, he proceeded to the temple of Castor and Pollux, which his soldiers surrounded carrying concealed daggers. Cannutius addressed the People first, speaking against Antonius. Afterwards Octavius also reminded them of his father and of what he had himself suffered at the hands of Antonius, on account of which he had enlisted this army as a guard for himself. He declared himself the obedient servant of his Republic in all things and said that he was ready to confront Antonius in the present emergency.*[17]

Meanwhile, Octavius had been on a recruitment campaign in the region of Campania, amongst the settled veterans of his father former legions, and had amassed himself a private army (clearly following a Pompeian / Crassan model). He had also sent emissaries to Antonius' newly-arrived legions at Brundisium and, with the addition of some monies and the promise of more to come, stirred up a revolt amongst Antonius' legions. Antonius reacted with his usual brutal efficiency and had the ringleaders executed, which hardly endeared him to the legions themselves. Antonius then returned to Rome and called a meeting of the Senate to confront Octavius, but at that point two of his five legions mutinied (in a well-orchestrated manoeuvre) and joined Octavius. Thus, Antonius had three legions, compared to five for Octavius (two of Antonius', two composed of veterans and one of new recruits). Clearly finding himself outmanoeuvred, Antonius soon left Rome to pursue the war against Brutus in Gaul, again leaving Octavius in control of Rome. He crossed into Gaul and started a siege of D. Brutus at Mutina in late 44 BC, but interestingly Octavius chose to leave Rome and soon set off in pursuit.

Whilst these events were taking place in Italy, overseas Cleopatra was also consolidating her position. Under Caesar's settlement she was technically only joint ruler of Ptolemaic Egypt, along with her younger brother Ptolemy XIV. However, with Rome otherwise distracted she had her younger brother murdered and, in his place, elevated her son (and Caesar's) to joint Pharaoh (as Ptolemy XV). Thus 44 BC ended with Caesar's two sons (legal and biological) holding power in both Rome and Alexandria respectively.

4. The Collapse and Recovery of the Western Republic (43 BC)

Although the Republic had held together during the months that followed Caesar's murder, the year 43 BC marked another collapse of government and cohesion in the Western Republic and culminated in a new form of Republican government, accompanied by widespread bloodshed. No sooner had the new Consuls taken power than the Senate was convened to discuss the issue of Antonius. By this point Antonius was in Gaul, laying siege to D. Brutus, Lepidus was in Spain, and Octavius and his private army was following Antonius towards Gaul. Within days Antonius' opponents, led by Cicero, had moved that Antonius be declared an 'enemy of the state'. This proposal was only blocked by a Tribune (Salvius) using his veto (*intercessio*). The charges labelled against Antonius were that he had illegally usurped the province of Gaul and brought his army over from Macedonia to pursue war against a fellow Roman. Furthermore, he was accused of aiming for a tyranny similar to that of his late mentor.

It does not take much to see the staggering hypocrisy being displayed here. The Senate itself had passed a motion removing Brutus from his Gallic command and transferred it to Antonius whilst supporting his move to dislodge Brutus, who was refusing a Senatorial command. Yet the second Antonius' back was turned they were happy to condemn him for this. Antonius' key mistake had been to leave Rome in pursuit of military control of the west, for in doing so he lost all political power and allowed his enemies control of the Senate. This soon turned him from being a duly-authorised Proconsul fighting a legitimate war, to a rebel and 'enemy of the state'.

Just months after voting to remove D. Iunius Brutus from his Gallic command, the Senate now voted that he be encouraged to remain in command and resist Antonius. They further voted that Octavius use his (illegally assembled) private army to assist the Consuls Vibius and Hirtius to defeat Antonius, with the power of a Propraetor. Thus, we have the extraordinary situation of Antonius being duly authorised to remove Brutus from Gaul, and then Vibius, Hirtius and Octavius being subsequently duly authorised to remove Antonius. Furthermore Octavius, with now the largest army in Italy/Gaul, received unprecedented honours from the Senate for a nineteen-year-old without any military success:

> *They* [the Senate] *awarded him a gilded statue and the right to declare his opinion among the consulars in the Senate even now, and the right to stand for the Consulship itself ten years before the legal period and voted from the public treasury to the legions that deserted from Antonius to him the same amount that he promised to give them if they should be victorious.*[18]

In the space of a year, and in a move which bore some resemblance to the early career of Pompeius, Octavius went from being a little-known teenager to the most powerful man in Rome. The Senate duly sent envoys to Antonius to deliver their decision, which was duly rebuffed. Antonius then apparently made counter-proposals to the Senate, which stated that he would indeed quit Gaul and disband his army if M. Iunius Brutus and C. Cassius Longinus were made Consuls. Even though the proposal would be rejected, this showed how far the political pendulum had swung in under a year. Naturally enough the Senate rejected these terms and duly declared war on Antonius, upon which a number of the elected magistrates quit Rome to join him. Dio states: *Many of those, therefore, who favoured Antonius' cause, went straight to him, among them a few Tribunes and Praetors.*[19]

These men too were declared enemies of the state. To support this war against Antonius, the Senate had to find additional funds, with the nobles of Rome expected to contribute:

And since there was need of much money for the war, they all contributed the twenty-fifth part of the wealth they possessed and the senators also four obols for each roof-tile of all the houses in the city that they either owned themselves or occupied as tenants. ... These contributions were given readily by those who favoured Caesar and hated Antonius; but the majority, being burdened alike by the campaigns and the taxes, were irritated.[20]

The Consul Hirtius was dispatched to join Octavius, whilst the other Consul (Pansa), stayed in Rome to levy fresh legions and pass domestic legislation. With Antonius declared an 'enemy of the state', his legislative reforms of the previous year were declared null and void and so Pansa had to pass similar measures to enter them back into statute. We hear of a measure confirming Caesar's acts, the abolition of the Dictatorship, and the confirmation of Caesar's veteran colonies. He also passed measures regarding the commands of M. Brutus, Sex. Pompeius and Dolabella (see below).

With these measures passed and an army of new recruits he set off to Gaul to join Hirtius and Octavius. With negotiation having failed, both sides resorted to battle. What followed next were two battles, Forum Gallorum and Mutina. Whilst the military details of the campaign fall outside of this work, Orosius provides a tidy summary:

On being declared an enemy of the state by the Senate, Antonius had blockaded Decimus Brutus, besieging him at Mutina. Caesar [Octavius] was sent along with the Consuls Hirtius and Pansa to free Brutus and defeat Antonius. Pansa arrived first and fell into an ambush. In the midst of his army's defeat he was gravely wounded by a javelin and died of his wounds a few days later. Hirtius, on bringing reinforcements for his colleague, destroyed Antonius' great army with enormous slaughter. Caesar merely guarded their camp. In a second battle against Antonius, both sides suffered heavy losses. It was then that the Consul Hirtius was killed, Antonius was defeated and put to flight and Caesar emerged victorious.[21]

Heavily outnumbered, Antonius fell back on his military skill and acted quickly to prevent the two Consular armies from joining forces, ambushing the weaker force (Pansa's) which was composed of new recruits. Unfortunately for him the other Consul (Hirtius) arrived and turned this victory into a defeat. In a second battle Antonius was defeated outright and retreated.

Though there were clear victors on the battlefield, the aftermath somewhat diluted the result. The greatest military plaudits went to the Consul A. Hirtius, who had twice defeated Antonius, but as he was killed toward the end of the Battle of Mutina he was not able to build on this success, though he was (along with his colleague Pansa) given a splendid public funeral in the Campus Martius. Thus, on the face of it, the obvious winner was Octavius: Antonius had been defeated and was on the run, whilst the two Consuls had been killed nobly in action leaving him as senior commander.

Yet, just as both his adopted father and opponent had done, Octavius underestimated the Senate. Caesar had assumed that the Senate had been pacified, following his string of victories on the battlefield, yet he found out (all too late) that the Senatorial oligarchy had merely been biding their time. Antonius too fell into this trap. As Consul in 44 BC and with troops in the city, the Senate readily acquiesced to Antonius' demands, yet the second his back was turned and he had left the city, the Senate were all too eager to designate him an enemy of the Senate and People of Rome. Once again, as with Antonius' downfall, the Senate were all too eager to acquiesce to Octavius' demands, especially when faced with his five legions, but following Mutina they no longer needed him, and he was deemed surplus to requirements.

Thus, Octavius would have been dismayed to find out that the Senate had decreed a Triumph, and command of Cisalpine Gaul and the Senatorial armies there had been awarded, not to himself, but to D. Iunius Brutus, one of his father's assassins. It was Brutus who was given the task (ironically) of hunting down the renegade Antonius. Furthermore, a Senatorial delegation was sent to Sex. Pompeius, who was stationed in the city of Massilia along with a substantial fleet. The Senate granted him Proconsular command of the Mediterranean, which Appian states was equal to his father's Mediterranean command in the 60s.[22] The Senate also made overtures to Lepidus, Antonius' colleague, to persuade him not to support Antonius but to side with the Senate:

> *The Senate and People of Rome, in return for the important and numerous services of Marcus Lepidus to the Republic, declares that it places great hopes of future tranquillity and peace and concord, in his virtue, authority, and good fortune; and the Senate and People of Rome will ever remember his services to the Republic; and it is decreed by the vote of this order, that a gilt equestrian statue be erected to him in the Rostra, or in whatever other place in the Forum he pleases.*[23]

Seemingly the chaos in the west had been quelled and the Senate seemed to be in control of the situation, with Antonius defeated, Octavius sidelined, and D. Brutus and Sex. Pompeius in command of the armies and navy. Yet as the events of the previous eighteen months had shown, the situation in the Republic could change in an instant and fortunes could easily be reversed.

5. The Collapse and Recovery of the Eastern Republic (43 BC)

Yet we need to briefly consider the civil war raging in Rome's eastern empire, as it had a material effect on events in the west and at Rome. The situation in the east in 43 BC was every bit as confused as that in the west. Central to this chaos were the successful campaigns of M. Iunius Brutus and C. Cassius Longinus, the two key leaders of the anti-Caesarian faction of the Senate. In theory they faced the Caesarian sponsored Governors, C. Antonius (brother of Marcus) and P. Cornelius Dolabella (M. Antonius' Consular colleague in 44 BC). Again, the full military details fall outside the scope of this present work, but we can outline the key events.

Despite being Governor of the province of Macedonia, C. Antonius found himself in a considerably weakened position when M. Iunius Brutus launched his invasion of Greece, as the bulk of the province's legions had been transferred to Italy to help his brother Marcus attack D. Iunius Brutus in Gaul. Furthermore, the outgoing Governor of Macedonia (Q. Hortensius) sided with Brutus. Thus, very quickly Antonius found himself besieged in Apollonia and forced to surrender to Brutus by the end of March 43 BC. Therefore, whilst D. Iunius Brutus was gaining command of Gaul, on the back of the defeat of M. Antonius,

M. Iunius Brutus had gained control of Macedonia having defeated
C. Antonius. As they had done in the west, the Senate seized on this
turn of fortune and rapidly confirmed M. Iunius Brutus as Proconsular
Governor of Macedonia, Illyricum and Achaea.

His colleague, C. Cassius Longinus had met with equal success in the
Roman province of Syria, where he had formerly held a command in the
First Romano–Parthian War. He too soon won over the local garrisons
without needing to fight the incumbent governor, as Cornelius Dolabella
had not even made it to his province yet; he was still coming overland
through Asia Minor. Once again, the Senate were all too eager to confirm
Cassius as Governor of Syria, even though Dolabella was still on route.

It was only as he travelled through Asia Minor that Dolabella found
his tardiness had cost him, and that the prize province of Syria was now
under the (Senatorially-authorised) command of Cassius. Dolabella,
however, who had never had strong ties to the Caesarian regime, seemingly
determined to regain control of 'his' province by force. The Governor of
Asia was C. Trebonius (Cos. 45 BC), who had been one of the conspirators
of 44 BC though not seemingly an active assassin. Trebonius, far from
taking sides in the impending clash between Dolabella and Cassius,
seemingly remained neutral, agreeing to provide Dolabella with supplies
but barring him from the major cities. Either taking offence at this, or
thinking that Trebonius was plotting with Cassius, Dolabella attacked
the city of Smyrna and captured it by surprise, along with Trebonius,
whom he promptly had executed. Thus, one former Consul ordered the
execution of another former Consul without trial.

When news reached the Senate, they were all too eager to seize on
the excuse and declared Dolabella an enemy of the Senate and People
(along with his consular colleague of 44 BC, M. Antonius). Nevertheless,
Dolabella was able to raise several legions and attacked Cassius in Syria
but proved to be no match on the battlefield and lost his army, soon after
committing suicide.

6. The Bloody Rise of the Triumvirate (43 BC)

Thus, by mid-43 BC the situation had seemingly stabilised and the
anti-Caesarian faction found itself in command of the bulk of Rome's

empire (both militarily and politically). In the west D. Iunius Brutus had command of the Senatorial armies chasing down M. Antonius, whilst in the east M. Iunius Brutus held command of Macedonia and Greece and Cassius held command in Syria. Furthermore, all these commands had been confirmed by the Senate (though that meant little these days). Their only rivals were M. Antonius, who was on the run in Gaul, Octavius, sulking in Cisalpine Gaul, and Lepidus in Spain. A third faction was represented by the last of the Pompeian forces commanded by Sex. Pompeius, who now had a Senatorial command of the Mediterranean.

There must have been many in the Senate, especially Cicero, who had reasons to be optimistic. Caesar was dead, his key lieutenant was on the run, his Roman son was seemingly neutralised, and they could call upon substantial military forces under the command of the anti-Caesarian faction and the Pompeian faction. Yet as the pendulum in Roman politics had suddenly swung in favour of the Senate and the anti-Caesarian faction, it suddenly swung against them.

The reason that this occurred was the simple fact that their military position in the west was not as strong as it looked on paper. Antonius had been defeated but was able to retreat into Gaul and towards the provinces of Gallia Norbonensis and Nearer Spain, both governed by Lepidus, Antonius' colleague. Although there was no love lost between the rivals Antonius and Lepidus, they had far more in common than with a Senate so clearly favouring the anti-Caesarian faction of Brutus and Cassius. In addition, Octavius was not entirely powerless in Gaul, as a number of the Senatorial legions refused to serve under Brutus, especially the Caesarian veterans. This left Octavius with the nearest military force to Rome itself, with all the other armies in the west across the Alps and moving towards a clash in southern Gaul or Spain.

Furthermore, there was the matter of the other Governors of the region, all of whom had been appointed by Antonius, notably C. Asinius Pollio in Farther Spain and L. Munatius Plancus in Transalpine Gaul. The key event took place in Gaul, where Lepidus marched to intercept Antonius. Given the disparity of their respective forces, Lepidus was in a position to crush Antonius, yet what did he have to gain by such an act, given that the Senate was hardly likely to provide him with any further rewards beyond meaningless votes of thanks? The Senate seemed to be firmly in the grip of the those opposed to the Caesarian faction, whether they be the faction of Brutus and Cassius or those biased neutrals, like Cicero.

Once more, a Roman nobleman associated his own good with the ultimate good of the Republic and decided that it was only his faction that could save the Republic from its enemies. Therefore, Lepidus renewed his Duumviral alliance with Antonius and the two men joined forces, though as equals, with Antonius clearly not in the position he had occupied throughout 44 BC. Thus, Antonius stopped running and now had a fresh army with which to face D. Iunis Brutus. The two men thus re-forged the Caesarian faction, which soon drew in the Caesarian-appointed Governors of Farther Spain (C. Asinius Pollio) and Transalpine Gaul (L. Munatius Plancus). Antonius and Lepidus now had command of the bulk of the forces of the Western Republic and could face D. Iunius Brutus with superior military strength.

As we can see, it was Lepidus who swung the war back in favour of the Caesarian faction by allying with Antonius once more. Yet Lepidus pulled off one more masterstroke which would seal their temporary dominance in the west: he contacted Octavius and proposed that he join with him and Antonius in a three-way alliance; a fresh Triumvirate. Octavius too had much to gain and nothing to lose from splitting from a Senate that had already discarded him. Furthermore, although only nineteen and no great military leader, he had the one thing that Lepidus and Antonius did not: the strategic position. He and his army sat in Cisalpine Gaul (thus on the Italian side of the Alps) and had an unguarded path between him and Rome. With control of Rome came control of the Senate and the Assemblies, and thus the levers of the Republican government, and most of all the legitimatisation of their position. Thus, whilst Antonius and Lepidus prepared to face D. Iunius Brutus, Octavius emulated his father and crossed the Rubicon, invading Italy and marching on Rome.

The Senate saw the danger too late: all that lay between Octavius and Rome was one legion left behind by the (now-deceased) Consul Pansa. As usual the Senate attempted to negotiate with Octavius, who sent a deputation of centurions from his army to press his demands: pay for the troops and the Consulship for himself (despite only being nineteen). At the same time, the Senate recalled two legions from Africa to bolster the one that was stationed near Rome. According to Appian the two legions arrived at Rome at the same time as Octavius and his main army. Thus, Octavius faced three legions defending Rome.[24]

Yet, wherever possible Octavius preferred to negotiate rather than fight and soon enough all three legions defected to his side, seemingly swayed by the promise of a large pay-out to the soldiers and the loyalty that Octavius now earned from being Caesar's son and heir. Two of the legionary commanders defected along with the soldiers, whilst the other (the Praetor M. Caecilius Cornutus) committed suicide. With total military control of Rome and Italy, Octavius' advancement was ensured and at the age of nineteen he was elected as a Consul of Rome. His colleague (of his choice) was an old ally of his adopted father; Q. Pedius.

Octavius immediately secured his military position by ensuring that the legions received their pay from the confiscated state treasury. With political control of Rome, the balance of legitimacy swung back in the favour of the Caesarian faction. The decrees declaring Lepidus, Antonius (and Dolabella) as enemies of the Republic were overturned (too late in Dolabella's case) and Q. Pedius passed a law establishing a special court to try the murderers of Caesar. Presided over by Octavius himself, the court convicted all those involved in the assassination in absentia and even included Sex. Pompeius for good measure. Thus, having only been confirmed in their newly acquired provinces by the Senate a few months earlier, D. Iunius Brutus, M. Iunius Brutus, C. Cassius Longinus and Sex. Pompeius were now all enemies of the state.

Furthermore, Octavius secured his own position by having a *lex curiata* passed by the People which legally confirmed his adoption by Caesar in his will. Thus, he took the adopted name of his father and became C. Iulius Caesar Octavianus. With his and his allies' position secured, Octavianus left Pedius in control of the city (backed up by his legions) and moved back to Cisalpine Gaul to link up with Lepidus and Antonius to face D. Brutus. For Brutus in Gaul, this reversal of fortune was all too obvious. From pursuing a defeated Antonius through Gaul, he now found himself facing the combined might of the armies of both Spanish provinces and two Gallic ones (Narbonensis and Transalpine) and an alliance of three Roman Governors, Lepidus, Asinius Pollio and Munatius Plancus. In addition to Antonius' remaining forces and those of Lepidus, Pollio brought a further two legions and Plancus a further three.

According to Appian, Brutus had ten legions at his disposal, but only four had seen combat, with the other six being freshly levied.[25] Rather than stand and fight (and be annihilated) Brutus turned and attempted to retreat from Gaul and join his kinsman (and fellow conspirator) M. Iunius Brutus in Macedonia. Yet facing him was Octavianus coming from Italy. Rather than fight the untested Octavianus, Brutus again chose flight and attempted the overland route between Gaul and Macedonia, through non-Roman-controlled tribal territories.

Naturally enough, Brutus' ten legions soon started deserting in droves, clearly sensing the swing in power in favour of the Caesarians. The freshly levied men returned to their own towns and villages and then his four veteran legions deserted as a whole to Antonius, the man they had fought at the Battles of Forum Gallorum and Mutina. With only a handful of men to his name, Brutus was captured by a Gallic chieftain, who sent word to Antonius, who in return sealed Brutus' fate; with Brutus' head being sent to Antonius. Thus, in a remarkable year in Roman politics, the Caesarian faction in the shape of Lepidus, Antonius and Caesar Octavianus now found themselves in military and political control of the Western Republic.

Clearly the last few months had shown these three men the danger of acting in an uncoordinated manner. Octavianus had completely undermined Antonius' position (with the help of the Senate) only to find himself side-lined and the anti-Caesarian faction being promoted by the Senate. Furthermore, despite being enemies of the Republic once more, and convicted murderers, Brutus and Cassius and their allies held the bulk of the Eastern Republic, whilst Sex. Pompeius had a fleet controlling the Mediterranean. Thus, it was clear that cooperation was central to their survival and continued prosperity. Therefore, they met and formally battered out a political alliance to rule the Republic, dispensing with the niceties of Republic *mos maiorum*.

Recent history had all too clearly shown the dangers of anyone trying to hold supreme power in Rome. Caesar had held extraordinary power and been assassinated by members of the Senate. Antonius had held the ordinary power of the Consulate, but had been outmanoeuvred by the Senate the second he had stepped down from the Consulship and left Rome. Thus, the three men agreed on a new constitutional order; a formal division of power between the three of them with a new office specially created for them. This was to be accompanied by a bloody purge of the Senate, which time and again had shown itself ready to oppose anyone trying to subvert the normal running of the Republic.

The first stage was achieved in November 43 BC by Tribunician law. The Tribune P. Titius put an extraordinary bill before the People:

> *Publius Titius proposed a law providing for a new magistracy for settling the present disorders, to consist of three men to hold office for five years, namely, Lepidus, Antonius, and Octavianus, with the same power as Consuls.*[26]

Thus, a new office was established in the Republic; the *Triumviri Rei Publicae Constituendae*, which held consular imperium and the right to appoint city magistrates, for a period of five years. These three officials carved up the Governorships (and thus the military resources) of the Western Republic between them. Lepidus remained in command of Nearer Spain and Narbonensis Gaul, Antonius received Transalpine and Cisalpine Gaul, whilst Octavianus received Sicily, Sardinia and Africa.

Clearly this office held greater powers than the Consulate, but the men ensured that Consuls were still elected, to maintain Republican tradition and have officials in Rome when they were not. Octavianus resigned his Consulship, whilst Pedius had died of natural causes (old age). In their place for the remainder of 43 BC new Consuls were elected: C. Carrinas and P. Ventidius Bassus, who was Praetor at the time of his election/ selection; a unique feat. Thus 43 BC saw the Republic have a record six Consuls, in three different pairings. For 42 BC Lepidus himself was selected as one of the Consuls (in addition to his Triumviral office) along with L. Munatius Plancus.

The Triumvirs had military and political control of Rome and the Western Republic. They cemented this position by learning from Caesar's (and their own) mistakes and swiftly moved to eliminate the one consistent source of domestic opposition: the Senate. Caesar had pardoned many of his enemies and appeased many others and had been rewarded by twenty-three stab wounds. Both Antonius and Octavianus had tried to work with the Senate but had then been outmanoeuvred.

As has been seen throughout this period, control of the Senate brought political legitimacy, but the question was how could one control the Senate? Although the hardcore anti-Caesarians had fled east, there still remained many neutrals who were not pro-Caesarian. Thus, the Triumvirs took a leaf out of recent Roman history and the rule of Sulla, and published a proscription list; a legitimate death list of political enemies to be murdered.[27]

Once more, Roman politicians turned to the state-sanctioned murder of their political opponents in the name of bringing stability to the Republic (or at least their version of it):

> *That same night, the proscription of one hundred and thirty men in addition to the seventeen was proclaimed in various parts of the city, and a little later one hundred and fifty more, and additions to the lists were constantly made of those who were condemned later or previously killed by mistake, so that they might seem to have perished justly.*[28]

Some three hundred men were slaughtered to secure the new regime. Amongst the victims were a number of serving magistrates, notably the Tribune Salvius, the Praetors Q. Gallius and Minucius and the Aedile Volusius, along with the Governor of Africa Q. Cornificius. (see Appendix Three).[29] Being related to the Triumvirs was no guarantee of safety:

> *Lepidus was the first to begin the work of proscription, and his brother Paullus was the first on the list of the proscribed. Antonius came next, and the second name on the list was that of his uncle, Lucius Caesar. These two men had been the first to vote Lepidus and Antonius public enemies. The third and fourth victims were relatives of the consuls-elect for the coming year, namely, Plotius, the brother of Plancus, and Quintus, the father-in-law of Asinius. ... When the lists were published, the gates and all the other exits from the city, the harbour, the marshes, the pools, and every other place that was suspected as adapted to flight or concealment, were occupied by soldiers; the centurions were charged to scour the surrounding country. All these things took place simultaneously.*[30]

In total it is said that over one hundred Senators found themselves on the proscription lists, but a number were able to escape, finding sanctuary either with Brutus and Cassius in the Eastern Republic or Sex. Pompeius, in the Mediterranean. The most prominent victim however was none other than the elder statesman M. Tullius Cicero himself, a long-time opponent of Antonius. Cicero, along with his brother Quintus and Quintus' son, were all proscribed and made a half-hearted effort to escape eastwards, despite not being in Rome when the announcements were made. All three were captured and executed with Cicero's head and hands being displayed in the Forum. Cicero's son Marcus escaped death due to his being in Greece at the time, and he joined the army of Brutus. He survived the subsequent civil wars and ironically held a Consulship in 30 BC with none other than Octavianus himself.

It was around this time that Caius Antonius (brother of M. Antonius), who had been held prisoner by M. Brutus in Macedonia was put to death on Brutus' orders, ostensibly for attempting to raise a rebellion against him, but it can be seen as retaliation for the Triumvirs, bloodshed.

Thus, the Triumvirs rid Rome and the Senate of all those they believed would oppose them, leaving behind them a Senate that could be relied upon not to double cross them the minute they left Rome (or so they hoped). The Proscriptions also gave the Triumvirs the chance to replenish the empty state coffers by confiscating and selling off the property of the proscribed men. Thus, the year 43 BC ended with the Triumvirs in control of the Western Republic, Brutus and Cassius the Eastern Republic, and Sex. Pompeius the Mediterranean.

Summary

We can see that the aftermath of the assassination of Caesar threw the Republic into turmoil and plunged it back into civil war. Whilst the immediate aftermath saw an uneasy truce emerge and all parties agree to work within the Republican framework, this soon collapsed into total anarchy. The subsequent events of 44 and 43 BC cannot be broken down into a tidy split between Caesarian and anti-Caesarians, with Octavius and Antonius going to war and the Senate playing both off against each other, not to mention Dolabella in the east and Pompeius in the Mediterranean.

Clearly no one (outside of the conspirators) was expecting there to be such a vacuum in power, and the various figures and factions continued to make swift alliances for greatest advantage.

It is difficult to say how long this truce would have held: as soon as the key figures had recovered from the rapidity of events in 44 BC, they soon set about ensuring their own dominance. Both Antonius and Lepidus clearly fancied stepping into Caesar's shoes as the dominant figure in Rome, though with a lower profile than Caesar. Initially it seemed that they would do so in a (relatively) peaceful manner, as seen by their accommodation with Pompeius (overlooking their murder of the pseudo-Marius). Yet it was their pursuit of D. Iunius Brutus that plunged the Republic back into chaos and throughput this period it is the shadow of Caesar and the clear example he had set when he crossed the Rubicon from Gaul into Italy that dominates.

What happened next was an amazing series of changes of fortune, with Antonius' dominance being undermined by Octavius, who was in turn undermined by the Senate who allied with the anti-Caesarian faction in the east, who were then undermined by the Triumvirate. Throughout these many twists and turns we can see the role of the Senate, trying to manoeuvre its way through these divisions yet not blessed with enough loyal commanders to field a force capable of facing down the various factions. At best, in late 43 BC they managed to summon three legions to defend Rome, with the rest of Rome's military forces split between the various oligarchs and factions. This in itself was a damning indictment of the weaknesses of the New Republic.

The tyrant had been removed, only for the survivors to vie for his crown. In the immediate aftermath, the various individuals and factions cancelled each other out and no one man emerged victorious. After eighteen months of warfare, however, there emerged three factions: the Triumvirate in the west, the Brutan-Cassian faction in the east, and the Pompeian faction in the Mediterranean.

Chapter Ten

The Rise and Fall of the Triumviral Republics: From Philippi to Actium (42–30 BC)

1. The War of the Three Factions

With complete military and political control of the Western Republic, the next step for the Triumvirs was the showdown with the forces of Brutus and Cassius, who controlled the Eastern Republic. Given their purging of the moderate elements of the Senate, there was little prospect of a peace accord between the factions vying for control of the Republic. The Triumvirs focused on raising more money to fund an eastern campaign, by introducing a punitive regime of taxation on the Roman oligarchy, be they Senatorial or Equestrian. They also took steps to further legitimatise their rule, through the honours bestowed on their former patron, C. Iulius Caesar. What followed was the creation of a cult to a deified Iulius Caesar, with Caesar being officially confirmed into the Roman pantheon as a deity:

> *They also laid the foundation of a shrine to him, as hero, in the Forum, on the spot where his body had been burned, and caused an image of him, together with a second image, that of Venus, to be carried in the procession at the Circensian games. And whenever news came of a victory anywhere, they assigned the honour of a thanksgiving to the victor by himself and to Caesar, though dead, by himself. And they compelled everybody to celebrate his birthday by wearing laurel and by merry-making, passing a law that those who neglected these observances should be accursed in the sight of Jupiter and of Caesar himself, and, in the case of Senators or Senators' sons, that they should forfeit a million sesterces.*[1]

In death Caesar became immensely useful to the politicians who succeeded him. It was not a case that any of the Senate believed he was a god, but his posthumous elevation (which the man himself would have enjoyed immensely) was a useful political tool both to legitimise the bloody seizure of power by his followers and the condemnation of his murderers; the opponents of the Triumvirs. Clearly had Brutus and Cassius won the subsequent war then this deification would most likely have been swiftly repealed. Furthermore, the Triumvirs swore an oath (and made all the surviving Senators swear it) to uphold all the acts passed by Caesar, despite Antonius himself having undone a good many of these during his year as Consul (44 BC). This had been an infrequent procedure since the time of Saturninus and was of doubtful practical success, given the standard double-dealing in Roman politics, but nevertheless it brought a religious gloss to the whole proceeding.

Having secured both economic and religious support, the Triumvirs set about a campaign against Brutus and Cassius. The war followed a similar pattern to the one Caesar had fought against Pompeius, with Brutus and Cassius holding the east and the chosen battleground for the two forces being Greece once more. During the First Civil War this had been the plan of the Consul Cinna (to fight Sulla in Greece), but the former's murder had allowed the latter to invade Italy. There seemed to be little appetite to allow a similar war to be fought in Italy, with both sides thinking it was far better to use the provinces as their battleground.

If anything, the choice of commanders for this war was a strange one. Of the three Triumvirs, Antonius and Lepidus were the battle-hardened commanders, with the young Caesar Octavianus showing far less aptitude on the battlefield. Yet it was Antonius and Octavianus who were to command the Triumviral forces in the east and Lepidus (the Consul) who was to stay in Rome. It is clear that one of the Triumvirs needed to stay in Rome, for both political and military reasons. Even with a purged Senate there was no guarantee that this body would remain loyal to them the moment that they left Italy, and in fact experience suggested that they would turn on them (as they had done throughout 43 BC), showing the underlying strength of the Republican ideal, even though it kept being overwhelmed militarily.

Furthermore, whilst Brutus and Cassius were the main threat, there was a secondary one; namely Sex. Pompeius and his fleet, who would likely use this clash between the two other factions to further his own power. In the event this is exactly what happened, as Pompeius attacked Sicily in late 43/early 42 BC. Sicily was commanded by Octavianus, and one of his legates (Q. Salvidius Rufus Salvius) was able to defeat Pompeius at Rhegium but was defeated by him in a subsequent naval battle. Thus, it is clear that the Triumvirs had to leave at least one of their number behind, but on paper Octavianus seemed the obvious choice; he had limited experience in commanding large armies but excellent political skills, and Pompeius was attacking his provinces.

Yet we must not forget that even though these three men had united to seize control of the Western Republic, they were still rivals and both Lepidus and Antonius had seen all too well what Octavianus was capable of when he had control of Rome, when the previous year he completely outmanoeuvred both men and had Antonius declared an enemy of the Republic. Furthermore, we must not forget that this Triumvirate (as with the one of Pompeius, Crassus and Caesar) was not an alliance of equals. Lepidus and Antonius were the senior men, both veteran commanders under Caesar, and both in their late 30s/early 40s,[2] whilst Octavianus was a different generation and a nineteen-year-old who was part of the alliance because he was Caesar's adopted son. It must have seemed safer to have Octavianus travel with one of the senior men, where he could be kept under watch, rather than leave him in sole control of Rome.

Lepidus (one of the serving Consuls) stayed in Rome, but it meant that the bulk of his military resources (some seven legions) were handed over to Antonius and Octavianus. He himself kept three legions to guard Rome and Italy. Overall this made strategic sense, allowing Antonius and Octavianus to field some twenty legions in Greece, but it did deplete the military resources of both the Western Republic (still faced with fighting the third faction led by Pompeius) and Lepidus himself compared to his two Triumviral colleagues (something which would come back to haunt him).

In terms of domestic politics, the Triumvirs appointed fresh Censors; P. Sulpicius and C. Antonius (Cos. 63 BC), the latter being the uncle of Marcus Antonius, but they failed to complete a Census. The Consuls, meanwhile, passed a law regarding the grant of citizenship and exemption from taxes in the provinces (the *lex Munatia Aemilia*) and began a programme of land distribution to veterans.

Whilst these preparations were being made in the Western Republic, in the East Brutus and Cassius had not been idle and had been engaging in minor campaigns to bring the unrulier parts of the provinces back under their control, increase their own economic resources and give their legions some battle experience. They too seemed happy to let the Triumvirs come to them in Greece or Macedon, and then, if victorious, return to Rome as liberators. To those ends Cassius brought his armies from Syria into Asia Minor and then Greece for what they hoped would be the conclusive showdown.

Again, whilst a detailed analysis of the military aspects of this war falls outside the remit of this present work, we can summarise the overall details. The Triumviral forces had sent an advance guard of eight legions to Greece (under the command of L. Decidius Saxa and C. Norbanus Flaccus) with the armies of Antonius and Octavianus to follow. They advanced through Macedonia into Thrace but encountered the forces of Brutus and Cassius and withdrew to the city of Philippi, on the Via Egnatia,[3] where they were joined by the armies of Antonius and Octavianus. In the first battle, Antonius' army fought that of Cassius, whilst in a separate clash, Octavianus' army fought that of Brutus.

In the first Antonius' army 'fought Cassius', whilst in a separate battle Octavianus 'fought Brutus'. Of the two clashes, Brutus scored a decisive victory over Octavianus, capturing both his camp and his legionary eagles and forcing him to flee (again confirming Octavianus' poor military leadership), whilst Antonius took Cassius' camp. Overall the result seemed to have been a stalemate, and Appian reports that Octavianus lost twice the numbers of Cassius.[4] Yet, in a bizarre twist, Cassius committed suicide, fearing the battle was lost overall and thus robbing their faction of their most accomplished commander.

Yet the Brutan-Cassian faction scored a notable victory that same day during a naval battle, when a naval convoy bringing two legions of reinforcements from Italy was defeated and destroyed by the commanders L. Staius Murcus and Cn. Domitius Ahenobarbus. Thus, the Triumvirs found themselves deprived of reinforcements and supplies from Italy and effectively cut off from their powerbase in the west. This victory gave Brutus the upper hand, as he could afford to wait and starve the Triumvirs' army, whilst he had a clear supply route from the east. The next few weeks saw the two armies manoeuvre around each other, with Brutus refusing to give battle and Antonius and Octavianus desperate to force a battle due to their dwindling supplies of food and money. Yet as with Pompeius at Pharsalus, Brutus eventually gave in and offered a battle, perhaps convinced of the weakness of his opponents and needing to strengthen his own position by delivering a decisive victory.

There was a second Battle of Philippi and this time there were clear victors, Antonius and Octavianus. Brutus, fighting on the wing of his army, was victorious, but the other wing and the centre collapsed and his army was destroyed. Brutus himself survived and retreated, but soon committed suicide rather than be captured and thus joined Cato and Cassius in martyrdom. A number of other prominent members of the Brutan-Cassian faction died too, either in battle or in the aftermath, most notably the son of Cato (see Appendix One). There were a number of survivors however, including the son of Cicero, who fled to the one remaining faction still fighting against the Triumvirs, namely that of Sex. Pompeius.

Thus, at the two Battles of Philippi, the Triumvirs destroyed the armies of Brutus and Cassius and thus (nominally) gained control of the Eastern Republic. Yet in reality it was not a victory for the three Triumvirs but only two (Antonius and Octavianus), and these two rivals/allies took it upon themselves to subtly re-negotiate their alliance. It was here that Lepidus' weak position showed, stuck in Rome with only a handful of legions. The two men agreed to take command of Lepidus' provinces for themselves, Octavianus taking Spain and Antonius Norbonensis Gaul. Thus, the balance of power between the Triumvirs shifted, with Lepidus (the eldest) now finding himself the junior partner.

Furthermore, they effectively kept the division between the Western and Eastern Republics in place with Antonius taking command of the East and Octavianus the West, though each man faced significant challenges. Antonius had the responsibility to bring the eastern provinces of the Republic back under the control of Rome, or at least the Triumvirate, which was no easy feat given that the eastern provinces had consistently supported the anti-Caesarian factions, firstly with Pompeius, and then with Brutus and Cassius. This was not to mention the rising threat of the Parthian Empire to Rome's eastern provinces, eager to exploit the Roman

Civil War and the rising power of Egypt under Cleopatra and Ptolemy XV (Caesar's natural son).

Octavianus meanwhile was given the responsibility of dealing with Pompeius and his growing faction, not to mention dealing with Lepidus himself, who suddenly found himself relegated. Furthermore, there was still the fleet of the Brutan-Cassian faction leaders Staius Murcus and Domitius Ahenobarbus to deal with. Aside from these continuing threats Antonius and Octavianus had agreed to disband a number of their legions, along with the survivors of the legions of Brutus and Cassius, all of which would need overseeing.

Sex. Pompeius meanwhile had not been idle and had launched a full scale attack on the island of Sicily, then commanded by A. Pompeius Bithynicus. Sex. Pompeius was successful in seizing military control of the island and sent two proscribed Roman Senators (Fannius and Hirrus) to negotiate with Bithynicus, who promptly switched sides to Sex. Pompeius, giving the latter complete control of Sicily. Bithynicus paid for his treachery when he was later murdered by Pompeius.

Sicily had not been the only province to see further civil war, as another theatre of conflict had opened in Africa. When the Triumvirs took Rome, the two African provinces, Vetus (old Carthage) and Nova (old Numidia) were governed by different men; Q. Cornificius and T. Sextius respectively. Of the two, Sextius was trusted by the Triumvirs and appointed to command both provinces. Given the prevailing climate it was not a surprise when the other governor (Cornificius) resisted by force, defeating Sextius. A second campaign however saw Sextius victorious and Cornificius dead. Thus, both African provinces fell to the Triumvirs.

2. Land Reforms and Civil War in the Western Republic (41–40 BC)

Of the two leading Triumvirs it is clear that Octavianus had been given the most difficult assignment. Control of Rome was a double-edged sword; on the one hand, it put him in nominal control of the key organs of the Republic, the Senate and People, but on the other it meant that he could not simply ride roughshod over everyone and impose his will, in the way which Antonius could do, in the eastern provinces of the Republic. Octavianus' position was further weakened by two additional factors. Firstly, the Roman fleet of the Brutan-Cassian commanders Murcus and Ahenobarbus, which had done so much damage to the Triumviral campaign in Greece, now left the Adriatic and joined forces with Sex. Pompeius in Sicily. Secondly, the chosen Consuls of the year were P. Servilius Isauricus and more importantly L. Antonius, the surviving younger brother of Marcus.

It was the Consul Antonius, rather than Octavianus' Triumviral colleague Lepidus, who proved to be the main source of opposition to Octavianus' control of Rome. Lepidus, although of technically equal power to Octavianus, soon found himself isolated by being cut out of the post-Philippi settlement, with his formal commands reduced to the two provinces of Africa (separated from Italy by the Pompeian-held Sicily). Having successfully side-lined Lepidus, who had few military resources of his own to challenge the armies of his two colleagues, Octavianus had two pressing challenges remaining, one military and one political. Before he could face Pompeius he first chose, perhaps wisely, to settle political matters in Italy and secure the position of the Triumvirs by successfully discharging the victorious (and defeated) armies from Philippi.

As in all military matters, victory in battle brought its own problems; namely that the Triumvirs had way too many men under arms for the wars that remained. Antonius only needed an army to pacify the eastern provinces, not that any were in open rebellion, and should he need an army for a Parthian War then it would be more sensible to recruit it from the eastern provinces and not the western. Octavianus needed enough legions to attack Sicily and no more.

The problem Octavianus faced was that the victorious soldiers demanded lands to be settled on, but where was this land to come from? As we have seen issues of land reforms and re-distributions had plagued the Republic for the last century, ever since the Tribunate (and murder) of Ti. Sempronius Gracchus. When Sulla faced this issue in the First Civil War he simply confiscated the lands from the Italian communities who had opposed him (which in itself created the tensions that helped spark the Second Civil War – see Chapter Three). Yet during this latest civil war, the number of Italian cities that rebelled were minimal. Octavianus had to resort to forcible confiscations of land throughout Italy, naturally alienating the existing communities and landowners. Furthermore, it is clear that the soldiers' demands would have to be moderated for the sake of the existing communities, which in turn alienated the soldiers.

Therefore, Octavianus found himself in a lose/lose situation, and alienated both Italians and veterans, as Appian and Dio detail in some length.[5] This whole situation was made worse by the economic effects brought about by the loss of Sicily to Pompeius. Sicily was the bread basket of the Western Republic and its loss brought about food shortages in Italy (and Rome) greatly increased by the piratical activities of Pompeius' fleet. Italy found itself effectively under siege.

Nevertheless, given his constitutional power and control of the armies in Italy, Octavianus on paper had a strong-enough hand to push through these unpopular land reforms. That was of course unless some figure with a strong-enough powerbase to rival that of Octavianus chose to oppose him and become a fulcrum for the opposition. On paper the only individual with enough constitutional power in Italy was Lepidus, but he chose not to openly challenge Octavianus, having no military powerbase to back up his constitutional power. The only man who had both was L. Antonius (the Consul) who was supported by his sister-in-law (M. Antonius' wife) and chose to be a figurehead for those affected by Octavianus' land reforms. Antonius clearly held an inferior position to Octavianus, in both constitutional and military terms. The Consul's power was inferior to that of a Triumvir, and Octavianus had more legions in Italy than Antonius, who had just returned to Rome and received a Triumph for fighting Alpine tribes.

Yet obviously Lucius was the brother of the most senior Triumvir and could not easily be brushed aside without consideration of his brother. We will never know to what extent Lucius (and Marcus' wife Fulvia) were acting with the approval of Marcus, or simply acting in his name to defend what they believed were his interests. Certainly, Marcus Antonius would have been happy to see Octavianus in political trouble and floundering, whilst he himself was in the east. Naturally, however, given the prevailing spirit of the times, these political clashes between the two men soon escalated. Lucius accused Octavianus of sending armed men against him and gathered himself a bodyguard of Antonine veterans. It was at this point that a group of senior Triumviral army veterans stepped in to arbitrate:

> *When the officers of the army learned these facts, they arbitrated between Lucius and Octavianus at Teanum and brought them to an agreement on the following terms: That the Consuls should exercise their office in the manner of the fathers and not be hindered by the Triumvirs; that the land should be assigned only to those who fought at Philippi; that of the money derived from confiscated property, and of the value of that which was still to be sold, Antonius' soldiers in Italy should have an equal share; that neither Antonius nor Octavianus should draw soldiers from Italy by conscription hereafter; that two of Antonius' legions should serve with Octavianus in the campaign against Pompeius; that the passes of the Alps should be opened to the forces sent by Octavian into Spain.[6]*

Yet this arbitration, an interesting intervention into Roman politics by the Roman army, proved to be illusionary and soon both men started levying armies in Italy. Although we must always be wary of generalisations, it seems that the discharged veterans sided with Octavianus and the Italian communities sided with L. Antonius:

> *Octavianus sent a legion of soldiers to Brundisium and hastily recalled Salvidienus from his march to Spain. Both Octavianus and Lucius sent recruiting officers throughout Italy, who had skirmishes with each other of more or less importance, and frequent ambuscades. The good-will of the Italians was of great service to Lucius, as they believed that he was fighting for them against the new colonists. Not only the cities that had been designated for the army, but almost the whole of Italy, rose, fearing like treatment. They drove out of the towns, or killed, those who were borrowing money from the temples for Octavianus, manned their walls, and joined Lucius. On the other hand, the colonised soldiers joined Octavianus. Each one in both parties took sides as though this were his own war.[7]*

Just one year after the victory at Philippi the Western Republic (and the Triumvirate) collapsed into further civil war (in addition to the ongoing

Pompeian/Triumvirate clash) with one of the Triumvirs going to war with the brother of his colleague. Lepidus chose to back Octavianus and was given two legions to guard Rome, whilst the Senate's attitude is again interesting. Having been purged of all opponents of the Triumvirate, they were split between those who supported Octavianus and those who supported the Antonine brothers, and a number defected to join Lucius' army.

It was L. Antonius who seized the initiative in the war which followed, as he was able to seize Rome without a fight. An advance guard was granted admittance through the gates by treachery and Lepidus chose to retreat to Octavianus rather than fight in Rome itself (though he may have lost no sleep in undermining Octavianus' position). This of course gave Lucius access to the Senate. If we are to believe Appian, then Lucius promised the Senate the abolition of the Triumvirate and the restoration of 'normal' Republican government.[8] This apparently included a promise from his brother (Marcus) to lay down his Triumviral power for a Consulship, though again we will never know whether this originated from Marcus himself or merely Lucius.

The attitude of the governors of the western provinces is an interesting one, split as they were between Octavianus' placements and those of M. Antonius. Here Octavianus had a distinct tactical advantage, as his supporters, men such as Q. Salvidienus Rufus Salvius, hastened to Italy to actively support him whilst those who owed their allegiance to M. Antonius merely took a neutral stance and tried to block Octavianus getting reinforcements. Importantly, they did not actively support Lucius, obviously waiting to see what Marcus Antonius' orders would be. Thus, when Salvidienus advanced into Italy with reinforcements for Octavianus, Lucius left Rome to face him. However, he chose not to engage Salvidienus when he was also faced with an army commanded by Octavianus' friend M. Vipsanius Agrippa. Thus, Lucius turned away from both armies and chose to set up base in the city of Perusia, which soon came under siege from Octavianus' forces.[9]

Outside of Italy, Africa once again fell into civil war and reflected the confusion that reigned in the Western Republic during this period. T. Sextius, the governor of the two provinces, had seized control of Africa in a short civil war the year before (see above) but had been ordered (by

L. Antonius) to hand them over to a C. Fuficius Fango, a supporter of Octavianus, which he did. When however civil war broke out in Italy, Lucius then ordered him to recover the provinces, and so for the second time in two years Sextius fought a civil war in Africa to gain control of the two Roman provinces.

Whilst the rest of the Western Republic's forces hesitated to join in with the civil war in Italy, Sex. Pompeius naturally saw his opportunity. Domitius Ahenobarbus launched an assault on the Italian port of Brundisium, the traditional crossing point to Greece, whilst Pompeius persuaded Bogud, the King of the Mauri (the only remaining independent North African kingdom) to attack Octavianus' governor of Spain (C. Carrinas).

The one participant that everyone was waiting for however was Marcus Antonius. He had spent the year travelling the eastern provinces of the Republic restoring them to Roman (Triumviral) control, first in Asia Minor and then Syria. He also had to contend with the fact that a number of survivors of the Brutan/Cassian alliance had fled east to the court of the Parthian Empire (mirroring the First Civil War, when a group of the Marian faction fled to Mithridates of Pontus).

Relations between the two empires were fragile at best. Rome had utilised a Parthian dynastic civil war to launch an invasion and attempted conquest in the 50s BC under M. Licinius Crassus. This invasion had ended spectacularly at the Battle of Carrhae in 53 BC, when the forces of the Parthian general Surenas had unexpectedly wiped out the Roman army of Crassus, forcing the Romans into a full-scale retreat into Syria.[10] A subsequent Parthian invasion of Syria had been defeated by none other than C. Cassius Longinus himself, which had led to a de-facto armistice between the two empires. Caesar had been planning a further invasion of Parthia in 44 BC and his imminent departure to the east brought about his assassination by Brutus and Cassius.

In the intervening years, the Parthians must have looked on with glee as not only did Caesar's invasion not take place, but the Republic collapsed into a further bout of civil war. The Parthians had refused an invitation from Brutus and Cassius to join their alliance against the Triumvirate but did receive a number of their supporters fleeing the defeats at Philippi. From their perspective the Parthians faced a weakened Rome whose eastern provinces had twice backed the losing side in a civil war (first Pompeius and now Brutus and Cassius), and now had a Roman general to lead their campaign (much as Mithridates VI had done in the First Civil War with M. Marius) in the form of Q. Labienus.

Therefore, M. Antonius was facing the prospect of a full-blown Parthian invasion and attempted annexation of Rome's eastern empire. To prepare for this, Antonius would have to rely on the resources of the Eastern Republic, itself recovering from the Parthian invasion of the late 50s BC and the civil wars of Dolabella and Cassius (43 BC). The greatest resources in the east however lay not under Roman control, but Ptolemaic; namely the kingdom of Cleopatra and Ptolemy XV (Caesarion). As his brother faced a siege at Perusia in Italy, Antonius was wintering in Egypt with Cleopatra, 'negotiating' for her support for his campaigns in the east.

With all this in mind, the last thing that Antonius needed was a civil war in Italy between his brother and Octavianus. This, and the distance, would explain his slow reaction to events in Italy. Antonius' position was further complicated in early 40 BC when the expected Parthian invasion of the Eastern Republic took place, commanded by the Roman general, Q. Labienus.[11] With Marcus Antonius occupied in the east and his supporters in Italy unsure of their orders in the civil war, Lucius Antonius received no reinforcements and eventually Perusia fell after a long siege (in March 40 BC). Whilst Lucius himself was spared, Octavianus ordered the deaths of three hundred of his most prominent supporters, including a number of Senators (again see Appendix One):

> *The leader and some others obtained pardon, but most of the Senators and knights were put to death. And the story goes that they did not merely suffer death in an ordinary form but were led to the altar consecrated to the former Caesar and were there sacrificed, three hundred knights and many Senators, among them Tiberius Cannutius, who previously during his Tribunate had assembled the populace for Caesar Octavianus.[12]*

Following this massacre a number of Antonius' other supporters, in both Rome and Italy (including his wife Fulvia), wisely took the hint and fled for Greece. Octavianus' mastery of Italy was reinforced when the pro-

Antonine Governor of Transalpine Gaul (Q. Fufius Calenus) died of natural causes, with Octavianus seizing the opportunity and taking control of the province and its eleven legions. This act was a clear breach of the post-Philippi agreement between Octavianus and Antonius. Faced with the complete unravelling of his position in Italy and the west, Antonius had no choice but to act, and leaving the situation with Parthia in the hands of his legates he returned westward to face Octavianus. Thus, for the second time in three years, Antonius and Octavianus prepared to go to war with each other.

Despite Octavianus' success at Perusia and in Gaul, his position in Italy was not as strong as it looked. As noted above, the bulk of Antonius' allies had chosen not to intervene in the war between Octavianus and Lucius and still held military forces in the west. C. Asinius Pollio now held Venetia with seven legions, P. Ventidius Bassus had withdrawn into southern Italy, whilst Ti. Claudius Nero now attempted a rebellion in Campania. Furthermore, Antonius controlled the resources of the Eastern Republic and was allied to Ptolemaic Egypt. Finally, there was the issue of Sex. Pompeius, who exploited this civil war in Italy to the full and by mid-40 BC had annexed the two African provinces from Q. Fuficius Fango, and Sardinia and Corsica from M. Lurius. This gave Pompeius his own empire in the mid-Mediterranean (Sicily, Africa, Sardinia and Corsica), not to mention control of the Mediterranean itself with his fleet. Octavianus actually made overtures to Pompeius and even married a lady named Scribonia, a relative of Pompeius.

However, Octavianus' position was further weakened when the Consul C. Asinius Pollio, another supporter of Antonius, brokered a deal with the rebel commander Cn. Domitius Ahenobarbus who controlled the former Brutan/Cassian fleet, and who was now nominally supporting Pompeius. Ahenobarbus now changed sides and supported Antonius, giving the latter control of the Adriatic; the launch pad for an invasion of Italy. Antonius gathered his forces in Macedonia and then attacked Brundisium along with Domitius Ahenobarbus, hoping to secure a crucial foothold in Italy, whilst at the same time Sex. Pompeius launched attacks on the Italian coast. Faced with no alternative, Octavianus moved his army to Brundisium to repel Antonius' invasion, whilst Agrippa successfully repulsed Antonius' attack on the city of Sipontium.

Whilst Rome's three leading figures were fighting a civil war in the Western Republic, the Eastern Republic was being overrun by the Parthian invasion, which swept through Syria and into Asia Minor, aided by the weakness of the Roman forces stationed there and a number of desertions by soldiers and commanders formerly of the Brutan-Cassian faction. L. Decidius Saxa, legate of Syria, was driven into Cilicia, captured and executed, whilst his brother suffered the desertion of his army to Labienus and the Parthians.

For Antonius it was perhaps this threat from the east that made him seek a peaceful solution. Even if he could capture Brundisium and invade Italy, he would still have to fight his way through Octavianus' forces to Rome and beyond. All the time, his eastern command was being reduced to nothing by the Parthians, who had penetrated further into the Roman east than ever before and were aiming for its total annexation. It would only have been a matter of time before the Parthians turned their attention to Egypt, the richest prize in the east.

For Octavianus too, a war against both Pompeius and Antonius was hardly likely to end well, due to defending Italy on two fronts. This added to the fact that the soldiers in both Antonius' and Octavianus' armies were all former comrades, either from Caesar's campaigns or Philippi, which made a rapprochement between the two men more likely, especially as they had worked together before. Thus was born the Peace of Brundisium, between Octavianus and Antonius, which re-founded the Triumvirate, though a Duumvirate in reality, and cast Pompeius back into the cold.

The agreement which cemented this alliance built on the one which followed Philippi, but simplified matters immensely. The Republic was effectively split into two, with Octavianus controlling the Western Republic and Antonius the Eastern Republic, with the dividing line down the Adriatic. This removed the anomaly of Antonius still controlling Gaul. Italy however was to be open to both men to recruit from (neutral territory as it were).

Lucius Antonius was given a command in Spain, where he promptly disappears from all records, whilst Lepidus was re-affirmed as commander of Africa and, armed with fresh legions, was dispatched to recover it from Pompeius. Octavianus was to secure the Western Republic by defeating

Pompeius, and Antonius was to secure the Eastern Republic by defeating the Parthians. This agreement was cemented by the traditional marriage alliance. With Antonius' wife Fulvia having died in Greece, Antonius was free to marry Octavia (Octavianus sister), though the shadow of Cleopatra must have hung over this agreement. Thus, once again, the two leading Caesarian faction leaders formed an alliance and carved the Roman Republic up between them.

The two men returned to Rome together, where they were awarded Ovations for ending the civil war (between them), the first-time Roman generals had been awarded honours for not fighting. Antonius was also married to Octavia (all sides tactfully overlooking the matter of Cleopatra). As well as the marriage the alliance was also cemented in blood when Antonius revealed that Octavianus' supposedly loyal general, Q. Salvidienus Rufus Salvidius (who had come to Octavianus' rescue the year before), had actually been negotiating with Antonius about switching sides just before the attack on Brundisium. Salvidienus was swiftly summoned to Rome and even more swiftly executed (or allowed to commit suicide)[13] for his attempted betrayal.

The two Triumvirs soon set about restoring peace to the portions of the Republic which they still controlled. Upon their return to Rome, they ordered the Consuls (Cn. Domitius Calvinus[14] and C. Asinius Pollio) and Praetors to stand down and fresh men were elected in their place:[15] a symbolic renewal of the Republic. Both Calvinus and Pollio received prize Proconsular commands (Spain and Macedonia respectively). P. Ventidius Bassus was appointed by Antonius to command the war against the Parthians, whilst M. Vipsanius Agrippa received command against Pompeius.

Unfortunately for the Triumvirs, the balance of power had shifted since the last time they had forged an agreement. There were indeed three leading men in the Republic, but the third was not Lepidus, but Sex. Pompeius, who had no intention of sitting back whilst his two rivals carved up the Republic. Now outmanned by the combined forces of the Triumvirs, he fell back on his policy of laying siege to Italy by cutting off its food supply from the rest of the empire. Thus, the population of Italy and Rome itself began to starve, which in turn undermined the leadership of the Triumvirs, who found that they had gone from being feted as peacemakers to being held responsible for Rome's economic woes:

> *Thus, there was a great rise in the cost of provisions, and the people considered the cause of it to be the strife between the chiefs and cried out against them and urged them to make peace with Pompeius. As Octavianus would by no means yield, Antonius advised him to hasten the war on account of the scarcity. As there was no money for this purpose, an edict was published that the owners of slaves should pay a tax for each one, equal to one-half of the twenty-five drachmas that had been ordained for the war against Brutus and Cassius, and that those who acquired property by legacies should contribute a share thereof. The People tore down the edict with fury. They were exasperated that, after exhausting the public treasury, stripping the provinces, burdening Italy itself with contributions, taxes, and confiscations, not for foreign war, not for extending the empire, but for private enmities and to add to their own power (for which reason the proscriptions and murders and this terrible famine had come about), the triumvirs should deprive them of the remainder of their property.*[16]

Therefore, despite their military dominance on land, two of the Triumvirs were being held to ransom by Pompeius' control of both Sicily, the islands and the wider Mediterranean, and found themselves with no choice but to open negotiations.

3. A Tale of Two Republics: Pompeius and the Parthians

Antonius and Octavianus opened the year (39 BC) by further securing their constitutional position, which involved the Senate ratifying all their respective acts to date, the enrolment of a number of new Senators (to make up for the numbers killed) and the levying of new taxes (on top of the existing financial crisis) to pay for all the legions under arms. They also passed acts setting out who was to hold senior magistracies for the next eight years. This included the formalisation of the policy of having more than two Consuls a year selected, with the new norm being two sets of Consuls a year. Dio states that this second set of Consuls were known as 'Lesser Consuls'.[17] Thus, the Senate approved the establishment of a true oligarchy, with the Republic being ruled by three Triumvirs who selected their supporters to hold the various magistracies, usually for a term of less than a year.

With their constitutional position re-affirmed, the two Triumvirs (Lepidus remaining in Africa) set off to meet Pompeius and settle the siege of Italy by negotiation. The two sides met at Misenum in the Gulf of Puteoli and there they battered out a peace treaty between the three of them (the true Triumvirate of the Republic). In return for his lifting of the blockade of Italy, the withdrawal of his troops from the peninsula, and the guarantee of open (pirate-free) commerce, Pompeius received handsome reward. He was to keep command of Sicily, Sardinia and Corsica and was to be handed control of the Peloponnese. All Roman exiles were allowed to return to Rome (except those directly implicated in the murder of Caesar) and have their estates restored, with some directly selected for magistracies. Runaway slaves in Pompeius' forces had their freedom confirmed, though Pompeius was to guarantee not to continue this practice. Pompeius himself secured the Consulship for 33 BC, an immediate elevation to his father's Augurate, and seventy million sesterce compensation for the loss of his father's estates.

On the face of it, the Treaty of Misenum brought an end (albeit temporarily) to the civil war which had been raging since 49 BC. In reality there were now four oligarchs, with the Western Republic being split into three: Gaul, Italy and Spain under the control of Octavianus, Africa under the control of Lepidus and Sicily and the islands (and the Peloponnese) under the control of Pompeius. The Eastern Republic fell under Antonius, who returned to Greece to coordinate the Second Romano-Parthian War, a task made much easier by the spectacular victories of his general P. Ventidius Bassus, who defeated the Parthians twice in quick succession, driving them from Asia and then from Syria, and resulting in the death of the Roman rebel general Q. Labienus.[18] These feats (and the victories that were to follow) made Ventidius the most successful Roman general against the Parthians until the time of the Emperor Trajan, some one hundred and fifty years later.[19]

Whilst relations between Octavianus and Lepidus remained cordial but chilly, almost inevitably the son of Caesar and the son of Pompeius fell out, with both sides accusing the other of bad faith, and the peace treaty soon fell apart with the civil war resuming in the Western Republic. Resumption of hostilities between Octavianus and Pompeius soon saw Antonius call a meeting of the Triumvirate at Brundisium (for he was still in Greece), yet he was the only one to turn up. Octavianus remained in northern Italy and Lepidus in Africa, thus showing that the three men had already started to go their separate ways.

Again, the full military details of this war fall outside the scope of this work, but Octavinaus secured Sardinia and Corsica from Pompeius by treachery but was then defeated by Pompeius in a naval battle, which was followed by the total destruction of his fleet in a storm. Wisely, Octavinaus then admitted his limitations as a military commander and handed command of this war over to his close friend M. Vipsanius Agrippa, who had successfully defeated a rebellion in Gaul. In the Eastern Republic the opposite happened when Ventidius scored Rome's greatest victory to date over a renewed Parthian invasion at the Battle of Mount Gindarus, killing the Parthian prince Pacorus. His reward was to be packed off to Rome by Antonius, where he celebrated Rome's first Triumph over the Parthians, with Antonius then taking command of the subsequent war – with disastrous consequences.[20] Thus, we can see that the civil war was already producing another golden generation of Roman generals (Agrippa and Ventidius), outside of the leading oligarchs.

4. The Degeneration of the Republic

Whilst the civil wars continued, at least in the Western Republic, what passes nearly unnoticed is the evolution of the Republican institutions in Rome. By 38 BC the Republic had already been under the rule of the constitutionally-recognised Triumvirate for five years. The Senatorial aristocracy had been purged and then counter-purged; first of Pompeians, then of Caesar's enemies, then of Antonius' supporters. The high casualty rate had seen the Triumvirs promote a new generation of men into the aristocracy from amongst their military forces, men with no discernible Senatorial background. The Roman magistracies had been first overshadowed by the position of Triumvir and then debased both in terms of election (selected by a Triumvir in advance) and then length of term; less than year.

Elements that had been key to the Republic, such as competition for office and security of tenure, had been undermined. In many ways this was both expedient for the Triumvirate and removed the more combustible elements from Republican politics. All the key episodes of political violence and bloodshed in the last century of the Republic had seen various politicians vying with each other in the Assemblies and clashing over political office or legislation. Under the Triumvirate this had been removed; laws were issued by Triumviral decree and rubber stamped by the Senate and People. In many ways, Rome had the Princeps that had been foreshadowed by Sulla and then Pompeius and Caesar. Yet on paper the Republic did not have one ruler, but three, all of equal power. In practice however, Rome itself only ever saw one Triumvir on a regular basis: Octavianus, with Antonius away in the east and Lepidus in Africa. The poor state of Roman politics can be seen from a passage of Dio for 38 BC:

> *But in the Consulship of Appius Claudius* (Pulcher) *and Caius Norbanus* (Flaccus), *who were the first to have two Quaestors apiece as associates, the populace revolted against the tax-gatherers, who oppressed them severely, and came to blows with the men themselves, their assistants, and the soldiers who helped them to collect the money; and sixty-seven Praetors one after another were appointed and held office. One person was chosen to be Quaestor while still accounted a boy and did not obtain the standing of a juvenis until the next day; and another, who had been enrolled in the Senate, desired to fight as a gladiator. Not only was he prevented, however, from doing this, but an act was also passed prohibiting any Senator from fighting as a gladiator, any slave from serving as a Lictor.*[21]

We can see already how debased Roman magistracies had become under the Triumvirate, with underage Quaestors, sixty-seven Praetors in one year, and the Senate needing to pass laws to prevent Senators fighting as Gladiators and slaves from serving as Lictors.

The year 37 BC saw a fresh meeting of the Triumvirate at Tarentum, which saw the agreement extended for a further five years (though the exact termination date is unclear, see Chapter Ten). The allocation of provinces remained the same between the Triumvirs, but the Treaty of Misenum was now rendered void and Octavianus (nominally) controlled the Western Republic, aside from Africa (Lepidus) and in practice Pompeius. The years that followed saw the split of the Roman Republic into two separate states in all but name (anticipating the split into Eastern and Western Empires by four hundred years). The Western Republic was ruled from Rome, with Octavianus as its Princeps, whilst the Eastern Republic was ruled from Alexandria and had Antonius as its Princeps.

The political cultures of the Two Republics also took on divergent tones, with the Western Republic still having the Senate and People (albeit as a rubber stamp) whilst the Eastern Republic was ruled from the court of the Ptolemies in Alexandria. Antonius' 'alliance' with Cleopatra had seen the fusion of the Ptolemaic Empire with the Eastern Republic, whilst Antonius had the full resources of Egypt to support his attempt to annex the Parthian Empire to this new eastern hybrid.

The most obvious manifestation of this new eastern alliance were three children: Alexander Helios, Cleopatra Selene, and Ptolemy Philadelphus, who in 34 BC were all granted royal titles and control over Roman, Ptolemaic and Parthian regions. Alexander became King of Armenia, Media and Parthia (despite the latter not being under Roman control), Cleopatra Selene received the Roman provinces of Cyrenaica and Libya, whilst Ptolemy Philadelphus received the Roman provinces of Syria and Cilicia. Antonius remained Triumvir and Proconsul of Greece, Macedonia and Asia, whilst Cleopatra was Queen of Egypt and Caesarion (Ptolemy XV) was King of Kings (the old Persian title) and heir to Caesar.

5. The End of the Triumvirate and the War of the Two Republics

By 34 BC both Antonius and Octavianus were undisputed masters of their own Republics. Antonius had failed in his first invasion and attempted conquest of Parthia (just as Crassus had) but had managed to annex Armenia, though not to Rome, and secured an alliance with

Media. The civil war in the Western Republic between the Triumvirs (Octavianus and Lepidus) and Pompeius had ended in 36 BC with the defeat of Pompeius at the Battle of Naulochus and the conquest of Sicily, which had seen Octavianus and Lepidus working together (along with Agrippa), and supported by a fleet from Antonius. Octavianus followed this victory up by the final betrayal of Lepidus, whose army betrayed him to Octavianus. Lepidus was summarily expelled from the Triumvirate by Octavianus and stripped of his African provinces, though he retained the role of Pontifex Maximus and returned to Rome. We know little of Lepidus' subsequent activities, though we must assume that he did take this demotion lying down but was plotting a return to power. With Pompeius and Lepidus both defeated, Octavianus now controlled the Western Republic. Pompeius survived and fled to the Eastern Republic, where he briefly ignited a fresh civil war against the forces of Antonius, exploiting Antonius' indecision over whether to treat him as an enemy or an ally. However, after initial gains, his forces were overwhelmed and he was captured and executed by the Antonine General M. Titius, with Antonius' tacit approval.

The Triumvirate was now a Duumvirate in practice though not in name and the Republic was now clearly two Republics, with two rulers, two capitals and two diverse political cultures. Clearly Antonius with his 34 BC constitutional settlement was aiming to convert the Eastern Republic into a new Ptolemaic/Roman (Antonine) Empire, with designs of effectively rebuilding the great Hellenistic empires of Alexander the Great and the Seleucids. Octavianus meanwhile had mastery of the west and was apparently contemplating an invasion of Britannia. The key question was whether these two men would be happy to leave the other alone and build up their own Republics or got to war (for a third time) for mastery of the whole Mediterranean. Antonius seems to have been happy with his eastern project for now but had named Caesarion (Caesar's natural born son) as Caesar's heir, a position occupied (under Roman law) by Octavianus. Octavianus meanwhile, having gained sole control of the Western Republic, was highly unlikely to allow the east to break away from the control of Rome and form a new entity.

The years 33–32 BC saw an interesting constitutional development as it seems that the five-year tenure of the Triumvirate (renewed in early 37 BC) ended. Technically this meant that neither man held any constitutional power nor command of any Roman armies, though neither man showed any inclination of giving up their practical power. Both Antonius and Octavianus briefly held additional Consulships, (Antonius in 34 BC, though he resigned on the first day, and Octavianus in 33 BC). Of the two, Antonius seems to have continued to use the title of Triumvir, whilst Octavianus did not. Both men were scheduled to hold the Consulship jointly in 31 BC, but it meant that during 32 BC both men seem to have reverted to private citizens, whilst still running their respective Republics and their armed forces. Gabba argues against this however and believes that the Triumvirate did not expire until late 32 BC.[22] In any event, the important aspect is that the Triumvirate had either expired or was due to expire shortly, which threw into sharp relief questions about the future.

It is clear that both men had their supporters chosen as Consuls, and presumably as Tribunes as well (though we are far less well informed of the Tribunes of the 30s BC – see Appendix Two). In the east Antonius still had the Ptolemaic power to fall back on. In the west, it seems that Octavianus did receive additional powers in 36 BC, following his victory over Sex. Pompeius in Sicily.[23]

> *Thereupon he was chosen Tribune for life by acclamation, the People urging him, by the offer of this perpetual magistracy, to give up his former one.*[24]
>
> *The Senate decreed that he should have the power of a Tribune permanently.*[25]
>
> *Hence they voted him the house and also protection from any insult by deed or word; anyone who committed such an offence was to be liable to the same penalties as had been established in the case of a Tribune.*[26]

Both Appian and Orosius state that Octavianus was made a Tribune for life (despite being an adopted Patrician) and despite this also happening in 30 and 23 BC (see Conclusion). However, Dio, who is the more accurate of the three, especially when it comes to political matters, only has Octavianus receiving the equivalent to Tribunician sacrosanctity and thus no additional political powers (see below).[27]

It seems that both men were content to allow the Triumvirate to officially expire without renewing it. In effect it had long been a Duumvirate, with the eclipse of Lepidus. The alliance was last renewed in the face of a clear threat from Sex. Pompeius and his faction, who may well have seized control of the Republic (with the compliance of the Senate). With Pompeius dead and Lepidus humbled, there were now just the two men left, both apparently powerful enough in their own right not to need to observe the constitutional niceties, though this would have been easier to accomplish in the Eastern Republic than in Rome itself.

The formal end of the Triumvirate also coincided with the final break between the two men and their respective Republics. Matters came to a head at a meeting of the Senate, where Antonius had the two Consuls (both his supporters; an interesting comment on Octavianus' control of the Western Republic) present his eastern settlement (see above). Despite his long-standing control of the Western Republic, Octavianus finally faced determined opposition in the Senate, a considerable portion of which (some three hundred Senators) supported Antonius, including the two Consuls (Cn. Domitius Ahenobarbus and C. Sosius). Furthermore, technically Octavianus now no longer held Triumviral power, weakening his constitutional position.

Both men brought charges against each other; Octavianus accused Antonius of ordering the murder of Sex. Pompeius, whilst Antonius charged Octavianus with deposing Lepidus. The Consul C. Sosius immediately opened his Consulship with an attack on Octavianus in the Senate (a novelty in the last decade) and prepared to bring legislation against him, though we do not know its content; perhaps relating to the expiration of his Triumviral power. Given that he now held no formal power, Octavianus seems to have relied upon a Tribune (Nonius Balbus) to use his Tribunician veto (*ius intercessio*) to prevent Sosius from introducing his legislation. Octavianus, who was not present at this time, then returned to Rome with an armed guard, entered the Senate, and in a show of force brought charges against both Sosius and Antonius.

This show of force brought the matter to a head and shortly afterward the two Consuls and a large body of the Senate, said to be three hundred Senators, left Rome to join Antonius in the east. In the opposite direction came two of Antonius' former allies, M. Titius and Munatius Plancus, who defected to Octavianus' side and tipped him off about the contents of Antonius' will, being held in the Temple of Vesta. Octavianus illegally seized the will, broke it open and read it to the remaining Senate: its contents confirmed the inheritance of the eastern provinces by his children and his wish to be buried in Alexandria with Cleopatra.

This allowed Octavianus the excuse to have the Senate (now composed of his allies and neutrals) declare war on Cleopatra (not Antonius). Again, control of Rome and the Senate gave Octavianus the chance for the Republic (theoretically indivisible) to declare Cleopatra (and presumably her children) as enemies of Rome. Antonius, according to Octavianus' propaganda, was being led astray by the wiles of an Egyptian queen, overlooking the matter of Octavianus' adopted father's liaison with Cleopatra and his subsequent stepbrother.

As we have seen, it was hardly as if the two men needed an excuse to go to war with each other, having done so twice already, and whoever won would commission men to write the history books extolling their position. Octavianus' position was that Antonius had betrayed Rome for Cleopatra, whilst Antonius' position was that Octavianus had usurped the title of Caesar's son and attacked his allies. Once again however, whilst the two Republics prepared to go to war with each other, the Parthian Empire choose to exploit these divisions and launched an attack on Rome's eastern allies, overrunning both Media and Armenia.[28]

With the civil war renewed (for the first time since 35 BC), Antonius stole a march and mobilised his forces in Greece, the western most part of his Republic and the springboard for an invasion of Italy. As we have seen, throughout the Third Civil War Greece had been a favoured battleground for Rome's battles, with Caesar fighting Pompeius and the Triumvirs fighting the Brutan-Cassian faction. Clearly no Roman wished to inflict the destruction upon Italy that had been seen in the First Civil War, when Sulla had invaded Italy from Greece, which would itself have been prevented had Cinna not been murdered by his own soldiers when preparing to face Sulla in Greece.

Octavianus, and more importantly his close friend and general, M. Vipsanius Agrippa, crossed to Greece with their forces in 31 BC, the year that, ironically, Antonius and Octavianus had agreed to hold the Consulship together. What followed is the well-known Battle of Actium, a naval battle, followed by the defeat of Antonius' forces, the subsequent surrender of his army in Greece and his own flight (along with Cleopatra) back to his Egyptian powerbase.[29]

Following this victory, Agrippa was dispatched back to Italy, whilst Octavianus moved into Asia to dismantle Antonius' Eastern Republic, simultaneously negotiating with Antonius himself. Agrippa's dismissal was no mere snub but an important strategic move, as the soldiers from both armies which had been demobilised after Actium and returned to Italy had apparently threatened to mutiny, upset at the lost opportunities of not being part of the invasion of Egypt. This clearly showed the inherent instability that Octavianus still faced, even though he now had military control of both Republics.

Once again, military control of Rome did not bring political control. As it was, the threat of mutiny was so severe that Octavianus had to break off his pursuit of Antonius and return to Italy himself. This threat of mutiny was dealt with by another round of land confiscations (from those communities who had voiced support for Antonius) and fresh distribution to the veterans, along with additional pay.

To bolster his constitutional power Octavianus was again chosen as Consul, alongside a certain M. Licinius Crassus, both a symbolic and practical choice. Crassus was the grandson of the Triumvir M. Licinius Crassus (son of Crassus' surviving son) and was not only heir to the vast Crassan fortune but was a former follower of Antonius, and thus a symbolic choice for Octavianus' colleague. With his position in Italy and Rome secured once more, Octavianus set off in 30 BC for the much-anticipated Roman invasion of Egypt (the last of the great Hellenistic kingdoms).

Following his defeat at Actium, it is not surprising to find that Antonius' remaining forces melted away and his legions stationed in Syria and Cyrene defected to Octavianus without bloodshed. Octavianus' general C. Cornelius Gallus launched an invasion of Egypt from Cyrene and defeated Antonius at Parethonium, on the Libyan border and then again at Pharos. Antonius was able to muster enough Romano-Egyptian forces to defend Alexandria against Octavianus and for one last time proved his superiority as a general over Octavianus by routing his cavalry. However, this victory proved to be short lived and was followed by the defection of his fleet, ending any thoughts of flight by sea, swiftly followed by the defection of his own cavalry and the defeat of his infantry. Thus, giving up all hope, Antonius retreated into the imperial palace and committed suicide, shortly followed by Cleopatra. Egypt soon fell to the Roman army and the Eastern Republic was re-unified with the Western, with Octavianus ending the latest round of civil war in military control of the whole Roman Republic and the Ptolemaic Kingdom of Egypt.

Summary

We can see that the period started with a breakdown of relations between Antonius and Octavianus (and a proxy civil war) and ended with the final break between the two men and a major civil war. The key difference being that in the late 40s/early 30s both men realised that they still needed the other. The break in the late 40s nearly gave Sex. Pompeius the opportunity to gain power in the Republic, aided no doubt by a willing Senate. Thus, the Triumvirate was renewed and again in 37 BC.

By 32 BC however, both men were masters of their own Republics and thus had no common threat to bind them together. Initially, however, both seemed content with expanding the empire of their Republics; Octavianus in Illyria, Gaul and possibly Britannia and Antonius with his (doomed) dream of emulating Alexander and conquering the east (Parthia). The formal expiration of the office of Triumvir in late 33/early 32 BC, however, seems to have brought matters to a head and both men came to the conclusion that they no longer needed the other and that there was no reason to co-operate. Thus, they plunged the Republic into another bout of civil war, which ended (at least in the short term) with Octavianus victorious.

Conclusion: The Roman Evolution

A s we have seen, throughout this period of Roman history there are two clear lessons. Firstly, victory in a set-piece battle, no matter how overwhelming, did not automatically mean the end of a period of civil war, which had a habit of flaring up again within a few years. Secondly, military control of the Republic did not automatically translate into political control, as Caesar himself had proven (to his cost). Thus, for Octavianus, the defeat and death of Antonius and the annexation of the Eastern Republic did not automatically mean the end of his struggle.

1. A Bloody Peace

Furthermore, the deaths of Antonius and Cleopatra did not bring an immediate end to the bloodshed, as there were still a number of scores to be settled. The two most notable casualties were M. Antonius Antyllus (the Roman son and legal heir of M. Antonius) and Caesarion (Ptolemy XV), Caesar's natural son and Octavianus' stepbrother (by adoption). Both were young men and in themselves neither constituted a danger to Octavianus' position (yet). However, Antyllus, as Antonius' legal heir, would inherit not just his father's wealth but all of his political support, and thus could be a beacon for those surviving supporters of Antonius and thus a potential rival to Octavianus. Caesarion represented something far more dangerous: Caesar's natural-born son (albeit illegitimate in Roman law) and the last crowned Pharaoh of Egypt. Thus, both statuses ensured that Octavianus would not allow them to live. By contrast, Antonius' three Egyptian children, all crowned heads of Romano–Ptolemaic possessions (see Chapter Ten), were spared, none holding a position under Roman law.

Whilst many supporters of Antonius had switched sides to Octavianus and were pardoned, there were some that were not so lucky and were swiftly butchered. Orosius tells us that three other Romans met their deaths on Octavianus' orders; P. Candidus Crassus, Q. Ovinius[1] and C. Cassius Palmensis, the latter of whom was recorded as the last surviving murderer of Caesar.[2]

Having settled these scores, the Ptolemaic dynasty was abolished and Egypt fell under the direct rule of Octavianus himself, thus in some ways continuing Antonius' policy. The eastern provinces were brought back under Roman control and Octavianus eventually conducted a treaty with the Parthian Empire, which had itself lapsed into another bout of civil war. Yet re-organising Rome's empire was the far easier task than the one which faced him in Rome, as events were soon to show.

2. The Problem of Peace (30–27 BC)

Of all of Octavianus' rivals, the only prominent one still living was his old Triumviral colleague, M. Aemilius Lepidus. Lepidus had been stripped of his Triumviral powers but still held the position of Rome's Chief Priest, the Pontifex Maximus, a position in which he had succeeded Iulius Caesar. Clearly the man represented a challenge to Octavianus, yet murdering Rome's Chief Priest seems to have been a step too far for polite Roman society. Yet, it seems that a conspiracy against Octavianus was being organised, by none other than Lepidus' son, M. Aemilius Lepidus. The details are scant and only Velleius preserves any details, but the younger Lepidus was apparently organising another political assassination, this time of Octavianus, when he returned to Rome. The plot was uncovered by C. Maecenas, who had been placed in charge of Rome by Octavianus and the younger Lepidus was executed, perhaps making him the last victim of this civil war. The elder Lepidus seemingly escaped without any involvement in this plot, which seems unlikely to say the least. Initially he was exiled but later returned to Rome.

Nevertheless, whilst his office made it inauspicious to murder him, he lost his son and heir, which placed his family on the back foot politically, though the murdered man did have a son (Manius) who became Consul in 11 AD. With the few details we have, we will never know how serious the assassination plot was, but the message to Octavianus was clear: no matter how many victories he won on the battlefield (or others did on his behalf), there would always be opposition and potential danger to his life in Rome from the Senatorial aristocracy – no matter how many times it was culled.

In the summer of 29 BC Octavianus returned to Rome, celebrated three Triumphs (Illyria, Actium and Alexandria), but tactfully not over Antonius, and even had the Senate ceremonially close the Gates of the Temple of Janus, signifying that Rome was at peace (only the third time that had been done and the first for two hundred years).[3] Yet, despite his military control of a unified Republic, he faced the same problem that all great generals had faced, since at least the time of Scipio Africanus, nearly two centuries before: how to turn military power into political power during peacetime. When the Triumvirs had been appointed, Rome was in turmoil, with at least three factions tearing the Republic apart and a clear external threat. Yet Rome in 29 BC had peace both within and outside of its borders (excluding the usual frontier campaigns).

Octavianus' problem was just that: peace; and if Rome was at peace and without an emergency situation, why would there be a need for an individual to hold supreme power? This is the conundrum that had faced both Sulla and Caesar before him. Sulla had taken supreme power, remodelled the Roman Republic and then resigned, probably hoping to take a guardianship role in the background, a hope that was dashed by terminal ill health. Caesar seemingly had none of Sulla's political astuteness and went for the direct approach of amassing as many offices and powers as he could and being a very obvious Princeps of the Republic; an attitude that brought about his subsequent murder and another fifteen years of civil war.

Furthermore, both Caesar and Sulla had been older men when they sized supreme power (50s) whereas Octavianus was only in his mid-30s. Having spent the last fifteen years fighting to gain supremacy in the Republic, he was hardly likely to give it up now and retire quietly, especially as he seemed also to have a clear image of the Republican system and its empire that he wanted to implement. There was also the problem that civil wars are far easier to start than to stop and Rome had spent the last sixty years in periods of civil war (91–70, 63, 49–27 BC), totalling over forty years out of the last sixty. Furthermore, as we have seen, the twenty years without civil war (69–64 and 62–49 BC) were ones of political turmoil and bloodshed.

As with the First Civil War, some of Rome's key political families were now on the second generation of men involved in the conflict. In fact, families such as the Pompeii and Lepidii were on their third generation of men involved in a civil war. Thus, whilst the victory over Antonius had ended this round of civil war, Octavianus' problem (and he clearly saw it as his problem) was how to prevent further civil warfare, despite the fact that his powers had only come from civil warfare.

In constitutional terms, with the expiration of the Triumvirate the Roman constitution resumed its pre-civil war shape once more, with the Consulship as the supreme position. For Octavianus this allowed him the chance to make a public declaration that the emergency had indeed passed and the Republic was indeed back to normal, by holding the Consulship, in consecutive years from 30 to 23 BC, amassing eleven in total. Furthermore, after 30 BC he seems to have abandoned the concept of shortened Consulships and numerous Suffect Consulships, with only one in 29 BC and none between 28–24 BC, Thus, when it suited him (i.e. when he needed it), Octavianus restored the Consulship to its full powers and prestige. Furthermore, he only shared it with men whom he could trust, including M. Vipsanius Agrippa (Rome's greatest living general), who shared the Consulships of 28 and 27 BC with him.

On top of this use of the Consulship came a special grant of powers from the Senate in 30 BC to celebrate his victory at Actium: *They also decreed that Caesar should hold the Tribunician power for life, that he should aid those who called upon him for help both within the Pomerium and outside for a distance of one mile, a privilege possessed by none of the Tribunes, also that he should judge appealed cases, and that in all the courts his vote was to be cast as Athena's vote.*[4]

This is apparently the second of the three stages of Octavianus receiving the powers of the Tribunate. It is reported that he received Tribunician sacrosanctity in 35 BC, and the powers of the Tribunate in 30 BC and again in 23 BC (below). Yet there is a way to reconcile these separate incidents. In both 44 BC, and again in 35 BC, Tribunician sacrosanctity had apparently been conferred on non-tribunes (first Caesar[5] and then Octavia and Livia[6]).However, as Bauman points out, on both occasions Dio uses an analogy to Tribunician sacrosanctity, rather than saying that it was actually Tribunician sacrosanctity that they received.[7] He speculates that

Caesar and then Octavia and Livia were voted sacrosanctity similar to that enjoyed by the Tribunes, but that this did not represent a separation of the powers from the office.

If we accept that Octavianus received sacrosanctity in 36 BC similar to his father but not that of the Tribunate, then we are left with three different dates for him receiving *tribunicia potestas* (36 BC – Appian only, 30 BC and 23 BC). We can start by discounting Appian's version of him receiving full powers in 36 BC as this was early for Octavianus to gain, or even want, full *tribunicia potestas*, as his position was far too weak to attempt something as radical compared to his position in 23 BC. Appian frequently betrays his own lack of a detailed understanding of the Republican constitution, being a product of his time.

This leaves the two grants of power in 30 and 23 BC and if Octavianus was granted it in 30 BC then why did he not use it until 23 BC or need it re-issued to him? The answer lies in the nature of the *tribunicia potestas*, which was not composed on one power but two: the *ius auxilli*, the right to intervene physically (the oldest of the Tribunate's powers) and the *ius intercessionis*, the right to intervene constitutionally (via veto or legislation). Thus, it becomes entirely possible that Octavianus received the *ius auxilii* in 30 BC as an honorific (the right to protect the people), which would augment his sacrosanct nature, whilst it was not until 23 BC. that he received the full *tribunicia potestas* including the right to propose legislation.[8]

The Consulship gave Octavianus control of Rome's political and military establishment, albeit as one of a pair, not sole rule, whilst observing the connotational niceties of not looking like he was Rome's ruler. His grant of Tribunician powers and sacrosanctity would effectively make him a Tribune each year. Thus, he effectively unified the posts of Consul and Tribune, making him the most powerful man in the Republic politically, albeit without obviously abusing the constitution and thus fuelling opposition. This is not to say that there weren't men opposed to his rule of the Republic, but he had not offended *mos maiorum* as clearly as his father had done, and therefore did not present his opponents with such an obvious rallying cry to defend the Republic.

In 28 BC he supplemented this Consular with a further grant of Censorial power, granted to both Consuls (himself and M. Vipsanius

Agrippa, his closest ally). The two men undertook the first full Census of the Roman population since 42 BC. This Census clearly used some different measurements of Roman citizen numbers, as it recorded 4,063,000 citizens, as opposed to 900,000 for the last census we have figures for (69 BC).[9] More importantly, this grant of Censorial power allowed Octavianus to revise the Senate, removing some two hundred Senators (presumably who's loyalty he suspected) and even allowed his own name to be placed as first on the list of Senators; the *Princeps Senatus*, the most senior Senator (and first amongst equals).[10]

3. The Rise of the Augustan Republic (27–23 BC)

Having been back in Rome for eighteen months (mid-29 to the end of 28 BC) and having secured his short-term position, Octavianus clearly turned his thoughts to a longer-term solution. Thus, he opened the year 27 BC with a very public renunciation of all his powers and the restoration to the Republic. This was followed by an equally public plea by the Senate for Octavianus not to retire from public life, but to continue his service to the *res publica*.[11] Thus, he was 'persuaded' to continue to hold the Consulship (until 23 BC) and retain Proconsular imperium over Rome's largest provinces (and thus the bulk of her military forces), namely Spain, Gaul and Syria. Administration of the other provinces fell once more to the Senate and its appointees, three of which held armies (Illyricum, Macedonia and Africa), whilst Octavianus' provinces continued to be governed by his legates.

Furthermore, Octavianus was officially granted a new name, his third so far: Augustus. This new identity drew a line under his previous activities and allowed him a fresh start. C. Iulius Caesar Octavianus had been a Triumvir and one of the key (and bloodiest) oligarchs in the civil war which had wracked the Republic. Augustus, with its obvious connotations of Romulus, the quasi-mythical founder of Rome, was thus publicly disassociated with the bloodshed of the civil wars and had a new identity as father of the state. Thus he attempted to draw a line under the civil wars and we may argue that it was in 27 BC that the Third Civil War ended (see Appendix Three).

The settlement of 27 BC was a clear attempt by Augustus (as he now was) to find the balance between having enough power to guide the Republic and ensuring that no rivals appeared, without looking like he was dominating the Republic and thus stoke up the very opposition and potential bloodshed he was hoping to avoid. For the next four years Augustus dominated the Republic through his repeated Consulships and his superior Proconsular imperium over the largest Roman provinces, thus commanding the bulk of the Republic's armies. He was ably supported by a faction of young ambitious Romans who could help him in his project of restoring the Republic, most notably, M. Vipsanius Agrippa and C. Maecenas.[12]

Therefore, Augustus avoided his adopted father's fundamental problem of looking like he was ruling the Republic; the Senate debated, Consuls were elected (albeit only one new man a year, Tribunes were elected (or nominated),[13] and the Assemblies met and passed legislation. Furthermore, there were no Dictators or Triumvirs. Thus, to all intents and purposes the machinery of the Republic continued as it should, albeit without the bloodshed and chaos that had marked the Republic since the 50s. Thus, the Republic was restored, albeit with Augustus as *Princeps Senatus*. The new system even allowed for individuals from the Senatorial aristocracy to seek military success and personal glory; the best example being M. Licinius Crassus (Cos. 30 BC), grandson of the Triumvir, who fought a distinguished campaign in Macedonia and Thrace and was awarded with a Triumph in 27 BC, though he was denied the *spolia opima* by Augustus.

Having implemented his blueprint for the political aspect of the Roman Republic, Augustus moved onto the next phase of his project, the implementation of his blueprint for Rome's empire. He now felt secure enough to leave Rome for a number of years and go campaigning, most notably finishing the two-hundred-year Roman conquest of Spain. Yet Augustus' control of the Republic proved not to be as secure as he had hoped, and yet again the absence of the key figure from Rome allowed others to develop their own plans.

The year 23 BC saw two important challenges to Augustus' domination, both politically and militarily. Firstly, the Governor of Macedonia (one of Augustus' provinces), M. Primus, went to war with a Thracian tribe without Augustus' permission, thus seeking military glory for himself. He was soon brought to trial and convicted of treason, but it did show that Augustus' control of the Roman military was not as solid as he might have hoped. Secondly, in Rome there arose another conspiracy against Augustus' life; this time organised by one Varro Murena.[14] Again, as with that of Lepidus seven years before, this conspiracy was nipped in the bud and soon ended, yet the threat clearly remained. Roman politics had the ultimate example of a tyrant slaying for any aspiring 'true' Republican to live up to.

A further crisis blew up shortly afterwards when Augustus himself fell dangerously ill and was not expected to survive. This raised the key issue of the 'succession', and the implicit dangers of a renewed civil war. In many ways, the situation was reminiscent of that of 44 BC. Like his adopted father, Augustus had no natural son to inherit his wealth and status. Yet, as in 44 BC, there were two obvious candidates, one a family member, and one a colleague. Augustus did have a daughter, Iulia, who was married to a certain M. Claudius Marcellus, making him Augustus' son-in-law. Yet clearly Augustus' right hand man and the finest general of Rome was his colleague M. Vipsanius Agrippa. This is not to mention that Augustus had two step-sons from his latest marriage to Agrippina: Ti. Claudius Nero and Nero Claudius Drusus. Given that Rome was a restored Republic there could be no formal talk of a succession, but Augustus did publicly hand his signet ring to Agrippa. Fortunately for all concerned (except perhaps Agrippa) Augustus recovered with the help of a new doctor and the crisis was averted, though it did foreshadow the succession crisis that was to dog Augustus' later years. Marcellus however caught a similar illness and died before the year was out, simplifying the question of the succession.

It was this brush with mortality that seemed to spur Augustus on to make another major change to the constitutional settlement, one which was to be his final. He gave up the Consulship and rarely held it again, thus removing the one very visible sign that he was dominating power in the Republic and hopefully some of the source of the resentment within the Senatorial oligarchy.[15] In its place he fully embraced the notion of taking powers from existing offices without holding the actual office itself. His new position lay on two foundations; the grant of Tribunician power (*tribunicia potestas*) granted to him in 31 BC and enhanced Proconsular imperium.

It is not clear whether Augustus sought a fresh grant of Tribunician power from the People or fell back on the earlier grant of 31 BC. In whichever case, he made the powers of the Tribunate central to his new position and thus in a wonderful piece of historical symmetry used the power of that office, which over a hundred years earlier had started the collapse of the Republic into bloodshed and violence, as the central platform upon which he would ensure peace in Rome. Thus, Augustus became the eleventh Tribune (he still could not hold the office himself) and thus had unlimited ability to propose legislation to the Assembly and initiate prosecutions.

Traditionally there were but two limitations on the Tribunate's powers; a one-year term and a colleague's veto, both of which were issues during the Tribunate of Ti. Sempronius Gracchus in 133 BC. Augustus now effectively became that which Gracchus' enemies had feared, a perpetual Tribune (albeit one without the actual office). Of the second limitation, we hear of no formal provision for Augustus' proposals not being subject to the vetoes (*ius intercessiones*) of the ten Tribunes each year, and this limitation may well have stayed in theory. In reality though, no one seems to have ever been foolhardy enough to publicly block one of Augustus' proposals. Even if they had, the Tribunician veto was never the termination of a proposal that some seem to believe, but merely a temporary halt to proceedings, allowing for further discussion and negotiation, until such time as it could be removed.

The importance of Tribunician power to Augustus and his position was ably, and very publicly, demonstrated when he instituted the practice of numbering his years in terms of how long he had held the power. Thus, we find in his own autobiography (the *res gestae*) terms such as: '*in the twelfth year of my Tribunician power*' (*tribunicia potestate duodecimum*).[16] This format became familiar for all public pronouncements and inscriptions, a practice which continued throughout the subsequent Roman Empire, with all emperors dating their reigns from the grant of Tribunician power. Thus, Augustus was publicly stating each time that the power he held was legitimate and that he was an officer of the People, not a king or a tyrant.

In many ways Augustus became a perpetual, or Imperial Tribune. There is more than a little synchronicity here. Just one hundred-and-ten years earlier, the cycle of political bloodshed was started when Ti. Gracchus' enemies murdered him, fearing he was aiming for a consecutive Tribunate and thus breaking the founding principle of the Republic that no man should hold power for more than one year. Now Augustus was doing just that and using the perpetual power of the Tribunate to govern the Republic. In many ways it was both the Triumph of the office of Tribune – its powers became central to the Roman Emperors (and all their successors) – and also its ultimate downfall, as the office itself was now effectively powerless and meaningless, with a perpetual eleventh (and superior) Tribune.

Augustus' military position was secured by a special grant of Proconsular imperium. Throughout the Republic men had held Proconsular imperium without holding the office, but Augustus had the Senate grant him regular periods (of five or ten years) of *maius* (greater) *imperium*. The concept of *maius imperium* was nothing new, as Pompeius himself had been granted similar in 57 BC when he was placed in charge of Rome's grain supply (see Chapter Five). This greater imperium meant that it (and he) were superior to all other holders of Proconsular imperium, meaning he outranked them and could issue them orders, thus putting him in effective command of the whole of Rome's military, but without actually looking like it. Furthermore, this imperium was also applicable within the Pomerium of Rome, unlike any other commander, meaning he could legally command troops within the sacred boundaries of Rome itself and thus legally use them to secure Rome itself.

Another key aspect in this grant of *maius imperium* was that it technically was not an unlimited grant but was time specific. It was renewed by the Senate in 18, 13, and 8 BC and again in AD 3 and 13. Specific grants of special imperium were nothing new to the Republic and Pompeius himself had used them on several occasions. Thus, it did not look as though Augustus was receiving unlimited control of the Republic's military, though in practice this is exactly what it was.

Augustus united the two key foundations of his new position, Tribunician power and Proconsular imperium, giving him complete control (should he so wish) of Roman legislation, judicial proceedings and the Roman military, along with the earlier grant of sacrosanctity, giving him religious status. He also had one grant of power from the People and one by the Senate, thus embodying the *senatus populusque romanus* in one person. Furthermore, these powers were bestowed on him by the Senate and People of Rome, as opposed to having been seized or inherited. Thus, in theory at least, the Senate and People had the ability to take these powers away or bestow them on somebody else.

These two central grants of power were enhanced by the further grant of the right for Augustus to nominate candidates to the various Assemblies for election. In terms of political stability, this power removed the dangerous and combustible element from Roman elections which had frequently led to outbreaks of violence and bloodshed. It also ensured that no men with a radical agenda for reform would ever be chosen. Away from the argument of stability, though, we can clearly see another step away from the democratic element of the Republic, with the Assemblies becoming a rubber stamp for elections, just as they were becoming for legislation.

The genius of this political settlement was that Augustus seized full control of all the levers of power in the Republic – military, legislative, judicial and electoral – whilst not looking like he was ruling the Republic or creating a tyranny. In theory Augustus held no office in the Republic; no Dictatorship, no repeated Consulships and no Triumvirate. Furthermore, the Republic looked like it had indeed been restored to its classical form. The highest offices were the Consuls, magistrates were elected annually by the various Assemblies,[17] the Senate deliberated on matters, and the Assemblies legislated. Yet as we can clearly see, and as many at the time did, this was merely a façade. No law could be passed, official be elected, or campaign be fought without the approval of one man. This was rule by stealth. With this settlement Augustus had finally been able to do that which all of his predecessors had failed – establish a stable one-man rule of a fiercely Republican system. Augustus showed that the key to ruling the Republic was not to look like you were ruling at all, a lesson which his successors virtually all failed to heed.

4. The Architect of Rome's Empire

As well as receiving *maius imperium* over Rome's empire, the Senate also surrendered their control (such as it was) over Rome's foreign policy by granting Augustus the right to conclude foreign treaties without submitting them to the Senate or People, and having all incoming magistrates swear to uphold all of his acts. Thus, Augustus became the sole source of foreign policy, a right the Senate and People never recovered. This had both positive and negative effects for the Republic. On the positive aspect there was now a central guiding policy behind all military and diplomatic activities, as seen with the massive and planned expansion of the Roman empire in Europe. No longer was military expansion done on an ad-hoc basis, guided by the desires of individual generals.

Throughout the last century, Rome's northern borders had been their most troublesome with no set boundary between the rule of Rome and the tribal societies which lay beyond it. Whilst the Alps gave Italy some protection, the Macedonian border had no such physical impediment, leading to over a century of perpetual low-level warfare in Macedon. Now, guided by Augustus' vision, Rome conquered vast swathes of tribal Europe and established a clear frontier on the Danube. Further to the west, the plan was for a German frontier on the Elbe, though after subsequent defeats in Germania this changed to the Rhine. In the east, rather than begin a Third Romano-Parthian War, Augustus chose to conduct a peace treaty with the Parthian Empire, effectively setting out the boundary between the two empires as the Euphrates. This led to an outbreak of peace between the two previously-expanding empires, which lasted for eighty years (until the time of Nero). Thus, considering the positive aspect, for the first time, Rome's empire now had firm boundaries.

However, there was a clear downside to this change. The setting of foreign policy was now down to one man and hinged on his mentality and ability. Whilst Augustus oversaw a huge expansion of Rome's empire, it was done clearly with a defensive mentality in mind; to create firm and defensible borders; Rhine-Danube-Euphrates. However, the empire which Augustus left behind was one whose borders barely moved for the next four hundred years. With a few exceptions Roman expansion came to a halt and the Republic lost its expansionist drive.

The history of the Republic is one of perpetual and ill-planned expansion; 'empire by accident'. The Roman mentality was forged in the early years of the city's existence; an endless struggle to survive in the perpetual warfare that marked out the existence of the small city states of Italy. When Rome, in the early-fourth century BC, found a way to tap into the manpower of the states it defeated, mastery of Italy soon followed. However, the Roman mentality did not change, and new threats emerged, this time from outside Italy. Rome could not be safe unless it mastered (not necessarily ruled) the other states of Italy. When that had been accomplished, then Rome would not be safe unless it mastered the states which were expanding towards Italy: Carthage, Syracuse, Macedon, the Gallic tribes of Northern Italy. Yet Rome found that defeating these states and leaving them free just seemed to lead to them becoming a renewed threat within a few decades and so the policy of annexation began. Furthermore, once the states surrounding Italy had been defeated and annexed, then the neighbouring states to those became potential threats, drawing Rome into mainland Europe and the Near East. It was Augustus that brought this endless insecurity and expansion to an end by giving Rome clearly defined and defensible borders.

Warfare continued on a smaller scale, with expeditions beyond Rome's boundaries to ensure that her neighbouring states and tribes would not be a threat. However, with the exception of a handful of Emperors, there was to be no further expansion; Claudius added Britannia, Trajan annexed a large swathe of central Europe and temporarily the Parthian Empire. The majority however were content to sit back and defend. Over the subsequent centuries, though, this defence turned into stagnation and newer threats were allowed to emerge both in Tribal Europe, beyond Rome's borders and in the east where a new Persian Empire rose from the ashes of the decayed Parthian one. Under the classical Republican system, individual generals seeking glory would have continued this expansion. Pompeius, Crassus, Caesar and Antonius all wanted to conquer the Parthian Empire and expand Rome's empire eastwards, following in the footsteps of Alexander, and ultimately it would have been better for Rome if they had. The only Roman it seemed who did not share his compatriots thirst for conquest for its own sake was Augustus, content to conquer and rule his own civilisation. If Augustus was the architect of the Roman Empire he was also the architect of its ultimate demise.

5. Empire by Stealth and Time

Whilst the constitutional settlement of 23 BC laid the foundations for Augustus' domination of the Republic, over the next thirty-seven years he continued to amass powers, all of which went to shape the new role of Princeps and lay the foundations for the future Roman Emperors. During the winter of 23/22 BC he exploited food shortages in Rome which led to the call for him to accept a more formal and perpetual role, such as Dictator or Consul for life, all of which gave him another opportunity to publicly decline them. What he did 'accept' was the role of guardian of the corn supply (*cura annonae*), a role which Pompeius had himself taken, giving him low level but wider powers over the whole empire and also placing Augustus as the guardian of the People's food supply.

On his return from the east in 19 BC, having recovered the legionary standards lost to the Parthians (by both Crassus and Antonius), he seems to have accepted the need for a more conspicuous display of his role by being 'granted' the right to sit between the Consuls and have twelve lictors. Dio goes further and states that he accepted a grant of Consular power for life, though this is argued.[18]

The death of Lepidus, in 12 BC, not only removed the last of Augustus' contemporaries but opened up a vacancy in the role of Pontifex Maximus (Rome's Chief Priest), a position held previously by Caesar. Thus, Augustus added this religious office to his collection of powers, so combining spiritual and temporal authority in one person. From this point onwards, the role of Pontifex Maximus would never be held independently until the time of the Popes: all future Emperors would also automatically hold the office of Pontifex Maximus. This religious authority now invested in the figure of Augustus was enhanced in 2 BC when he was 'awarded' the title of *pater patriae* or father of the nation.

In addition to these grants of titles and offices, Augustus also subtly subverted existing features of Roman life and slowly absorbed them into his own sphere, most notably Triumphs and the Censorship. In the early years of the Augustan Republic, Triumphs continued to be awarded to members of the Senate, most notably M. Licinius Crassus in 27 BC. Between 30 and 23 BC we have surviving records of five different Senatorial Triumphs (actually all between 28 and 26 BC).[19] Yet there were only to be two more such Triumphs, the last coming in 19 BC.[20] This was to be the last Triumph to be celebrated by someone not of the ruling family. Though there was no formal announcement of a new policy, from that point on, the public acknowledgement of military successes was limited to those connected to the family of Augustus (by marriage or blood). Henceforth it was only the ruling family that could bring about military success, and though others could hold commands and fight successful wars, it would not be acknowledged in such a public display.

The Censorship too initially continued to be open to members of the Senatorial nobility. However, the last Censors who were not members of the ruling family were Paul. Aemilius Lepidus and L. Munatius Plancus in 22 BC, after which that too was only to be held by those related to Augustus. Thus, though the office was not abolished, the powers to revise the Senatorial membership, the citizen lists, became exclusive to the Princeps.

This process of slow evolution continued and by AD 5 Augustus felt secure enough to introduce a major change to the Roman constitution concerning the election of magistrates. The Consuls L. Valerius Messalla Volesus and Cn. Cornelius Cinna Magnus (son of none other than L. Cornelius Cinna)[21] introduced a law which created ten new centuries in the Comitia Centuriata, the Assembly which elected the senior magistrates. The new ten centuries (named after Augustus' grandsons Caius and Lucius) were to be composed of senior Senators and Equestrians and were to vote first on the selection of magistrates and present their choices to the wider Comitia Centuriata, who would be expected to vote accordingly. Thus again, Augustus removed another 'democratic' element from the Roman constitution, whilst leaving the institutions intact.

However, by far the greatest factor involved in the evolution of the Augustan Republic was the longevity of the man himself. Both Sulla and Caesar had been at the end of their careers when they seized control of the Republic, and Sulla as it turned out was in poor health. Augustus however was young and lived a long life (dying at the age of seventy-five). There can be little doubt that had Augustus died in 23 BC then his vision of the Republic would have died with him, most likely followed by another round of civil war. As the decades rolled by, there was always Augustus, the steady hand on the tiller, ever present to guide the Republic into a new age of peace and prosperity.

This was all accompanied by continued exercises in public relations. The civil wars had ended and the political violence which accompanied Roman politics had ceased. Rome's empire was at its height and Rome itself was rebuilt to be a fit imperial capital, encapsulated by the comment ascribed to Augustus' that he '*found it of brick, but left it of marble*'.[22] The dividends of peace and prosperity were a massive building programme, throughout the Roman world, but especially in Rome itself, all of which helped to enhance the myth that Rome under Augustus was a new golden age, all thanks to the man himself.

Yet, having ruled Rome for nearly sixty years (43 BC to AD 14) and having built this new position of Princeps, Augustus faced one crucial dilemma: namely, what to do when he died. Here was the crux of the problem; technically no new office had been created, Augustus held personal grants of power but those were subject to renewal. If his new Republic were to survive then it would need to continue to have a new man take charge upon his death.

Yet this in itself could spark another civil war and undo all his work. Furthermore, in a historical parallel, Augustus, like Caesar before him, had no natural son to inherit his position and his *auctoritas*. In fact, Augustus initially had the opposite problem: there were too many possible successors. In the early years there was Augustus' son-in-law M. Claudius Marcellus, and Augustus' right-hand man and Rome's leading general, Agrippa. Then there were Augustus' two steps-sons, Tiberius and Drusus, both of the gens Claudii and thus with impeccable Republican ancestry.

The story of the succession is a well-known and sometimes lurid one. Marcellus died young (23 BC) and Augustus tried to solve his problem by marrying his widowed daughter (Iulia) to his closest ally, Agrippa (died 12 BC). This union produced two sons, Caius and Lucius, whom Augustus adopted as his own and thus seemingly secured the succession. All concepts of Republican *mos maiorum* disappeared in the promotion of these two young men, with both being awarded the right to be Consuls whilst still in their teens. Yet fate, or perhaps human agent, intervened and both young men died before Augustus (Lucius in AD 2 and Caius in AD 4). Natural (or unnatural) selection left Augustus with just one choice: Ti. Claudius Nero (known today as Tiberius); his brother Drusus having died in 9 BC.

Despite a history of antagonism between the two men, Augustus laid the plans for Tiberius to succeed him and receive the same grants of power which he himself had held. As it turned out, Tiberius was probably a far better choice (on paper) than Augustus' preferred options. He had not been born to the role and had impeccable Republican ancestry (the gens Claudii). Furthermore, he was one of Rome's leading generals, having fought campaigns in Gaul, Germania and on the Danube. and was clearly one of the leading men of the Republic.

Tiberius was invested by the Senate and People to hold the role of Princeps and become the guardian of the Republic. There is no clear answer to the question: was this the moment that the Republic died, and the Roman Empire was born? The Senate and People accepted a recommendation from their outgoing Princeps about the choice of a new one, one who had excellent credentials to be selected. Others would argue that it was hereditary succession, yet the Republic had always had the hereditary principle at its very heart. Perhaps it was only when Tiberius was succeeded as Princeps by a twenty-five-year-old C. Iulius Caesar (or Caligula as he is more popularly known) that the Republic perished. The Augustan Republic was not an empire, but clearly laid the foundations for one.

Summary

After over a hundred years of bloodshed and sixty years of civil war, the cycle of violence was brought to an end by Augustus, who seemed to be the only man who could win both the war and the peace (something that neither Sulla nor Caesar had been able to manage). He seems to have learnt the lessons of his predecessors well; namely that the trick to ruling the Republic was not to look like you were ruling it. By taking no obvious monarchical office he was able to reconcile the twin needs of the Senate and People, for peace and stability without tyranny. However, there was no moving away from the fact that it was through warfare and bloodshed that he had achieved his position of dominance, as many at the time were only too aware. Yet as Caesar had shown, military might was not enough to rule Rome: one needed the tacit approval of the Senate and People, and it is a testament to the genius of Augustus that this settlement not only outlasted him but brought about one hundred years of stability in Rome and her empire.

Yet the year AD 14 marked the high-point of the Augustan settlement; a peaceful transition of power. What followed was the return of political bloodshed in Rome, from the rise and fall of Sejanus to the assassination of Caligula and the instability of Nero. The whole system collapsed in AD 68/69, one hundred years after Actium, and saw the return of civil war. Yet even then, the strength of the Augustan settlement can be seen. Having dispensed with the hereditary principle, the Senate appointed Galba as the new Emperor (though he was soon disposed of). The hereditary principle returned briefly under the Flavians but was replaced by a new version: empire by adoption, where one Emperor would choose a leading candidate for the role and adopt him; a principle which brought about the golden age of the Roman Empire, an age which only fell when the principle was abandoned and hereditary succession (in the form of Commodus) returned.

At best, Augustus brought about a temporary breathing space in the chaos and bloodshed that was to plague Roman society for the rest of its existence, a fact which ultimately showed that he had failed in his attempt to cure the Republican system of its tendencies for bloodshed and civil war. His solution centred all the power (however disguised) on one individual. Whilst that individual was himself, all was well, but few of his successors showed the balance and temperament needed to oversee a system such as Rome. Ultimately, therefore, all he had done was create a new office for the Roman nobles to compete for, a prize far greater than any before it and thus one worth shedding more blood for. Thus, the competitive element within the Roman nobility proved to be its greatest asset (building up the largest empire that had ever been seen) but also its greatest weakness, periodically leading to collapses into civil war and bloodshed and ultimately leading to the downfall of the Western Empire, showing how far they had come from the murder of a Tribune in 133 BC.

Appendix I

The Butcher's Bill:
Murdered Roman Politicians (70–27 BC)

66   Outbreak of violence at the Assembly – multiple fatalities from amongst supporters of the Tribune C. Manilius

63   *P. Cornelius Lentulus Sura*   (Cos. 71, Pr. 74 & 67 BC)
     M. Caeparius
     C. Cornelius Cethegus
     P. Gabinius Capito
     L. Statilius
     Executed without trial for their role in the attempted coup

     Aulus Fulvius
     A Senator murdered by his own father for his suspected involvement in the coup

62   *L. Sergius Catalina*   (Pr. c. 68 BC)
     C. Manlius
     Killed during the Battle of Pistoria

59   *L. Vettius*
     Murdered whilst in prison

58   Outbreak of violence at Legislative Assembly – multiple fatalities

55   Outbreak of violence at the Aedile elections – multiple fatalities
     Outbreak of violence at Legislative Assembly – multiple fatalities

53   'Battle' of Via Sacra between supporters of the Consular candidates Hypsaeus and Milo – multiple fatalities

52   *P. Clodius Pulcher*   (Tr. 59/58 BC)
     Killed during a clash on the Via Appia, by the supporters of Milo
     Outbreak of violence at a Trial – multiple fatalities

49   *C. Scribonius Curio*   (Tr. 51/50 BC)
     Killed in battle fighting the Pompeians / Numidians

48   *T. Annius Milo*   (Tr. 57 BC)
     Killed in battle with Caesarian forces, having invaded Italy

M. Caelius Rufus   (Pr. 48 BC)
Killed whilst attempting to subvert a Caesarian garrison in Italy

L. Domitius Ahenobarbus   (Cos. 54 BC)
Killed during the aftermath of the Battle of Pharsalus

Cn. Pompeius Magnus   (Cos. 70, 55, 52 BC)
Murdered by Roman soldiers upon landing in Egypt

L. Cornelius Lentulus Crus   (Cos. 49 BC)
Murdered by the Egyptians whilst a prisoner
Outbreak of violence at Legislative Assembly – eight hundred killed
by soldiers of M. Antonius

47 *C. Cosconius*   (Pr. 54 BC)
    Galba
    Killed during a mutiny of Caesarian soldiers in Italy

46 *Q. Caecilius Metellus Pius Scipio Nasica*   (Cos. 52 BC)
    M. Porcius Cato   (Pr. 54 BC)
    M. Petreius
    Committed suicide following Caesar's victory at the Battle of
    Thapsus

    Faustus Cornelius Sulla
    L. Iulius Caesar
    L. Afranius   (Cos. 60 BC)
    Murdered by Caesarian forces following the Battle of Thapsus

    Sex. Iulius Caesar
    Killed during a Pompeian revolt in Syria

    C. Considius Longus   (Pr. 58 BC)
    Killed during a mutiny

45 *P. Attius Varus*   (Pr. 53 BC)
    T. Labienus
    Killed during the Battle of Munda

    Cn. Pompeius
    Murdered by Caesarian forces following the Battle of Munda

44 *C. Iulius Caesar*   (Cos. 59, 48, 46, 45, 44 BC)
    Murdered in the Senate House

    Outbreak of violence in Rome at news of Caesar's murder – multiple
    fatalities including an unknown number of Senators

C. Helvius Cinna (Tr. 45/44 BC)

Murdered by a mob at Caesar's funeral

C. Marius

The man purporting to be Marius' grandson was executed by M. Antonius

Outbreak of violence in Rome between Antonius' forces and the supporters of the pseudo-Marius. Multiple fatalities, including executions of captured slaves and freedmen

43 *C. Trebonius* (Cos. 45 BC)

Murdered by Cornelius Dolabella in Asia

D. Carfulenus (Tr. 45/44 BC)

Believed killed during the Battle of Forum Gallorum

C. Vibius Pansa Caetronianus (Cos. 43 BC)

Died of wounds received in the Battle of Forum Gallorum fighting M. Antonius

A. Hirtius (Cos. 43 BC)

Killed during the Battle of Mutina fighting M. Antonius

C. Peducaeus

Pontius Aquila

L. Roscius Fabatus (Pr. 49 BC)

Killed during the Battle of Mutina

P. Cornelius Dolabella (Cos. 44 BC)

Committed suicide following defeat to Cassius

M. Iuventius Laterensis (Pr. 51 BC)

Committed suicide when Lepidus allied with M. Antonius

D. Iunius Brutus Albinus (Pr. 45 BC)

Murdered on the orders of M. Antonius by a Gallic Chieftain

M. Caecilius Cornutus (Pr. 43 BC)

Committed suicide when Octavius seized Rome

Proscription lists published (containing 17, 130, then 150 individuals) to be murdered[1]

Salvius (Tr. 44/43 BC)

A serving Tribune, the first victim of the Proscriptions

M. Aquilius Crassus	(Pr. 43 BC)
Q. Gallius	(Pr. 43 BC)
Minucius	(Pr. 43 BC)
L. Plotius Plancus	(Pr. 43 BC)

All serving Praetors, all murdered during the Proscriptions

M. Tullius Cicero	(Cos. 63 BC)
Q. Tullius Cicero	(Pr. 62 BC)
Q. Tullius Cicero	

Murdered during the Proscriptions

C. Antonius   (Pr. 44 BC)

Brother of M. Antonius murdered by Q. Hortensius, whilst M. Brutus' prisoner

42   C. Cassius Longinus   (Pr. 44 BC)

Committed suicide following the First Battle of Philippi

P. Cornelius Lentulus Spinther

Believed killed during the Battles of Philippi

M. Porcius Cato

Son of the famous Cato, killed during the Second Battle of Philippi

M. Terentius Varro Gibba   (Tr. 44/43 BC)

Killed during the Second Battle of Philippi

M. Iunius Brutus   (Pr. 44 BC)

Pacuvius Antistius Labeo

L. (Quinctilius) Varus   (Pr.)

Committed suicide following the Second Battle of Philippi

Q. Hortensius

Murdered following the Second Battle of Philippi, in retaliation for the death of C. Antonius

Q. Cornificius   (Pr. 45 BC)

Died (either killed in battle or suicide) following Sextius' victory in Africa

Ventidius

Killed fighting Sextius in Africa

D. Laelius Balbus

Roscius

Committed suicide following Sextius' victory in Africa

A. Pompeius Bithynicus   (Pr. 45 BC)
Murdered by Sex. Pompeius following his capture of Sicily

Villius Annalis   (Aed. 43 BC)
Killed in office by Triumviral soldiers

40   *Three Hundred Senators and Equestrians*
Murdered on the orders of Octavianus following the fall of Perusia

Ti. Cannutius   (Tr. 45/44 BC)
Murdered on the orders of Octavianus following the fall of Perusia

C. Velleius
Committed suicide after the fall of Perusia

Q. Fuficius Fango
Committed suicide when Pompeius captured the African provinces

Q. Salvidius Rufus Salvius   (Cos. Des. 39 BC)
Executed by Octavianus (or committed suicide) after Antonius revealed his attempted betrayal

39   *Q. Labienus*
Murdered on the orders of Ventidius after being captured following a defeat

L. Staius Murco   (Pr. 45 BC)
Murdered on the orders of Sex. Pompeius

35   *Sex. Pompeius*   (Cos. Des. 33 BC)
Murdered by M. Titius after being captured (possibly on the orders of M. Antonius)

Curius
Executed for conspiring with Pompeius

31   *Aquilii Flori*
Curio
P./D. Turullius
Murdered on the orders of Octavianus following the Battle of Actium

30   *M. Antonius*   (Cos. 44, 34, 31 (Des) BC)
Committed suicide following Octavianus' invasion of Egypt

P. Candidus Crassus   (Cos. 40 BC)
Q. Ovinius
Supporters of Antonius, all murdered on the orders of Octavianus following his conquest of Egypt

M. Antonius Antyllus

Son of M. Antonius, murdered on the orders of Octavianus following his conquest of Egypt

Caesarion (Ptolemy XV)

Son of Caesar, murdered on the orders of Octavianus following his conquest of Egypt

C. Cassius Parmensis

Murdered on the orders of Octavianus for being the last of the killers of Caesar

M. Aemilius Lepidus

Son of the Triumvir, murdered on the orders of Octavianus having been accused of a conspiracy to murder him

Appendix II

Who Were the Tribunes? (70–27 BC)

1. Tribunician Fasti

Determining just who held the Tribunate in the Roman Republic is not as easy as it may sound. Unlike the holders of the Consulship, there is no surviving list from antiquity (though several existed) and so the holders must be compiled from a trawl through the surviving sources. However, unlike the holders of the Consulships, there are many occasions where the sources are ambiguous over what office a particular Roman politician was holding and so there is no certain attestation that they were indeed a Tribune. Furthermore, we are aware of a number of men attested as holding the Tribunate, but their year of office is uncertain and there also exists a number of references to Tribunes and their activities, but not their identity. Thus, we have the following categories:

- Named and Attested to a Year
- Un-named and Attested to a Year
- Named and Unattested to a Year
- Possible Tribunes

In a number of cases whether a person was a Tribune or what year he held the office is a matter of individual analysis, which means that each person looking at it can come to a different conclusion or even change their mind over time. To date there have been seven works identifying and listing the various holders of the Tribunate, from 1599 to 2005, and their results are below:

Author	Strongly Attested	Uncertain Date	Total Number	% Total of all
Pighius[1]	452	122	574	13.0
Garofalo[2]	407	–	407	9.2
Ziegler[3]	81	–	81	–
Pais[4]	462	–	462	10.5
Niccolini[5]	456	93	549	12.5
Broughton[6]	490	53	543	12.3
Sampson[7]	493	93	586	13.3

2. The Tribunes 70–27 BC

The list below is an amended one, based on the 2005 listing, and details all the attested, anonymous and possible Tribunes from 70 to 27 BC.[8] As Tribunes traditionally took office on 10th December of the year they were elected, their year in office straddles two calendar years, as shown below.[9]

71/70	*Plautius/Plotius*	*(Possible)*
	Anonymous – Single	
70/69	Q. Cornificius	
	Q. Manlius	
69/68	C. Antius	
or 73/72	C. Antonius	
	Q. Caecilius (*Metellus*)	
	Cn. Cornelius (*Lentulus*)	
	C. Fundanius	
	L. Hostilius	
	Q. Marcius	
	C. Popilius	
	M. Valerius	
	L. V[*olcatius*]	
74–67	Q. (*Caecilius*) Metellus	
	Cn. (*Cornelius*) Lentulus	
	C. Falcidius	
	Q. Caelius Latiniensis	
68/67	C. Cornelius	
	A. Gabinius	

	C. Papirius Carbo	
	L. Roscius Otho	
	P. Servilius Globulus	
	L. Trebellius	
	Anonymous – Multiple	
67/66	C. Manilius	
	C. Memmius	*(Possible)*
	Anonymous – Multiple	
c.67	C. / Cn. Papirius Carbo	
66/65	C. Papius	
	Anonymous – Multiple	
65/64	Q. Mucius Orestinus	
64/63	T. Ampius Balbus	
	L. Caecilius Rufus	
	T. Labienus	
	P. Servilius Rullus	
	Anonymous – Multiple	
63/62	Q. Caecilius Metellus Nepos	
	L. Calpurnius Bestia	
	L. Marius	
	Q. Minucius Thermus	
	M. Porcius Cato	
62/61	C. Caecilius Cornutus	
	Q. Fufius Calenus	
	Lurco (*M. Aufidius Lurco*)	
61/60	L. Flavius	
	C. Herennius	
	Anonymous – Multiple	
60/59	C. Alfius Flavus	
	Q. Ancharius	
	Q. Caecilius Metellus Pius Scipio Nasica	
	C. Cosconius	
	Cn. Domitius Calvinus	
	C. Fannius	
	P. Vatinius	
59/58	Aelius Ligus	
	L. Antistius	

               L. Ninnius Quadratus
               L. Novius
               Q. Terentius Culleo
               P. Claudius (Clodius) Pulcher
               Anonymous – Multiple

58/57   T. Annius Milo
               Sex. Atilius Serranus Gavianus
               C. Cestilius
               M. Cispius
               C./M. Curius Peduceanus
               Q. Fabricius
               T. Fadius
               C. Messius
               Q. Numerius Rufus
               P. Sestius

57/56   Antistius Vetus
               L. Caninius Gallus
               C. Cassius
               M. Nonius Sufenas
               Cn. Plancius
               A. Plautius
               C. Porcius Cato
               L. Procilius
               L. Racilius
               P. Rutilius Lupus

56/55   P. Aquilius Gallus
               C. Ateius Capito
               C. Trebonius
               Anonymous – Multiple

55/54   D. Laelius
               C. Memmius
               Q. Mucius Scaevola
               Terentius

54/53   M. Coelius Vinicianus
               C. Lucilius Hirrus
               P. Licinius Crassus Dives Iunianus
               Anonymous – Multiple

53/52	M. Caelius Rufus	
	Manilius Cumanus	
	T. Munatius Plancus Byrsa	
	Q. Pompeius Rufus	
	C. Sallustius Crispus	
	Anonymous – Multiple	
52/51	C. Caelius (*Rufus*)	
	P. Cornelius	
	C. Vibius Pansa	
	L. Vinicius	
51/50	C. Furnius	
	Servaeus	Tribune Elect, disqualified for bribery
	C. Scribonius Curio	Suffect Tribune
40s	P. Decius	
	P. Ventidius Bassus	
	Valerius Siculus	
50/49	M. Antonius	
	L. Caecilius Metellus	
	C. Cassius Longinus	
	Q. Cassius Longinus	
	Cotta (*Aurelius Cotta*)	
	L. Marcius Philippus	
49/48	Anonymous – Multiple	
48/47	P. Cornelius Dolabella	
	L. Trebellius	
	C. Asinius Pollio	*(Possible)*
47/46	*C. Antonius*	*(Possible)*
	Anonymous – Multiple	
46/45	L. Pontius Aquila	
	Caecilius or Pomponius	*(Possible)*
45/44	L. Antonius	
	Asprenas (*Nonius Asprenas*)	
	Ti. Cannutius	
	(D.) Carfulenus	
	L. Cassius Longinus	
	C. Helvius Cinna	Killed whilst in office.

	C. *(Servilius)* Casca	
	L. Caesetius Flavus	Removed by Caesar
	C. Epidius Marullus	Removed by Caesar
	L. Decidius Saxa	Suffect Tribune
	(C./P.) Hostilius Saserna	Suffect Tribune
	Flaminius	*(Possible)*
c.43–35	Tillius *(Cimber)*	
44/43	P. Appuleius	
	Salvius	
	M. Servilius	
	P. Servilius Casca Longus	Removed from Office
	M. Terentius Varro	
	P. Titius	Died in Office
	Anonymous – Multiple	
c.42	L. Clodius	
	M. Insteius	
	Tullus Hostilius	
42/41	*(C./P.)* Falcidius	
40s/30s	M. Vipsanius Agrippa	
33/32	Nonius Balbus	
30/29 or 29/28	Q. Statilius	
28/27	Sex. Apudius/Pacuvius	

Undatable – Late Republic[10]

M. Ampudius
C. Appulleius Tappo
L. Caecina
Q. Carellius
C. Cestius Epulo
M. Fruticius
Q. Haterius
L. Memmius
P. Paquius Scaeva
L. Precilius
Q. Sanquinius

When is a Civil War Not a Civil War?

W hen is a civil war not a civil war? Although this may sound like the opening line of a particularly unfunny academic joke, the question is a fundamental one for anyone studying this period of Roman history. Throughout, we see bloodshed and violence (between Romans) on a scale not seen before, everything from individual murders, to battles in the streets of Rome and full-scale clashes between Roman armies. Although we use the term civil war there is no clarity over how it can be applied to the events covered in these volumes.[1] Furthermore, the traditional historiography of this period seems to contain a number of marked inconsistencies and downright nonsensical statements.

In modern historiography of the Roman period, the First Civil War is said to have started in 88 BC, when Sulla and his consular colleague Pompeius Rufus (though he is often overlooked), marched their army on Rome in 88 BC, and ended in 82 BC, following Sulla's victory at the Colline Gate and Pompeius' re-conquest of Sicily and North Africa. Yet this leaves us with the ridiculous situation that a Consul (Cinna) marching his army on Rome in 87 BC and fighting another Consul (Octavius) is classed as a civil war, whilst the same situation just ten years later (in 77 BC, between Lepidus and Catulus) is not classed as a civil war, and is most commonly referred to as the 'Lepidian revolt'.

Thus, modern historiography seems to be following a Sullan approach and agreeing that Sulla ended the civil wars in 82 BC with his victory at the Colline Gate. This overlooks the fact that Roman fought Roman throughout the 70s BC, first in Spain (with Sertorius) and then in Asia Minor (with M. Marius).

This brings us to the vexed question of what is a civil war? The traditional answer is a war within a country or state between the various groups within that region. Yet the key question is how do we apply this definition to Rome and the events covered in this period? Ancient historians fared no better with this question than those of us today and we can see a range of opinion; everything from Appian, who classed all the events from 133 to 31 BC as one *Bellum Civile*, down to Florus, who classes each conflict as a separate *Bellum*, including the civil wars of Marius, Lepidus and then Caesar and Pompeius.

All too often, modern historiography ignores this question and seems to follow the Florine route, wanting to separate these various conflicts into nice self-contained wars. This is not just a problem with Roman history. Modern historiography seems to demand that civil wars be clearly defined between two opposing sides each with a different ideological standpoint. Thus, English history only has one civil war (1642–1651) with two clearly defined sides, with separate ideological stand points (monarchy vs parliament) and even clearly defined costumes. Yet this war was at least the fifth fought between the English in the last thousand years. We have the civil war between Stephen and Maud for the crowns of England and Normandy (1135–1153), the two civil wars fought between Kings John and Henry III and their rebellious nobles (1215–1217 and 1264–1267), and the bloodiest civil war fought between the various branches of the Plantagenet dynasty for the English crown in 1403 and again between 1455 and 1487 (dubbed the War of the Roses).

Thus, English history had at least five civil wars in the last thousand years, yet only one makes the cut as an 'official' civil war. The obvious question is, why are the others ignored and downgraded into non-civil wars, each with a meaningless title (Baron Wars, Wars of the Roses)? Is it because they don't fit into a nice ideological framework, or is it an unwillingness to admit that societies collapse more often than we would like to admit?

If we look at history, we can discern two broad types of civil war. One is the 'modern' version, where we have a clash between two clear sides, each with an ideological standpoint, usually centred on a question of governance. Thus, we have the classic English, American, Spanish and Chinese Civil Wars. Yet the second type is where there is a complete breakdown of government and a society collapses into anarchy with various competing warlords emerging and fighting for supremacy. These types can most commonly be seen in modern Africa.

Yet returning to Rome, which type of civil wars can we see? All too often modern historians want them to be the clear-cut ideological civil wars, between optimates and populares (terms which have been grossly distorted). Thus, our two official civil wars of the period (Sulla vs Marius and Caesar vs Pompeius) are often painted in these terms. Yet having reviewed these events, such terms are meaningless. The various protagonists did not go to war over differing views of government, but turned to their armies to defend their own positions from the attacks of their enemies. The events of the 80s and 40s both snowballed out of everyone's control, with the Republican system collapsing and leading to periods of anarchy where various Roman generals fought for supremacy amongst themselves until a victorious individual emerged who could rebuild central authority and calm the bloodshed i.e. dominate without looking like they were doing so. For example, Pompeius and Crassus in 71–70 BC and Octavianus in 30–27 BC.

Thus, modern Roman historiography leaves us with a Florine-like patchwork of different wars:

Social War	(91–88 BC)
First Civil War	(88–81 BC)
Sertorian Rebellion	(81–72 BC)
Lepidian Revolt	(78–77 BC)
Catiline Conspiracy	(63–62 BC)
Second Civil War	(49–31 BC)

The clear danger of following such an approach of course is that it shifts focus away from the underlying causes of these conflicts and onto individuals and thus blurs the line between symptom and cause. Should we be focusing on Sulla, Lepidus, Catilina, Caesar or the underlying issues that were at work behind them? Clearly, having read this volume, the reader will understand that focussing on the individuals at the expense of the wider picture is not a method I chose to pursue. Not one of these men woke up one morning and thought that they would like to march their army against their own state simply to gain power for themselves, but Republican politics had forced them to believe that they had no alternative and that what they were doing was for the benefit of the Republic.

Ultimately, as these events proved, the Republican system did not provide a robust-enough framework to keep the various tensions between the Senatorial oligarchy from spilling over into violence and civil war. Various attempts were made to modify the Republic, be it Triumvirate (official or unofficial) or sole rule (subtle or obvious). The one version that emerged victorious from this period was sole rule, with one figure guiding and overseeing the smooth running of the Republic and acting as arbiter to keep the others in check. Yet this too was flawed and laid the foundations for a role of Emperor, first on a hereditary basis and then merit or force.

Yet, if we are to reject the Florine version of the wars in this period; what are we to replace it with? Do we simply follow the Appianic version and state that all this period was one giant civil war, or do we reject the notion of a civil war in a society such as Rome altogether? I have and will continue to argue that within this period of Roman history there were distinct periods of civil wars, when the clashes and tensions within the Republican system boiled over into full-blown military conflict and in two out of the three cases, total system wide (and empire wide collapse).

Civil war within a country is one thing, but civil war in a society that had a full-blown empire is another matter altogether and magnified the chaos and fighting on a Mediterranean-wide level. As we have seen, in two out of three cases Rome's empire became a battleground for the various parties of the civil war and led to the extinction of several independent kingdoms, who became too closely associated with a losing side (namely Numidia and Egypt).

Having rejected the modern Florine notion of multiple separate wars, I would like to offer up a fresh framework for the civil wars within this period, if only to stimulate further debate on a subject that can never have a right answer.

First Civil War, 91–70 BC

All too often, discussions of the First Civil War ignore the fact that Italy had been riven by civil warfare for three years with two rebel factions fighting the Republican government. This is the very reason that Sulla had an army of battle-hardened veterans in Italy within marching distance of Rome and citizen distribution was at the heart of the political manoeuvring which led to Sulla's loss of command. Thus, the war that broke out in 91 BC between the various societies that made up the Roman system must be classed as a civil war, with neighbour fighting neighbour and, if we are to believe the more dramatic sources, brother fighting brother.

The First Civil War period saw a number of different phases, which were not neat separate conflicts but were all intertwined. The war in Italy led to the Consular attack on Rome in 88 BC, both of which mixed together to spark off the war of 87 BC. There then followed a lull whilst at least two different Roman armies separately fought off a foreign invasion. When that invasion had been dealt with, then all sides engaged in a fight for supremacy, which brought about another lull as Sulla consolidated his control of Italy and the Western Republic. Some regions were forcibly reunited (Sicily, Africa) whilst others (Spain and Gaul) were brought back through negotiation between warlords. Yet the faction that lost Italy soon stoked a rebellion in Spain, where the civil war continued (mixed in with a native rebellion, as it had done in Italy) for another nine years. Whilst the civil war continued in the west (Spain), other elements of the faction that lost Italy spearheaded another foreign invasion of Rome's empire, again blurring the lines between civil war and foreign war.

Thus, we can see that during this period there were no neat delineations between civil war, native rebellion and foreign wars, but all became inexorably interlinked in one great collapse of the Republican system. It is also not a coincidence that the largest slave rebellion in Roman history happened during this period of chaos, when a certain slave named Spartacus took advantage of the devastation in Italy, disaffection with Rome and overseas wars to launch his rebellion.

By 71 BC there emerged another lull, with the fighting ended in Spain, Italy and Asia. Yet it took the actions of Pompeius and Crassus, who chose to unite Rome rather than continue the divisions (and personally benefit from it). Their Consulship not only set an example that two oligarchs could work in a peaceful manner, especially if they cooperated but the constitutional settlement they introduced also removed a number of tension points (though some would say reintroduced them) and saw a very public recall of all Romans exiled during the previous twenty years of tumult. Thus, it can be argued that a lull became a definite end.

Second Civil War, 63–62 BC

That the events of 63/62 constitute a civil war should not be difficult to argue. Although the ancient sources and modern histography choose to focus on events in Rome, the key facts are that there were widescale rebellions against Rome throughout Italy and native rebellions in Gaul (again mixing the two), and two Romano-Italian armies fought one another in a set piece battle. That there was only one set piece battle, and that it was over relatively quickly, should not disqualify this from being classed as a civil war. In fact, the surviving sources paint a picture of wider military action across Italy, but we only have the barest of detail for it. Had we fuller sources for this fighting then we would be able to see the true scale of the civil war in Italy.

The other argument is that if this was a civil war, was it a continuation of the first war and thus can we extend the First Civil War down to 62 BC?[2] As we have reviewed, the causes of this war did have its roots in the first war, be they disgruntled Sullan politicians and veterans or displaced Italian communities. Yet I would argue that it was a separate conflict from that of 91–70 BC and that the years 69–64 were not merely a lull in the first war, but that the Pompeian-Crassan Consulships did end the First Civil War. That a war can be finished but still leave matters unsettled can be seen frequently throughout history; most recently in the First and Second World Wars (at least in Europe). So, although the Second Civil War had its roots in the first they were, I believe, separate conflicts. This can also be seen by the fact that the New Republic reconstituted out of the ashes of the First Civil War did not collapse as it had done in 91–70 or 49–27 BC.

Third Civil War, 49–27 BC

This is perhaps the most uncontentious of the three, with it being widely accepted that the events between the crossing of the Rubicon in 49 BC and the victory of Octavianus constitute another period of one civil war, which again saw a total collapse of the Republican system, and the emergence of various factions and warlords. It also saw the blurring between civil war and foreign war, again most easily seen in the east with the attack by the Parthian Empire being spearheaded by a Roman general. This period too saw lulls in the fighting between the various overlapping conflicts. There was no certainty that Octavianus' victory at Actium in 31 BC would be the final major battle of the war, anymore than the Battle of Pharsalus in 48 BC or Philippi in 42 BC.

If there is one contentious issue, then it must be the end date of this civil war. It clearly did not end with the Battle of Actium in 31 BC, as Antonius still fought on with his defence of Egypt, which only fell in 30 BC. Yet as we have explored above, winning a campaign did not bring about victory, especially in a civil war; it was winning the peace. This is where both Sulla and Caesar failed when they had military control of the Republic. Roman civil wars did not seem to end when one side was victorious in battle, as new opponents soon emerged. Roman civil wars only ended when everyone agreed that there was no more need to fight and that the imbalances in the Republican system that they had believed were there, had been corrected. For that reason, I would argue that the Third Civil War did not end until the First Constitutional Settlement of the newly-renamed Augustus in 27 BC, with the intervening years 30–27 being merely a lull in the fighting. Thus, Republican politics was both the cause of the civil wars and the solution (however temporary).

Notes

Introduction

1. G. Sampson, (2005). *A re-examination of the office of the Tribunate of the Plebs in the Roman Republic (494–23 BC)* (Unpublished Thesis).

Chapter One

1. For a more detailed analysis of this period, see G. Sampson, (2017). *Rome, Blood and Politics. Reform, Murder and Popular Politics in the Late Republic 146–70 BC* (Barnsley).
2. For a more detailed analysis of this period, see G. Sampson, (2010). *The Crisis of Rome. The Jugurthine and Northern Wars and the Rise of Marius* (Barnsley).
3. For a more detailed analysis of this period, see G. Sampson, (2013). *The Collapse of Rome, Marius, Sulla and The First Civil War 91–70 BC* (Barnsley).
4. Cic. *ND.* 3.81.
5. See R. Smith. (1957). 'The Lex Plotia Agraria and Pompey's Spanish Veterans', *Classical Quarterly* 7, pp. 82–85; B. Marshall, (1972). 'The Lex Plotia Agraria', *Antichthon* 6, pp. 43–52.
6. There is no clear detail as to what new criteria were used to enroll the new citizens. By 28 BC Augustus' census registered 4,063,000 citizens. See T. Frank, (1924). 'Roman Census Statistics from 225 to 28 BC', *Classical Philology* 19, pp. 329–341, and P. Brunt, (1971). *Italian Manpower 225 BC–AD 14* (Oxford).
7. These included C. Antonius (Cos. 63 BC) and P. Cornelius Lentulus Sura (Cos. 71 BC) who both played a part in the Second Civil War (63–62 BC).

Chapter Two

1. When Marius and Cinna took control of Rome (see Chapter One).
2. The exact criteria used to determine a Roman citizen is much debated and seems to have changed over time. See T. Frank, (1924) and P. Brunt, (1971).
3. Liv. *Per.* 84.
4. See G. Sampson (forthcoming). *Rome's Great Eastern War. Lucullus, Pompey and the Conquest of the East 74–63 BC* (Barnsley).
5. See E. Gruen, (1971). 'Pompey, Metellus Pius, and the Trials of 70–69 BC: The Perils of Schematism', *American Journal of Philology* 92, pp. 1–16.
6. See W. McDonald, (1929). 'The Tribunate of Cornelius', *Classical Quarterly* 23, pp. 196–208; R. Seager, (1969). 'The Tribunate of Cornelius. Some Ramifications', in J. Bibauw (ed.), *Hommages à Marcel Renard II* (Brussels), pp. 680–686; M. Griffin, (1973). 'The Tribune C. Cornelius', *Journal of Roman Studies* 63, pp. 196–213.
7. Ascon. 57–59C.
8. Ascon. 58C.
9. *Ibid.*
10. Ascon. 59C.
11. *Ibid.*
12. Cic. *Leg. Man.* 26.
13. Plut. *Luc.* 33.5.

14. See E. Badian, (1959) 'The Early Career of A. Gabinius (Cos. 58 BC)', *Philologus* 103, pp. 87–99; E. Sanford, (1939). 'The Career of Aulus Gabinius', *Transactions and Proceedings of the American Philological Association* 70, pp. 64–92; R. Williams, (1978). 'The Role of "Amicitia" in the Career of A. Gabinius (Cos. 58)', *Phoenix* 32, pp. 195–210.
15. Plut. *Pomp.* 25.2–3.
16. Vell. 2.31.
17. See S. Jameson, (1970). 'Pompey's Imperium in 67: Some Constitutional Fictions', *Historia* 19, pp. 539–560.
18. Dio. 24.1.–2.
19. Dio. 24.3–4.
20. Ascon. 72C.
21. Ascon. 45C.
22. Dio. 36.42.1–4.
23. Dio. 36.4.4.
24. See J. Ramsey. (1980), 'The Prosecution of C. Manilius in 66 BC and Cicero's "pro Manilio"', *Phoenix* 34, pp. 323–336, & (1985). 'Asconius P.60 (Clark), Prima Pars: The Trial and Conviction of C. Manilius in 65 BC', *American Journal of Philology* 106, pp. 367–373.
25. A later version of his defence speech the pro Cornelio was published and preserved by Asconius.
26. Ascon. 76C.
27. See E. Hardy, (1916). 'The Transpadane Question and the Alien Act of 65 or 64 BC', *Journal of Roman Studies* 6, pp. 63–82.
28. We have no record of his younger brother (Servius) ever holding office either, although he was a Senator, which means he must have held a junior office on the *cursus honorum*.
29. Dio. 37.9.4.
30. T. Broughton, (1952). *The Magistrates of the Roman Republic Volume 2* (New York), p. 162 & 164, suggests that there was a Fabius this year, based on Niccolini's argument on the dating of the Lex Fabia on the number of candidate's attendants allowed at elections (p. 266).
31. See R. Ridley, (2000). 'The Dictator's Mistake: Caesar's Escape from Sulla', *Historia* 49, pp. 211–229.
32. L. Marius (Tr. 62 BC) and Sex. Marius (Legate 43 BC).
33. See. G. Sampson (2013), pp. 197–211.
34. Plut. *Caes.* 5.2–5 states it was before his Quaestorship, whilst Suetonius (*Caes.* 6.1) states he was Quaestor. If we wanted to marry both accounts perfectly then it could be argued that he had already been elected, but had not taken up office; especially as he served in Spain.
35. Plut. *Caes.* 5.2–3.
36. Plut. *Caes.* 5.4–5.
37. Plut. *Caes.* 6.
38. Vell. 2.43.1.

Chapter Three

1. Plut. *Luc.* 37.1.
2. Plut. *Cat.* 17.4–5.
3. *Ibid.*
4. Dio. 47.6.4.
5. See T. Broughton, (1952). 2, p. 162.
6. Dio. 37.10.2.
7. Suet. *Iul.* 11.

8. Ascon. 90–91C.

9. *Sen. Dial.* 5.18.1–3. See. B. Marshall, (1985). 'Catilina and the Execution of M. Marius Gratidianus', *Classical Quarterly* 35, pp. 124–133.

10. Dio. 47.10.3. Also see Ascon. 91C.

11. Dio. 36.44.3.

12. Suet. *Iul.* 9.

13. His Praetorship was most probably in 68 BC, along with Sulla and Autronius.

14. See J. Ramsey, (1982). 'Cicero, pro Sulla 68 and the Catiline's Candidacy in 66 BC', *Harvard Studies in Classical Philology* 86, pp. 121–131; F. Ryan, (1995). 'The Consular Candidacy of Catiline in 66', *Museum Helveticum* 25, 45–48.

15. See C. Damon and C. Mackay, (1995). 'On the Prosecution of C. Antonius in 76 BC', *Historia* 44, pp. 37–55.

16. Ascon. 86C.

17. See A. Drummond, (1999). 'Tribunes and Tribunician Programmes in 63 BC', *Athenaeum* 77, pp. 121–167.

18. Dio. 37.24.3.

19. See E. Hardy, (1913). 'The Policy of the Rullan Proposal in 63 BC', *Journal of Philology* 32, pp. 228–260: G. Sumner, (1966). 'Cicero, Pompeius and Rullus', *Transactions and Proceedings of the American Philological Association* 97, pp. 569–582.

20. The only previous Servilius Rullus who is recorded as holding office was a Monetales c. 100 BC.

21. Dio. 37.25.4.

22. Cic. *Off.* 2.84.

23. Cic. *Att.* 2.1.3.

24. Plin. *NH.* 7.117.

25. Cic. *Leg. Agr.* 2.10.

26. Cic. *Sull.* 63, 65.

27. Dio. 37.26–27.

28. See E. Phillips, (1974). 'The Prosecution of C. Rabirius in 63 BC', *Klio* 56, pp. 87–101.

29. Cic. *Pis.* 4.

30. Dio 37.30.1.

31. Cic. *Mur.* 49.

32. Plut. *Cic.* 17.

33. *Ibid.*

34. Plut. *Cic.* 14.

35. Sall. *Cat.* 16.4.

36. Despite Pompeius previously having been married to Faustus' stepsister. See B. Marshall, (1984). 'Faustus Sulla and Political Labels in the 60's and 50's BC', *Historia* 33, pp. 199–219.

37. Sall. *Cat.* 30.

38. See T. Mitchell, (1971). 'Cicero and the Senatus "consultum ultimum"', *Historia* 20, pp. 47–61.

39. Q. Annius (Chilo), L. Cassius Longinus, P. Umbrenus. See G. Botsford, (1913). 'On the Legality of the Trial and Condemnation of the Catilinarian Conspirators', *Classical Weekly* 6, pp. 130–132: A. Drummond. (1995). *Law Politics and Power. Sallust and the Execution of the Catilinarian Conspirators* (Stuttgart).

40. Dio. 37.36.4.

41. Sall. *Cat.* 28.4.

42. Sall. *Cat.* 33.

43. Sall. *Cat.* 30.3.

44. Sall. *Cat.* 42.

45. Sall. *Cat.* 56.

46. Oros. 6.6.7.
47. Sall. *Cat.* 42.
48. Sallust ends with monograph just after their deaths.
49. I. Harrison, (2008). 'Catiline, Clodius, and Popular Politics at Rome during the 60s and 50s BC', *Bulletin of the Institute of Classical Studies* 51, pp. 95–118.

Chapter Four

1. Dio. 37.41.2–3.
2. Suet. *Iul.* 17.
3. See E. Salmon, (1935). 'Catiline, Crassus, and Caesar', *American Journal of Philology* 56, pp. 302–316.
4. See G. Sampson, (2017).
5. Plut. *Cic.* 23.
6. Ascon. 6.
7. Plut. *Cic.* 24.1–3.
8. Dio. 37.42.1–5.
9. Plut. *Cat. Min.* 26.1, *Caes.* 8.4.
10. See G. Sampson (forthcoming).
11. See G. Sampson, (2010).
12. Suet. *Caes.* 16.1.
13. Plut. *Cat. Min.* 27.1.
14. Dio. 37.43.2–4.
15. Plut. *Cat. Min.* 27.1.
16. Plut. *Cat. Min.* 29.2.
17. See G. Sampson (forthcoming).
18. See S. Haley, (1985). 'The Five Wives of Pompey the Great', *Greece & Rome* 32, pp. 49–59.
19. See T. Rising, (2013). 'Senatorial Opposition to Pompey's Eastern Settlement. A Storm in a Teacup?' *Historia* 62, pp. 196–221.
20. See R. Williams and B. Williams, (1988). 'Cn. Pompeius Magnus and L. Afranius. Failure to Secure the Eastern Settlement', *Classical Journal* 83, pp. 198–206.
21. See T. Wiseman, (1971). 'Celer and Nepos', *Classical Quarterly* 21, pp. 180–182.
22. Cic. *Har. Resp.* 45.
23. Plut. *Cat. Min.* 31.3–4.
24. Suet. *Caes.* 19.2.
25. See G. Stanton and B. Marshall, (1975). 'The Coalition between Pompeius and Crassus 60–59 BC', *Historia* pp. 205–219.
26. See H. Sanders, (1932). 'The So-Called First Triumvirate', *Memoirs of the American Academy in Rome* 10, pp. 55–68.
27. App. *BC.* 2.10.
28. Dio. 38.1.3–4.
29. Dio. 38.2.1.
30. Dio. 38.3.2.
31. Dio. 38.5.2.
32. Dio. 38.4.1.
33. Plut. *Cat. Min.* 33.1.
34. Suet. *Iul.* 28. Also see App. *BC.* 2.26; Cic. *Att.* 5.11.2; Plut. *Caes.* 29; Strabo. 5.1.6.
35. Suet. *Iul.* 20.
36. See G. Sampson (2010).
37. Plut. *Luc.* 42.7–8.
38. App. *BC.* 2.12.

39. Cic. *Vat.* 10–11. Also see. Cic. *Vat.* 10–11; Dio. 38.9.2–4; Suet. *Iul.* 20.5; *Schol. Bob.* 139 & 148.

40. See W. McDermott, (1949). 'Vettius Ille, Ille Noster Index', *Transactions and Proceedings of the American Philological Association* 80, pp. 351–367; L. Taylor, (1950). 'The Date and Meaning of the Vettius Affair', *Historia* 1, pp. 45–51; W. Allen, (1950). 'The "Vettius Affair" Once More', *Transactions and Proceedings of the American Philological Association* 81, pp. 153–163.

41. Plut. *Cat. Min.* 33.7.

42. See W. Tatum, (1999). *The Patrician Tribune: Publius Clodius Pulcher* (Chapel Hill).

43. Suet. *Iul.* 20.4.

44. Cic. *Att.* 8.3.3.

45. Dio. 38.12.2.

Chapter Five

1. See E. Gruen. (1966). 'P. Clodius: Instrument or Independent Agent?', *Phoenix* 20, pp. 120–130.

2. Suet. *Iul.* 23. Also see Suet. *Nero.* 2.2, and *Schol. Bob.* 130, 146, 151.

3. Cic. *Vat.* 34. Also see *Schol. Bob.* 150.

4. See G. Sampson, (2017), pp. 241–243.

5. This law is only known in a passing reference in Suetonius (*Dom.* 9).

6. See A. Greenidge, (1893). 'The Repeal of the Lex Aelia Fufia', *Classical Review* 7, pp. 158–161; W. McDonald, (1929). 'Clodius and the Lex Aelia Fufia', *Journal of Roman Studies* 19, pp. 164–179; S. Weinstock, (1937). 'Clodius and the Lex Aelia Fufia', *Journal of Roman Studies* 27, pp. 216–222; G. Sumner, (1963). 'Lex Aelia, Lex Fufia', *American Journal of Philology* 84, 337–358; A. Astin, (1964). 'Leges Aelia et Fufia', *Latomus* 23, pp. 421–445.

7. Cic. *Red. Sen.* 11.

8. Ascon. 8.

9. See J. Bellemore, (2008). 'Cicero's Retreat from Rome in Early 58 BC', *Antichthon* 42, pp. 100–120.

10. Dio 38.12.7.

11. Plut. *Cic.* 29.1–2.

12. See E. Badian, (1965). 'M. Porcius Cato and the Annexation and Early Administration of Cyprus', *Journal of Roman Studies* 55, pp. 110–121.

13. See R. Evans, (2004). 'Clodius and Milo; more equals than opposites', *Questioning Reputations* (Pretoria), pp. 161–191.

14. Dio. 39.6.

15. Cic. *Sest.* 77.

16. Dio. 39.8.

17. Plut. *Cic.* 33.

18. Ascon. 48C.

19. Dio. 39.9.2.

20. Cic. *Att.* 4.1.6–7.

21. Cic. *Mil.* 38.

22. Cic. *Att.* 4.1.7.

23. Plut. *Pomp.* 49.

24. App. *BC.* 2.18.

25. Dio. 39.9.3.

26. See R. Ridley, (1983). 'Pompey's Commands in the 50s: How Cumulative?' *Rheinisches Museum für Philologie* 126, pp. 136–148.

27. See I. Shatzman, (1971). 'The Egyptian Question in Roman Politics (59–54 BC)', *Latomus* 30, pp. 363–369; M. Siani-Davies, (1997). 'Ptolemy XII Auletes and the Romans', *Historia* 46, pp. 306–340.

28. Dio. 39.18.1.
29. Cic. *QF*. 2.3..1
30. *Ibid*.
31. Cic. *QF*. 2.3.2.
32. See R. Rowland, (1960). 'Crassus, Clodius, and Curio in the Year 59 BC', *Historia* 15, pp. 217–223.
33. See G. Sampson, (2017).
34. Cic. *QF*. 2.3.2.
35. Dio. 39.21.1.-2.
36. Dio. 39.21.3–4.
37. Plut. *Cic*. 40.
38. *Ibid*.
39. Plut. *Pomp*. 50.
40. Plut. *Pomp*. 49.6.

Chapter Six

1. See J. Lazenby, (1959). 'The Conference of Luca and the Gallic War; A Study in Roman Politics 57–55 BC', *Latomus* 18, pp. 63–76; E. Gruen, (1969). 'Pompey, the Roman Aristocracy and the Conference at Luca', *Historia* 18, pp. 71–108; C. Luibheid, (1970). 'The Luca Conference', *Classical Philology* 65, pp. 88–94.
2. Plut. *Crass*. 14.
3. Plut. *Pomp*. 51.
4. *Ibid*.
5. Plut. *Crass*. 15.
6. Dio. 39.29.
7. Dio. 39.27.3.
8. Dio. 39.31.
9. Dio. 39.32.1–3.
10. Plut. *Pomp*. 53.3.
11. Dio. 39.33.2.
12. Dio. 39.33.4.
13. *Ibid*.
14. Berenice being the daughter of Ptolemy XII.
15. Plut. *Crass*. 16.4.
16. See E. Fantham, (1975). 'The Trials of Gabinius in 54 BC', *Historia* 24, pp. 425–443; R. Williams, (1985). 'Rei Publicae Causa: Gabinius' Defense of His Restoration of Ptolemy Auletes', *Classical Journal* 81, pp. 25–38.
17. There were also prosecutions of M. Aemilius Scaurus (Pr. 56), Caelius Rufus, Sufenas, Procilius, Lucretius, and Domitius Calvinus. This may be an abnormally-high number, or it may just be that (primarily thanks to Cicero), we have a fuller picture than we do for most years.
18. Suet. *Nero*. 2.2. The great irony here is that this note comes from a biography of the Emperor Nero, a direct descendant of Domitius, being born into the Domitii Ahenobarbus family but adopted into the Iulian family and thus being the last of the Iulio-Claudian Emperors.
19. Dio. 39.64.
20. Cic. *Att*. 4.17.3.
21. Plut. *Cat. Min*. 44.2.
22. *Ibid*., 44.3.
23. See E. Gruen, (1969). 'The Consular Elections for 53 BC', in J. Bibauw (ed.), *Hommages à Marcel Renard II* (Brussels), pp. 311–321.
24. Cic. *Att*. 4.18.
25. Plut. *Pomp*. 54.2.

26. *Obseq.* 63.
27. Cic. *Fam.* 8.4.3.
28. We must note that due to the inaccurate measurement of the length of a year, the Roman calendar at this point was somewhat confused. See D. Feeney, (2007). *Caesar's Calendar: Ancient Time and the Beginnings of History* (London).
29. Dio. 40.45–46.
30. See G. Sampson, (2008), pp. 94–147.
31. Crassus' father and elder brother had both been killed in the aftermath of the Battle of Rome in 87 BC.
32. Cic. *Mil.* 25.
33. *Schol. Bob.* 172.
34. Cic. *Phil.* 2.21 and also 2.49.
35. Ascon. 30.
36. Ascon. 48.
37. Dio. 40.46.
38. Plut. *Cat. Min.* 47.
39. Ascon. 31–32C.
40. See G. Sumi, (1997) 'Power and Ritual: The Crowd at Clodius' Funeral', *Historia* 46, pp. 80–102.
41. Dio. 40.49.5.
42. Ascon. 34C.
43. Presumably aside from the more junior Plebeian Aediles.
44. Plut. *Caes.* 28.

Chapter Seven
1. Ascon. 36C.
2. App. *BC.* 2.23.
3. Dio. 40.52.
4. *Ibid.*
5. Cic. *Mil.* 47.
6. Plut. *Pomp.* 55.4.
7. App. *BC.* 2.24.
8. See R. Husband, (1915). 'The Prosecution of Milo', *Classical Weekly* 8, pp. 146–150; J. Ruebel, (1979). 'The Trial of Milo in 52 bc: A Chronological Study', *Transactions of the American Philological Association* 109, pp. 231–249.
9. See A. Lintott, (1974). 'Cicero and Milo', *Journal of Roman Studies* 64, pp. 62–78.
10. App. *BC.* 2.24.
11. He had had four prior marriages. See S. Haley, (1985).
12. Plut. *Pomp.* 55.4.
13. Dio. 40.56.
14. *Ibid.*
15. App. *BC.* 2.25.
16. Dio. 40.59.
17. Cic. *Fam.* 8.8.6–8. C. Caelius, L. Vinicius, P. Cornelius and C. Vibius Pansa on the first motion and C. Caelius and C. Vibius Pansa on the second and third motions.
18. Dio. 40.59.
19. *Ibid.*
20. Dio. 40.59.
21. App. *BC.* 2.26.
22. Caes. *BC.* 8.5.1–2.
23. App. *BC.* 2.32.
24. Dio. 40.62.4.
25. App. *BC.* 2.30.
26. App. *BC.* 2.31.

27. Dio, 40.64.4.
28. Dio. 40.66.1.
29. Dio. 40.66.2.
30. See R. Evans, (2004). 'Caesar's use of the tribuni plebis', *Questioning Reputations* (Pretoria), pp. 65–92.
31. Dio. 41.2.
32. See H. Appel, (2012). 'Pompeius Magnus: his Third Consulate and the senatus consultum ultimum', *Biuletyn Polskiej Misji Historycznej* 7, pp. 341–360. Also see L. Pocock, (1959). 'What Made Pompeius Fight in 49 BC?', *Greece & Rome* 6, pp. 68–81.
33. App. *BC*. 2.34.
34. See G. Stanton, (2003). 'Why Did Caesar Cross the Rubicon?', *Historia* 52, pp. 67–94.
35. Dio. 41.5.
36. Caes. *BC*. 1.5. Also see. R. Evans, (2004). 'Caesar's use of the tribuni plebis', *Questioning Reputations* (Pretoria), pp. 65–92.
37. Plutarch (*Caes*. 37.1) has the Senate appoint him, Appian (*BC*. 2.48) states it was by a law passed by the People, Dio (41.36) also has the People pass the motion at the order of the Praetor Lepidus, whilst Eutropius (6.20.1) has Caesar appoint himself Dictator. Caesar (*BC*. 3.1.1) himself glosses over the mechanism used to appoint him Dictator but stressed his constitutional position.
38. Cic. *Att*. 9.9.3, 15.2; Dio. 41.36.1.
39. Both Cinna and Carbo had ruled Rome via the Consulship in the 80s BC with Cinna choosing a junior colleague (Carbo) and then Carbo himself ruling for most of 84 BC as sole Consul.

Chapter Eight
1. App. *BC*. 2.43.
2. Plut. *Caes*. 37.
3. See G. Sampson, (2017).
4. Dio. 46.
5. Dio. 42.22.
6. Caes. *BC*. 20.
7. Dio. 42.23.1.
8. Dio. 42.23.
9. Caes. *BC*. 23.
10. Dio. 42.29.1.
11. See T. Broughton, (1952). 2, p.287.
12. Dio. 42.29.2.
13. Plut. *Ant*. 9.
14. Liv. *Per*. 113.
15. Full details of this campaign can be found in G. Sampson (forthcoming). *Rome and Parthia. Empires at War* (Barnsley).
16. Dio. 42.51.1–2.
17. Dio. 43.14.3–4.
18. App. *BC*. 2.102.
19. Dio. 43.47.
20. All collegia had been disbanded by the Senate in 64 BC and then reinstated by Clodius.
21. Suet. *Iul*. 41.3.
22. Suet. *Iul*. 42.1.
23. *Ibid*.
24. Suet. *Iul*. 44.3.
25. Suet. *Iul*. 40.
26. This civil war proved to be disastrous for the kingdoms of North Africa, with Numidia being annexed due to its support for Cn. Pompeius, followed, fifteen years later, by Egypt thanks to its support of M. Antonius.

27. Dio. 43.48.

28. Cic. *Att.* 13.20.1, 13.33.4, 13.35.1; Suet. *Iul.* 44, Dio. 43.49.

29. Cic. *Att.*12.49 & 14.6.1.

30. Val. Max. 9.15.

31. Liv. *Per.* 116.

32. App. *BC.* 3.2.

33. Nic. Dam. 128.14.

34. See A. Pappano, (1935). 'The Pseudo-Marius', *Classical Philology* 30, pp. 58–65; F. Meijer, (1986). 'Marius' Grandson', *Mnemosyne* 39, pp. 112–121.

35. See A. Powell & K. Welch, (2002). *Sextus Pompeius* (London).

36. Suet. *Iul.* 41.2.

37. Dio. 43.47.

38. See W. McDermott, (1982/3). 'Caesar's Projected Dacian-Parthian Expedition', *Ancient Society* 13/14, pp. 223–231; J. Malitz, (1984). 'Caesars Partherkrieg', *Historia* 33, pp. 21–59.

39. App. *BC.* 2.106.

40. Dio. 43.45.

41. See R. Bauman, (1981). 'Tribunician Sacrosanctity in 44, 36 and 35 BC', *Rheinisches Museum für Philogie* 124 (1981), pp. 166–183.

42. See M. Zeev, (1996).'When was the title "Dictator perpetuus" given to Caesar?', *L'antiquité classique* 65, pp. 251–253.

43. Plut. *Caes.* 57.

44. Nic. Dam. 130.67.

45. Plut. *Caes.* 61.4–9.

46. See R. Syme, (1937). 'Who was Decidius Saxa?', *Journal of Roman Studies* 27, pp. 127–137.

47. Plut. *Caes.* 60.

48. Plut. *Caes.* 58.

49. The historic date for the start of the new Consuls taking office (though no longer in practice).

50. Here we are excluding Cicero, who, though still alive, was never a major player in the power games of the 60s and 50s, despite his posthumous reputation.

Chapter Nine

1. App. *BC.* 2.118.

2. See J. Moles, (1987). 'The Attacks on L. Cornelius Cinna, Praetor in 44 BC', *Rheinisches Museum für Philologie* 130, pp. 124–128.

3. App. *BC.* 2.122.

4. Dio. 44.25.1.

5. Dio. 44.34.

6. See M. Deutsch, (1925). 'The Murder of Cinna, the Poet', *Classical Journal* 20, pp. 326–336.

7. App. *BC.* 2.147.

8. Dio. 44.51.2.

9. Val. Max. 9.15.1.

10. App. *BC.* 3.3.

11. *Ibid.*

12. App. *BC.* 3.4.

13. App. *BC.* 3.49.

14. See R. Ridley, (2000).

15. See M. Toher, (2004). 'Octavian's Arrival in Rome, 44 BC', *Classical Quarterly* 54, pp. 174–184.

16. App. *BC.* 3.31; Dio. 45.6.3; Plut. *Ant.* 16.2.
17. App. *BC.* 3.41.
18. App. *BC.* 3.51.
19. Dio. 46.31.2.
20. Dio. 46.31.3.
21. Oros. 6.18.3–5.
22. App. *BC.* 4.84.
23. Cic. *Phil.* 5.41.
24. App. *BC.* 3.90.
25. App. *BC.* 3.97.
26. App. *BC.* 4.7.
27. See F. Hinard, (1985). *Les Proscriptions de la Rome Républicaine* (Rome), pp. 413–552.
28. *Ibid.*
29. See F. Hinard, (1985), pp. 413–552.
30. App. *BC.* 4.12.

Chapter Ten

1. Dio. 47.18–19.
2. Antonius was born in 83 BC whilst Lepidus was born in c. 89 BC.
3. The Roman road which ran the length of Greece and connected the Adriatic to the city of Byzantium, on the Bosphorus.
4. App. *BC.* 4.112.
5. App. *BC.* 5.12–18; Dio. 48.5.4–9.5.
6. App. *BC.* 5.20.
7. App. *BC.* 5.27.
8. App. *BC.* 5.29.
9. This has led this conflict to be called the Perusine War by many; see M. Reinhold, (1933). 'The Perusine War', *Classical Weekly* 26, pp. 180–182; and E. Gabba, (1971). 'The Perusine War and Triumviral Italy', *Harvard Studies in Classical Philology* 75, pp. 139–160.
10. As detailed in G. Sampson, (2008).
11. See G. Sampson (forthcoming), *Rome & Parthia: Empires at War. Ventidius, Antonius and the Second Romano-Parthian War (40–20 BC)* (Barnsley).
12. Dio. 48.14.3.
13. Appian (*BC.* 5.66), Dio (48.33.2) and Suetonius (*Aug.* 66) state he was executed whilst the Periochae of Livy (127) states suicide.
14. His second Consulship, his first being in 53 BC.
15. L. Cornelius Balbus and P. Candidius Crassus as Consuls.
16. App. *BC.* 5.67.
17. Dio. 48.35.3.
18. See J. Seaver, (1952). 'Publius Ventidius. Neglected Roman Military Hero', *Classical Journal* 47, pp. 275–280 & 300.
19. G. Sampson, (forthcoming).
20. *Ibid.*
21. Dio. 48.43.
22. E. Gabba, (1971), pp. 157–158.
23. See R. Palmer, (1978). 'Octavian's First Attempt to restore the Constitution (36 BC)', *Athenaeum* 56, pp. 315–328.
24. App. *BC.* 5.132.
25. Oros. 6.18.34.
26. Dio. 49.15.5–6.
27. See R. Bauman, (1981).

28. G. Sampson, (forthcoming).
29. See L. Fratantuono, (2016). *The Battle of Actium 31 BC: War for the World* (Barnsley).

Conclusion
1. A possible descendant of the Ovinius who held the Tribunate in the 4th Century BC and passed the *lex Ovinia* on the composition of the Senate.
2. Oros. 6.19.20.
3. See C. Lange, (2013). 'Triumph and Civil War in the Late Republic', *Papers of the British School at Rome* 81, pp. 67–90.
4. We do not know when Ventidius died.
5. Dio. 51.19.6.
6. Dio. 44.5.3.
7. Dio. 49.38.1.
8. See R. Bauman, (1981), p.167.
9. See G. Sampson, (2005), pp. 328–330.
10. See T. Frank, (1924) and P. Brunt, (1971).
11. R. Evans, (1997). 'The Augustan "Purge" of the Senate and the Census of 86 BC', *Acta Classica* 40, pp. 77–86.
12. See R. Syme (1939). *The Roman Revolution* (Oxford), for a detailed account of this alliance.
13. See W. Lacey, (1974). 'Octavian in the Senate, January 27 BC', *Journal of Roman Studies* 64, pp. 176–184.
14. Suetonius (*Aug.* 40) refers to a law Augustus passed allowing for nomination of equestrians to the positions, if not enough members of the Senatorial aristocracy stood for the Tribunate. The interesting aspect is that the post should have been open to every Plebeian not just those of the Senatorial order. This could just be Suetonius' misunderstanding or it could be a sign of a more interesting change to the Tribunate from Augustus, restricting it to the Plebeian aristocracy only.
15. The dating of 23 BC is open to question; see K. Atkinson, (1960). 'Constitutional and Legal Aspects of the Trials of Marcus Primus and Varro Murena', *Historia* 9, pp. 440–473; R. Bauman, (1966). 'Tiberius and Murena', *Historia* 15, pp. 420–432; M. Swan, (1967). 'The Consular Fasti of 23 BC and the Conspiracy of Varro Murena', *Harvard Studies in Classical Philology* 71, pp. 235–247; S. Jameson. (1969). '22 or 23?', *Historia* 18, pp. 204–229.
16. See W. Lacey, (1985). 'Augustus and the Senate: 23 BC', *Antichthon* 19, pp. 57–67.
17. Aug. *Res. Gest.* 3.15.
18. See A. Jones, (1955). 'The Elections under Augustus', *Journal of Roman Studies* 45, pp. 9–21.
19. A. Jones, (1951). 'The Imperium of Augustus', *Journal of Roman Studies* 41, pp. 112–119.
20. 28 BC; C. Carrinas (Gaul) and L. Autronius Paetus (Africa): 27 BC; M. Licinius Crassus (Thrace) and M. Valerius Messalla Corvinus (Gaul): 26 BC; Sex. Appuleius (Spain).
21. 21 BC; L. Sempronius Atratinus (Africa): 19 BC; L. Cornelius Balbus (Africa).
22. His mother being the daughter of Pompeius himself.
23. Suet. *Aug.* 29.

Appendix I
1. See F. Hinard, (1985). pp. 413–552 for a full list of the victims.

Appendix II
1. S. Pighius, (1599). *Annales Magistratuum et Provinciarum SPQR ab urbe condita 1* (Antwerp), & (1615). *Annales Romanorum 1–3* (Antwerp).
2. F. Garofalo, (1889). *I fasti dei tribuni della plebe*, (Catania).
3. M. Ziegler, (1903). *Fasti Tribunorum Plebis 133–70*, (Ulm).

4. E. Pais, (1918). 'I fasti dei tribuni della plebe', *Ricerche sulla storia e sul diritto pubblico di Roma Volume III*, (Pisa).
5. G. Niccolini, (1934). *I fasti dei tribuni della plebe*, (Milan).
6. T. Broughton, (1951/2). *Magistrates of the Roman Republic Volumes 1 & 2*, (New York); (1960). *Supplement to the Magistrates of the Roman Republic*, (New York); (1986). *Supplement to the Magistrates of the Roman Republic*, (New York).
7. G. Sampson, (2005), pp. 39–181.
8. For the full list with explanations, see G. Sampson, (2005), pp. 39–181.
9. For simplicity's sake, only the substantial year is referred to in the main text.
10. These are listed by Niccolini (1934), pp. 444–449 and Broughton (1952) 2, pp. 468–474.

Appendix III

1. See G. Sampson, (2017).
2. This was an argument put to me in 2002 at the Classical Association Conference in Edinburgh during a paper on the First Civil War.

Bibliography

Adcock, F. (1966). *Marcus Crassus, Millionaire* (Cambridge).

Alexander, C. (2017). *The Second Triumvirate: Augustus, Marc Antony, Marcus Aemilius Lepidus, And The Founding Of An Empire* (London).

Allen, W. (1950). 'The "Vettius Affair" Once More', *Transactions and Proceedings of the American Philological Association* 81, 153–163.

Appel, H. (2012). 'Pompeius Magnus: his Third Consulate and the senatus consultum ultimum', *Biuletyn Polskiej Misji Historycznej* 7, 341–360.

Astin, A. (1964). 'Leges Aelia et Fufia', *Latomus* 23, 421–445.

Atkinson, K. (1960). 'Constitutional and Legal Aspects of the Trials of Marcus Primus and Varro Murena', *Historia* 9, 440–473.

Badian, E. (1959) 'The Early Career of A. Gabinius (Cos. 58 BC)', *Philologus* 103, 87–99

——. (1965). 'M. Porcius Cato and the Annexation and Early Administration of Cyprus', *Journal of Roman Studies* 55, 110–121.

——. (1996). 'Tribuni Plebis and Res Publica', in J. Linderski (ed.) *Imperium Sine Fine* (Stuttgart), 187–214.

Balsdon, J. (1939). 'Consular Provinces under the Late Republic I. General Considerations', *Journal of Roman Studies* 29, 57–73.

——. (1939b). 'Consular Provinces under the Late Republic II. Caesar's Gallic Command', *Journal of Roman Studies* 29, 167–183.

——. (1957). 'Roman History, 58–59 BC: Three Ciceronian Problems', *Journal of Roman Studies* 47, 15–20.

——. (1962). 'Roman History, 65–50 BC Five Problems', *Journal of Roman Studies* 52, 134–141.

Barlow, J. (1994). 'Cicero's Sacrilege in 63 BC', *Studies in Latin Literature and Roman History VII*, 180–189.

Bauman, R. (1966). 'Tiberius and Murena', *Historia* 15, 420–432.

——. (1981). 'Tribunician Sacrosanctity in 44, 36 and 35 BC', *Rheinisches Museum für Philogie* 124 (1981), 166–183.

Bellemore, J. (1995). 'Cato the Younger in the East in 66 BC', *Historia* 44, 376–379.

——. (2008). 'Cicero's Retreat from Rome in Early 58 BC', *Antichthon* 42, 100–120.

Belot, E. (1872). *De tribunis plebis de origine et vi forma et modo tribuniciae potestatis* (Paris).

Bispham, E. (2008). *From Asculum to Actium: The Municipalization of Italy from the Social War to Augustus* (Oxford).

Bleicken, J. (1955). *Das Volkstribunat der klassischen Republik* (Munich).

——. (1981). 'Das römische Volkstribunat', *Chiron* 11, 87–108.

Boak, A. (1918). 'The Extraordinary Commands from 80 to 48 BC: A Study in the Origins of the Principate', *American Historical Review* 24, 1–25.

Botsford, G. (1909). *The Roman Assemblies from their Origin to the End of the Republic* (New York).

——. (1913). 'On the Legality of the Trial and Condemnation of the Catilinarian Conspirators', *Classical Weekly* 6, 130–132.

Brennan, T. (2000). *The Praetorship in the Roman Republic Volumes 1 & 2* (Oxford).

Broughton, T. (1951/2). *The Magistrates of the Roman Republic Volume I & 2* (New York).

——. (1960). *Supplement to the Magistrates of the Roman Republic* (New York).

——. (1986). *Supplement to the Magistrates of the Roman Republic* (New York).

——. (1989). 'M. Aemilius Lepidus: His Youthful Career', in R. Curtis (ed.). *Studia Pompeiana and Classica in Honour of Wilhelmina F. Jashemski* (New York), 13–23.

——. (1991). 'Candidates Defeated in Roman Elections: Some Ancient Roman "Also-Rans"', *Transactions of the American Philological Society* 81, 1–64.

Brunell, N. (1698). *De Tribunis Romanae Plebis* (Holmiae).

Brunt, P. (1971). *Italian Manpower 225 BC–AD 14* (Oxford).

——. (1971). *Social Conflicts in the Roman Republic* (London).

——. (1988). *The Fall of the Roman Republic* (Oxford).

Bucher, G. (1995). 'Appian BC 2.24 and the Trial "de ambitu" of M. Aemilius Scaurus', *Historia* 44, 396–421.

Cary, M. (1929). 'Notes on the Legislation of Julius Caesar', *Journal of Roman Studies* 19, 113–116.

——. (1937). 'The Municipal Legislation of Julius Caesar', *Journal of Roman Studies* 27, 48–53.

Clarke, M. (1981). *The Noblest Roman: Marcus Brutus and His Reputation* (London).

Cocchia, E. (1917). *Il tribunato della plebe* (Rome).

Collins, H. (1953). 'Decline and Fall of Pompey the Great', *Greece & Rome* 22, 98–106.

Corrigan, K. (2015). *Brutus. Caesar's Assassin* (Barnsley).

Damon, C and Mackay, C. (1995). 'On the Prosecution of C. Antonius in 76 BC', *Historia* 44, 37–55.

Dando-Collins, S. (2010). *The Ides. Caesar's Murder and the War for Rome* (New Jersey).

De Ruggiero, P. (2013). *Mark Antony. A Plain Blunt Man* (Barnsley)

Deutsch, M. (1925). 'The Murder of Cinna, the Poet', *Classical Journal* 20, 326–336.

Dunkle, J. (1967). 'The Greek Tyrant and Roman Political Invective of the Late Republic', *Transactions and Proceedings of the American Philological Association* 98, 151–171.

Drummond, A. (1995). *Law Politics and Power. Sallust and the Execution of the Catilinarian Conspirators* (Stuttgart).

——. (1999). 'Tribunes and Tribunician Programmes in 63 BC', *Athenaeum* 77, 121–167.

Eder, W. (1990). 'Augustus and the power of tradition', in K. Raaflaub and M. Tohler (eds.) *Between Republic and Empire* (Berkeley), 71–122.

——. (1996). 'Republicans and Sinners. The Decline of the Roman Republic and the End of a Provisional Arrangement', in R. Wallace and E. Harris (eds). *Transitions to Empire. Essays in Greco-Roman History 360–146 BC in Honour of E. Badian* (London), 439–461.

Ehrhardt, C. (1995). 'Crossing the Rubicon', *Antichthon* 29, 37–41.

Epstein, D. (1987). *Personal Enmity in Roman Politics 218–43 BC* (London).

Evans, R. (1988). 'A Note on the Consuls from 69 to 60 BC', *Acta Classica* 31, 97–105.

——. (1997). 'The Augustan "Purge" of the Senate and the Census of 86 BC', *Acta Classica* 40, 77–86.

——. (2004). 'Caesar's use of the tribuni plebis', *Questioning Reputations* (Pretoria), 65–92.

——. (2004). 'Clodius and Milo; more equals than opposites', *Questioning Reputations* (Pretoria), 161–191.

Everitt, A. (2006). *The First Emperor. Caesar Augustus and the Triumph of Rome* (London).

Fantham, E. (1975). 'The Trials of Gabinius in 54 BC', *Historia* 24, 425–443.

Feeney, D. (2007). *Caesar's Calendar. Ancient Time and the Beginnings of History* (London).

Flower, H. (2010). *Roman Republics* (Princeton).

Frank, T. (1924). 'Roman Census Statistics from 225 to 28 BC', *Classical Philology* 19, 329–341.

Fratantuono, L. (2016). *The Battle of Actium 31 BC. War for the World* (Barnsley).

Frederiksen, M. (1966). 'Caesar, Cicero and the Problem of Debt', *Journal of Roman Studies* 56, 128–141.

Gabba, E. (1971). 'The Perusine War and Triumviral Italy', *Harvard Studies in Classical Philology* 75, 139–160.

Galassi, F. (2014). *Catiline. The Monster of Rome* (Yardley)

Garofalo, F. (1889). *I fasti dei tribuni della plebe della repubblica romana* (Catania).

Gelzer, M. (1980). *Caesar: Politician and Statesman* (London).

Golden, G. (2013). *Crisis Management during the Roman Republic: The Role of Political Institutions in Emergencies* (Cambridge).

Goldsworthy, A. (2006). *Caesar: Life of a Colossus* (Yale).

——. (2010). *Antony and Cleopatra* (London).

——. (2014). *Augustus: From Revolutionary to Emperor* (London).

Goodman, R and Soni. J. (2012). *Rome's Last Citizen* (New York).

Greenhalgh, P. (1980). *Pompey. The Roman Alexander* (London).

——. (1981). *Pompey. The Republican Prince* (London).

Greenidge, A. (1893). 'The Repeal of the Lex Aelia Fufia', *Classical Review* 7, 158–161.

——. (1893b). 'The Lex Sempronia and the Banishment of Cicero', *Classical Review* 7, 347–348.

Griffin, M. (1973). 'The Tribune C. Cornelius', *Journal of Roman Studies* 63, 196–213

Gruen. E. (1966). 'P. Clodius: Instrument or Independent Agent?', *Phoenix* 20, 120–130.

——. (1969). 'Pompey, the Roman Aristocracy and the Conference at Luca', *Historia* 18, 71–108.

——. (1969). 'Notes on the "First Catilinarian Conspiracy"', *Classical Philology* 64, 20–24.

——. (1969). 'The Consular Elections for 53 BC', in J. Bibauw (ed.) *Hommages à Marcel Renard II* (Brussels), 311–321.

——. (1971). 'Pompey, Metellus Pius, and the Trials of 70–69 BC: The Perils of Schematism', *American Journal of Philology* 92, 1–16.

——. (1974). *The Last Generation of the Roman Republic* (Berkeley).

Haley, S. (1985). 'The Five Wives of Pompey the Great', *Greece & Rome* 32, 49–59.

Hardy, E. (1913). 'The Policy of the Rullan Proposal in 63 BC', *Journal of Philology* 32, 228–260.

——. (1916). 'The Transpadane Question and the Alien Act of 65 or 64 BC', *Journal of Roman Studies* 6, 63–82.

——. (1917). 'The Catilinarian Conspiracy in Its Context: A Re-Study of the Evidence', *Journal of Roman Studies* 7, 153–228.

Harrison, I. (2008). 'Catiline, Clodius, and Popular Politics at Rome during the 60s and 50s BC', *Bulletin of the Institute of Classical Studies* 51, 95–118.

Hillard, T. (1981). 'Crassus in 61', *Liverpool Classical Monthly* 6, 127–130.

——. (1982). 'P. Clodius Pulcher 62–58 BC: "Pompeii Adfinis et Sodalis"', *Papers of the British School at Rome* 50, 34–44.

Hinard. F. (1985). *Les Proscriptions de la Rome Républicaine* (Rome)

Holland, R. (2004). *Augustus. Godfather of Europe* (Stroud).

Hooke, N. (1738–1771). *The Roman History from the Building of Rome to the Ruin of the Commonwealth* (London).

Husband, R. (1915). 'The Prosecution of Milo', *Classical Weekly* 8, 146–150.

Huzar, E. (1978). *Mark Antony; A Biography* (Minneapolis).

Isayev, E. (2007). 'Unruly Youth? The Myth of Generation Conflict in Late Republican Rome', *Historia* 56, 1–13.

Jameson, S. (1969). '22 or 23?', *Historia* 18, 204–229.

——. (1970). 'Pompey's Imperium in 67: Some Constitutional Fictions', *Historia* 19, 539–560.

Jones, A. (1951). 'The Imperium of Augustus' *Journal of Roman Studies* 41, 112–119.

——. (1955). 'The Elections under Augustus', *Journal of Roman Studies* 45, 9–21.

——. (1970). *Augustus* (London).

Keaveney, A. (2007). *The Army in the Roman Revolution* (London).

Lacey, W. (1974). 'Octavian in the Senate, January 27 BC', *Journal of Roman Studies* 64, 176–184.

——. (1985). 'Augustus and the Senate: 23 BC', *Antichthon* 19, 57–67.

Lange, C. (2008). 'Civil War in the Res Gestae Divi Augusti: Conquering the World and Fighting a War at Home', in E. Bragg, L. Hau and E. Macaulay-Lewis (eds.). *Beyond the Battlefields: New Perspectives on Warfare and Society in the Graeco-Roman World* (Newcastle), 185–204.

——. (2013). 'Triumph and Civil War in the Late Republic', *Papers of the British School at Rome* 81, 67–90.

Lazenby, J. (1959). 'The Conference of Luca and the Gallic War; A Study in Roman Politics 57–55 BC', *Latomus* 18, 63–76.

Leach, J. (1978). *Pompey the Great* (London).

Levi, M. (1978). *Il Tribunato della Plebe* (Milan).

Levick, B. (2015). *Catiline* (London).

Lintott, A. (1967). 'P. Clodius Pulcher – "Felix Catilina?"' *Greece & Rome* 14, 157–169.

——. (1968). *Violence in Republican Rome* (Oxford).

——. (1974). 'Cicero and Milo', *Journal of Roman Studies* 64, 62–78.

——. (1999). *The Constitution of the Roman Republic* (Oxford).

Lobrano, G. (1983). *Il potere dei tribuni della plebe* (Milan).

Long, G. (1864). *The Decline of the Roman Republic Volumes 1–5* (London).

Luibheid, C. (1970). 'The Luca Conference', *Classical Philology* 65, 88–94.

Malitz, J. (1984). 'Caesars Partherkrieg', *Historia* 33, 21–59.

Marin, P. (2009). *Blood in the Forum. The Struggle for the Roman Republic* (London).

Marsh, F. (1927). 'The Chronology of Caesar's Consulship', *Classical Journal* 22, 504–524.

Marshall, B. (1972). 'The Lex Plotia Agraria', *Antichton* 6, 43–52

——. (1976). *Crassus: a Political Biography* (Amsterdam).

——. (1984). 'Faustus Sulla and Political Labels in the 60s and 50s BC', *Historia* 33, 199–219.

——. (1985). 'Catilina and the Execution of M. Marius Gratidianus', *Classical Quarterly* 35, 124–133.

Marshall. B and Beness, J. (1987). 'Tribunician Agitation and the Aristocratic Reaction 80–71 BC', *Athenaeum* 65, 361–378.

Mattingly, H. (1930). 'Tribunicia Potestate', *Journal of Roman Studies* 20, 78–91.

McDermott, W. (1949). 'Vettius Ille, Ille Noster Index', *Transactions and Proceedings of the American Philological Association* 80, 351–367.

——. (1977). 'Lex De Tribunicia Potestate (70 BC)', *Classical Philology* 72, 49–52.

——. (1982/3). 'Caesar's Projected Dacian-Parthian Expedition', *Ancient Society* 13/14, 223–231.

McDonald, W. (1929). 'The Tribunate of Cornelius', *Classical Quarterly* 23, 196–208.

——. (1929). 'Clodius and the Lex Aelia Fufia', *Journal of Roman Studies* 19, 164–179.

Meier, C. (1982). *Caesar. A Biography.* translated by D. McClintock (New York).

Meijer, F. (1986). 'Marius' Grandson', *Mnemosyne* 39, 112–121.

——. (1993). 'Cicero and the Costs of the Republican Grain Laws', in H. Sancisci-Weerdenburg (ed.) *De Agricultura: In Memoriam Pieter Willem de Neeve* (Amsterdam), 153–163.

Millar, F. (1973). 'Triumvirate and Principate', *Journal of Roman Studies* 63, 60–67.

——. (1994). 'Popular Politics at Rome in the Late Republic', in I. Malkin and Z. Rubinsohn (eds.) *Leaders and Masses in the Roman World: Studies in Honor of Zvi Yavetz* (Leiden), 91–113.

Mitchell, T. (1971). 'Cicero and the Senatus consultum ultimum', *Historia* 20, 47–61.

——. (1984). 'Cicero on the moral crisis of the late Republic', *Hermathena* 136, 21–41

——. (1986). 'The Leges Clodiae and obnuntiatio', *Classical Quarterly* 36, 172–176

Moles, J. (1987). 'The Attacks on L. Cornelius Cinna, Praetor in 44 BC', *Rheinisches Museum für Philologie* 130, 124–128.

Morrell, K. (2017). *Pompey, Cato, and the Governance of the Roman Empire* (Oxford).

Mouritsen, H. (2001). *Plebs and Politics in the Late Roman Republic* (Cambridge).

Munzer, F. (1999). *Roman Aristocratic Parties and Families*, trans. T. Ridley (Baltimore)

Murray, R. (1966). 'Cicero and the Gracchi', *Transactions and Proceedings of the American Philological Association* 97, 291–298.

Niccolini, G. (1932). *Il tribunato della plebe* (Milan).

——. (1934). *I fasti dei tribuni della plebe* (Milan).

Orlin, E. (2007). 'Augustan Religion and the Reshaping of Roman Memory', *Arethusa* 40, 73–92.

Osgood, J. (2006). *Caesar's Legacy. Civil War and the Emergence of the Roman Empire* (Cambridge).

Palmer, R. (1978). 'Octavian's First Attempt to restore the Constitution (36 BC)', *Athenaeum* 56, 315–328.

Pappano, A. (1935). 'The Pseudo-Marius', *Classical Philology* 30, 58–65.

Parrish, E. (1973). 'Crassus' New Friends and Pompey's Return', *Phoenix* 27, 357–380.

Pettinger, A. (2012). *The Republic in Danger: Drusus Libo and the Succession of Tiberius* (Oxford).

Phillips, D. (1997). 'The Conspiracy of Egnatius Rufus and the Election of Suffect Consuls under Augustus', *Historia* 46, 103–112.

Phillips, E. (1974). 'The Prosecution of C. Rabirius in 63 BC', *Klio* 56, 87–101.

——. (1976). 'Catiline's Conspiracy', *Historia* 25, 441–448.

Pocock, L. (1959). 'What Made Pompeius Fight in 49 BC?', *Greece & Rome* 6, 68–81.

Podesta, G. (1895). *Il tribunato della plebe in Roma* (Parma).

Powell, A & Welch, K. (2002). *Sextus Pompeius* (London).

Powell, L. (2014). *Marcus Agrippa: Right-Hand Man of Caesar Augustus* (Barnsley).

Raaflaub, K. and Tohler, M. (1990). *Between Republic and Empire: Interpretations of Augustus and His Principate* (Berkeley).

Ramsey, J. (1980). 'The Prosecution of C. Manilius in 66 BC and Cicero's "pro Manilio"', *Phoenix* 34, 323–336.

——. (1982). 'Cicero, pro Sulla 68 and the Catiline's Candidacy in 66 BC', *Harvard Studies in Classical Philology* 86, 121–131.

——. (1985). 'Asconius P.60 (Clark), Prima Pars: The Trial and Conviction of C. Manilius in 65 BC', *American Journal of Philology* 106, 367–373.

Reinhold, M. (1933). 'The Perusine War', *Classical Weekly* 26, 180–182.

Rocher, L. (1984). *El Tribunado de la Plebe en la Republica Arcaica (494–287 a. C.)* (Zaragoza).

Rice-Holmes, T. (1931). *The Architect of the Roman Empire 27 BC–AD 14* (Oxford).

Ridley, R. (1981). 'The Extraordinary Commands of the Late Republic: A Matter of Definition', *Historia* 30, 280–297.

——. (1983). 'Pompey's Commands in the 50s: How Cumulative?' *Rheinisches Museum für Philologie* 126, 136–148.

——. (2000). 'The Dictator's Mistake: Caesar's Escape from Sulla', *Historia* 49, 211–229.

Rising, T. (2013). 'Senatorial Opposition to Pompey's Eastern Settlement. A Storm in a Teacup?' *Historia* 62, 196–221.

Rotondi, G. (1912). *Leges Publicae Populi Romani* (Milan).

Rowe, G. (2013). 'Reconsidering the "Auctoritas" of Augustus', *Journal of Roman Studies* 103, 1–15.

Rowland, R. (1960). 'Crassus, Clodius, and Curio in the Year 59 BC', *Historia* 15, 217–223.

——. (1964). *Roman Grain Legislation 133–50 BC* (Michigan).

Rubino, J. (1825). *De tribunicia potestate* (Kassel).

Ruebel, J. (1979). 'The Trial of Milo in 52 BC: A Chronological Study', *Transactions of the American Philological Association* 109, 231–249.

Ryan, F. (1995). 'The Consular Candidacy of Catiline in 66', *Museum Helveticum* 25, 45–48.

——. (1996). 'The Lectio Senatus after Sulla', *Rheinisches Museum für Philologie* 139, 189–191.

——. (1998). *Rank and Participation in the Republican Senate* (Stuttgart).

Sage, E. (1920). 'The Senatus Consultum Ultimum', *Classical Weekly* 13, 185–189.

Salmon, E. (1935). 'Catiline, Crassus, and Caesar', *American Journal of Philology* 56, 302–316.

——. (1976). 'Augustus the Patrician', in A. Dunston (ed.) *Essays on Roman Culture* (Toronto), 3–33.

Sampson. G. (2005). *A re-examination of the office of the Tribunate of the Plebs in the Roman Republic (494 – 23 BC)* (Unpublished Thesis).

——. (2008). *The Defeat of Rome. Crassus, Carrhae and the Invasion of the East* (Barnsley).

——. (2010). *The Crisis of Rome. The Jugurthine and Northern Wars and the Rise of Marius* (Barnsley).

——. (2013). *The Collapse of Rome, Marius, Sulla and The First Civil War 91–70 BC* (Barnsley).

——. (2017). *Rome, Blood and Politics. Reform, Murder and Popular Politics in the Late Republic 146–70 BC* (Barnsley).

——. (forthcoming). *Rome & Parthia: Empires at War. Ventidius, Antony and the Second Parthian War 40–20 BC* (Barnsley).

——. (forthcoming). *Rome's Great Eastern War. Lucullus, Pompey and the Conquest of the East 74–63 BC* (Barnsley).

Sanders, H. (1932). 'The So-Called First Triumvirate', *Memoirs of the American Academy in Rome* 10, 55–68.

Sanford, E. (1939). 'The Career of Aulus Gabinius', *Transactions and Proceedings of the American Philological Association* 70, 64–92.

Scott, K. (1933). 'The Political Propaganda of 44–30 BC', *Memoirs of the American Academy in Rome 11*, 7–49.

Seager, R. (1969) (ed.) *The Crisis of the Roman Republic* (Cambridge).

——. (1969). 'The Tribunate of Cornelius. Some Ramifications', in J. Bibauw (ed.) *Hommages à Marcel Renard II* (Brussels), 680–686.

——. (1973). 'Iusta Catilinae', *Historia* 22, 240–248.

——. (1979). *Pompey. A Political Biography* (Oxford).

Seaver, J. (1952). 'Publius Ventidius. Neglected Roman Military Hero', *Classical Journal* 47, 275–280 & 300.

Shatzman, I. (1971). 'The Egyptian Question in Roman Politics (59–54 BC)', *Latomus* 30, 363–369.

Siani-Davies, M. (1997). 'Ptolemy XII Auletes and the Romans', *Historia* 46, 306–340.

Smith, R. (1955). *The Failure of the Roman Republic* (Cambridge).

——. (1957). 'The Lex Plotia Agraria and Pompey's Spanish Veterans', *Classical Quarterly* 7, 82–85.

——. (1957). 'The Conspiracy and the Conspirators', *Greece & Rome* 4, 58–70.

——. (1958). *Service in the Post Marian Roman Army* (Manchester).

——. (1977). 'The Use of Force in Passing Legislation in the Late Republic', *Athenaeum* 55, 150–174.

Southern, P. (1998). *Augustus* (Oxford).

——. (1998). *Mark Antony* (Stroud).

——. (2001). *Julius Caesar* (Stroud).

——. (2002). *Pompey the Great* (Stroud).

——. (2009). *Antony & Cleopatra* (Stroud).

Stanton, G. (2003). 'Why Did Caesar Cross the Rubicon?', *Historia* 52, 67–94.

Stanton, G. and Marshall, B. (1975). 'The Coalition between Pompeius and Crassus 60–59 BC', *Historia* 24, 205–219.

Steel, C. (2012). 'The "Lex Pompeia de Provinciis" of 52 BC: A Reconsideration', *Historia* 61, 83–93

——. (2014). 'Rethinking Sulla; The Case of the Roman Senate', *Classical Quarterly* 64, 657–668.

Stevenson, T. (2014). *Julius Caesar and the Transformation of the Roman Republic* (London).

Strack, P. (1939). 'Zur tribunicia potestas des Augustus', *Klio* 32, 358–381.

Sumi, G. (1997) 'Power and Ritual: The Crowd at Clodius' Funeral', *Historia* 46, 80–102.

——. (2005). *Ceremony and Power: Performing Politics in Rome between Republic and Empire* (Michigan).

Sumner, G. (1963). 'Lex Aelia, Lex Fufia', *American Journal of Philology* 84, 337–358.

——. (1963b). 'The Last Journey of L. Sergius Catalina', *Classical Philology* 58, 215–219.

——. (1966). 'Cicero, Pompeius and Rullus', *Transactions and Proceedings of the American Philological Association* 97, 569–582.

——. (1971). 'The Lex Annalis under Caesar', *Phoenix* 25, 246–271.

——. (1971b). 'The Lex Annalis under Caesar (Continued)', *Phoenix* 25, 357–371.

Sunden, J. (1897). *De tribunicia potestate a L. Sulla imminuta quaestiones* (Upsala).

Swan, M. (1967). 'The Consular Fasti of 23 B. C. and the Conspiracy of Varro Murena', *Harvard Studies in Classical Philology* 71, 235–247.

Syme, R. (1937). 'Who was Decidius Saxa?', *Journal of Roman Studies* 27, 127–137.

——. (1939). *The Roman Revolution* (Oxford).

——. (1963). 'Ten Tribunes', *Journal of Roman Studies* 53, 55–60.

——. (1980). 'The Sons of Crassus', *Latomus* 39, 403–408.

——. (1986). *The Augustan Aristocracy* (Oxford).

Talbert, R. (1984). 'Augustus and the Senate', *Greece & Rome* 31, 55–63.

Tatum, W. (1999). *The Patrician Tribune: Publius Clodius Pulcher* (Chapel Hill).

——. (1990). 'Cicero's Opposition to the Lex Clodia de Collegiis', *Classical Quarterly* 40, 187–194.

Taylor, L. (1941). 'Caesar's Early Career', *Classical Philology* 36, 113–132.

——. (1949). *Party Politics in the Age of Caesar* (Berkeley).

——. (1950). 'The Date and Meaning of the Vettius Affair', *Historia* 1, 45–51.

Tempest, K. (2013). *Cicero: Politics and Persuasion in Ancient Rome* (London).

——. (2017). *Brutus: The Noble Conspirator* (Yale).

Thommen, L. (1989). *Das Volkstribunat der späten römischen Republik* (Stuttgart).

Toher, M. (2004). 'Octavian's Arrival in Rome, 44 BC', *Classical Quarterly* 54, 174–184.

Tuori, K. (2014). 'Augustus, Legislative Power and the Power of Appearances', *Fundamina* 20, 938–945.

Twyman, B. (1972). 'The Metelli, Pompeius and Prosopography', *Aufsteig und Niedergang der Römischen Welt 1.1*, 816–874.

Ward, A. (1972). 'Cicero's Fight Against Crassus and Caesar in 65 and 63 BC', *Historia* 21, 244–258.

——. (1977). *Marcus Crassus and the Late Roman Republic* (Columbia).

Warde-Fowler, W. (1900*). Julius Caesar and the Foundation of the Roman Imperial System* (London).

Weigel, R. (1992). *Lepidus: The Tarnished Triumvir* (London).

Weinstock, S. (1937). 'Clodius and the Lex Aelia Fufia', *Journal of Roman Studies* 27, 216–222.

Williams, R. (1978). 'The Role of "Amicitia" in the Career of A. Gabinius (Cos. 58)', *Phoenix* 32, 195–210.

——. (1985). 'Rei Publicae Causa: Gabinius' Defence of His Restoration of Ptolemy Auletes', *Classical Journal* 81, 25–38.

Williams, R. and Williams, B. (1988). 'Cn. Pompeius Magnus and L. Afranius. Failure to Secure the Eastern Settlement', *Classical Journal* 83, 198–206.

Wirszubski, C. (1968). *Libertas as a political idea during the Late Republic and Early Principate* (Cambridge).

Wiseman, T. (1969). 'The Census in the First Century BC', *Journal of Roman Studies* 59, 59–75.

——. (1971). 'Celer and Nepos', *Classical Quarterly* 21, 180–182.

Wistrand, E. (1968). *Sallust on Judicial Murders in Rome. A Philological and Historical Study* (Gothenburg).

Woolf, G. (2006). *Et tu, Brute? The Murder of Caesar and Political Assassination* (London)

Yakobson, A. (1999). *Elections and Electioneering in Rome* (Stuttgart).

Yarrow, L. (2006). *Historiography at the End of the Republic* (Oxford).

Yavetz, Z. (1969). *Plebs and Princeps* (Oxford).

Zeev, M. (1996). 'When was the title "Dictator perpetuus" given to Caesar?' *L'antiquité classique* 65, 251–253.

Ziegler, M. (1903). *Fasti Tribunorum Plebis 133–70* (Ulm).

Index